Penguin Handbooks

The Penguin Guide to
Prehistoric England and Wales

James Dyer was born in 1934 in Bedfordshire, where he has lived most of his life. He took part in his first excavation at the age of fifteen and published his first paper two years later. Since then he has written frequently for specialist journals and has published eleven books on archaeological subjects. He is particularly interested in visible prehistoric remains and has travelled extensively in Britain and Western Europe, making a special study of British iron age hillforts and Scandinavian megalithic sites.

After training as a school teacher, James Dyer graduated in archaeology at Leicester University, and was appointed Principal Lecturer in archaeology at the former Putteridge Bury College of Education. In 1976 he returned to school teaching, and is now Head of Archaeology at Harlington Upper School in Bedfordshire. Deeply committed to the teaching of archaeology in schools, he is a member of the Schools Committee of the Council for British Archaeology. He has served on the Council of the Prehistoric Society and is a Fellow of the Society of Antiquaries.

His other books include, *Discovering Archaeology in England and Wales* (1969), *Discovering Archaeology in Denmark* (1972), *Southern England: an archaeological guide* (1973), *Your Book of Prehistoric Britain* (1974) and *Hillforts of England and Wales* (1981).

By the same author

Discovering Archaeology in England and Wales (1969)
Discovering Archaeology in Denmark (1972)
Southern England: an archaeological guide (1973)
Your Book of Prehistoric Britain (1974)
Hillforts of England and Wales (1981)

With J. G. Dony
The Story of Luton (1975)

Editor for R. H. Cunnington
From Antiquary to Archaeologist (1975)

The Penguin Guide to
Prehistoric England and Wales

James Dyer

Penguin Books

Penguin Books Ltd, Harmondsworth, Middlesex, England
Penguin Books, 625 Madison Avenue, New York, New York 10022, U.S.A.
Penguin Books Australia Ltd, Ringwood, Victoria, Australia
Penguin Books Canada Ltd, 2801 John Street, Markham, Ontario, Canada L3R 1B4
Penguin Books (N.Z.) Ltd, 182-190 Wairau Road, Auckland 10, New Zealand

—

First published by Allen Lane 1981
Published in Penguin Books 1982

—

Copyright © James Dyer, 1981
All rights reserved

—

Reproduced, printed and bound in Great Britain by
Hazell Watson & Viney Ltd, Aylesbury, Bucks
Set in Linotron 202 Times by
Western Printing Services Ltd, Bristol

C. W. Parry, BA
In memoriam,
1914–80

Contents

Contents

WALES

List of Plates

1. Victoria Cave near Settle in North Yorkshire was occupied by man in the upper palaeolithic period (*S. W. Feather*)
2. The Cheddar Gorge in Somerset contains at least three caves occupied by man in the upper palaeolithic period (*J. E. Hancock*)
3. At least five of the caves in the limestone gorge at Creswell Crags in Derbyshire were occupied by stone age man (*The author*)
4. A cup-and-ring marked stone near Lordenshaws hillfort in Northumberland (*S. W. Feather*)
5. An aerial view of native settlements of iron age and Roman date at Crosby Garrett in Cumbria (*Cambridge University collection*)
6. Iron age courtyard houses at Chysauster in Cornwall (*Cambridge University collection*)
7. The plateau fort of Uffington Castle beside the Ridgeway in Oxfordshire (*J. E. Hancock*)
8. In this aerial view, part of the excavations can be seen at Danebury Ring in Hampshire (*J. E. Hancock*)
9. The contour fort of Caer Caradoc, strongly sited above Church Stretton in Shropshire (*Cambridge University collection*)
10. Tre'r Ceiri hillfort with massive stone walls and groups of huts stands high above the Gwynedd countryside (*Cambridge University collection*)
11. The entrance to Yarnbury hillfort in Wiltshire (*The author*)
12. The rampart and ditch of Stanwick fort in North Yorkshire, which was attacked by the Romans around AD 70 (*S. W. Feather*)
13. The multiple ramparts of Maiden Castle, Dorset, possibly built as a defence against sling warfare (*Society of Antiquaries*)
14. Three lines of rampart and ditch isolate the Rumps promontory fort in Cornwall (*The author*)
15. Lanyon Quoit in Cornwall, the remains of a once much higher burial chamber, was restored in 1815 (*The author*)
16. Dyffryn Ardudwy chambered cairn, Gwynedd, contains two burial chambers (*RCHM, Wales*)
17. The massive chamber of Plas Newydd in Anglesey has long since lost its covering mound of earth (*The author*)
18. The weathered stones of Maesyfelin, Glamorgan, stand over two metres high (*RCHM, Wales*)

List of Figures

Foreword

Visiting prehistoric sites is one of the best ways I know of exploring the countryside. Frequently one is taken off the beaten track and away from large crowds of holiday-makers to the quiet byroads and field paths. A purpose is given to climbs over more difficult terrain, and a sense of achievement when a site is reached. Often one is rewarded with an exceptional view and a feeling of discovery.

The sites described in this book are my personal selection. Others would have chosen differently and I am conscious that I may have done less than justice to areas that I do not know very well. However, I have tried to reach a fair balance, and if I have erred, then perhaps it may be corrected at a later time.

I have not given details of the best way to reach a site as this would have required a considerably longer book. Nor have I included details of rights of way, land ownership, etc., which are likely to change from time to time. Suffice to say that in almost all cases the monuments are on private land, and I would stress that permission is needed to visit them. Please respect the owner's rights, so that others may be permitted to follow you. Where sites are in state care, they are normally open at standard times, and in some cases a charge is made for admission. National Grid references have been given for all sites and they should not prove too difficult to find using the Ordnance Survey 1:50,000 maps, which show public footpaths and rights of way.

Every county has its museums with material from many of the sites described. Up-to-date details of these with opening times can be found in the annual publication *Museums and Art Galleries in Great Britain and Ireland* published by ABC Historic Publications Ltd. Where the visitor has limited time then the prehistoric galleries in the British Museum, London, and the National Museum, Cardiff, should certainly be visited, and if possible the Museum of the Wiltshire Archaeological and Natural History Society at 41 Long Street, Devizes, in Wiltshire (closed Sundays and Mondays), which has an exceptional prehistoric collection.

All the sites described in this book are scheduled ancient monuments protected by law. Sometimes they are very remote and damage to them often goes unnoticed for a long time. Vandalism, unauthorized ploughing or earth-moving, and the unfortunate craze of metal-detecting are all illegal on such sites and should be instantly reported to the local police and the Department of the Environment, Fortress House, 23 Savile Row, London W1X 2AA.

Acknowledgements

A number of people have helped me in compiling this book and checking information for me. I would particularly like to thank the following: Owen Bedwin, B. M. Beeby, Tom Clare, L. V. Grinsell, Graeme Guilbert, Joseph Hughes, Nicholas Johnson, Andrew Lawson, Frances Lynch, W. H. Manning, Barry Marsden, Jeffrey May, Peter Reynolds and my father, F. J. Dyer, who read the whole work and compiled the index for me.

For photographs I am indebted to the Department of the Environment, S. W. Feather, J. E. Hancock, Professor J. K. St Joseph (Cambridge University Collection, Crown Copyright Reserved), the Society of Antiquaries and the Royal Commission Historical Monuments (Wales).

The maps and plans were drawn from a variety of sources by Reginald Piggott.

Note on the Use of Ordnance Survey Maps

In order that any site in this book can be found accurately on the Ordnance Survey maps its National Grid reference number is given (eg, Stonehenge SU 122422). In order to use this the following points should be observed. The two letters SU refer to the 100 kilometre square in which the site occurs. This is shown in the key of the appropriate Ordnance Survey map. Along the top and bottom edge of the map are a series of numbers at 1 km intervals called *eastings*. Similarly up the sides of the map are other numbers called *northings*. To use the grid reference for Stonehenge, take the first three numbers 122 and insert a decimal point before the last digit: 12·2. Find the easting 12 at the foot of the page and move beyond it for 0·2 of a kilometre. Similarly to use the second three numbers 422 find the northing 42 on the side of the map and then move up the square 0·2 km. Where the eastings and northings cross is the location of the site.

Note on Metric Units

These equivalents are approximate only.

$$1 \text{ cm} = 2/5 \text{ inches}$$
$$1 \text{ m} = 39\tfrac{1}{2} \text{ inches}$$
$$1 \text{ km} = \tfrac{5}{8} \text{ mile}$$
$$1 \text{ ha (hectare)} = 2\tfrac{1}{2} \text{ acres}$$
$$1 \text{ tonne} = 0·98 \text{ ton}$$
$$2·5 \text{ cm} = 1 \text{ inch}$$
$$0·9 \text{ m} = 1 \text{ yard}$$
$$1·6 \text{ km} = 1 \text{ mile}$$
$$0·4 \text{ ha} = 1 \text{ acre}$$
$$1·016 \text{ tonnes} = 1 \text{ ton}$$

Maps Showing Prehistoric Sites in England and Wales

The following maps are designed to give a general indication of the distribution and concentration of prehistoric sites over the area covered by this guide, and may be found useful when planning a holiday or tour in a particular area.

The sites described in the guide are represented here by dots, numbered according to their appearance in the relevant county section. For more exact details of location the reader should refer to the appropriate Ordnance Survey map (a note on the use of map references is given opposite).

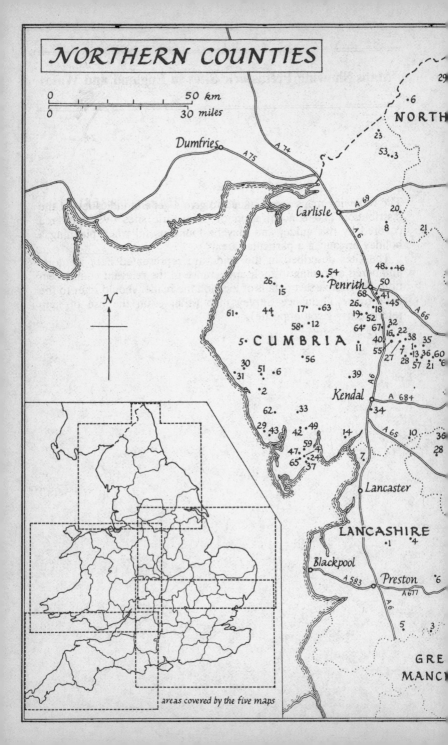

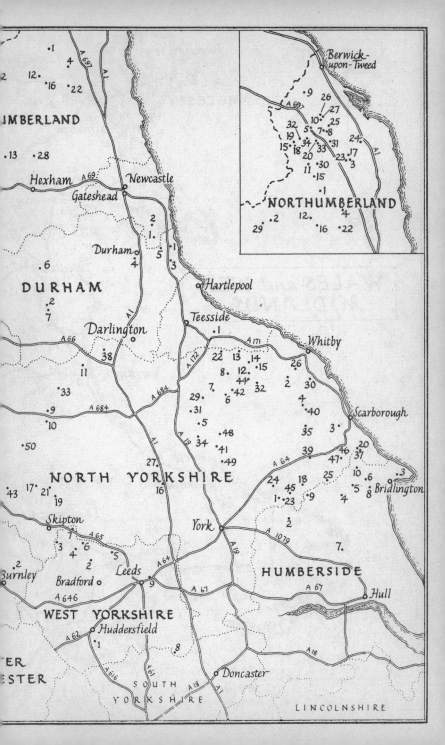

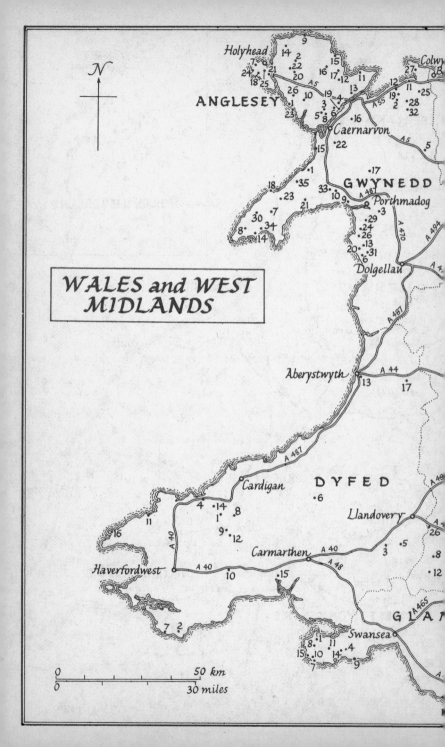

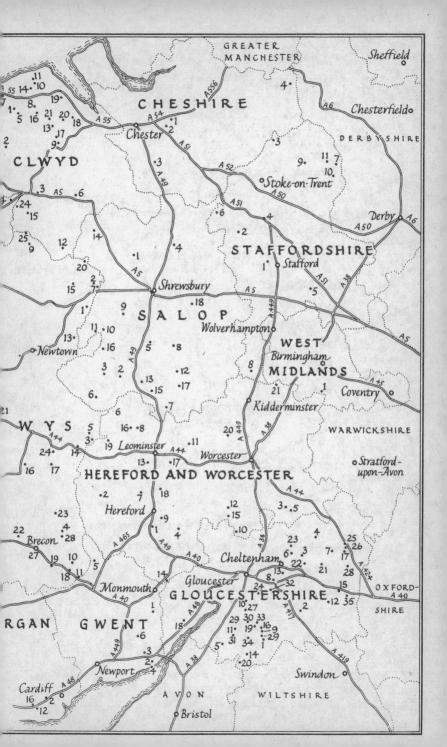

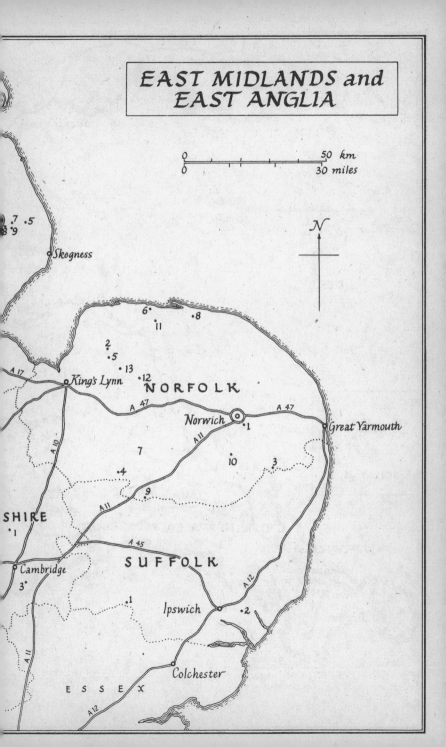

EAST MIDLANDS and EAST ANGLIA

0   50 km
0   30 miles

N

.7 .5
.8 .9

○ Skegness

.6   .8
.11

.2
.5
.13

A 17   .12

○ King's Lynn   N O R F O L K

A 47   A 47

Norwich ◎ .1   ○ Great Yarmouth

A 10   A 11   7

.4   10   3

.9

A 11

SHIRE
.1

○ Cambridge

3.

A 45

S U F F O L K

.1   Ipswich ○ .2   A 12

A 11

○ Colchester

E S S E X

A 12

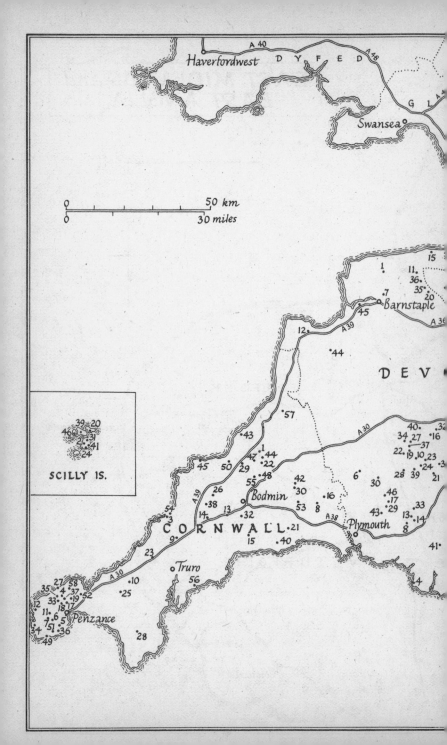

Haverfordwest D Y F E D

A 40

A 48

G L A

Swansea

15

0   50 km
0   30 miles

1   11.
          36.
7   35. 20
          Barnstaple

45   A 36

12   A 39

44   D E V

57

43   40. 32
          34 27 16
1   37
47 44   22. 19 10 23
50 29   6   28 39 24
48   30   21
42
55 Bodmin 30   46
26   53 8   17
38   16   29 33
54   13   43   13
3   14   32   8 14
C O R N W A L L 21   Plymouth
9   15
23   40   41

Truro
56

35 27 58   10
4 37
33 19 52   25
12 18 17
11 6
7 5 Penzance
4 51
49 36   28

SCILLY IS.

39 20
46 2 31
24 41

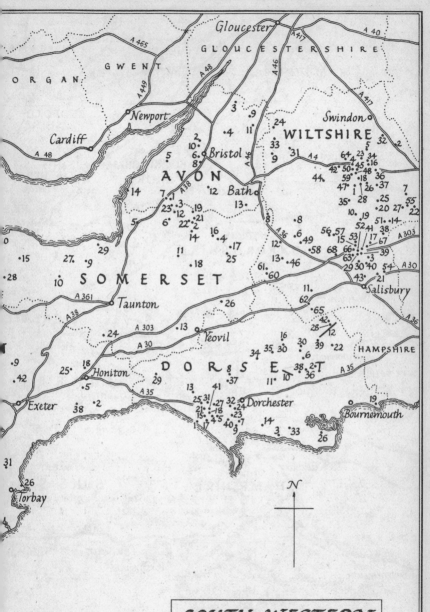

SOUTH-WESTERN
COUNTIES

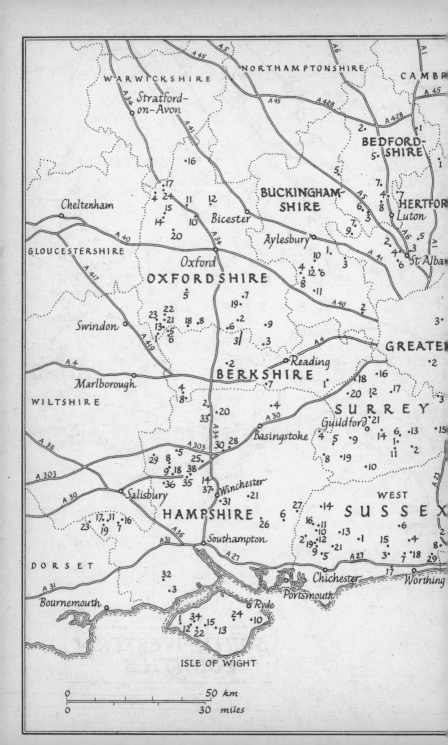

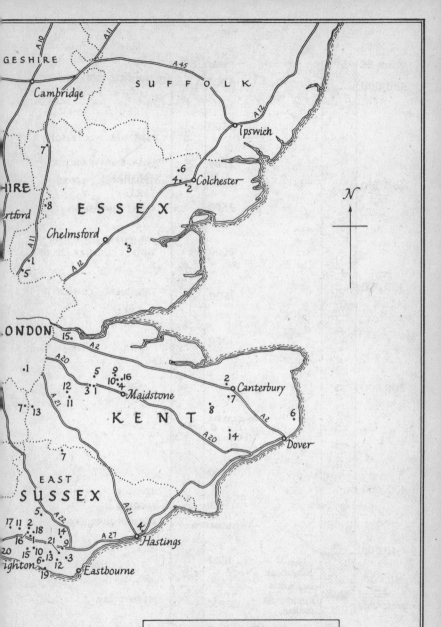

GESHIRE

Cambridge

S U F F O L K

A 45

A 11

A 10

A 12

Ipswich

N

.6

4. Colchester
.2

E S S E X

.8

rtford

Hertford

Chelmsford

.3

A 12

A 11

.1

.5

LONDON

15.

A 2

A 20

.1

.5   .9 .16
12. 10..4
3 .1
.11

Maidstone

2.   Canterbury
.7

A 21

7. 13

K E N T

.8

6.

Dover

A 2

7.

.14

A 20

EAST

SUSSEX

A 22

5.

17 11 .2
.18
16   21 14
20   .10   .9
15 6. 13 .3
righton 19 12

A 27

4.

Hastings

Eastbourne

SOUTH-EASTERN
COUNTIES

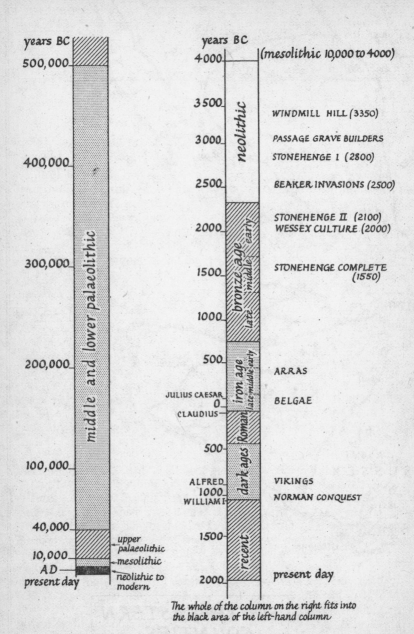

years BC

500,000

400,000

300,000

200,000

100,000

40,000

10,000

AD
present day

middle and lower palaeolithic

upper palaeolithic
mesolithic
neolithic to modern

years BC

4000 (mesolithic 10,000 to 4000)

3500   WINDMILL HILL (3350)

3000   PASSAGE GRAVE BUILDERS
        STONEHENGE 1 (2800)

2500   BEAKER INVASIONS (2500)

2000   STONEHENGE II (2100)
        WESSEX CULTURE (2000)

1500   STONEHENGE COMPLETE
                    (1550)

1000

500   ARRAS

JULIUS CAESAR
0   BELGAE
CLAUDIUS

500

ALFRED
1000   VIKINGS
WILLIAM I NORMAN CONQUEST

1500

2000   present day

neolithic

bronze age late middle early

iron age late middle early

Roman

dark ages

recent

*The whole of the column on the right fits into
the black area of the left-hand column*

Fig. 1. Time chart

28

Introduction

This book is concerned with the visible monuments of prehistoric times that can be clearly found in the countryside. The sites have been grouped by counties to make it easier to find them. This has meant that hut circles and burial mounds, hillforts and flint mines are all mixed together without any background information. It is the purpose of this introduction to go some way to supplying this, by looking at the prehistoric inhabitants of Britain, and then considering the various types of monuments they built, and observing their development in chronological order.

The People

The inhabitants of the first sites that I have described were hunters who lived some 50,000 years ago in an interglacial period during what archaeologists call the palaeolithic period (or old stone age). Contrary to common belief these folk looked very similar to ourselves, though they may have been a little shorter and their life span was little more than thirty years. Although a number of their sites are known in southern England, few would prove worth visiting since they are now little more than contorted layers of clay or gravel in a pit that is frequently overgrown and inexplicable to the layman.

The palaeolithic period lasted until about 10,000 BC. During that time the greater part of Britain was covered with ice or a tundra environment in which it would have been difficult for man to survive for any length of time. Summer camps were made in the mouths of caves during the final centuries of the palaeolithic, at a time when the climate was already becoming warmer. These have left their traces and a few have been included in this book. The most famous is the cave which contained the so called 'Red Lady' of Paviland with a radiocarbon date of 16,510 ± 340 bc (Goat's Cave, Paviland).

By about 10,000 BC much of the ice had left Britain, though a little remained on the tops of the highest mountains in Wales and Scotland. The countryside was dotted with small lakes and pools and clumps of birch trees, amongst which small groups of men hunted and fished. Such people belong to the culture known as mesolithic. They had few settled homes, but tended to lead a nomadic life following herds of deer that provided them with food and clothing. Somewhere between 6000 and 5000 B C the English Channel formed, thus separating Britain from the Continent, and by about 4000 B C the neolithic period had begun. This phase is characterized by the arrival in Britain of agriculturalists from Europe, bringing with them corn and stock animals, as well as the art of pottery making. Such farmers arrived in small family groups, travelling in skin boats and settling all over the British Isles at roughly the same time, mixing with the indigenous population. In all probability the lowland chalk hills supported arable farming, whilst stock rearing developed in the highlands and mountains of the west and Wales. It was these neolithic people who built ceremonial sites like causewayed camps and henge monuments, long barrows for their dead, and rectangular dwelling houses. They also introduced industry in the form of flint mining and stone axe making. All of this is described in more detail later.

Around 2500 B C new groups of immigrants arrived on the eastern shores of Britain, bringing with them a characteristic drinking vessel known as a beaker, as well as the first knowledge of metal to reach these islands. These beaker folk spread rapidly along the river valleys of eastern and southern England, frequently stopping to bury their dead singly in crouched positions under small round barrows. Unfortunately little is known of their daily life and domestic sites are rarely found. In central southern England there developed by 2000 B C a group of people who can best be described as a localized hierarchy whose graves contained small quantities of gold and fine metalwork, and which were covered by elaborate burial mounds with a variety of fancy shapes. This development is known as the Wessex culture and is almost exclusively found in that area, although there are a few remains in East Anglia and south-west England. Amongst other things the Wessex folk are believed to have been responsible for building the final stages of Stonehenge.

The bronze age had dawned in Britain about 2300 B C and imperceptibly developed, following ideas taken from neolithic, beaker and Wessex culture sources. Round barrow burial became universal and farming seems to have been the main way of life, with isolated farmsteads and small villages spreading along the hillsides of England and into Wales. Stone circles and rows marked the ceremonial side of life. Towards the end of the period fortification began to develop in a simple way with the occasional fencing of hilltop farms and villages.

Conventionally the bronze age ended around 750 B C when the iron age began, but in reality there was no obvious change, save for the widespread replacement of bronze by iron. The farming life went on as before. Cremation was almost the only burial rite, and barrows went out of fashion. Flat cemeteries or the scattering of ashes took their place. Defended hilltops now proliferated in Wales, the Marches and northern Britain, and a whole group of sites loosely termed hillforts emerged, though by no means all of them were literally forts, but should properly be seen as defended farms, villages and towns, depending on their size and situation. Who they were defended against is a difficult question to answer; presumably neighbouring tribesmen, since incursions from abroad, or internal warfare on a large scale is not clearly demonstrated in the archaeological record. In southern Britain the hillforts developed later, and in eastern England scarcely at all. By the first century B C it is likely that immigrant groups from the continent were moving into southern England, and settling in Essex, Hertfordshire and Hampshire. These were the Belgae. Other immigrants had settled on the Yorkshire Wolds. By Caesar's invasions of 55 and 54 B C Britain was divided into a number of tribal areas broadly identified today, and during the following century a number of dominant tribal leaders emerged, often with headquarters in oppida (see page 34), all of which were to be subdued by the might of Rome in A D 43 or the years that followed.

Fig 2. The main iron age tribes of southern Britain

Settlement

The earliest forms of settlement described in this book are the *rock shelters and caves* of the palaeolithic and mesolithic periods (i.e. prior to 4000 BC). A suitably overhanging rock face or the mouth of a cave made an acceptable shelter during early prehistory. Windbreaks of sticks and skins offered protection against the elements, and a wood fire made the habitation cheerful and provided light. A stream was invariably close at hand to provide drinking water both for man and for the animals that he hunted. These were by no means the only homes occupied by palaeolithic people, indeed they were in the minority, but more ephemeral houses in the open countryside have failed to survive. The majority of occupied caves belong to the upper palaeolithic, and particularly good examples occur at Gough's Cave, Cheddar, and Kent's Cavern in Torquay, as well as at Creswell Crags in Derbyshire. At the latter site mesolithic occupation is also found, as well as at High Rocks in East Sussex. A mesolithic hut in the open countryside is still visible at Abinger, Surrey.

Evidence of settlement in the neolithic period is sadly lacking. Excavations of isolated round and rectangular houses have left no trace for the visitor to see. Only at Carn Brea in Cornwall are there scattered huts enclosed by a stone wall. Whether causewayed camps should be discussed under this heading is open to doubt and I have chosen to consider them as ceremonial sites.

Bronze age settlement, like the neolithic, is hard to find. Scatters of flints and pottery in a field are frequently the only indication that a site exists, and areas like Wessex where dense concentrations of burial mounds indicate a large population are almost totally lacking in signs of settlement. On the chalk hills of southern Britain one can occasionally find the low banks and ditches of undefended farmsteads or hamlets, such as Itford Hill in Sussex, with perhaps a dozen round house platforms, and traces of fields and hollow trackways. Only in the granite areas of the west country have circular house foundations called hut circles survived in large numbers, though it is not always possible to say whether they are of bronze or iron age date. On Dartmoor large walled enclosures called pounds still exist, containing circular huts. So close together are some of the pounds that they are unlikely to represent villages, but rather the sheep farms of extended family groups. The best-known example is Grimspound on Dartmoor. In the same part of the country open villages of round houses without protective walls can be found; Rough Tor in Cornwall is an example.

It is also in the west country and Wales that the *circular huts* of the iron age are found, often enclosed with stone walls designed to keep cattle in and wild animals out. These are not defensive in the same sense as the hillforts, although the huts are of similar shape and size. In

Cornwall there is a group of stone-built houses arranged around courtyards that may have been open to the sky. The best known is at Chysauster. Sometimes semi-underground passages called fogous are attached. These were probably store-chambers, though some may have been connected with defence. In the lowlands a wooden palisade would have surrounded a group of huts and we can see them as farmsteads and small villages. They range from Staple Howe in Yorkshire to Smacam Down in Dorset. At the centre of these farms and villages were circular huts with pointed thatched roofs and walls of wattle and daub, erected on a skilfully carpentered framework. Entrance porches with double doors kept out the wind and rain and made the home reasonably warm, especially when the central fire was burning and heating the clay oven. Around the walls were benches covered with furs for sitting and sleeping. Outside were square wooden granaries and storage huts, pig-sties and cattle-sheds, and all the accoutrements of a well-run farm. Beyond the enclosure fence were the fields, small rectangles of neatly ploughed land forming the characteristic Celtic fields, or, on the sloping hillside, the stepped flights of lynchets.

Fortification

When did man first need to construct a defence? The answer might be as early as the neolithic period, about 3500 BC. Earthworks called *causewayed camps* were being constructed at that time, consisting of concentric rings of ditches broken by causeways and enclosing banks of more continuous character. These were sometimes closed by wooden gates. At the Crickley Hill causewayed camp in Gloucestershire a rectangular wooden hut had been burnt down. Around it were scattered two hundred leaf-shaped arrowheads. However, such evidence is not common on similar sites and it may be that defence proper did not begin until the later bronze and iron ages.

Strictly speaking *hillforts* are hilltops defended by walls of stone, banks of earth or fences of wood, usually accompanied by one or more external ditches. The word fort might be more accurately reserved for defensive works on low-lying ground.

Traditionally associated with the iron age, a number of hillforts are known to have begun in the late bronze age, often on sites with an even earlier history of occupation. The fortification of a farmstead or village as protection against wild animals or hostile neighbours may have led to the idea of hillfort construction. At first this would have taken the simple form of a ditch and wooden stockade, but as time went by this became more elaborate. The stockade became two parallel fences forming a row whose interior was filled with soil. Rampart walks for sentries were developed on top of it. Entrances were simple straight-through affairs, but these evolved into diagonal passages or long inturned entrances with guard chambers, like medieval city barbicans. Often bridges ran over the entrance, carrying the rampart walk, and all the time efforts were made to make them stronger and more attack-proof.

The commonest hillforts are known as contour forts, since their defences faithfully follow the contours of the hills on which they are built. These hills can be of any height, which may vary from a few metres above fenland to hundreds of metres in mountainous areas. Where the ground is usually low-lying forts are often called plateau forts. Sometimes a hill spur with steep natural slopes on all sides is only defended across its neck: these are known as promontory forts. Similarly, where a coastal headland juts out to sea, the cliffs may form a natural defence, whilst only the neck where the headland joins the mainland is artificially protected with banks and ditches. This type of fort is called a cliff castle. There are numerous variations on these simple themes. In the north-west timbers within the stone walls were sometimes ignited, causing the stone to melt and create vitrified forts. In the south-west of England and west Wales there are hill-slope forts that are overlooked from above, and consist of a series of linked enclosures, probably used for cattle penning.

Why the hillforts were defended calls for some comment. To erect hundreds of metres of wooden fencing and to dig many cubic metres of ditches is a lengthy and time-consuming process. It could not have been done quickly. 'The Romans are coming, build a fort' could not have been answered by immediate action. In many cases two or three years' work at least is involved, and it is reasonable to see hillforts being constructed in times of peace as a natural part of the environment of iron age man, to be called upon in times of strife, but normally acting only as a safeguard, like the medieval city wall, to be kept in good repair and to give confidence to those who dwelt within. This parallel with the medieval city may often have been justified, and one can visualize the larger forts occupied permanently by many families, with artisans making pottery and leather goods, working in wood and producing metalwork. For some this was a full-time occupation; for others there were fields outside the fort to be farmed. If war developed the walls were manned with slingers, and bands of soldiers formed up at the gates to counter any attack. Many forts were impregnable; only the might of Rome could finally crush them.

Forts probably had their own political territories in which they were the centralized power over a group of farmsteads and open villages. The largest forts of all, the oppida, or walled towns, were literally tribal headquarters, the centres of administration and trade. They came into being in the later iron age, perhaps around 50 B C, and tended to be low-lying and protected by massive earthwork dykes, like those at Colchester and Chichester.

Burial

Although deliberate burial of the dead was practised in the palaeolithic and mesolithic periods, it is not until the neolithic that field monuments appear in the form of burial mounds. These take different shapes according to geographical location. In the south and east are found *long barrows* of earth and chalk, rectangular mounds, usually slightly higher and broader at one end, and often with traces of quarry ditches on either side. Such barrows contained collective burials that may once have laid in a mortuary chamber of wood or turf. As many as fifty bodies might be interred in a single long barrow and evidence shows that the remains of the dead were collected over a long period of time and brought together for burial under the mound at a single ceremony. In Yorkshire and Wiltshire early excavation reports indicate that sometimes the dead were cremated before the barrow was erected over the pyre.

Throughout the western part of Britain *chambered barrows* and cairns of stone were constructed for the neolithic dead. Here the mortuary hut seems to have been built of stone and incorporated into the long barrow mound as a burial chamber to which successive interments could be added over very long periods of time. The group is known geographically as the Severn–Cotswold tombs. The West Kennet long barrow (Wilts.) is the best example of this kind. Sometimes the burial chamber was at the highest end of the barrow, at other times it was incorporated into the side (lateral chamber), then often with a false portal or doorway at the higher end. At Belas Knap in Gloucestershire the barrow has three lateral chambers as well as a fine false portal. At the higher end of the chambered barrows there is a tendency for horns or lobes to protrude on either side of the entrance, enclosing a funnel-shaped forecourt, where some kind of ceremonial seems to have taken place, often involving fires and ritual deposits. It seems probable that the chambered tombs were opened not only for burial, but for other ceremonies to be performed, in which gifts of food, pottery, weapons and even earth were deposited in the burial chambers and entrance passage.

In Kent a small group of chambered long barrows known as the Medway group are separated from those in the west of Britain and should perhaps be seen as belonging to a continental tradition, in which a rectangular mound edgèd with a kerb of stones was constructed, with a small burial chamber at one end.

Circular cairns with stone burial chambers are rare in England and Wales. A small group called entrance graves occurs in the Scilly Isles and the extreme western tip of Cornwall. There are half a dozen circular barrows with burial chambers in the Peak District of Derbyshire. True cairns of passage-grave type can be found in Anglesey at Bryn-Celli-

Ddu and Barclodiad-y-Gawres, the latter with a series of decorated wall stones reminiscent of the passage graves of Ireland.

By far the most common surviving field monuments in England and Wales are the *round barrows* or cairns of the bronze age; estimates of their number vary between 30,000 and 40,000. In most cases the barrow consists of a circular turf-covered mound or cairn of earth or boulders, the latter sometimes with a stone cist or kerb of stones around its edge. A great many of these barrows show the hollows of nineteenth-century excavators' trenches in their summits.

During the early part of the bronze age a series of exceptional barrows were constructed in Wessex with a few outliers in East Anglia and Sussex; these are the bell-, disc-, saucer- and pond-barrows of the Wessex culture, which seem to represent the graves of an aristocracy whose achievement included the construction of Stonehenge in its final form. Bell-barrows tend to cover adult male internments and disc-barrows the remains of women.

Round barrows generally are fewer in Wales. In Yorkshire and Northumbria the cairns have resemblances to Scandinavian barrows and a number of them covered burials in tree-trunk or boat-shaped wooden coffins. They are often surrounded by kerbs, often with cup-marked stones.

The later bronze age grave mounds covered Deverel-Rimbury urns and tend to be rare in England. Barrows disappear and cremation and the dispersal of the ashes seems to have followed. Throughout the iron age burial is rare, though the finds of damaged human bones on settlement sites suggests that sometimes the dead were exposed and their remains allowed to litter the ground. Only in east Yorkshire was formal burial continued with the construction of clusters of several hundred small burial mounds, often surrounded by circular or square ditches, and linked culturally to the Marne region of France.

Surviving princely burial mounds of the later iron age are rare, though the Lexden tumulus at Colchester should be noted. Other similar monuments have probably been destroyed.

Ceremonial Monuments

In the century or so following 3600 BC a series of earthworks were constructed in southern Britain that are known as *causewayed camps*. They consist of concentric circles or ovals of ditches, broken at frequent intervals by causeways of undug earth. The quarried material was piled on the inner side to form a bank. The outer ditch is usually the most massive and at the type site, Windmill Hill near Avebury, this ditch alone produced 13,000 tons of chalk. The whole site, with its three ditches, involved about 65,000 man hours of work, and must have been undertaken for some very special purpose. We can only guess

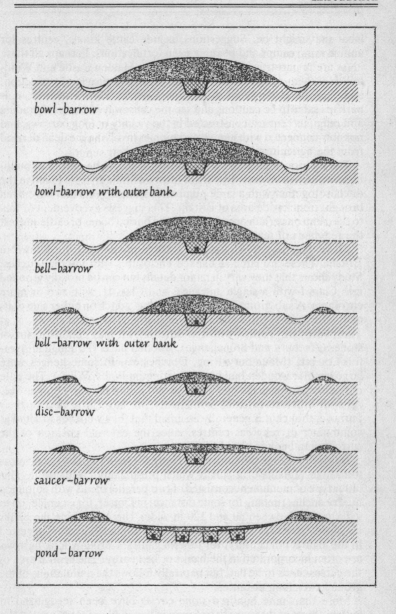

bowl–barrow

bowl–barrow with outer bank

bell–barrow

bell–barrow with outer bank

disc–barrow

saucer–barrow

pond – barrow

Fig 3. The chief types of round barrow

what that might be. Suggestions include cattle kraals, centres for annual fairs, camps and possibly even fortifications. Perhaps all these ideas are in part true. The larger sites, like Maiden Castle and Windmill Hill, with massive outer ditches may have provided protection, and there is evidence of warfare at Crickley Hill. However, it is perhaps safer to be cautious and see the causewayed camps as trading and religious centres, constructed in the vicinity of long barrows, and possibly connected with annual ceremonies involving the dead derived from the agricultural background of the makers.

The interior of most causewayed sites seems to be devoid of buildings or other structures. Pottery of most neolithic styles is found in the ditches, together with a large number of stone objects that have been brought from a wide area of Britain. This suggests a movement of folk to the camp on certain occasions, and the buried bones of cattle suggest the remnants of feasting.

More than seventy examples of *henge monuments* are known in Britain. These are circular banked enclosures with internal ditches. Study shows that they vary in minor details but can be broadly grouped into Class I with a single entrance, and Class II, with two or more entrances. A sub-group IIa in Yorkshire has a ditch on either side of its bank. Sometimes the central area of the henge is quite empty, as at Thornborough, Yorks., whilst at other sites it may contain a ring of stones (Avebury and Stonehenge), wooden posts (Arminghall, Norfolk) or pits (Maumbury Ring, Dorchester). In some henges were large circular wooden buildings (Durrington Walls, Wilts.). The date of the henges spans the end of the neolithic into the early bronze age. As with other ceremonial monuments, we have little idea of their purpose, though it is generally assumed that they were constructed as community or religious centres, since the external position of the surrounding bank is non-defensive.

Beneath a henge monument at Thornborough (Yorks.) excavators found the remains of a *cursus* which presumably pre-dated it. This latter type of monument consisted of two parallel banks with adjoining quarry ditches running for some distance; in Dorset, for example, up to 9·7 km, and between 60 and 120 m wide. The area inside the banks may have been used for processions, or as William Stukeley suggested in the eighteenth century, for funeral games. Certainly long barrows are often incorporated in the banks or lie nearby. The central area of the cursus tends to be flat, but naturally follows the undulations of the ground over long distances.

More than nine hundred *stone circles* have been recognized in Britain. Most of these are to be found in the highland zone, west of the line from the Tees to the Exe, with a few outliers in Wiltshire and Somerset. In eastern England wooden circles may have existed once and disintegrated leaving little trace.

Most circles have suffered damage in the past and have stones missing, but enough remains to show that they are not always true circles, some are flattened along one side or are distinctly egg-shaped. The reasons are not known, but sometimes they seem to have been made deliberately to counteract perspective on a sloping site, thus making the ring look more truly circular from a particular viewpoint.

Stone circles seems to have been built for about 1800 years between 3000 BC and 1200 BC. Considering the number of existing circles in Britain that is only one every two years.

There is a tendency to divide circles into two groups: the larger ones which are often early and probably neolithic: and the smaller ones, later and of bronze age construction. The early rings are markedly circular, often with a single entrance marked by portal stones, and with an outlying stone nearby. They are usually found on open, low-lying ground. The later circles are sometimes concentric with a central stone; they may be more oval in shape and surrounded by a bank of earth or rubble. Such circles tend to be found in remote upland areas. Of course there are exceptions to this scheme.

Professor Alexander Thom suggested that all circles were constructed according to a standard unit of 2·72 feet ('megalithic yard'), but this does not seem to have been used throughout Britain. Whilst it may hold good for parts of Scotland and south-west England, there are other areas that must have had their own regional units.

It is noticeable that in many circles the stones have been graded in size: often with larger stones marking approximately north, south, east and west. An outlier has often been set up for the observation of astronomical phenomena: the summer or winter solstice or the spring and autumn equinoxes. Such information could be used by early agriculturalists to plan their seasonal work, as well as to warn them of the approach of special ceremonies in their yearly calendar which had to be performed in the circular enclosure, perhaps accompanied by music and dancing. On the other hand, too much attention has certainly been given to trying to attach non-existent astronomical properties to stone circles. Only a few are aligned on astronomical phenomena, and these can be verified only when the correct viewing position is known. It is tempting to try to give the circles properties which they never had. Most British churches are aligned east-west, but this does not mean that they were deliberately set up for the observation of the midsummer sunrise!

Standing stones and stone rows seem to belong to the end of the neolithic and the bronze age. Single upright stones are a common sight in the west country and Wales. Often they are rubbing stones erected by a farmer for his cattle, but many are of ancient origin and must once have acted as markers, perhaps connected with cross-country travel or astronomy, or they may indicate the position of particular mineral outcrops.

Stone rows tend to be low in the heather and difficult to find, being seldom more than a metre high. The rows can be double or treble and often lead to or from a round barrow or cairn. The best examples will be found on Dartmoor.

True avenues consist of much larger blocks of stone and may stretch for some way; 2·5 km at Avebury in Wiltshire, where the avenue links two stone circles, or 3 km at Shap in Cumbria, where a circle and a barrow are linked by a trail of stones. Sometimes the stone row is both massive and short as at the Devil's Arrows near Boroughbridge (Yorks.) or Harold's Stones at Trellech (Gwent). The purpose of the rows is difficult to interpret; they may be direction indicators, perhaps showing the path a spirit must follow to reach the next world, or they may be more mundane markers indicating an earthly route to grazing or hunting grounds.

Often the stones of avenues, circles and tombs have been decorated with simple incised or pecked designs, of which the most common are the *cup-and-ring marks*. These consist of circular hollows 4–5 cm across surrounded by one or more incised rings. Many variations occur producing maze-like patterns that have given rise to heated debates as to their meaning. Many designs occur on outcrops of living rock, particularly in Northumbria. Some would see 'schools' of designers, others groups of doodlers. Unlike the rock-art of Scandinavia, where some of the patterns also occur, British rock art seems to be non-representational. Whatever the meaning of these designs, it is no longer clear to us.

Industry

Igneous rock, suitable for *stone axe manufacture*, had been located in Cornwall, Wales and Cumbria. Outcrops were attacked with hammer-stones and tons of material removed for polishing into axes and adzes. The remaining debris was strewn down the mountainside where it can still be found today. The most accessible site for the energetic visitor is the lower slope of the Pike of Stickle in Langdale (Cumbria). Dozens of axes from the highland areas of Britain have been found all over southern Britain, which they had reached presumably as the result of trade in the form of barter.

The most popular material for tool manufacture was flint. In order to obtain the best-quality stone, *mines* had to be dug into the chalk of southern and eastern England, and these have left deep depressions in numerous places, particularly Cissbury in Sussex and Grimes Graves in Norfolk. It is difficult to know how neolithic man first recognized that flint occurred in the chalk. Perhaps he saw it in the cliffs along the sea-shore. This does not explain how he identified it in the chalk of Norfolk, buried beneath a layer of Breckland sand. The flint was extracted either by open-cast mining or by sinking shafts from above until the seams of stone were found, and then following them horizontally for some metres until the safety limit was reached.

Traces of prehistoric *metalworking* seem to have been largely swept away by later mining, although mention must be made of the iron mines at Lydney (Glos.) which may have been worked in iron age times and certainly pre-date the Roman buildings that overlie them.

Agriculture

The whole landscape of England and Wales is a palimpsest of agricultural patterns developed over the past four thousand years. The earliest visible examples of note probably date from the early bronze age, although there is plenty of excavation evidence of agriculture being practised in neolithic and even mesolithic times. It is generally assumed that the earliest *fields* were irregular plots of land, best observed in the highland areas of Devon and Cornwall, Cumbria and Wales, whilst rectangular fields appeared around the tenth century B C, towards the end of the bronze age, and developed during the iron age and later periods. Most fields were formed as a result of ploughing. In order to clear the land large stones were moved to the edge of the plot and these became field banks, particularly when loose soil began to pile up against them. On sloping ground the soil crept down to the bank and created lynchets. At Itford Hill in Sussex the first rectangular fields appeared about 1000 B C, close to a palisaded enclosure containing houses. Over the next millenium rectangular fields, each about $\frac{1}{2}$ ha,* became normal in southern Britain, and early workers gave them the name 'Celtic fields'. Examples can frequently be seen on aerial photographs, but are often not particularly visible on the ground. Good examples occur in Dorset at the Valley of Stones and at Fyfield Down in Wiltshire. For the animal husbandry and crop production practised in these fields we must turn to the excavated material in museums, where the bones of animals and grain from storage pits fill in the background to the story.

Communications

Roads and trackways are outside the scope of this book. They are almost impossible to date and what frequently appears to be an ancient routeway is often of relatively recent formation. However, it is worth

---

* ha = hectare. (1 ha is approximately 2·47 acres. There is a note on metric/imperial equivalents on page 16.)

mentioning what are considered to be the major prehistoric route-
ways. In south-east England the Pilgrims' Way and the Harroway run
from Canterbury to Salisbury Plain. A good section to visit lies on either
side of the Mole gap to the north of Dorking (TQ:150506 to 187514).
Further south the South Downs Ridgeway passes from Beachy Head
to Old Winchester Hill in Hampshire. It is not entirely prehistoric,
but connects many ancient monuments. The best-known routeway
is the Icknield Way with its continuation, the Berkshire Ridgeway,
which runs from the Norfolk coast near Wells-next-the-Sea to Salisbury Plain. There is a good walkable section north of Luton and
Hitchin (TL:080265 to 178313), and a 38 km length from Streatley
(SU:589815) to Wanborough (SU:231814) passes Uffington Castle
and Wayland's Smithy. A less easily found route is the Jurassic Way
between Lincoln and Somerset.

Bibliography

Ordnance Survey, *Field Archaeology in Britain*, London, HMSO, 1973.
Eric S. Wood, *Collins Field Guide to Archaeology in Britain*, London, Collins,
1979.

A Note on Dates
Historical dates and corrected radiocarbon dates are expressed in years BC;
uncorrected radiocarbon dates in years bc. This distinction has to be made
because it is now thought that the true dates are substantially earlier than the
dates given by radiocarbon for prehistoric times.

England

AVON

1 AVELINE'S HOLE, Burrington ST:476587

This cave consists of two chambers, both of which have been excavated and are now empty. Nothing of archaeological importance seems to have been found in the inner chamber, but the outer one seems to have been a living site of the late upper palaeolithic period. Here were found a series of flints, a harpoon and a necklace of sea-shells, as well as a number of human skeletons, two of which had been crushed by a roof fall. The cave occupation can probably be dated to around 12,000 BC, though a radiocarbon date for one of the skeletons suggests later mesolithic occupation. The finds are in the University of Bristol Spelaeological Society Museum.

2 BLAISE CASTLE, Bristol ST:559784

An oval fort of 2·8 ha which crowns Blaise Hill lies in the grounds of Blaise Castle. Its defences are slight on the south and south-east where the steepness of the ground provides a natural defence, but on the north and west there are two strong tree-covered banks and ditches. There is uncertainty about the position of the entrances. Trial excavations by Philip Rahtz have produced iron age B pottery, brooches and storage pits, indicating that settlement had begun by the third century BC. The site has been much altered by early nineteenth-century landscaping. [P. Rahtz, *PUBSS*, 8 (1959), 147.]

3 BLOODY ACRE CAMP, Cromhall ST:689915

A diamond-shaped promontory of some 4 ha is cut off by multiple defences on the north-west, where there are double banks and ditches, and in the south-west, where triple banks and ditches are present. The north-east and south-east sides are protected by steep natural slopes. There may have been an entrance at the north-eastern end of the rampart where it bends eastwards forming one side of an inturn. The site is covered with trees.

BURWALLS, see Clifton Promontory Forts.

4 BURY HILL CAMP, Winterbourne Down ST:652791

Pear-shaped in plan and enclosing 2 ha, this fort is surrounded by two walls of stone rubble separated by a U-shaped ditch 6 m wide and 1·5 m deep. Quarrying on the western side has damaged the defences. Of three entrances it is uncertain which are original. Excavations in 1926 produced only Romano-British material, including a house covered by a long mound in the centre of the fort and a well south of the north-west gate. [J. A. Davies and C. W. Phillips, *PUBSS,* 3 (1926), 8.]

5 CADBURY CAMP, Tickenham   ST:454725
This is an oval fort of 2·5 ha, with double ramparts and ditches, covered with bushes all round the site. There is an additional line of bank and ditch on the north side. The entrance is on the north and is well preserved. The outer bank and ditch swing outwards to form a hornwork which prevents a direct approach to the entrance. Limestone dug from the ditches was used to face the drystone walls. Excavations by H. St George Gray in 1922 produced iron age and Roman material suggesting that the site was in continuous use throughout those periods. A dyke 135 m to the west cuts off the easiest approach to the camp. [H. St George Gray, *P Somerset AS,* 68 (1923), 8.]

6 CLIFTON PROMONTORY FORTS, Bristol
Three promontory forts face each other across the Avon Gorge.
Clifton Down Camp (ST:566733). Three banks and ditches enclose some 1·2 ha forming an arc, which is broken by a probable entrance on the east side. There may have been another entrance close to the cliff edge on the north-west. This is a public open space and footpaths follow the ditches, though the ramparts have been disturbed by quarrying and trees and bushes. On the north-west side of the interior is a low bank and a rectangular enclosure, which, although unexcavated, is more recent than the fort.
Burwalls (Borough Walls) (ST:563729). Like Clifton Down, originally defended by three banks and two ditches, but now partly destroyed. It may have had two entrances on the south. It is mostly in the grounds of Burwalls House.
Stokeleigh Camp (ST:559733). The third arc-shaped fort, nearly 3 ha in size, has three banks and ditches like the rest. The inner rampart is massive, standing 10 m above the bottom of the ditch. A stone core is exposed. The entrance was probably at the northern end close to the Avon Gorge. [J. W. Haldane, *PUBSS,* 11, i (1966), 31.]

7 DOLEBURY, Churchill   ST:450590
A fine hillfort on the northern edge of the Mendips. Its wall of tumbled limestone and its external ditch surrounds an area of 7·5 ha, whilst a counterscarp bank gives added strength on the north, east and west. There is a good entrance at the west end which is inturned for 3·5 m. That at the east seems more likely to be recent, possibly connected

with lead mining in that part of the fort. A bank 75 m to the east is also of doubtful origin. Half a kilometre further east along the hilltop is a cross-ridge dyke (possibly unfinished). The long north-south mounds inside the hillfort are almost certainly rabbit warrens, hence the name Dolebury Warren to the east. [D. P. Dobson, *Archaeology of Somerset* (1931), 196.]

8   DRUID STOKE, Bristol   ST:561762
A possible chambered long barrow composed of a rectangular group of stones, one covered by a potential capstone, and close by a massive coverstone 3 m long supported by a smaller upright slab. Excavation in 1913 failed to produce any finds or positive information. [L. V. Grinsell, *TBGAS*, (1979).]

9   HORTON CAMP, Horton   ST:765845
Also known as The Castles, this site of 2 ha forms a promontory fort overlooking Horton. The west and the south are defended by natural scarps. On the north and east a bank curves round, its ditch now silted up. Midway along the rampart fire-reddened limestone is exposed in the outer face. The original entrance is not clear, but was probably at the south-eastern corner. A hollow way climbs up the scarp on the south side and may have provided an alternative approach. [RCHM, *Gloucs.*, I (1976), 65.]

10   KING'S WESTON, Bristol   ST:557782
This is a tiny promontory fort of 0·4 ha defended by steep slopes on the north and east. There is a rampart and ditch on the south and west, and another slighter bank 275 m further west that is an additional protection. Between this bank and the fort is a circular earthwork 18 m in diameter with a shallow ditch and low bank. It may surround a farmstead. Its ditch contained early iron age pottery. The ditch of the main fort was cut into solid rock. It was 1·8 m deep and 4·5 m wide with a flat floor and vertical sides. Its closeness to Blaise Castle hillfort 0·4 km to the north-east led its excavator, Philip Rahtz, to suggest that the owners of King's Weston might have been driven away by slingstones from the larger fort. [P. Rahtz, *PUBSS*, 8 (1956), 30.]

11   SODBURY CAMP, Little Sodbury   ST:760826
This is one of the finest multivallate hillforts on the Cotswold escarpment. Rectangular in shape, it encloses about 4·5 ha. There are widely spaced double ramparts and ditches on all sides except the west. The gap between them, about 30 m, is a feature of many south-western forts. The inner rampart appears to be of glacis construction and stands 1·5 m above the interior of the camp, and 4 m above the exterior. This bank curves round the north-west corner and runs halfway along the

west side where the steep hill scarp makes it unnecessary. The main entrance is midway along the east side where the rampart ends are slightly overlapped. At this point it is possible to see the fire-reddened core of the rampart, indicating that the gate has been burnt at some time. The outer rampart seems to be unfinished, being irregular in height. A wide berm separates it from an equally irregular outer ditch, which disappears on the north side. There are two gaps in the outer eastern rampart. That opposite the inner entrance is probably an original gateway, although the northern gap is out-turned and seems to show a guard chamber on the north side. [RCHM, *Gloucs.*, I (1976), 103.]

12   STANTON DREW   ST:601634

(Department of the Environment; closed Sundays). 'This noble monument is vulgarly called the Weddings; and they say 'tis a company that assisted at a nuptial solemnity thus petrify'd.' So wrote William Stukeley in 1743 of this group of three stone circles, which includes the second largest circle in Britain. Yet the low-lying siting of Stanton Drew, at the end of a modern farmyard with the church hiding the cove from view, makes it far from impressive.

The monument consists of three circles, a cove to the west, two short stone avenues, and an outlying stone called Hautville's Quoit. The north-east circle, the great circle and the cove are on the same alignment to the north-east, and a line can be projected from the centre of the south-west circle, through the centre of the great circle to Hautville's Quoit.

Only three stones of about thirty in the great circle are still standing; most of the rest are lying on their sides, marking a circle 113 m across. The majority of these stones are made of local dolomitic conglomerate, although one or two may be sarsen. From the great circle an avenue runs slightly north of east, its eight stones getting tangled with those of the north-east circle. This latter ring is much smaller and is oval in shape, measuring some 30 m by 32 m. It contained only eight stones, four of them still standing. Like the great circle, it too has an avenue, also containing eight stones and running eastwards. Two fields away to the south-west is the south-west circle, another oval some 43 m by 40 m. All its dozen stones are fallen.

South of the footpath behind the Druid's Arms Inn is the cove, a box-like setting of three great stones originally opening to the south, although the back stone is now fallen. Its purpose is unknown, though it resembles a burial chamber. Similar coves occur at Avebury and Arbor Low.

Hautville's Quoit lies fallen 360 m north-north-east of the great circle and east of Hautville's Quoit Farm (ST:602638). It now stands

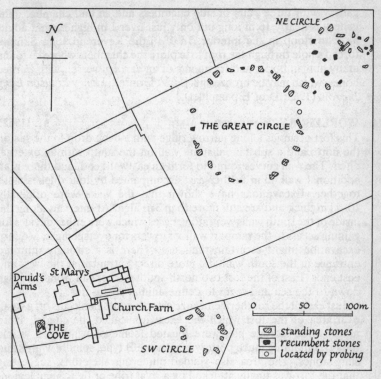

Fig 4. Stanton Drew circles, Avon

2·1 m high and was originally taller. It is possibly aligned astronomi-
cally, but this is unproven.

The sites have not been excavated, but they almost certainly date
from the late neolithic period, around 2600 BC. [A. Burl, *Rings of
Stone* (1979), 264.]

STOKELEIGH CAMP, see Clifton Promontory Forts.

13 STONEY LITTLETON, Wellow   ST:735572
(Department of the Environment; admission charge). 'The most perfect specimen of Celtic antiquity still existing in Great Britain' reads
the inscription just inside the entrance to this splendid chambered long
barrow, commemorating its careful restoration in 1858. The grass-
covered mound enclosed behind a drystone wall measures 30 m long
and 15 m wide. At the south-east is a horned entrance with a fine fossil
ammonite cast on the western door jamb. The entrance leads into a

gallery with three pairs of side chambers and an end chamber. The gallery is nearly 16 m long but only just over 1 m high so that adults have to stoop in the interior. In 1816 the Reverend John Skinner forced a hole through the roof to explore the chambers where he found many human bones and fragments of an earthen vessel, with burned bones, which may be bronze age. [L. V. Grinsell, *Stoney Littleton Long Barrow* (1963; D of E pamphlet).]

14 WORLEBURY, Weston-super-Mare   st:315625

This fort occupies a long narrow ridge with a deep drop to the sea on the north and a substantial stone wall on the south with an external ditch. The wall curves round to form an eastward end, and there is an additional wall 40 m further east accompanied by four ditches close together. Excavations have shown that the walls were originally 10–11 m thick and are still more than 3 m high. At intervals along the inside of the south walls were stone bases which were either devices for gaining access to the rampart walk or towers for overseeing it. Modern excavation might ascertain their use. There is a strongly inturned entrance in the south wall and more direct entrances at the west and east ends. East of the fort two north-south ditches run from the ridge down to the sea and seem to define animal enclosures.

Just east of the southern entrance a north-south bank cuts off a small oval area of the fort which the excavator called the citadel. Here ninety-three storage pits were located (some of which are visible today) containing much pottery of iron age B type, spindle whorls and sling-stones. The area also yielded numerous skeletons, suggesting that the fort was finally attacked by a rival tribe or by Roman legionaries. [C. W. Dymond, *Worlebury* (1902).]

BEDFORDSHIRE

1 CAESAR'S CAMP, Sandy TL:179490

This is a sandy spur facing south-west over the valley of the Ivel, and was an iron age promontory fort at least 3 ha in extent. It is protected by steep slopes on all sides, except on the north where any original defence has now been destroyed. On the west is a rampart and terrace, where a ditch may have been cut. This continues along the south-east side until an oblique original entrance is reached, at which point a rampart and ditch continue north-eastwards and fade out. [B. Wadmore, *Earthworks of Bedfordshire* (1920), 39.]

2 DEVIL'S JUMP STONE, Marston Moretaine SP:999409

Scarcely worthy of note in stone country, this small standing stone 0·6 m high is unusual in this part of Britain. It is a glacial erratic – originally one of three – erected beside the road at the spot where the Devil is traditionally said to have jumped on an unsuspecting landowner who played leap-frog on the Sabbath. It may be connected with the many prehistoric sites now only visible as crop-marks in this part of the Ouse valley.

3 FIVE KNOLLS, Dunstable TL:007210

This is the finest round barrow cemetery in the Chilterns; it contains two bowl-barrows, three bell-barrows enclosed within one ditch and two pond-barrows.

The most northerly bowl-barrow was excavated in 1928 by Gerald Dunning and Sir Mortimer Wheeler. In a central grave pit was a crouched female skeleton with a late neolithic knife at her shoulder. A secondary cremation burial in a collared urn was added later. The finds are all in Luton Museum. During the Saxon period about thirty bodies were buried in rows with their hands tied behind their backs, the victims of an unrecorded massacre. Some centuries later yet more bodies, gallows victims, were added to the mound.

The three joined bell-barrows have not been properly excavated but may date from the Wessex culture. There is no record of the southern bowl-barrow or the pond-barrows having been opened. [J. Dyer, *Bedfordshire Magazine*, 8 (1963), 15.]

4   GALLEY HILL, Streatley   TL:092270
Two small bowl-barrows on Galley Hill have both been excavated.
The southern one had been robbed but seemed to be of iron age date.
The northern barrow was kidney-shaped and covered a neolithic primary burial with Windmill Hill Pottery. A central burial pit was empty.
In the fourth century AD the barrow formed a slaughter cemetery for
about fifteen bodies, eleven men, three young women and a boy. In the
fifteenth century a gallows stood on the site and six of its victims were
found at its foot, buried head downwards, together with a witchcraft
deposit consisting of a horse's skull and dice. [J. Dyer, *Beds. A J,* 9
(1974), 13.]

5   HOUGHTON CONQUEST   TL:055405
Unusual on the sand hills of this area, a long barrow runs south-east to
north-west down the hill slope. It is 50 m long, 10 m wide and 1·5 m
high, with traces of side ditches. About 90 m east is a round barrow
18 m in diameter. Both are being encroached upon by scrub.

6   MAIDEN BOWER, Houghton Regis   SP:997224
This small iron age plateau fort encloses 4·4 ha within a single bank and
filled-in ditch. Only the rampart, 2 m high in places, is accessible, the
interior being ploughed. Excavations in 1913 suggest that the only
entrance, on the south-east side, was funnel-shaped, perhaps with a
bridge over the top. During the middle iron age the fort was the scene
of fighting with sling-stones and subsequent slaughter.
   Beneath the fort lies a neolithic causewayed camp. Several flat-
bottomed ditch sections were found in the last century and can still be
seen in the side of the modern quarry that is eroding the fort on the
northern side. These have produced bones and Windmill Hill pottery.
The iron age V-shaped ditches are also clearly visible. [J. Dyer,
Bedfordshire Magazine, 7 (1961), 320.]

7   SHARPENHOE CLAPPER, Sharpenhoe   TL:066302
A magnificent north-facing spur of the Chilterns appears to have been
formed into a promontory fort by a line of rampart which partially cuts
off its neck. Recent trial excavations by Brian Dix have shown that the
rampart is of early medieval date and possibly a rabbit warren, but
below it was a footing trench for a timber palisade of middle iron age
date, with a possible external ditch also buried beneath the medieval
bank. There are lynchets on the hillside to the south-west.

8   WAULUD'S BANK, Luton   TL:062247
Now difficult to trace, a semicircular bank, still 2·5 m high in places, and
a silted outer ditch 6 m wide sweep in an arc from the source of the Lea,
past the blocks of flats, and round the hill crest to Youth House.

Excavations in recent years show that the site is neolithic in date and exhibits similarities with henge monuments, particularly Marden in Wiltshire, where the river forms part of the circumference of the enclosure. No entrances or internal structures have been located, though grooved ware has been found and many arrow-heads, suggesting hunting in the marshes or warfare. [A. Selkirk, *Current Archaeology*, 3 (1972–3), 173.]

BERKSHIRE

1 CAESAR'S CAMP, Easthampstead   SU:863657

This is probably the best example of a true iron age contour fort in
England. So rigidly do the defences follow every valley along the 122 m
line that the plan resembles an oak leaf. It is relatively straight only on
the southern side, where it is most easily accessible. Two of the valleys
on the east and west seem to form simple entrances, and there are two
others on the north and south. The site is unexcavated. [M. A. Cotton,
Berks. A I, 60 (1962), 43.]

2 GRIMSBURY CASTLE, Hermitage   SU:512723

Belonging to the group sometimes called multiple enclosure forts,
Grimsbury is triangular in plan, its earthworks reflecting the contours
of the hill. They enclose 3·2 ha and are broken by three probable
entrances. One, on the west, is slightly incurved with a northward
curving outer line of defence 120 m long. There is a second simple
entrance gap on the north, and a third on the south-west, which may
have led to springs. To the west of the fort is a second curved line of
rampart and ditch forming an enclosure. Excavations date the fort's
occupation to the third and second centuries BC. [P. Wood, *Trans-
actions of the Newbury and District Field Club*, 11 (1963), 53.]

3 GRIM'S DITCH, Aldworth   SU:546785 to 570792

It is now generally accepted that the earthworks that run through the
Berkshire Downs and the Chilterns are all of iron age date, though they
may not all be part of the same system. One of the best preserved
sections of bank and ditch lies east of Beche Farm. About 1 km east it
makes a right-angled turn north. It splits into two where the road from
Hungerford Green crosses it. Both branches end after a further
0·8 km.

Another tree-covered section lies to the south on Hart Ridge, in
Brooms Wood and Bowler's Copse (SU:585775). Yet another stretch
about 1 km in length lies between the A417 near the Grotto (on the
Thames) and Hurdle Shaw (SU:593796). In this area the ditch climbs
steeply from the Thames valley, and takes the unusual form of having
its ditch facing up the hill slope. Such a work was almost entirely
intended as a boundary and not for defence. At all times the ditch is on

the north side of the bank, and the greatest height from ditch bottom to crest of bank is about 1·8 m.

4 INKPEN LONG BARROW (Combe Gibbet)   SU:365623
Lying east to west, this long barrow is 60 m in length, 22 m wide and 2 m high. It is flanked by ditches 4·5 m wide and 1 m deep. It is crowned by a wooden gibbet which is a modern reconstruction.

5 LAMBOURN LONG BARROW   SU:323834
At the south end of Wescot Wood lies a mutilated long barrow about 80 m long and 20 m wide, still standing a metre high at its eastern end. Martin Atkins dug into it a century ago and found skeletons, but left no details. Recently John Wymer found a crouched female skeleton, with a necklace of dog whelk shells, in a sarsen stone cist at the eastern end. It did not form part of the primary deposit, but had been tucked into the core of sarsen stones. Charcoal from the barrow gave a radiocarbon date of 3415 bc ± 180. [J. Wymer, *Berks. AJ*, 62 (1965–1966), 1.]

6 LAMBOURN SEVEN BARROWS, Lambourn   SU:328828
This is one of the most accessible groups of round barrows in southern England. Although there are some forty barrows in the vicinity altogether, only those in the enclosure beside the road may be visited without permission, and these are described in some detail. These barrows lie in two rows running north-west to south-east, and were numbered by L. V. Grinsell and Humphrey Case. Commence at the north-west end of the row nearer the road.

38 A small saucer-barrow 13 m in diameter with a ditch 0·9 m deep and a slight outer bank.

10 Two barrows enclosed by a single ditch. A hollow on top of the north mound was made by Martin Atkins about 1850. He found the bones of an ox and a dog.

11 A bowl-barrow 3 m high and 30 m in diameter. Its contents are unknown.

12 A bowl-barrow with an earthen tree-planting ring (a bank intended to protect newly planted trees from animals) around it.

13 A fine disc-barrow 30 m across, with a central mound 18 m in diameter and 0·3 m high. Again there are no records of its contents.

The second row lies further from the road; from the north-west:

4 A large disc- or saucer-barrow 36 m in diameter.

5 A bowl-barrow 21 m in diameter and 1·8 m high.

6,7 A large bowl-barrow with a tiny barrow on its south side.

8 Two barrows enclosed within a single ditch, their mounds overlapping, suggesting that one is earlier than the other.

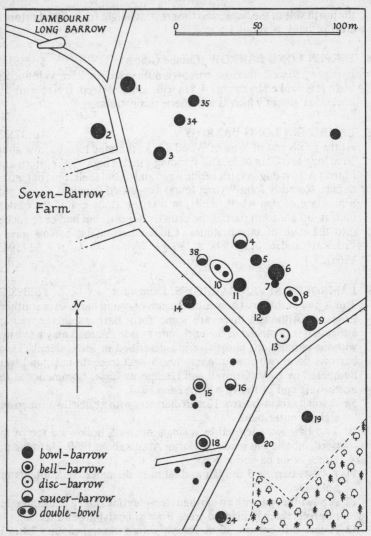

Fig 5. Lambourn Seven Barrows, Berkshire

9   A bowl-barrow 18 m in diameter and 1·8 m high contained a sarsen stone cist holding a female cremation in a collared urn.

About 180 m south of the above group and beside a trackway is the largest bell-barrow at Lambourn (18). Partly covered by trees, the mound is 1·8 m high and 18 m wide. In a sarsen cist at the centre was a cremation burial accompanied by a bronze awl and a small jet pendant. Beside the Kingston Lisle road 230 m to the north of the main group is a reconstructed bowl-barrow (1). At its centre were two cremations with a small bronze knife, a bronze awl and a pygmy cup. The surface of the barrow was covered with a late bronze age urnfield consisting of 122 cremation burials, fifty-four protected by sarsen stones and fifty-eight in fragmentary cinerary urns. [H. Case, *Berks. AJ*, 55 (1956–7), 15.]

7 MORTIMER COMMON, Stratfield Mortimer   su:643651
A linear cemetery of five barrows running from north-west to south-east. At the north-west is an easily overlooked disc-barrow, overlapped by a small bell-barrow, then a second bell-barrow 42 m in diameter and 1·8 m high, and finally two small bowl-barrows. There is no record of the contents of any of the barrows.

8 WALBURY, Combe   su:374617
Walbury fort is situated on Combe Hill, the highest chalk hill in Britain at 297 m above sea-level. Enclosing 33 ha it is the largest hillfort in Berkshire. It is trapezoidal in shape and is surrounded by a single bank and ditch, with faint traces of an outer counterscarp bank. There are two entrances, a small one in the south-east side and a slightly inturned example at the north-west corner. From this corner minor earthworks connected with hollow ways run north-west down the hill, and in the same area two banks run across the hill spur. The larger western one, a cross-ridge dyke, seems to provide an extra line of defence, and the slighter bank, nearer the entrance, seem to have formed some kind of barbican. Various circular depressions inside the camp may have been hut circles. [M. A. Cotton, *Berks. AJ*, 60 (1962), 42.]

BUCKINGHAMSHIRE

1 BODDINGTON CAMP, Wendover   SP: 882080

The fort encloses about 7 ha at the end of a lemon-shaped promontory.
It is defended by a single bank and ditch on all sides except the
north-west, where it has been destroyed. An entrance gap at the
south-western end may be original although somewhere in the north-
western area would seem to be more logical. The rampart is built of
dumped chalk faced with turves and backed by a pile of flints. Aerial
photographs showed an inner enclosure, but tree planting has effectively stopped any hope of following this up. [RCHM, *Bucks. South*
(1912), 184.]

2 BULSTRODE CAMP, Gerrard's Cross   SU: 994880

Bulstrode is now a public open space. It is oval in shape, enclosing 9 ha,
and is defended by two banks with outer ditches except on the west and
north-west sides, where the outermost ditch has been destroyed. Excavation in 1924 suggested that the rampart was of dumped gravel and
sand. There are a number of gaps which might be original entrances.
That on the north-east seems most probable; that on the south-west
has been proved to be modern. The excavations failed to date the site,
which is the largest hillfort in Buckinghamshire. [C. Fox, *Records of
Bucks.*, 11 (1924), 283.]

3 CHOLESBURY CAMP, Cholesbury   SP: 930072

This tree-covered oval plateau fort encloses 4 ha within its circumference. The defences consist of a single bank, ditch and pronounced
counterscarp with a second line of ditch and counterscarp on the
southern half of the site. On the west the inner and outer ditches are
separated by a triangular berm which terminates suddenly at a low
cross-bank and ditch, about 100 m north of the church drive. Excavation in 1932 showed this cross-ditch to be the earliest feature on the
site. It possibly marks some earlier agricultural complex of which
traces can be found between Cholesbury and the Grim's Ditch 1·6 km
to the north. Pottery from the site was considered to be not earlier than
the second century BC and native in character. [K. Kimball, *J Brit.
Archaeol. Assn*, 39 (1933), 187.]

4   THE COP, Bledlow   SP: 773011
Hidden in the woods, this barrow is 18 m in diameter and about 1·8 m
high. Excavation showed that it had no ditch and had been constructed
by scraping soil from the surrounding area. A polished stone axe-head
and a tanged bronze dagger were found in the central grave, but the
burial seems to have been robbed. A cremation was added in the
bronze age, and more burials in the Saxon period. [J. F. Head,
Records of Bucks., 13 (1938), 328.]

5   DANESBOROUGH, Wavendon   SP: 922348
This little hillfort of 3·4 ha lies in thick woodland. It is roughly rectangular in shape and is protected by a bank, ditch and counterscarp
except at the north-east, where the rampart is either unfinished or
destroyed. A hollow way leads to the original south-western entrance,
where iron age pottery has been found. A second sunken track leads to
the north-east, where there may once have been another entrance.
Extensive earthworks outside the fort to the west have recently been
wantonly destroyed without record by a golf course. They seem to
have formed some of the most extensive cattle ranching boundaries
in Britain. [J. Berry, *Records of Bucks.*, 11 (1924), 363.]

6   GRIM'S DITCH, Chilterns
This prehistoric dyke runs intermittently for 40 km from Naphill near
West Wycombe to Dunstable (Beds.), seeming to mark the boundary
of iron age expansion, perhaps of the tribe of the Catuvellauni. The
gaps in the dyke, sometimes three or four kilometres in length, were
possibly filled by forest land or ancient boundaries, such as fences
or hedges, long since destroyed. The best sections to visit are those
near Great Hampden (Bucks.), especially the section running north-
east from Redland End (SP: 835023). South-east of Hampden House,
two earlier burial mounds have been incorporated in the ditch
(SP: 857020). Another fine length can be traced for some distance on
Pitstone Hill (SP: 949142 – not marked on the Ordnance Survey maps).
The section on Berkhamsted Common is now considered to be part of
a medieval boundary ditch of Berkhamsted Castle. [J. Dyer, *Antiquity,* 37 (1963), 46.]

7   IVINGHOE BEACON, Ivinghoe   SP: 960168
This rounded downland spur is capped by the slight remains of one of
the oldest hillforts in England. A single rampart and ditch form a pear-
shaped plan enclosing 2·2 ha. On the weaker south and western sides is
a second line of ditch facing the Icknield Way, which ran south of the
hill at this point. The entrance, about 3 m wide, was at the eastern end,
and the entrance passage was lined with posts. The ramparts were of
two lines of timbers erratically spaced, filled with chalk rubble and

faced by a chalk-cut ditch 3 m wide and deep. When excavated, the interior of the fort was very eroded, but enough post-holes survived to suggest that both circular and square buildings had existed, perhaps side by side. Although most of the pottery was of the earliest iron age, 500–400 BC, a bronze razor and pieces of sword could be dated to the eighth century BC, leading to the conclusion that Ivinghoe is one of the earliest forts in the country, an idea supported by the erratic construction of the rampart, suggesting inexperienced workers. [M. A. Cotton and S. S. Frere, *Records of Bucks.*, 18 (1968), 187.]

8 LODGE HILL, Saunderton   SP:789004
Ploughed down, but still clearly visible as mounds amongst the growing crop, these must once have been the finest bell-barrows in the Chilterns. They are best viewed from the hilltop to the south. [J. Dyer, *Arch. J*, 116 (1961), 23.]

9 PITSTONE HILL, Pitstone   SP:949142
Two flint mines have been recognized at the north-western end of the chalk escarpment. Both are still about 3 m deep and have piles of waste material on their lower edges. They would not be remarkable in Sussex but in the Chilterns are rare, though there are other inaccessible mines not far away in Whipsnade Zoo. Immediately east of the Pitstone mines traces of a causewayed ditch can be seen, which may be of neolithic date.

  Below the mines on the escarpment face is a section of the Chiltern's Grim's Ditch, a linear earthwork thought to be of iron age date. [J. Dyer and A. J. Hales, *Records of Bucks.*, 17 (1961), 49.]

10 PULPIT HILL, Great Kimble   SP:832050
Shield-shaped in plan, this little contour fort of 1·6 ha is defended by a double rampart and ditch. The north-eastern and south-western sides need only a single bank and ditch due to the natural steepness of the hill. The main entrance is on the east and is of the simple straight-through type. A break on the west might allow access to a look-out post. Numerous banks and ditches in the woods nearby may be connected with iron age agriculture or ranching. [RCHM, *Bucks. South* (1912), 164.]

11 WEST WYCOMBE CAMP, West Wycombe   SP:827949
A circular fort of 1·2 ha, its ramparts covered with trees, surrounds the churchyard at West Wycombe. The rampart still rises 3·5 m on the north-east side and is separated from an outer bank 2 m high by a ditch 15 m wide and still 1·6 m deep. The defences were destroyed on the south-east to make way for the large eighteenth-century Dashwood

mausoleum. The original entrance to the fort probably coincided with the north-west gate into the churchyard.

The caves below Church Hill are man-made and of medieval and later date. [RCHM, *Bucks. South* (1912), 318.]

12   WHITELEAF BARROW, Princes Risborough   SP:822040
On a false crest above the Whiteleaf Cross (medieval) are the disturbed and overgrown remains of a kidney-shaped barrow excavated in the late 1930s. It is surrounded by a circular ditch 24 m in diameter, but had a hollow forecourt on the east. Under the mound was a wooden burial chamber 2·4 m long and 1·7 m wide. The left foot of a middle-aged man lay in the chamber. The rest of his bones were scattered in the forecourt outside. Pieces of more than fifty neolithic pots and hundreds of flints were found scattered through the barrow mound, suggesting that they lay on the ground surface when the material for the barrow was scraped up. There are two other small barrows along the hill ridge to the east. [V. G. Childe and I. F. Smith, *PPS*, 20 (1954), 212.]

CAMBRIDGESHIRE

1 BELSAR'S HILL, Willingham TL:423703

This is an oval fort unusually placed on a slight island at the edge of the Fens. It consists of a single rampart and ditch, broken by entrances on the west and, possibly, east. Although now under pasture it has suffered much from ploughing in the past. It is linked by a causeway through the marshes to the Isle of Ely 14·5 km north-east. [C. Fox, *Archaeology of the Cambridge Region* (1923), 137.]

2 THORNHAUGH, Thornhaugh TF:066008

If this is a henge monument, as seems likely, then it is situated in a classic low-lying position. It consists of a wide but low bank with ditches inside and out, and traces of an inner bank. It has a diameter of about 85 m and entrances at the north-north-west and south-south-east. The ditches have neatly squared-off ends, like the Big Rings at Dorchester, Oxon. (destroyed). C. W. Phillips has suggested that the site might be an example of a seventeenth-century pleasance or water garden. [R. J. C. Atkinson and others, *Excavations at Dorchester, Oxon,* 1 (1951), 104.]

3 WANDLEBURY, Stapleford TL:493534

Two massive banks and ditches once enclosed a circular area of 6 ha. Sadly the inner bank was pushed into its ditch in the eighteenth century and the outer bank was breached a number of times, all in aid of landscape gardening. The only certain original entrance is the gap on the south-east.

Excavations in 1955–6 showed that in the fifth century BC the site was defended only by the outer rampart and ditch. At that time the rampart was 4 m wide and was faced with timber both inside and out. The external ditch had steep sides and a flat floor. In the fourth century BC, after a period of disuse, the ditch was recut and the material obtained was dumped outside to form a counterscarp. The original rampart was replaced and all the defences strengthened by the construction of an inner rampart and V-shaped ditch. The new ditch was 5 m deep and 11·5 m wide. The rampart was given a strong outer facing of timber. The interior of the camp was intensively occupied throughout its existence, which came to an end about 250 BC. [B. R. Hartley, *P Cambs. Ant. Soc.*, 50 (1957), 1.]

CHESHIRE

1 CASTLE DITCH, Delamere   SJ:553695

Situated on Eddisbury Hill is a fort of 4·5 ha surrounded by two lines
of ramparts and ditch. Excavations between 1936 and 1938 showed
four iron age phases. At first, in the second century BC, a palisade was
set up on the eastern half of the hill. This was renewed early in the first
century with a single stone rampart and ditch, and broken by a simple
entrance gap and wooden guard chamber on the south side. Later in
the iron age the camp was extended to take in the west side of the hill
and a second inturned entrance was constructed at the north-west. Just
inside the entrance a hut was uncovered with five successive clay
hearths. The rampart was of earth and stone and near the entrance it
had timber lacing. Outside was a ditch 7 m wide and 3 m deep. In its
final stage the second outer bank and ditch were constructed, the
entrances were more deeply inturned and the walls were refaced with
drystone walling. At the eastern side the entrance was remodelled in
stone with guard chambers both north and south of the gate. The
Romans slighted the fort late in the first century AD and it fell into
decay. It should be noticed that the site was reoccupied in the tenth
century AD when the outer ditch was recut and the rampart heightened. [M. A. Cotton, *Arch. J*, 111 (1954), 89.]

2 KELLSBORO' CASTLE, Kelsall   SJ:532675

This is an oval hillfort of 3 ha, with steep slopes on the west and
south-east. Only on the north does the fort need the protection of a
single bank and ditch 7·5 m wide. The entrance is a narrow gap
between the eastern end of the rampart and the natural slope defining
the promontory.

3 MAIDEN CASTLE, Bickerton   SJ:497528

This rectangular promontory fort of 0·5 ha is protected by steep cliffs
on the west and north, and there are two banks on the south and east. It
is probable that the outer rampart was first built in the early iron age,
when it consisted of a bank of sand faced with a stone wall. This wall
was strengthened by increasing its thickness to 2 m by adding a new
outer face and filling behind it with rubble. The height was raised by
digging out sand from the rear and setting a palisade on top. The later

inner rampart was 6·5 m thick and faced with stone on either side. Beams tied the two walls together and the space between them was filled with an earth and rubble core. The beams were found burnt. This later inner wall was probably built in the first centurv BC. The entrance in the east side was of a simple type with an inturn forming a passage 12 m long, with gateposts halfway along it. A hut was found behind one of the inturns. [W. J. Varley, *Cheshire before the Romans* (1964), 95.]

4 SPONDS HILL, Lyme Handley   sj:970803
A small round barrow about 14 m in diameter and 1·5 m high has been excavated, but only a cremation without accompanying grave goods was found. [*TLCAS*, 30 (1912), 184.]

CLEVELAND

ESTON NAB CAMP, Eston and Wilton   NZ:567183
This semicircular promontory fort is situated on a steep cliff edge at the
north-western corner of the Eston Hills, commanding wide views in all
directions. The rampart, ditch and counterscarp enclose about 1 ha.
The rampart consists of a clay bank backed by a stone wall 4·5 m thick,
some of which can still be seen in section on the cliff edge. There may
have been an original entrance near the Beacon. A palisade enclosure
inside the fort has been found by excavation. Bronze age pottery may
indicate that it pre-dates the hillfort. [*YAJ*, 42 (1969), 237.]

CORNWALL and the ISLES OF SCILLY

1   ADVENT BARROW, Advent   sx:137834
As far as is known, this triple bell-barrow is unexcavated. Three
flat-topped mounds are enclosed within the same oval ditch, whose
overall diameter is 61 m.

2   BANT'S CAIRN, St Mary's, Isles of Scilly   sv:911123
Probably the largest of the entrance graves in the Scilly Isles, it is
surrounded by two concentric walls of stone: a retaining wall for the
cairn and a lower outer 'collar'. The passage through the collar is 4·5 m
long; the chamber to which it leads is 4·5 m long and 1·5 m wide and
high. When excavated by George Bonsor in 1899 four piles of cremated bones were found at the end of the chamber, together with
pieces of neolithic and late bronze age pottery. [P. Ashbee, *Ancient
Scilly* (1974), 305.]

3   BARROWFIELDS, Newquay   sw:820623
Only three barrows remain today of a group of about eighteen. The
majority were destroyed in 1821.

4   BODRIFTY   sw:445354
A fourth-century-BC open settlement of circular huts was surrounded
in the second century BC by a pound wall enclosing 1·2 ha. The pound
was not very strong and probably served only to contain animals.
Inside were about eight huts, the largest with an external diameter of
14 m. They had central fireplaces and were probably lit from the
doorway or through cracks in the thatched roof. The walls were faced
internally and externally with stone and filled with rubble; some stood
a metre high. On the hillside above the village were small fields that
can still be seen as low banks today. Undecorated pottery was plenti-
ful; spindle whorls tell us that wool was spun and many pebbles suggest
that the sling was the main weapon in use. [D. Dudley, *Arch. J*, 113
(1956), 1.]

5   BOLEIGH FOGOU, Boleigh   sw:437252
Once enclosed within an earthwork, the fogou now stands alone. A
long passage, 1·5 m wide, runs south-west to north-east for about 12 m,

facing into the direction of the prevailing wind. There are entrances at both ends. On the western side there is a short L-shaped side passage with an air-shaft hole in the roof. The western door jamb is rather uneven and has been claimed by some to represent a carved figure. The purpose of fogous in general is obscure but the most acceptable explanation seems to be as a communal cellar or cold store. As hiding places they would have been veritable death-traps. [A. Fox, *South-West England* (1964), 151.]

6   BOSCAWEN-UN STONE CIRCLE, St Buryan   sw:412274

Nineteen very regularly spaced blocks of stone are enclosed within a modern field wall. This low-lying circle is 23 m in diameter, with a leaning pillar of stone 2·5 m at its centre. This may once have been the site of foundation deposits and offerings. It has no apparent astronomical significance.

7   BRANE, Sancreed   sw:402282

The best example in Cornwall of the entrance graves normally found in the Isles of Scilly. The barrow is 6 m in diameter and 2 m high and is held in position by a wall of large stone blocks. On the south-east is an entrance passage that leads directly into the chamber. The whole is 2·2 m long and 1 m wide, roofed with two capstones.

8   CADSON BURY, St Ive   sx:343674

This isolated hilltop due west of the river Lynher is encircled by a bank and ditch enclosing 2·8 ha. The bank is quite low, about 2 m, and the ditch is relatively shallow, but it gains an impression of strength from the steepness of the hillside in between. There is an apparently original entrance on the east with a claw-like inturn which suggests the presence of guard chambers.

9   CARLAND CROSSROADS, Mitchell   sw:845539

There were originally about thirty barrows in this group. Today the most accessible is the bell-barrow north of the A30. It has a deep 'robbers' pit in its mound, which is about 1·8 m high. There are three round barrows south of the road.

10   CARN BREA, Redruth   sw:686407

This large iron age hillfort (15 ha) dominated a rather derelict area of Cornwall. It is capped by a medieval castle on a summit to the east and a hideous monument to Sir Francis Basset on the west. Between these, along the north side of the hill, runs a single drystone wall, with two others looping round the south side. It seems likely that the fort was built in three stages: I, a small enclosure around the area of the Basset monument; II, the inner fortification on the central saddle of the hill and III, the outer circuit looping down the hillside, which appears to be incomplete. There are a number of entrance gaps. In stage I there is a gap due north of the monument which is lined with stone slabs. Another, probably of stage II, lies about 150 m south-west of the castle. Excavations have shown rock-cut ditches outside the walls and about a dozen circular iron age huts inside, producing iron age pottery of south-western B fabric and cordoned ware. In the mid-eighteenth century a hoard of Kentish gold staters were found on the hill suggesting far-reaching trade contacts.

Particularly interesting is the stone wall round the castle on the eastern summit. Excavation indicates that the wall is of neolithic origin. Within it are irregular huts, including one leaning up against the wall, which are undoubtedly the oldest in Britain. They have been dated by carbon-14 to between 3109 and 2687 BC. Considerable amounts of neolithic pottery have come from the whole area and it is not inconceivable that *all* the fortifications could be neolithic. [R. Mercer, *Cornish Archaeology*, 9 (1970), 53; 11 (1972) 5; 12 (1973), 57.]

11 **CARN EUNY, Sancreed**   SW:403288
(Department of the Environment). This little village began life around 400 BC with a group of timber huts, all traces of which have now disappeared. Later these were rebuilt in stone, and four courtyard houses and a few smaller huts from the first century BC can be seen today. The inhabitants seem to have been farmers and stock-breeders, but to have had some involvement in the local tin trade. Their pottery was of cordoned type and quantities of grinding stones and spindle whorls were excavated.

Perhaps the most interesting feature is the souterrain or fogou, entered along an underground passage 20 m long, with a low 'creep' passage at the west end and a circular corbelled chamber which seems to have been the first feature on the site. The fogou was probably an elaborate cold storage chamber for the whole village. [P. M. L. Christie, *PPS*, 44 (1978), 309.]

12 **CARN GLUZE (Ballowal), St Just**   SW:355313
One of the most dramatic archaeological sites in southern Britain. It was excavated by Borlase and Lukis in 1874, and from their discoveries we can try to reconstruct the original tomb. First a T-shaped pit 2 m deep was dug, with steps leading down to it. Since no burial was found it was presumably of ritual use. Around it stood four small stone cists (no longer visible) holding miniature middle bronze age urns. Over the pit and cists an oval corbelled dome was constructed 9 m by 11 m across and about 3·6 m high. It was completely sealed off, with no entrance, though a further small burial chamber was incorporated into it. Out-

side the dome were yet two more empty burial cists. Finally, a massive
wall was built round the whole structure, 20 m by 22·5 m in plan, 6 m
thick and 1·5 m high. In the south-west side of this a rectangular burial
chamber about 3 m long of neolithic entrance grave type was built.
[A. Fox, *South-west England* (1964), 52.]

13 CASTILLY, Luxulyan   sx:032627
An oval bank with an internal ditch encloses a small henge monument
with a single entrance on the northern side. The bank still stands 2 m
high but is covered with bushes, making it difficult to view. It is built
from local slate and seems to have been remodelled in medieval or
Civil War times. Round barrows close by support the assumption that
it is probably religious in character. [C. Thomas, *Cornish Archaeology*, 3 (1964), 3.]

14 CASTLE-AN-DINAS, St Columb Major   sx:946623
Wild and overgrown with gorse, this fort site has two rings of massive
stone-built ramparts, ditches and counterscarp banks. In parts the
inner ring has an additional ditch outside the counterscarp. Between
the two rings are traces of a third rampart and ditch, but this is quite
slight in contrast to the rest and is probably incomplete, though
whether it pre-dates or post-dates the other earthworks is uncertain.
The only original entrance seems to have been on the south-west,
although there are other gaps in the ramparts. The camp has its own
water supply feeding a pond in the centre, where a number of hut
circles can also be traced. [B. Wailes, *Cornish Archaeology*, 2 (1963),
51.]

15 CASTLE DORE, St Sampson   sw:103548
The two asymetrically placed ramparts and ditches of this circular fort
are densely overgrown. The inner circle encloses 0·5 ha and has a
counterscarp bank on the eastern annexe side. The outer circle lies
beside the inner on the west and forms a strong defence, though the
ditch has been almost filled in on the west. On the east the defences
diverge around a crescent-shaped enclosure, through which the fort
was entered by a barbican-like passageway. The fort has been excavated and shown to be of two periods. The earlier, about 150 BC, was
protected by the banks described above, each being about the same
height. Later, about 50 BC, the inner rampart was rebuilt with a vertical
stone outer facing, and the barbican passageway was flattened and a
new entrance tunnel constructed. At least five round houses were
associated with the first phase and a further four with the second.
Three rectangular buildings were attributed to the early medieval
period, perhaps the palace of King Mark of the Tristan and Isolde
legend. [C. A. R. Radford, *J R Inst. Cornwall*, NS 1 (1951), 1.]

16 CASTLEWITCH, Callington   sx:371685

On the summit of Balstone Down is an outcrop of Cornish greenstone, a source of polished stone axes in the neolithic period. Less than half a kilometre to the south is the Castlewitch henge monument which must have been constructed by the stone quarriers and used for their personal ceremonies. It is a small monument, oval in shape, with the usual bank and internal ditch. There is an entrance on the southern side. [A. Fox, *Ant. J*, 32 (1952), 67.]

17 CHUN CASTLE, Morvah   sw:405339

Remotely crowning a hill frequently shrouded in sea mist, this is one of my favourite forts. It is small and circular with an inner drystone wall 2·5 m high, separated by a slight ditch from an outer wall and ditch. The outer wall is 85 m in diameter and is broken on the south-west by an entrance. This is not directly opposite the entrance into the inner enclosure, but staggered so that an attacker must present his right flank to the defender. The inner gate has two massive gateposts, 1·5 m apart, and is strongly inturned. Examination of the outer wall opposite the inner gate shows a blocked-up entrance, so we may assume that this was originally of the straight-through type. Inside the fort are a well and a number of roughly rectangular enclosures which belong to the latest occupation of the fort, which, on pottery evidence, was probably between 550 and 650 AD. A furnace may also belong to this period. Earlier huts were circular, about 5 m in diameter and about a dozen in number. They were associated with iron age pottery with curvilinear decoration as well as with duck-stamped wares of the third and second centuries BC. A curiosity of the site are the pulpit-like features on the main rampart, set up in the nineteenth century as preaching places for open-air Methodist services. [C. Thomas, *Arch. J*, 130 (1973), 273.]

18 CHUN QUOIT, Morvah   sw:402339

A giant mushroom-shaped capstone 2·4 m square supported by four wallstones forms one of the finest surviving burial chambers in Cornwall. The chamber measures 1·8 m long by 1·7 m wide. A few scattered stones on the south might mark an entrance passage. Visit quietly; the tomb contained a sleeping tramp when I last saw it! [G. E. Daniel, *Prehistoric Chamber Tombs* (1950), 238.]

19 CHYSAUSTER, Madron   sw:472350

A steep climb up a narrow path leads to one of the best preserved of the Cornish courtyard villages. Eight houses, in pairs, line a village street; down an alleyway lies a ninth. The houses tend to be oval in plan, and an entrance passage, often 6 m long, leads into a courtyard out of which opens a series of circular and rectangular rooms, some for living and some for working. When they were excavated many of these

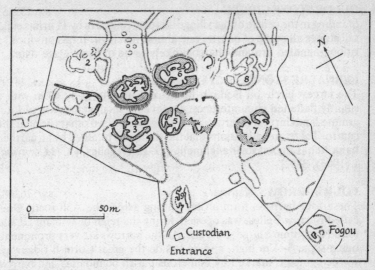

Fig 6. Chysauster, Cornwall

produced fireplaces and corn-grinding querns, as well as large quantities of pottery and other domestic rubbish. At least one of the houses had a drain under its floor. It is not clear how the houses were roofed; some were perhaps corbelled, others thatched, and the courtyard was left open to the sky. Gardens were attached to each house, with low stone walls dividing them from their neighbours. One ruined house at the south-eastern corner of the village covers a small fogou. While the village probably specialized in stock-rearing and some arable farming, it is noticeable that a track leads from the village to a stream where tin-working was carried out. Chysauster is less than 6 km from the sea, where the ore was shipped to the European continent. The village probably came into being about 100 BC and continued into Roman times. [H. O. Hencken, *Archaeologia*, 83 (1933), 237.]

20 CRUTHER'S HILL, St Martin's, Isles of Scilly   sv:929152
Three knolls run from north to south on Cruther's Hill, each with barrows on them. The northern is about 6 m in diameter, with a chamber that almost penetrates the cairn, and is entered from the south-west. There is a well-marked kerb around this barrow. On the central knoll the barrow is 8 m in diameter. The burial chamber is entered from the east, and widens towards the inner end. It is 4·5 m long. There are two barrows on the southern hill, both about 6 m in diameter, one with a good burial chamber, the other ruined. [P. Ashbee, *Ancient Scilly* (1974), 299.]

21 **DULOE STONE CIRCLE**   sx: 235583
Standing in the centre of the village this oval ring 12 m by 11 m has eight
tall stones all made of quartz, one almost 3 m high. It has produced a
ribbon-handled urn and charcoal likely to be of bronze age date.

22 **FERNACRE STONE CIRCLE, Fernacre**   sx: 144799
The largest circle on Bodmin Moor measures 46 m by 43 m with a
slightly flattened circumference. Its seventy small stones are of local
granite, and thirty-nine are still standing today. Two others lie near the
centre. There are indications that the circle was retained by an earthen
bank. It has a good solar alignment. [G. F. Tregelles, *VCH Cornwall*,
I (1906), 379.]

23 **FOUR BARROWS, Kenwyn**   sw: 762482
These four barrows form an arc cutting across the A30 road. One,
called Burrow Belles, was opened during the reign of William III and
found to contain a large stone cist. All the barrows are very prominent,
being some 3–4 m high, and lie beside the great Cornish ridgeway,
whose course is marked by numerous parish boundaries and barrow
groups.

24 **GIANT'S CASTLE, St Mary's, Isles of Scilly**   sv: 924101
This small promontory fort is defended by three lines of stone-built
ramparts and rock-cut ditches. The inner rampart utilized natural rock
outcrops. The site has been badly robbed of stone since it was described by Borlase in 1756. Duck-stamped pottery is reputed to have
been found in military trenches during the Second World War.
[P. Ashbee, *Ancient Scilly* (1974), 211.]

25 **GIANT'S FRYING PAN, Caerwynnen**   sw: 650373
It is just possible to make out traces of a mound around this collapsed
burial chamber. Its main feature is a 10-tonne capstone which fell in
1834, was restored, and fell again in 1967. It was originally supported
on three uprights. The site is unexcavated.

26 **GIANT'S QUOIT, Pawton**   sw: 966696
An enormous rectangular capstone, originally measuring 4 m by 2·1 m
and 0·8 m thick, is supported by three out of seven wallstones. Two
further stones would have supported the front of the stone, which has
broken off. The chamber is in a ploughed field and is difficult to reach
except in the winter. There are traces of an oval mound 21 m by 15 m.

27 **GURNARD'S HEAD, Zennor**   sw: 433387
This massive rocky headland was fortified with two banks and ditches
60 m long, which isolated an area of 3 ha. The inner rampart was the

main defence, consisting of a stone wall with steep batter, about 3 m wide and still 2 m high in places. The back of the wall was stepped. In front were two ditches, pecked into the hard rock, with a dumped bank of rubble between them. Another ditch, apparently unfinished, was separated from the main group. It was V-shaped, 3·5 m wide, and covered only half of the promontory. There appears to be an oblique entrance in the main rampart but it was not possible to excavate it. However, part of the rocky interior was examined where the eastern slope is more sheltered. Here traces of thirteen circular huts can still be seen. The pottery discovered can be dated to the beginning of the first century BC. The western slope is bare rock and is unlikely to have been occupied. [A. S. R. Gordon, *Arch. J,* 97 (1940), 96.]

28 HALLIGYE FOGOU, Mawgan-in-Meneage   SW:712238
A torch is needed to explore this fogou with its underground stone-lined passage 16·5 m long. A cross-passage joins it at the eastern end and is equally massive. At the north it originally ran into a ditch, but is now blocked. There is a short passage running south at the western end of the main corridor. A block of rock 0·6 m high lies across the floor of the main passage and it has been claimed that it was intended as a deliberate stumbling block to warn of approaching danger. This seems unlikely, since the fogou was probably the cold storage place of a small settlement now destroyed.

29 HELSBURY CASTLE, Michaelstow   SX:083796
This hillfort is circular in shape and contains 1·4 ha. It is defended by a single strong rampart and ditch. To the east there is a roughly rectangular annexe covering another 0·6 ha. Entrances to both enclosures are on the east and in line. There is a hollow way leading into the fort, but this could be connected with the later use of the hilltop as the site of St Syth's chapel. [J. Forde-Johnston, *Hillforts* (1976), 188.]

30 THE HURLERS, Minions   SX:258714
Three splendid circles lie in a line on the depressing, mine-scarred eastern side of Bodmin Moor. They almost touch one another and run from south-west to north-east up the hillside. The smallest circle is on the south side. It contains nine stones still standing and measures 35 m in diameter. Adjoining it is the largest circle, 42 m in diameter, egg-shaped and with an off-centre stone; it has seventeen stones still standing. To the north is a circle 33 m across consisting of thirteen stones. Excavation has shown that the interior of this circle is roughly paved with granite blocks. The stones of the circles were originally shaped and set up in pits of varying depths so that their tops would all be level. Two standing stones, the Pipers, lie 120 m west-south-west of the central circle. According to folklore the stones were all once men,

petrified for 'hurling the ball on the Lord's Day'. [C. A. R. Radford, *PPS,* 4 (1938), 319.]

31 INNISIDGEN CARN, St Mary's, Isles of Scilly sv:921127
A grass-covered entrance grave with stone retaining wall, 8·2 m in diameter. The entrance passage leads directly into the rectangular burial chamber which is 4·5 m long, 1·5 m wide and 1·5 m high. Five rounded blocks of stone roof the tomb. Paul Ashbee has suggested that the similarities of Innisidgen and Bant's Carn are such that the same architect might have been responsible for both.

Ninety metres north of Innisidgen Carn is Lower Innisidgen, close to the sea and roughly 6 m in diameter. The chamber on the north side can still be seen. It was illegally dug into in 1950 and its contents lost. [P. Ashbee, *Ancient Scilly* (1974), 304.]

32 LANIVET QUOIT, Lanhydrock sx:072628
Three stones survive in the middle of a ploughed field, of which one is an enormous capstone 4·5 m long and 2·7 m wide. The other stones are presumably the uprights on which it once rested.

33 LANYON QUOIT, Madron sw:430337
(National Trust). Like a giant table, a great capstone 5·8 m long is supported on three uprights, each 2·5 m high. Once you could have ridden a horse under the arch, 'a very short man on a very short horse', but the monument fell down in 1815 and its height was reduced when it was set up again nine years later. Other stones lie beneath it, and a few metres further south are others that probably belong to a burial cist. All are contained in a long north-south mound, which can still be seen in spite of being overgrown. It measures about 27 m by 12 m. Large human bones (a giant's) are reputed to have been found in the tomb, although cremation was more common in south-western graves.

Only two stones of the West Lanyon Quoit remain (SW:432338): one about 1·5 m square and a capstone leaning against it. [G. E. Daniel, *Prehistoric Chamber Tombs* (1950), 238.]

34 MAEN CASTLE, Sennen sw:347257
The most western promontory fort in England is protected by a ditch and granite wall 60 m long and 3·5 m thick. The entrance consists of a stone-lined passage with post-holes still visible at the inner end. The interior is less than a hectare in size and there are no signs of huts, though early iron age pottery has been found. There are field systems visible to the east. [C. B. Crofts, *Proceedings of the West Cornwall Field Club,* 1 (1954), 93.]

35   **MEN-AN-TOL, Madron**   sw:427349
Men-an-tol, 'the stone with the hole', is the central block of a line of
three. It is a thin slab with a perfectly circular hole at the centre wide
enough to pass a young child through – this was believed to be a cure
for rickets! On either side are upright pillar stones, one of which has
been moved in historic times. It is possible that the whole monument
once formed part of a burial chamber, but this is by no means certain
since there are other holed stones in Cornwall with other origins.

36   **MERRY MAIDENS, St Buryan**   sw:433245
This is one of the most perfect stone circles in Britain, and measures
some 24 m in diameter. It is composed of nineteen rectangular blocks
of stone, each about a metre high and evenly spaced except on the
north-east, where there is a possible entrance gap. Beside the B3315
and nearly half a kilometre to the north-east are two standing stones
known as the Pipers, one 4·6 m high and the other 4 m high. They
cannot be seen from the circle, though one to the west, called the
Fiddler, is in clear view. The Cornish name for the circle is Dans Maen,
or 'Stone Dance', which recalls the maidens who were turned to stone
for dancing on the Sabbath.

37   **MULFRA QUOIT, Madron**   sw:452353
Three upright stones form a rectangular cist and a large capstone leans
on the western side, one end firmly in the ground. There are traces of a
small circular mound about 12 m in diameter. [G. E. Daniel, *Prehistoric Chamber Tombs* (1950), 238.]

38   **NINE MAIDENS, St Columb Major**   sx:937676
The remnants of a row of nine standing stones, of which six are still
upright and three broken. The stones are each about 1·5 m high and
the line is about 110 m long. Almost 1 km further north of the stone
alignment is a single block of stone called the Magi Stone. There is a
round barrow a little to the south of it.

39   **OLD BLOCK HOUSE, Tresco, Isles of Scilly**   sv:896155
The Old Block House is a defensive building from the Civil War, but
the promontory on which it stands is cut off by the roughly semicircular
rampart of an iron age fort. Lower down the hill slope are two further
banks. No ditches are visible. There is an original entrance gap on the
southern side. [B. H. St J. O'Neil, *Isles of Scilly* (1949), 9.]

40   **PELYNT**   sw:200544
Once a group of ten round barrows, they are now much ploughed and
difficult to identify. They were dug into by Jonathan Couch in 1830 and
1845; he found cremations, one with an ogival dagger of bronze with

large rivets, another with a greenstone macehead and a third holding a dagger of late Mycenean type, which suggests contacts with the Mediterranean in the fourteenth or thirteenth centuries BC. [J. Couch, *27th Report, Royal Inst. Cornwall* (1845), 34.]

41 PORTH HELLICK DOWN, St Mary's, Isles of Scilly   sv:928108
One of the finest entrance graves of the Scillies, excavated by George Bonsor in 1899 and restored by the Department of the Environment. It is 12 m in diameter and 1·5 m high. An entrance on the north-west leads into a passage 4·3 m long and 0·9 m wide. This curves into the burial chamber, which is a further 3·7 m long and roofed with four cover slabs. Finds of late bronze age pottery suggest re-use of the tomb at that time. [P. Ashbee, *Ancient Scilly* (1974), 301.]

42 RILLATON, Linkinhorne   sx:260719
This barrow consists of a great pile of stones 36 m in diameter and 2·4 m high, standing on the highest point of the hill, 0·8 km north of The Hurlers stone circle. This is the Rillaton barrow, with a large robbers' hollow in the top and a stone-lined grave on the eastern side, opened in 1818. The grave, rebuilt about 1890, can still be seen, 2·3 m long, 1·2 m wide and 0·9 m high. In it lay a skeleton buried with a handled beaker made of corrugated sheet gold, a broken pottery vessel, a bronze ogival dagger and some faience beads. The gold beaker resembles specimens found at Mycenae and in Switzerland and Germany. It is now in the British Museum, together with the bronze dagger. [G. Smirke, *Arch. J*, 24 (1867), 189.]

43 ROCKY VALLEY, Tintagel   sx:073893
Tucked away in a narrow wooded gorge are two labyrinth-like carvings, each 23 cm across. They have been pecked out of the vertical rock face beside disused mill buildings. Although scheduled under the Ancient Monuments Act as bronze age, they could really be of any age and the reader should keep an open mind.

44 ROUGH TOR, St Breward   sx:141815
There are hut circles surrounded by small oval enclosures at the south-west end of Rough Tor between the stream and the hilltop. Stones cleared from fields have been piled up into walls which often link these enclosures.
  On the summit of the Tor between the two rock outcrops are the walls of a small hillfort. Two lines of defence can be traced on the west, but there is little to see on the east. Hut circles can be found inside the fort. It probably spans a period from about 1000 to 700 BC.

45 THE RUMPS, Pentire Head, Polzeath   sw:934810
(National Trust). An attractively sited cliff castle protected by three
ramparts and ditches which cut off the narrow neck of a spur with two
rocky headlands. The outer ditch is shallow and its associated bank not
particularly strong. It does not seem to be of the same construction as
the other two, of which the middle bank is the stronger, built of
weathered slate with a continuous kerb of boulders. Its ditch is 4·5 m
deep. The entrances were lined with timber and drystone walls and
follow the same positions as the modern breaks. A number of circular
huts were found in the hollow behind Rumps Point. The pottery
included cordoned vessels of a type common in Cornwall and north-
west France in the first centuries BC and AD, and Mediterranean wine
amphorae. All this points to continental contacts between Britain and
Cornwall at that time. [R. T. Brooks, *Cornish Archaeology*, 3 (1966),
26; 5 (1966), 4; 7 (1968), 38.]

46 SAMSON HILL, Bryher, Isles of Scilly   sv:879142
Glyn Daniel has written of the Scilly Isles: 'There are between a fifth
and a quarter of all the chamber tombs in southern Britain on the
island.' They are to be found on even the smallest islet. Bryher has at
least eight cairns; that on the south side of Samson Hill is 7 m in
diameter with a surrounding kerb of largish stones. The chamber is
entered from the north-east; it is 6 m long and 0·6 m wide at the
entrance, widening to 1·4 m in the centre. At least two other cairns can
be seen close by, though their chambers have been destroyed. There is
another on Gweal Hill and more to the north of Shipman Head Down.
[P. Ashbee, *Ancient Scilly* (1974), 296.]

47 STANNON, St Breward   sx:126800
A circle of forty-one closely spaced stones, 42 m in diameter. Originally there were about eighty stones. At the centre lies a single block.

48 STRIPPLE STONES, Blisland   sx:144752
An embanked henge monument 44·5 m in diameter with the usual
internal ditch, which was found to be very irregular when it was
excavated in 1905. The ditch averaged 2·7m wide and 1·2 m deep. An
entrance faces towards the Trippet Stones on the south-west. Inside
the henge is an irregular circle of fifteen (originally twenty-eight)
blocks of granite, of which four are still standing. A single block of
stone lies close to the centre of the circle, and three other stones lie
outside the circle, but within the enclosure. Since the site combines
features of a henge monument and a stone circle it probably dates from
the late neolithic or early bronze age. [H. St George Gray, *Archaeologia*, 61 (1906), 1.]

49 TREEN DINAS, Treen   sw:397222
(National Trust). This fine headland with its natural rocking Logan
Stone is made into a cliff castle by the presence of five ramparts with
ditches. They are obviously not all of the same date but without
excavation this cannot be verified. From the north one first encounters
a massive curved rampart and ditch. After a gap there are a further
three banks and ditches, of which the centre one is the strongest. Last
of all, a few metres north of the Logan Stone, is a massive stone-faced
defence with a great ditch, broken at the centre by an entrance. There
are the foundations of two huts just inside this entrance.

50 TREGEARE ROUNDS, St Kew   sx:033800
Two widely spaced concentric ramparts and ditches form this multiple
enclosure hill-slope fort of about 2 ha. There is a crescent-shaped
annexe on the south-east. The inner enclosure is defended by a bank
10 m wide and 3 m high; the outer by a bank 16 m by 3 m. The main
entrance to both enclosures is on the south-east and is approached
through the annexe by a hollow way which leads up from a stream. The
gaps on the west seem to be modern.
    Excavation in 1904 produced iron age B type pottery datable to
about 100 BC. [A. Fox, *Arch. J,* 109 (1952), 9.]

51 TREGIFFIAN, St Buryan   sw:431244
Although cut in half by the B3315 road, much still remains of this
circular barrow, about 17 m in diameter, defined by a kerb of granite
blocks. On the south side is a burial chamber 4·6 m long, 2 m wide and
1 m high. Its walls are a mixture of stone uprights and coursed walling.
The roof is composed of four capstones. The outermost eastern wall-
stone of the chamber was decorated with numerous deep cup marks. In
order to preserve it a concrete replica now stands in its place. The
original has been removed to the Museum of the Royal Institution of
Cornwall in Truro. Recent excavation found the burial chamber filled
with clean earth, but with two pits in the floor. Both contained collared
urns, one holding a cremation burial. [C. Thomas, *Arch. J,* 130 (1973),
259.]

52 TRENCROM, Ludgvan   sw:517363
(National Trust). A small fort of 0·4 ha is encircled by a single drystone
wall composed of great stone slabs and natural outcrops of rock. There
is no surrounding ditch, which is hardly surprising in such a subsoil. On
the east and west are entrances. There are a dozen overgrown hut
circles within the fort. It can be dated to the second century BC on the
evidence of surface pottery.

53 TRETHEVY QUOIT, St Cleer sx: 259688

'A little howse raysed of mightie stones, standing on a little hill within a feilde' wrote John Norden in 1584, and the description is still apt today. Seven upright stones form a rectangular burial chamber 2 m by 1·5 m and more than 3 m high on the southern side. Resting on top is a great sloping capstone 3·7 m long with a small hole piercing its highest corner. The chamber is divided into two parts by the great doorstone at the eastern end. The inside is almost completely sealed, except for a small rectangular hole in the corner of the doorstone, just big enough to pass a body through. Outside in an antechamber formed by the two side stones that jut forward to the east. Lukis records an oval mound 7 m by 6 m a hundred years ago. [G. E. Daniel, *Prehistoric Chamber Tombs* (1950), 239.]

54 TREVELGUE HEAD, Newquay sx: 827630

Six lines of rampart and ditch guard this excellent example of a cliff castle. Approaching from the road a single rampart and ditch is met at the end of the putting green. Beyond is an enclosure, with cliffs on either side, which contains a bronze age round barrow. Next, three close-set banks and ditches cut across the headland with a gap near the sea on the north that may have been an entrance before erosion cut through the headland and isolated the island at the western end. The narrow gorge is crossed by a modern bridge; the gap that it utilizes is certainly not ancient. Another rampart is met immediately, then another small enclosure and finally a defence cutting off the headland. There is another bowl-barrow on the end of the peninsula with a deep cutting in its side. Nothing is known of its contents. Excavations in 1939 produced material of bronze age and early iron age date, but have not yet been fully published. [*PPS*, 5 (1939), 254 (brief note).]

55 TRIPPET STONES, Blisland sx: 131750

These young maidens were turned to stone for dancing on the Sabbath. There were originally about twenty-six stones in a circle 33 m in diameter, of which eight remain standing and four are fallen. The stone in the centre is a modern boundary stone. [H. St George Gray, *Archaeologia*, 61 (1906), 25.]

56 VERYAN BARROW, Veryan sx: 913387

This is one of the largest barrows in southern England. Its scrub-covered surface is 4·5 m high and 113 m in diameter. Nothing is known of its contents.

57 WARBSTOW BURY, Warbstow sx: 202908

One of my favourite hillforts, it has wide views in all directions except the south-west. It belongs to the group of multiple enclosure forts. At

Warbstow Bury there are two concentric rings of ramparts, ditches and counterscarps with a wide space between the two, and traces of an intermediate bank on the south-west, where the ground is flatter. The inner rampart is about 4·4 m high. There are entrance gaps on the north-west and south-east. West of the centre is a long low mound that resembles a pillow mound.

58   ZENNOR QUOIT, Zennor   sw:469380
A large capstone, 5·5 m across, has fallen at forty-five degrees so that one end rests on the ground and the remainder completely covers the five wallstones of the burial chamber. On the east is a narrow antechamber in which a perforated whetstone was found. In front of that stand two large stones that give a straight facade to the barrow, the narrow gap between them forming the entry to the antechamber. There was an unsuccessful attempt to open the tomb with gunpowder in the nineteenth century. R. J. Noall later excavated it and found cremated bones, flints and neolithic pottery. [G. E. Daniel, *Prehistoric Chamber Tombs* (1950), 237.]

CUMBRIA

1 ASBY COMMON, Asby   NY:673109

A triangular enclosure overlooking Great Asby covers about half a hectare. It is defined by a stone bank with hut circles touching the inner face, and broken by what seems to be an original entrance on the south.

2 BARNSCAR, Muncaster   SD:135958

There are about half a dozen huts on Birkby Fell of which one was excavated in 1957. In it was a central hearth and a possible sling-stone. East of the huts is an extensive group of cairns or stone heaps; at least 360 have been counted. They vary in diameter from 1·5 m to 7·5 m and are very low. They are supposed to have contained burials and urns when they were dug into a century ago, but modern excavation has failed to find traces of either, and it is possible that they are simply piles of stones cleared from fields in medieval times.

3 BARRON'S PIKE CAIRN DITCH, Askerton   NY:595752

Only the well-marked ditch surrounding this flattened cairn now survives. It is about 18 m in diameter and 2 m wide, with an entrance break on the south-western side. Nothing is known of the contents.

4 BIRKRIGG COMMON, Urswick and Aldingham

There are five barrows, mostly on the north-east side of the common. Closest to the road is a low, flat-topped cairn edged with large limestone slabs (SD:282740). The remains of ten cremations have been found inside. At SD:286742 are four tiny barrows. Nothing has been found in them. At SD:289743 a barrow 12 m in diameter covered three skeletons and a bronze awl. On the eastern side was a ritual circle of boulders and slabs covering patches of black earth and all covered by the barrow mound. An oval mound at SD:288746 produced seven cremations, three in bronze age cordoned urns. The barrow at SD:285744 is nearly 1 m high and appears to have the capstone of a burial cist lying on it.

Two rectangular enclosures lie to the north-east and south-west of the barrow at SD:288746. That to the south-west is the largest, oval in shape, with an entrance at the north-west. The north-eastern enclosure has an entrance on the eastern side and traces of three internal huts. A wall about 4 m wide and half a metre high surrounds it. Both enclosures are probably of iron age date. [C. Geldered, *TCWAAS*, 12 (1911), 262.]

5 BLAKELEY RAISE, Ennerdale   NY:068132
This circle contains twelve stones, each about 0·5 m high; it may have surrounded a barrow 10 m in diameter.

6 BRATS HILL, Miterdale   NY:173023
A long, steep climb is required to reach this group of circles. The largest is flattened on its northern side and measures 32 m by 26 m. Of its forty-two stones only eight are now standing, though the rest can clearly be seen. The circle is unusual in that there are five cairns, each about 7 m in diameter, standing within its south-western half. The cairns, now very low, are surrounded by the remains of kerbs, and when two were excavated in 1827 they revealed domes of stones covering cremations, animal bones and antlers.

There are two circles 16 m in diameter 130 m north-west of Brats Hill at *White Moss*. Both appear to contain unopened central cairns. On *Low Longrigg* 450 m north and above White Moss are two more circles, one, 15 m across, containing a cairn. The second, to the north-east, is oval in shape, 22 m by 15 m, and contains two cairns, one with a well-defined kerb. [A. Burl, *Stone Circles of the British Isles* (1976), 93.]

7 BURWENS, Crosby Ravensworth   NY:621123
This is one of the best preserved settlements in the area and lies on a gentle north-facing slope. A wall, whose inner and outer faces are filled with rubble, surrounds a rectangular enclosure of about 0·4 ha. From an entrance on the north-west side a village street leads to a series of circular huts, some with attached courtyards. Although it is unexcavated the village probably dates from late in the iron age, continuing into the Roman occupation. To the north and east of the village are traces of fields stretching over about a hectare. [RCHM, *Westmorland* (1936), 86.]

8 CARDONNETH PIKE, Cumrew   NY:559520
High on the skyline of Cumrew Fell stands a cairn 22 m in diameter and 2 m high. It may originally have contained a burial cist on the north-west, and it is possible that this is where the forty 'urns' reputed to have come from the cairn were found.

9 CARROCK FELL, Mungrisdale   NY:343337
A steep climb of 650 m over difficult hillside is needed to reach this oval

fort situated on the eastern slopes of the Caldbeck Fells. It is remarkably strong, with precipitous crags at the south-western end. About
2 ha are enclosed by a drystone wall whose facing has survived in a
number of places. There is an entrance at the western end and another
midway along the southern side. A. H. A. Hogg suggests that other
breaks in the walls are the result of deliberate slighting.

Inside the eastern end of the fort is a cairn with its central cist
exposed. Numerous other cairns lie on the northern slope of Carrock
Fell beside the Carrock Beck. One, at NY:351349, produced a cremation and piece of bronze when it was excavated. [R. G. Collingwood,
TCWAAS, 38 (1938), 32.]

10   CASTERTON   SD:640799
This stone circle, 18 m in diameter, is possibly embanked. Twenty
stones, each less than 0·5 m high, surround what might have been a
cairn circle. A beaker burial may have come from this site. [RCHM,
Westmorland (1936), 66.]

11   CASTLE CRAG, Mardale   NY:469128
This minute fort still clings to its crag 120 m above the Haweswater
reservoir, but its original appearance has been completely altered. Its
oval site is protected on the north and north-east by the steepness of
the rock, although a rampart existed there. On the south side are two
rock-cut ditches with a fallen stone rampart above them. Although the
interior is only about 0·4 ha in area it has produced traces of hut floors
and hearths. The pathway on the west probably leads through the only
entrance.

12   CASTLE CRAG, Shoulthwaite   NY:300188
On the eastern side of Castlerigg Fell, in a rocky clearing in the
woodland, is a small hillfort commanding the precipitous slopes of
Shoulthwaite Gill. Although its authenticity has been challenged, it
has almost certainly been modified by man if not entirely constructed
by him. There are two lines of ditch below the rocky outcrop. On their
inner side is a rampart of earth and stone, 2·2 m high internally, with an
entrance on the eastern side. It has been suggested that from forts like
this iron age man could control the summer mountainside pastures as
well as watch the valley bottom below. [*Prehistoric Society Handbook*
(1977), 25.]

13   CASTLE FOLDS, Great Ashby   NY:650094
At 395 m above sea level this little fort looks north across Great Ashby
Scar. It is roughly rectangular, 0·5 ha in area and enclosed by a stone
wall once about 2·5 m thick. Against the inside of the wall are traces of

oval and circular huts. There is an entrance on the south approached by a rough path from outside.

There is a barrow 450 m south-east, 15 m in diameter and 1 m high. It contained four burials, one, in a central rock-cut pit, accompanied by a chert axe.

14   CASTLEHEAD, Grange   SD:421797
A low-sited promontory fort with steep scarps on all sides except the north. The only defence is a line of drystone-faced rampart cutting off the neck of the spur, but stopping short on the western side to make an entrance gap 3 m wide. There is no ditch accompanying the rampart. There may have been a triangular outwork in front of the entrance. [J. Forde-Johnston, *TLCAS,* 72 (1962), 32.]

15   CASTLE HOW, Wythop   NY:202308
Cut off from Bassenthwaite Lake by the new A66, this little fort of 0·5 ha is strongly sited on a narrow east-west ridge. The north and south sides are steep and naturally protected, so extra attention has been paid to the western end where there are four banks and ditches, as well as artificial scarping of the hillside. At the east there are two banks and ditches and an original entrance. The fort may have been occupied in Roman times by local folk imitating the Roman life-style. [W. G. Collingwood, *TCWAAS,* 8 (1908), 97.]

16   CASTLEHOWE SCAR, Crosby Ravensworth   NY:587155
A stone circle 6·4 m in diameter. Of the eleven stones, all save one are standing. [RCHM, *Westmorland* (1936), 90.]

17   CASTLERIGG, Keswick   NY:292236
There is no more beautifully sited stone circle in England than Castle-rigg, with its panoramic views of the north Lakeland hills. Almost every one of the thirty-eight stones still stands in its original position, marking out a slightly flattened circle 85 m in diameter. A gap 3·5 m wide on the north side flanked by two massive stones may indicate an entrance. Ten stones forming a rectangle touch the inside of the circle on the east. This is an unusual feature and its purpose is not clear. It has been suggested that they might have formed a burial chamber, but they seem to be too low and wide apart for effective roofing. To the east 3·5 km away stands the hill called Threlkeld Knott over which the equinoctial sun rises. Alexander Thom has demonstrated that a variety of other astronomical details may be worked out from the circle. [A. Thom, *Megalithic Sites in Britain* (1967), 145.]

18   CASTLESTEAD, Yanwath   NY:518252
On a wooded spur above the river Lowther this tiny enclosure of 0·1 ha

is defended by three concentric banks and two ditches, which have been damaged on the river side. Scarcely a kilometre north is another enclosure at Yanwath Wood (qv). Strictly speaking neither of these sites is a hillfort; they are best described as defended enclosures of a type often found in northern England.

19   THE COCKPIT, Waverton   NY: 483222
This may be either a stone circle or a ring cairn. Two concentric circles of stones a little over 25 m in diameter form the facings of a wall. There are traces of a cairn on the wall at the south-east.

20   COLD FELL CAIRN, Midgeholme   NY: 606556
A large heap of stones 15 m in diameter and a little over a metre high represent what appears to be an unopened cairn. There are traces of a ditch at the circumference.

21   CROSBY GARRETT   NY: 719064
Aerial photographs show that the fells around Crosby are covered with prehistoric field systems, interspersed with road systems and settlements. Three of the latter are worthy of closer inspection. The largest is on the south-east slopes of Begin Hill where a series of low banks form a subrectangular hut enclosure with field boundaries radiating out from it. About 640 m to the north-east is a smaller settlement with huts and paddocks, and 270 m further to the north-east above Crag Wood is a more regularly rectangular example. The date of the villages and their associated fields is unknown. To the east, across the Scandal Beck, are a number of barrows possibly connected with the settlements.

22   CROSBY RAVENSWORTH BARROWS   NY: 597148
There are two barrows, one underlying a stone wall to the north, about 13 m in diameter and 1 m high, with stones marking a kerb. A few metres to the south is a circle of twelve granite boulders enclosing a low mound. It is reputed to have contained an inhumation.

23   THE CURRICK, Bewcastle   NY: 537827
This cairn in Kershope Forest is difficult to find; it is 44 m long with a squared-off south-eastern end 18 m wide. Hollows in the sides may indicate the presence of burial chambers destroyed in the past. There are no recorded finds.

24   DRUIDS' TEMPLE, Birkrigg Common   SD: 292739
Here we have two concentric rings of limestone blocks, the outer circle, 26 m in diameter, consists of fourteen stones low in the bracken. The inner circle is 8·4 m in diameter with ten stones enclosing five

cremation pits, one containing an inverted urn. The tallest stone is on the north, whilst on the south-west two other high stones flank the lowest, as though forming a ceremonial doorway. Excavations in 1911 and 1921 uncovered burnt patches where the bodies may have been cremated, as well as a cobbled pavement, immediately outside the inner circle, which may have been used for processions or dances.

25 DUNMALLET, Dacre   NY:468246
Capping a conical tree-clad hill at the northern end of Ullswater is a tiny univallate hillfort with traces of a counterscarp. The entrance is at the south-west where access would have been easiest.

26 ELVA PLAIN, Setmurthy   NY:173317
The tallest of the fifteen stones in this circle is just over 1 m high. The ring is about 34 m in diameter with an outlying stone to the south-west pointing along the ridge that runs west to the coast. Originally there would have been about thirty stones. [K. S. Hodgson, *TCWAAS*, 63 (1963), 301.]

27 EWE CLOSE, Crosby Ravensworth   NY:609135
On the north-eastern slope of the hill is a large enclosure of about 0·5 ha containing two separate groups of huts and associated gardens. At the centre of the western group is a large circular hut with a paved floor. All the huts have massive stone walls at least 1·8 m thick. Roman objects came from the village but it seems likely that it was constructed in the later iron age. There is another village called *Ewe Lock* 640 m to the south, where two paddocks and hut groups 60 m apart can be seen.

28 GAMELANDS CIRCLE, Orton   NY:640082
This flattened and embanked stone circle, 42 m in diameter, lies on a saddle with extensive views. It once had forty stones around it, but ploughing a hundred years ago has damaged many and reduced them to thirty-three. The rounded boulders are of Shap granite. There is an entrance at the south-east. [C. I. Fell, *TCWAAS*, 64 (1964), 408.]

29 GIANT'S GRAVE, Lacra, Kirksanton   SD:137811
These stones form part of the Lacra complex of prehistoric sites (qv). One is 3 m high, the other 2·5 m. The larger has a cup mark cut into its face 8 cm across and 4 cm deep.

30 GRETIGATE CIRCLES, Gosforth   NY:058036
Part of a large circle 31 m in diameter survives in a field wall north-west of Sides Farm. Further west along the path are two other circles; one, about 21 m in diameter, originally contained about sixteen stones, of which nine remain; the other touching it on the north is 7 m in

diameter. Both the latter circles probably contained cairns. There are a number of other small cairns between the circles. [H. B. Stout, *TCWAAS*, 61 (1961), 1.]

31   GREY CROFT, Seascale   NY:034024
This ring of stones is oval in shape 27 m by 24 m. There were twelve stones when it was destroyed in the nineteenth century; it was excavated and restored in 1949, and ten of the stones were re-erected. A low cairn at the centre was excavated and produced a cremation burial and part of a jet ring. A partly polished stone axe made at Langdale was found beside one of the stones. Alexander Thom has suggested that an outlying stone is aligned on the setting of the star Daneb. [W. Fletcher, *TCWAAS*, 57 (1957), 1.]

32   GUNNERKELD, Rosgill   NY:568178
One of the Shap group of circles, it is most easily seen by looking down from the south-bound carriageway of the M6 motorway. This ring of two concentric ovals encloses a low mound and cist. The inner ring, 18 m in diameter, is the more complete. Of the outer ring of stones, 28 m in diameter, only three of some eighteen stones are still standing. This circle is sometimes called Shap Central.

33   HEATHWAITE FELL, Kirkby Irelith   SD:251880
Between the two roads is a settlement made up of a number of walled paddocks still standing 1–2 m high. There is an entrance on the south side. A number of small cairns in the area are more likely to be clearance heaps than burial mounds.

34   HELM HILL, Natland and Stainton   SD:531887
Sited on the southern end of The Helm above Saint Sunday's Beck is a small oval hillfort defended by two ramparts with an intervening bank. These are best preserved on the north and south; they are almost unnecessary on the east above the steep drop to the minor road below.

35   HOLBORN HILL, Great Asby   NY:682123
A somewhat damaged site on the western slope of the hill. It consists of a stone-walled oval enclosure about 135 m in diameter, divided into a series of paddocks and probably used for animal husbandry during the late iron age.

36   HOLLIN STUMP, Asby   NY:693085
This cairn is 1·5 m high and 21 m in diameter. It contains a stone cist in which a skeleton was found in the last century.

37 HOLME BANK, Urswick SD:276734

Overlooking Little Urswick is a stone-walled enclosure defended by great orthostats 4 m long and nearly a metre high, broken by an entrance on the east. There are traces of a ditch on the uphill side of the site and the remains of two huts 4·5 m and 7·5 m in diameter. The interior is divided into two by a cross-bank, which probably separated off the animals. Another isolated hut and attached paddock lies 22 m to the north-west.

38 HOWARCLES, Crosby Ravensworth NY:627132

On the slope above Woodfoot are a group of oval huts and gardens covering 0·6 ha. A roadway runs approximately north-south through them, and the whole settlement is commanded by a single large hut on the north-east side.

39 HUGILL NY:437010

On the hillside to the east of and above High Borrans is a settlement of 0·8 ha surrounded by a drystone wall that stands on top of a prehistoric bank. This is broken by three original entrances. The interior is divided into two parts: groups of circular huts lie to the west and small paddocks and cultivation terraces to the east.

40 KEMP HOWE, Shap NY:567133

Shap South circle, which lies beside the railway a few hundred metres east of the river Lowther, is now badly damaged and only six of the great Shap granite boulders now remain, each more than 2 m long. The circle was about 24 m in diameter. Traces of at least eight stones of an avenue 3000 m long can be found running north-west to the Skellaw Hill barrow and the massive *Thunder Stone* (NY:552157) more than 1200 m away. Avenue stones include examples at NY:562147, NY:559150 (Goggleby Stone), NY:558152 and NY:555152. [RCHM, *Westmorland* (1936), 206; T. Clare, *TCWAAS*, 78 (1978), 5.]

41 KING ARTHUR'S ROUND TABLE, Yanwath NY:523284

A mutilated henge monument 90 m in diameter, originally with two opposing entrances; only that on the south-east now survives. The northern was once flanked by two stones. The bank still stands 1·5 m high and is separated by a berm from a ditch 9 m wide and 1·5 m deep. Excavations by Gerhard Bersu suggested that there may once have been a stone circle on the berm. At the centre of the monument was a trench, 2·4 m long, 0·9 m wide and 25 cm deep, which had been used to cremate a corpse, using hazel wood as fuel. Above the trench was a stone structure that was too damaged to be interpreted. The low mound on the central platform is a recent addition. The *Little Round*

Table originally lay to the south (NY:324282). [G. Bersu, *TCWAAS*, 40 (1940), 169.]

42   KIRKBY MOOR, Kirkby Irelith   SD:251827
A bank of earth and stones 2–3 m wide and 0·5 m high delimits a circle 22 m in diameter. This is a ring cairn, partly retained on the inner eastern side by a kerb of stones. There is no obvious entrance, but 30 m to the north-east three pairs of small stones form the beginning of an avenue. About 300 m north-east (SD:251830) is a rough stone cairn 24 m in diameter and 1 m high. It has a burial cist on its south-west side in which a cremation was found.

43   LACRA CIRCLES, Millom   SD:150814
The five Lacra circles were excavated in 1947. Circle A is badly damaged. It lies 100 m east of the house and measures 15 m in diameter; six stones are still standing. The second circle, B, lies 360 m to the east. Six of its original eleven stones still stand in a circle 16·2 m in diameter. Its low central cairn covered a stack of turf which in turn covered a cremation burial with lots of charcoal. The cairn had a ring of stones placed on it. Circle C, 100 m east of the last, has only four surviving stones. It also produced charcoal. The most interesting circle was D, 150 m east-south-east. Oval in shape, 18 m by 16 m, it has a possible central stone and an avenue of stones running west-south-west with a single stone row on the opposite side to the east-north-east. An inverted overhanging rim urn was discovered in a shallow pit by the north-west stone. Oak and hazel charcoal was found and a hazel nut indicated an autumn burial. Circle E is a small ring of six stones, only 5 m across, with a central stone. It lies 8 m north-west of D and excavation proved unproductive. South-west of this are the remains of another avenue, 15 m wide, running for some 70 m. Most of the north side is missing. [J. A. Dixon and C. I. Fell, *TCWAAS,* 48 (1948), 1.]

44   LANGTHWAITE GREEN   NY:161209
Above the northern end of Crummock Water where the delta provided valuable grazing land is a settlement, now no more than a hollow 60 m across, with an entrance facing west. It is divided up into a number of sections which may have acted as paddocks for stock or maybe hut sites. [J. R. Mason and H. Valentine, *TCWAAS,* 24 (1924), 117.]

45   LEACET, Brougham   NY:563263
This is a cairn ring rather than a true stone circle. Seven stones retain the material of a badly damaged cairn 11 m in diameter. Excavations in the last century uncovered a cremation, together with some urns, a food vessel and an incense cup.

46   LITTLE MEG, Glassonby   NY:577375

This untidy pile of stones at the edge of the field consists of eleven
blocks that surrounded a cairn. An urn containing a cremation was
found in a central cist. Two of the stones have been decorated by
hollows and spiral engravings.

47   LITTLE URSWICK, Urswick   SD:262744

Little remains of this site save for two large boulders that support a
capstone. Additional strength is given by the use of packing stones.
More stones are scattered nearby and probably formed another burial
chamber.

48   LONG MEG AND HER DAUGHTERS, Hunsonby   NY:571373

A narrow country lane leads into one of Britain's largest stone circles,
where folklore tells us that a local witch and her coven were turned to
stone. Long Meg is a single narrow column of red sandstone 3·7 m tall,
decorated on its north-eastern face with a cup-and-ring mark, a spiral
and an incomplete concentric circle. These carvings face the stone
circle 18 m away. Oval in plan, the ring (the Daughters) measures
109 m by 93 m and slopes downhill from west to east. Here the shape
seems designed to counteract foreshortening by perspective. There
were originally about sixty-six stones in the ring, which has an entrance
at the south-west close to Long Meg. Two of the largest stones stand
east and west on the circumferences in the directions of the spring and
autumn equinoxes. There are traces of an earth bank on the west side
of the circle. Two cairns may have originally stood within the circle,
but this is open to doubt. [A. Burl, *Stone Circles of the British Isles*
(1976), 89.]

49   LOWICK RING CAIRN, Egton with Lowick   SD:279843

On the western side of the moor is a stone embankment forming a ring
cairn 30 m in diameter. The bank is 2·7 m wide and is broken by an
entrance on the south-west. Of an inner retaining wall only five stones
survive in their original position. Nothing is known of the contents of
the cairn.

LOW LONGRIGG, see Brats Hill.

50   MAYBURGH, Eamont Bridge   NY:519285

A great grey tree-crowned bank of rounded boulders 6 m high and 65 m
in diameter rises in height as it approaches the single entrance on the
eastern side facing King Arthur's Round Table (qv). Although it lacks
a quarry ditch this is a class I henge monument. At the centre stands
one only of the original group of four stones recorded by Stukeley –
Pennant refers to four others that once stood inside the entrance.

There are two projections of the bank outwards from the entrance; these may be original. [G. Clark, *PPS*, 2 (1936), 44.]

51   MECKLIN PARK CAIRN, Irton with Santon   NY:126019
This cairn may have been built in the beaker period as a sherd of beaker pottery was found when it was excavated. No burial was found; only a scatter of charcoal in a ring of granite boulders. The covering mound is 9 m in diameter and 1 m high. [*TCWAAS*, 37 (1937), 104.]

52   MOOR DIVOCK, Askham Fell (Fig 7, p. 92)   NY:497217
A group of small stone circles, avenues, ring cairns and barrows are strung out along a mile of moorland and have been explained by Aubrey Burl as 'a familial cemetery used over several generations . . . with ritual and sepulchral monuments intermingled'.

Sites include the Copstone standing stone (NY:496216), a monolith 1·5 m high on the south-east side of a circular depression with slight surrounding bank 21 m in diameter.

To the north-west are eleven standing stones (NY:494220) on a barrow. The site was dug by Simpson and Greenwell in the nineteenth century; they found a shallow central pit containing ashes and pot fragments. Above this was a food-vessel on its side.

At NY:493222 is a mutilated cairn opened by Simpson which contained a cremation in an inverted urn. Close by are traces of other cairn rings. The White Raise Barrow (NY:489224) is curiously star-shaped (though this need not necessarily have been its original shape) and is about 18 m in diameter. There are signs of a burial cist at the centre which contained a crouched skeleton. There is an oval barrow nearby, 7·5 m by 4·5 m, with a large stone at its west end.

South of the Cockpit (qv) is a group of cairns called Three Pow Raise. There are also the remains of alleged stone rows on the Fell, especially around NY:494220, but these are difficult to trace with accuracy. [M. W. Taylor, *TCWAAS* (1st S), 8 (1886), 323.]

53   MOUNT HOULIE, Askerton   NY:578746
Cutting into the hillside south of the Kirk Beck is a single hut 8 m in diameter. It has walls 0·75 m thick on a base 1 m wide, and an entrance on the southern side. Two post-holes inside the hut may have held the roof supports. A hearth was found, as well as a conical jet button and a ring pendant. The house is likely to be of middle bronze age date, 1700–1400 BC. [K. S. Hodgson, *TCWAAS*, 40 (1940), 162.]

54   MUNGRISDALE CAIRNS, Caldbeck   NY:353337
A group of about two hundred small cairns at the eastern foot of Carrock Fell. Excavation of one produced a cremation in a pit. A

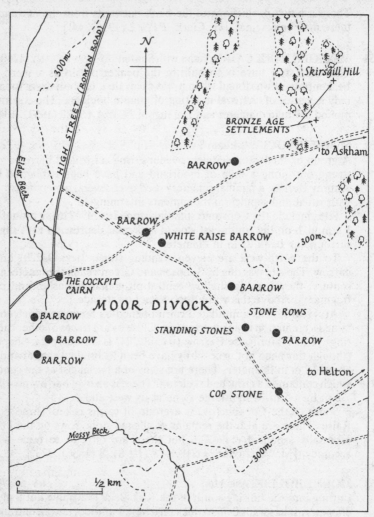

Fig 7. Moor Divock, Cumbria

number of ring cairns also exist in the group but excavation has failed to produce any dating evidence or burial.

55 ODDENDALE, Crosby Ravensworth   NY:593129

Situated on the exposed summit of Hardendale Fells, this circle consists of an outer ring 26 m across, and an inner kerb 7 m in diameter. On the east between the two circles is a single block of stone. The kerb encloses a small cairn which has produced a cremation.

56 PIKE OF STICKLE, Langdale NY:272072 (centre)
Around 3000 BC neolithic axe makers sat on large blocks of stone on the south-western slopes of Langdale Pikes roughing out thousands of stone axes. Their discarded flakes and broken implements can still be picked up today between the head of the Pike of Stickle at 600 m and the foot of the scree around 150 m. The rock is a tuff of the Borrowdale Volcanic Series and can easily be ground into a fine, sharp edge. Many axes from the site have been found widely scattered in Britain, with large numbers in Wessex. [B. Bunch and C. I. Fell, *PPS*, 15 (1949), 1.]

57 RAISET PIKE, Crosby Garrett NY:683073
This long cairn is badly damaged, probably due to the excavation of Canon Greenwell. It is 55 m long and 19 m wide at the south-western end. There seems to have been a mortuary building running along the spine of the barrow from near the south-west end up to a standing stone 2 m high. In it were the disarticulated bodies of three adults and three children mixed with plenty of wood. A flue trench enabled the wood and burials to be ignited and to burn within the cairn. North-west of the standing-stone other unburnt disarticulated bodies were found, many of them children. [W. Greenwell, *British Barrows* (1877), 510.]

58 REECASTLE CRAG, Borrowdale NY:275175
(National Trust). This tiny fort is on a crag above Wathendlath Beck. It is defended by triple banks on the west and a single bank on the east. The site is badly damaged, but an entrance seems probable on the south.

59 SKELMORE HEADS, Urswick SD:274754
A low grass-grown mound 18 m by 10·5 m. Two large stones protrude from the eastern end and two others were found in alignment towards the west. Excavation in 1957 showed that the site had been robbed in the past. If there had been a burial, it must have been between the eastern stones, but no trace remained. There were no signs of a kerb to the barrow, or its original shape.

The Tosthills burial chamber marked on the Ordnance Survey map at SD:262744 is a natural rock outcrop.

60 SMARDALE DEMESNE, Waithby NY:730072
On the moorland above Scandal Beck are two settlements. The larger contains a number of rectangular paddocks with huts in them. The other, 450 m to the north-east (NY:735075), is oval in plan with a single

hut and a cross-bank dividing the enclosure into two parts. The entrance was probably at the north-east.

61 STUDFOLD GATE, Dean   NY:040224
Eleven stones of this circle can still be traced; some of them are very low and one is actually incorporated in the modern wall which cuts the circle. [J. R. Mason, *TCWAAS*, 23 (1923), 34.]

62 SWINSIDE, Millom   SD:172883
A very fine stone circle 27 m in diameter, containing fifty-two close-set stones with two outlying portal stones to the south-east 2·7 m apart. Excavations have shown that the stones are bedded in a layer of small pebbles; fragments of charcoal and burnt bones were found. The circle is sometimes called Sunken Kirke, since the Devil is supposed to have caused the stones, which were used in building a church by day, to sink into the ground at night. [C. W. Dymond, *TCWAAS*, 2 (1902), 53.]

63 THRELKELD KNOTT, St John's in the Vale   NY:329241
On the northern slope of the moor is a rectangular enclosure about 120 m by 90 m, divided into about five paddocks with four or five small huts amongst them. Excavation of the largest hut, near the centre of the group, showed it to be 6 m across with walls about 1·5 m thick. On the slopes below the settlement are the remains of a field system, as well as about thirty small heaps of stones 6 m to 7·5 m across. Traces of charcoal found in some of these suggest that they were connected with burial, perhaps the bases of pyres on which bodies were cremated. [C. W. Dymond, *TCWAAS*, 2 (1902), 38.]

64 TOWTOP KIRK, Bampton   NY:494179
On the end of an east-facing spur is an oval enclosure labelled 'stone circle' on the Ordnance Survey maps. There is a U-shaped hut at the centre, with a second, smaller enclosure to the east. There is an entrance to the enclosure at the north-west, where there are traces of another hut, now covered by a later structure.

65 URSWICK STONE WALLS   SD:260741
An oval and a rectangular settlement lie side by side on the northern slope of a limestone hill. The oval enclosure is likely to be of iron age date and is surrounded by a stone wall about 3 m wide. The interior was divided into a number of paddocks and there are signs of at least three huts. One was excavated in 1906; it was shown to be 9 m in diameter and built of stone blocks. The method of roofing was uncertain. The adjoining rectangular enclosure has been badly destroyed by quarrying. It may be of Roman or later date. [W. G. Collingwood, *TCWAAS*, 7 (1907). 73.]

66 WAITBY   NY:755074
Overlain by the north side of the railway embankment is a remarkably rectangular earthwork, broken internally by subrectangular enclosures and with an inturned entrance on the west facing downhill. There is a second site to the south-east, also divided internally, but with signs of at least three hut circles inside.

67 WILSON SCAR, Thrimby   NY:550184
This small stone circle is really one of the Shap group. It contains thirty-two small stones and measures 15 m in diameter. It overlooks a quarry to the east.

WHITE MOSS, see Brats Hill.

68 YANWATH WOOD, Yanwath   NY:519260
This earthwork juts out on a D-shaped spur above the river Lowther. A north-south bank and ditch form the straight side about 220 m long, and banks loop out to the east with a ditch between them. There is an entrance at the north-west and possibly another at the south-east. The fort which is only 0·4 ha in area, contains a number of small enclosures.

DERBYSHIRE

1   ARBOR LOW, Middleton   sk:160636

An uphill climb leads to the grass-covered banks of this class II henge monument that encloses a circle of white weathered limestone blocks. The henge is oval in shape, measuring some 83 m by 75 m, with entrances at the north-north-west and south-south-east. The internal ditch was hewn out of solid limestone, producing about 1500 cubic metres of stone. This was built into the bank which today is a little over 2 m high and very irregular in appearance, especially on the eastern side where its surface has been robbed for the later building of a round barrow that overlies it, and which produced a cremation accompanied by two food vessels when it was excavated by Thomas Bateman in 1845.

On the flat internal area of Arbor Low lie some three dozen limestone blocks, that once presumably stood in an egg-shaped ring, 37 m by 41·5 m. Excavations have failed to produce any stone holes, so one imagines that the stones were originally propped in position with smaller stones. At the centre three larger stones formed a cove, whilst just to the east lay an extended male skeleton surrounded by stones. The site probably dates from early in the second millenium BC.

West from the southern entrance runs a long, low, curving bank which leads 320 m to the south-west, missing the large round cairn called *Gib Hill*. This was dug by Bateman in 1848 and produced a small limestone cist containing a cremation burial and a food vessel. [H. St George Gray, *Archaeologia,* 58 (1903), 461.]

2   BALL CROSS, Edensor   sk:228691

This is a roughly rectangular fort on a promontory of millstone grit, defended by precipitous natural slopes to the south and west above the river Wye. The north and east are protected by a stone wall still 1·2 m high and 1·5 m thick at its base, narrowing to 0·9 m at the top. This was built on top of material dug out of a V-shaped ditch 2·5 m deep. There is evidence that the fort had been permanently occupied and quantities of late bronze age and early iron age pottery have been found, together with quern stones. With the Roman advance into midland England after AD 43 the fort was flattened. A building was erected in the enclosure during the sixteenth century AD. [J. Stanley, *Derbys. Arch. J,* 74 (1954), 85.]

3 BARBROOK, Ramsley Moor   SK:278755
There are three circles in this group. The southern consists of thirteen
stones on the inner edge of a rubble bank 13 m in diameter. A circle of
similar size, 275 m north of the first, surrounded a burial mound. This
contained two cremations in urns dated by radiocarbon to 1500 ± 150
bc. A further 450 m north-north-east is another site with twenty-two
stones on the edge of a 30 m diameter bank [*VCH Derby*, I (1905),
181.]

4 BEELEY MOOR, Beeley   SK:281668
Three adjoining cairns neatly restored after excavation in 1967. Each is
about 7·5 m in diameter and under 1 m high. All were built on an
unusual layer of white sand. The western cairn had a cremation in an
urn at its centre, with another urn on the south side. The central cairn,
which was surrounded by a double kerb, had been robbed but traces of
two cremations were found. A collared urn was found in the eastern
cairn in 1963.
    There is a small rectangular cairn 11 m west of those described
above. At its centre was a cremation deposit buried with a segmented
faience bead. [J. Radley, *Derbys. Arch. J*, 89 (1969), 1.]

5 BEE LOW, Youlgreave   SK:192647
A partially tree-covered cairn 12 m across and 1·5 m high was dug into
twice by Thomas Bateman, in 1843 and 1851, and was re-excavated in
1966–8 by Barry M. Marsden. It seems probable that the barrow was in
use for about three centuries. The earliest burials were a group of six
inhumations in a stone cist, with a beaker. Two other cists were found,
as well as isolated burials, making a total of twenty-three inhumations
and five cremations. Three more beakers, bronze awls and a riveted
knife were discovered. [B. M. Marsden, *Ant.J.*, 50 (1970), 186.]

6 BULL RING, Dove Holes   SK:078783
A class II double-entrance henge monument badly damaged by quarrying. Today the outer bank of limestone rubble stands 1·2 m high and
is 75 m in diameter. Excavation in 1949 showed that the ditch was
about 2 m deep and about 10 m wide. There was once a ring of stones
within the monument, but by 1789 all except one had been removed.
This would have made the site look similar to Arbor Low. Another
similarity is a large barrow 2·4 m high that stands south-west of the Bull
Ring, and recalls Gib Hill at Arbor Low. [L. Alcock, *PPS*, 16 (1950),
81.]

7 CASTLE NAZE, Chapel-en-le-Frith   SK:054784
Promontory forts are a feature of this part of Derbyshire. Castle Naze
lies on a west-facing spur at 443 m above sea-level. The fort covers a

triangular area which has steep cliffs on the north and south, and two drystone walls and an outer ditch on the east. Field work suggests that the inner wall is the earliest, and that the outer wall and ditch belong to a later iron age phase. The entrance at the centre of the east side is unlikely to be original. A gap between the northern end of the walls and the cliff face, which is approached by a deep hollow way, is more likely to be the true entrance. [H. G. Ramm, *Derbys. Arch. J,* 77 (1957), 49.]

8   CASTLE RING, Harthill   SK:221628
This oval hillfort occupies a north-facing spur of the millstone grit. It is small, its bank, ditch and counterscarp enclosing only 0·4 ha. Much of the inside of the rampart has been damaged, but it is still possible to identify the site of the entrance on the south-east. [J. May, *Derbys. Arch. J,* (forthcoming).]

9   CRESWELL CRAGS, Whitwell   SL:538743 (Visitors' Centre)
Preserved as a Site of Special Scientific Interest, this narrow limestone gorge contains twenty caves of archaeological interest. They can be divided into two groups, those a little above river level and those much higher up the crag face, now severely eroded. Three groups of men occupied the caves. About 43,000 BC Neanderthal man made rough axes from Bunter sandstone pebbles. Between 30,000 and 28,000 years ago upper palaeolithic men of modern type lived around the caves making long laurel-leaf-shaped flint tools, which they used to hunt mammoth, woolly rhinoceros, bison and reindeer. A long time passed, during which the caves became dens for hyenas until, around 13,000–11,000 years ago, more modern men arrived, known to archaeologists as Creswellians. They also made skilled tools from flint blades and produced simple works of art carved on animal bone.

In order to preserve them, the caves are not open to the public, but metal grilles have been set across the entrances, allowing the interior of some to be inspected. Visitors can gain much information from the Visitors' Centre, where they can watch a slide programme and then follow a trail past the more important sites. (Allow 1½ hours.) These are:
Boat House Cave, excavated using explosives; it produced the bones of hyena, bison and horse.
Church Hole Cave, excavated by Rev. Magens Mello and William Boyd Dawkins in the 1870s. It too produced a lot of bone material. Stretching for 50 m into the hillside, it is one of the larger caves at the Crags, with side chambers near the entrance. Evidence of human occupation ranges from the tools of Neanderthal and early upper palaeolithic man to Roman material, whilst remains of vast numbers of animals include hyenas, bear, woolly rhinoceros, wolf and cave lion.

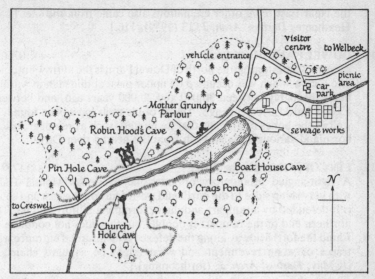

Fig 8. Creswell Crags, Derbyshire

Pin Hole Cave, excavated by Leslie Armstrong in 1924. A narrow fissure leads into a small chamber at the back; 15,000 pieces of bone were uncovered, revealing another hyena den. Men of Neanderthal and Creswellian type had occupied the site which was used again and again throughout prehistory. The cave produced a crudely engraved figure of a man on a piece of reindeer rib, which links it rather tenuously to the painted caves of southern France and Spain.

Robin Hood's Cave: five entrances lead into the largest of the Creswell caves. Its contents were similar to the others. A horse head engraved on bone was found, again linking these caves to the painted group.

Mother Grundy's Parlour, a horseshoe-shaped cave which produced many broken bones and flint blades, much of it coming from the platform at the cave mouth. Like the others the site was occupied by man almost continuously from Neanderthal to neolithic times. [R. D. S. Jenkinson, *Creswell Crags Visitors' Centre Research Reports No. 1* (1978).]

10 **DOLL TOR, Stanton** (Fig 9, p. 103)   sk:238628
A stone circle, about 7 m in diameter, composed of six stones, two fallen, and linked by a continuous ring of smaller stones. It has produced cinerary urns with cremations and incense cups in a low cairn on the eastern side. At the centre of this cairn a female cremation was found in a hollow accompanied by a faience bead which linked it with

the Near East. Five other cremations also came from the site. [J. P.
Heathcote, *Derbys. Arch. J*, 13 (1939), 116.]

11 DOWEL CAVE, Hartington   SK:075676
In a small limestone gorge north of Dowel Farm is the narrow entrance
into a cave which was occupied by upper palaeolithic man in warmer
times, probably between 30,000 and 20,000 years ago, and between
13,000 and 11,000 years ago. Traces of his tools have been found, as
well as the bones of animals that he hunted, such as reindeer, bison,
horse and various birds and fish from the nearby river Dove.

12 FIN COP, Ashford in the Water   SK:175710
A right-angled promontory of limestone overlooks Monsal Dale,
with very steep sides to the north and west. Only on the east and south
is it defended by a rampart and ditch, forming a hillfort of 4 ha. The
northern end of the rampart is double, but this does not continue all
round the fort. Midway along the defence is an inturned entrance with
traces of stone revetment and what might be a guard chamber.
[J. May, *Derbys. Arch. J*, (forthcoming).]

13 FIVEWELLS, Taddington   SK:124710
A circular cairn with two burial chambers back to back approached by
passages from east to west. Both chambers are roofless, with two
portal stones at the entrances to each. The eastern chamber is better
preserved. Thomas Bateman found a dozen skeletons in 1846, and five
others were uncovered later. Neolithic pottery, arrowheads and a flint
knife have also been discovered. The cairn is constructed of thin slabs
of limestone. [B. M. Marsden, *Burial Mounds of Derbyshire* (1977),
6.]

14 GREEN LOW, Aldwark   SK:233580
This roughly circular cairn, 18 m in diameter, was excavated in 1963–4.
It was shown to have a straight facade on the south side of the barrow
and, from the centre of this, a small narrow passage leading into a
chamber approximately 2 m square. In 1843 Bateman found fragments
of a skeleton in the chamber, and in 1964 the disarticulated remains of
another were found in the mound material. At the same time neolithic
pottery was found. [T. Manby, *Derbys. Arch. J,* 85 (1965), 1.]

15 HARTINGTON CAIRNS, Hartington
Parsley Hay (SK:144631). Bateman excavated this round cairn in 1848.
It is 1·8 m high and 18 m in diameter. A skeleton in a sitting position
was found in a rock-cut grave beneath stone slabs. Above the grave
was a secondary crouched burial with a bronze round-heeled dagger
and a granite battle-axe.

Lean Low (SK: 149622). Slightly smaller than Parsley Hay, and dug by Bateman in 1843, this barrow also produced a skeleton in a rock-cut grave, as well as another inhumation and a cremation. Further excavations in 1972 produced a skull and long bones, together with a biconical jet bead.

End Low (SK: 156605) is at the southern end of the group, standing 2 m high and 20 m in diameter. A great hole in the summit shows where Bateman dug a deep trench in 1848 to reach a burial 4 m below. There he found a crouched skeleton with a bronze round-heeled dagger and a flint knife. At a higher level was a child's skeleton. [B. M. Marsden, *Burial Mounds of Derbyshire* (1977), 44, 49, 50.]

16 HOB HURST'S HOUSE, Beeley   SK: 287692
A cairn 10 m in diameter and less than 1 m high, surrounded by a bank and ditch. At one time there was a circle of stones inside the bank. In the centre of the cairn was a stone cist 3 m by 2·7 m in which a body had been cremated. [B. M. Marsden, *Burial Mounds of Derbyshire* (1977), 20.]

17 MAM TOR, Castleton   SK: 128838
(National Trust). This is a tongue-shaped fort of 7 ha in an unusually high position on a hog-back ridge of the Peak District. A probable early timber palisade round the hilltop was later replaced by a dumped rampart revetted with a stone wall in front, together with a ditch and counterscarp bank. The weaker northern end is breached by an in-turned entrance, whilst at the south another entrance has a single inturn. Huts were found inside the enclosure, circular in shape and cut into platforms on the hilltop. Large quantities of bucket- and barrel-shaped pots have been found in excavations between 1965 and 1969. Radiocarbon dates for the interior occupation layers of 1180 bc are remarkably early and suggest a middle bronze age date, but it is emphasized that no dates have been obtained for the defences. There are two barrows inside the fort; one was examined in the nineteenth century and produced a bronze axe and urn. [D. G. Coombs, in D. W. Harding, *Hillforts* (1976), 147.]

18 MARKLAND GRIPS, Clowne   SK: 511752
Limestone crags up to 8 m high surround this 4 ha promontory fort on the north and south sides. The western neck is cut off by earthworks on the west, which have been badly disturbed by ploughing. There may at one time have been three lines of ramparts, but only the inner one still stands, 15 m wide and 3 m high, with a ditch 5 m wide to the west. The bank is made of dumped clay and gravel with a facing of limestone slabs. Internal excavations have found scarcely any iron age material,

but a substantial amount of second- to third-century Roman finds. chambers were added on the west and south-west. Most of these

19   MINNING LOW, Ballidon   sK:209573

The largest chambered barrow in the Peak District is one of two mounds in the plantation. Although it is now very ruined, it contains at least four burial chambers. The first, at the centre, approached by a drystone-walled passage, was built into a small cairn. This mound was later extended when the second chamber on the south side was added. Both of these chambers have their capstone still in position. Later chambers were added on the west and south-west. Most of these chambers were cleaned out by Thomas Bateman in 1851, although it seems clear that the tomb had been robbed from Roman times onwards. [B. M. Marsden, *Burial Mounds of Derbyshire* (1977), 4.]

20   NINE LADIES, Stanton Moor   sK:247634

Imprisoned within a low modern stone wall is a circle of nine (possibly ten) stones, each less than 1 m high, standing on the inner edge of a slight embankment, which is broken by entrance gaps on the north-east and south-west. There was once a small mound in the centre but this has now vanished. The stone circle is 10 m in diameter. To the south-west is an outlier, the King Stone, a block of millstone grit 58 cm high, also enclosed by a wall. Close by are three ring cairns (see Stanton Moor). [A. Burl, *Stone Circles of the British Isles* (1976), 291.]

21   NINE STONES CLOSE, Harthill   sK:225626

Only four enormous stones remain of this 13 m circle, though a block of stone in the wall to the south may perhaps have been one of the nine stones. A dig by Thomas Bateman in 1847 produced a few scraps of pottery and flints. [T. Bateman, *Vestiges* (1848), 102.]

22   RINGHAM LOW, Over Haddon   sK:169664

An oval-chambered barrow, now much ruined, lies mainly in a plantation with a field wall cutting off its northern end. Llewellynn Jewitt's engraving suggests that it once had a horned forecourt. It had four or five burial chambers that between them held some twenty human burials as well as animal bones, flint tools and arrowheads. [B. M. Marsden, *Burial Mounds of Derbyshire* (1977), 2.]

23   STANTON MOOR   sK:249623

About 60 ha of remote heath-covered sandstone plateau provide extensive views to the south and east. Here, in the bronze age, a necropolis of some seventy cairns, stone circles and a standing stone was erected. Many of the sites have been excavated by the Heathcote family, whose private museum in the village of Birchover contains

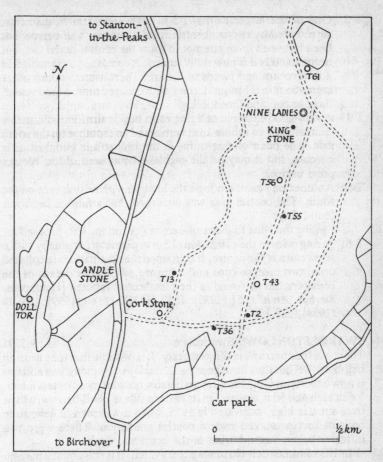

Fig 9. Stanton Moor, Derbyshire (after Heathcote)

most of the finds. There is not room to describe all the sites, nor would it be worthwhile, for even in the winter when the heather is low, many are difficult to find. Instead a brief selection is given here following a route approximately from south to north. Numbers are according to the plan, and will also be found marked on some of the sites.

T 13 A rectangular cairn 12 m by 7 m and 1 m high, covering thirteen cremations, most of them apparently young females, and six in collared urns. Four of the urns were inverted; one contained an incense cup and another a clay stud.

T 36 A cairn 9 m in diameter and 0·8 m high. In a pit south of the centre was a cremation lying over a dolerite battle-axe.

T 2 One of the larger cairns, 1·5 m high and 15 m in diameter, surrounded by two concentric rings of stones. The barrow has been left open in an attempt to show the central burial cist, but unfortunately it is now sadly ruined. It contained a cremation in a broken urn and pieces of bronze. There were a dozen other cremations in the mound, some with collared urns, a food vessel, incense cup and flint tools.

T 43 A very good example of a ring cairn beside the footpath, with a circular bank of rubble 18 m across and an entrance on the south side. The place of ring cairns in the bronze age burial ritual is obscure, but it may be the highland equivalent of the Wessex pond barrow.

T 56 Another ring cairn amongst the heather with an entrance on the south. The central area was disturbed, but a faience bead was found there.

Passing the Nine Ladies stone circle (qv) on the left, proceed to:

T 61 A ring cairn in the plantation, 12 m in diameter, originally with a small cairn at the centre. It contained nine cremations in collared urns, two incense cups and a bronze awl. Fuller details of the cemetery can be found in the Heathcotes' reports: [Heathcote, *Derbys. Arch. J,* 51 (1930), 1; 57 (1936), 21; 60 (1939), 105; 74 (1954), 128.]

24 SWARKESTON LOWS, Swarkeston sk:365295

There are four barrows in this cemetery. It is possible that they were all bell-barrows, but they have been badly damaged by ploughing and this is now uncertain. Only the western barrow remains more or less intact, 3·6 m high and 30 m across. On its eastern side is a bell-barrow, a little over a metre high, excavated in 1955, when it was seen to have been built of turves stacked over a central cremation. There were two intrusive pagan Saxon burials in the berm and ditch.

In 1956 another bell-barrow was excavated. It is still about 2 m high. It seems to have begun as a turf-built bowl-barrow covering a primary burial with a flint knife in a boat-shaped wooden coffin. Later enlarged as a bell-barrow with surrounding double ditch, it seems to have been designed to take three cremations in urns. Under the barrow traces of a beaker habitation site were disclosed. The final barrow in the group is only about 0·5 m high and unexcavated. [M. Posnansky, *Derbys. Arch. J,* 75 (1955), 123; E. Greenfield, ibid., 80 (1960), 1.]

DEVONSHIRE

1 BERRY DOWN, Berrynarbor ss: 569436 (centre)
A group of nine round barrows, some of which were opened in 1883 by George Doe. In one he found a large Trevisker-type Cornish urn, inverted over a cremation. [L. V. Grinsell, *Archaeology of Exmoor* (1970), 59.]

2 BLACKBURY CASTLE, Southleigh sx: 187924
(Department of the Environment). Blackbury Castle sits astride a narrow ridge with small streams to the north and south. It is oval in shape with a triangular annexe on the south side. Its single rampart, of dumped clay and flints, and V-shaped ditch enclose 2·6 ha. Only the entrance on the south is original. It probably had bastions on either side of a gate 2·5 m wide and may have been crossed by a bridge. The annexe, which is unfinished, was added later. It included an elongated entrance passage with a gate 4·5 m wide, between two triangular enclosures probably used as stock corrals. Limited interior excavation produced a rather flimsy hut or corn drying area. [A. Young and K. Richardson, *PDAES*, 5 (1954–5), 43.]

3 BLACK HILL, Manaton sx: 766792
Thirty metres north of the road from Haytor to Manaton are the remains of a ring cairn or truncated cairn 14 m in diameter. Leading northwards from it down the slope is a row of sixteen stones, nine of which have fallen. This was probably a double row originally, but there is no longer much evidence of that. The row stretches over a distance of about 120 m and ends at a larger stone set at right angles to the axis of the row. There is another ruined cairn beyond. [R. H. Worth, *Dartmoor* (1967), 227.]

4 BOLT TAIL, Malborough sx: 669397
(National Trust). Here is a promontory fort of about 5 ha commanding magnificent views across Bigbury Bay. In addition to steep rocky cliffs it is defended by a rampart 275 m long and 4·5 m high, faced with stone on the outer, eastern side. On the north side is an inturned entrance guarded by a semicircular outwork, from which a hollow way leads to a second minor fort that looks across Hope Bay and seems to guard a

fresh water supply. A line of rampart defines this fort, which is entered near the cliffs on the north-west side. [*VCH* Devon, I (1906), 578.]

5   BROAD DOWN BARROW CEMETERY, Farway
sy:147967 to 174935

Spread out along the ridges of Gittisham Hill, Farway Hill and Broad Down are about fifty round barrows forming one of the most remarkable linear cemeteries in England. Some are only a few centimetres high whilst others like the example at sy:151961 reach 3·5 m high. The barrows tend to concentrate in three main groups, some east of the Hare and Hounds Inn, others in the woods around a possible henge monument or afforestation ring in Farway Hill plantation (sy:161955) and the third group at Roncombe Gate crossroads. Some of the barrows were dug in the nineteenth century by the Rev. R. Kirwan of Gittisham and in 1898 by R. H. Worth, who dug four in a week. Four barrows on Ball Hill (sy:175946) had circles of stone around their circumference, and one yielded a shale cup. Since many barrows have been destroyed by ploughing it is difficult to identify the excavated barrows with certainty. [C. and A. Fox, *PDAES,* 4 (1948), 1.]

6   BURLEY WOOD, Bridestowe
sx:495876

This is a most complicated site on a north-facing spur above the springs of the river Lew. More than 6·0 ha are contained by a series of enclosures and cross-ridge dykes, and half the site is made more difficult to interpret by being tree-covered. The main enclosure is oval in shape with an inturned entrance on the south side. It is protected by a single rampart and ditch with traces of a counterscarp on east and west. Outside the southern entrance is a large annexe with a small enclosure on its eastern side, possibly designed as a cattle pen. The annexe entrance is on the west. Separating the spur from the main hill mass are three cross-ridge dykes. The nearest to the fort is relatively weak and broken by a central entrance gap. The same applies to the middle dyke. The southern dyke, broken by two entrances, is also the most massive. There is a medieval motte-and-bailey castle site north-east of the hillfort. [J. Forde-Johnston, *Hillforts* (1976), 205.]

7   BURRIDGE CAMP, Roborough
ss:569352

This is a damaged example of a multiple-enclosure fort, of which the main surviving features are a roughly oval enclosure of 1·2 ha defended by a single rampart and ditch. This is broken on the east by an entrance gap. The south side has been damaged. Some 370 m further along the ridge to the east is a second line of defence, which probably marks off a stock-raising area. Although almost certainly of iron age date, the fort may have been reused in late Saxon times as a *burh.* [L. V. Grinsell, *Archaeology of Exmoor* (1970), 83.]

8   BUTTERDON HILL, Harford   sx:655587
From a small round barrow 10·5 m in diameter leads one of the longest
stone rows on Dartmoor. It runs slightly west of north for about 1600 m
until it stops at a large fallen stone. The row originally went on past a
cross-marked stone called Hobajons Cross and ended after 1915 m at
the Longstone on Piles Hill, a menhir, now fallen, which measures
some 2·6 m in length. [R. H. Worth, *Dartmoor* (1967), 205.]

9   CADBURY CASTLE, Cadbury   ss:914053
This oval fort of 1·6 ha is defended by massive ramparts 6 m high on the
south-east to south-west side. On the north-west a steep slope makes
defence unnecessary. The original entrance seems to be on the
south-east; that on the north-east is almost certainly modern. Some
30 m inside the southern entrance is a marked terrace lying convex to
the main rampart and joining it on the east and west. It seems to
represent an earlier line of rampart, reduced by pushing it outwards
into a ditch that still survives as a distinct hollow.
   In 1847 a deep hollow in the centre of the fort was opened and a shaft
was revealed, lined with puddled clay and descending for 18 m. It
contained pottery, bones and ashes, twenty metal and four shale
bracelets, rings and beads and an iron knife blade. The shaft failed to
reach water and it seems likely that it was dug for votive purposes.
[J. M. Coles and D. Simpson, eds., *Studies in Ancient Europe* (1968),
262.]

10   CHALLACOMBE, North Bovey   sx:690809
Three rows of stones run downhill for a distance of 161 m. At the
southern end is a triangular blocking stone. The northern end was
destroyed by tin working. The large stone in the central row at this end
was probably turned at right angles when some restoration work took
place in the nineteenth century. Outside the rows to the west of this
stone are traces of what seems to be a stone circle. These too seem to
be the work of the restorer and are not original. [J. W. Brailsford,
Antiquity, 12 (1938), 463.]

11   CHAPMAN BARROWS, Challacombe   ss:695435
A linear cemetery of some nine round barrows, of which the eastern-
most was opened by J. F. Chanter in 1905. In it he found burnt bones
covered by a layer of turves. The barrow was enclosed by a stone kerb
though the mound had overspread it and obscured it. Four hundred
and fifty metres south-east of this barrow is the tallest standing stone
on Exmoor, the *Long Stone*, a block of Morte slate 2·7 m high. [L. V.
Grinsell, *Archaeology of Exmoor* (1970), 59.]

12   CLOVELLY DYKES   ss:311235
Three ancient trackways follow ridges which meet at this fort; the fort

seems to have been specially designed for herding cattle, possibly prior to exporting them to the continent from nearby estuaries and harbours. Two roughly rectangular enclosures, one within the other, were strongly defended, with entrances on the eastern side. Later, additions were made in the form of three strip-like enclosures on the west, and a semicircular annexe on the east. Entrances to the western enclosures were on the northern, seaward side facing nearby springs. The rampart ends are quite massive at the entrances, suggesting that they were designed to withstand considerable jostling by heavy cattle. Today the earthworks are overgrown and form field boundaries. [A. Fox, *Ant. J,* 109 (1952), 12.]

13 CORRINGDON BALL, South Brent   sx:666613
A stone row 152 m long is aligned on a cairn of stones. To the south-east of the cairn is a ruined ring of stones that once surrounded a barrow. Two triple rows of stones are aligned on this circle. One row stretches for 79 m, the other 67 m. Since few of the stones are more than 30 cm high the site is most easily found when the bracken is low. [R. H. Worth, *Dartmoor* (1967), 231.]

14 CORRINGDON BALL GATE, South Brent   sx:670614
A long barrow 40 m long and 20 m wide lies roughly south-east to north-west. At the higher, south-east end are the collapsed remains of a burial chamber. One stone still stands upright 1·3 m high and beside it lie two others measuring about 4 m by 2 m. There are some badly preserved alignments a short distance to the east, connected with a cairn. [L. V. Grinsell, *PDAS,* 36 (1978), 132.]

15 COUNTISBURY PROMONTORY FORT, Lynton   ss:741493
Wind Hill spur lies between the East Lyn river and the sea. Its neck is cut by a massive rampart 0·4 km long and 9 m high. An entrance is uncertain, but is probably the one through which the road passes. It has been suggested that Countisbury may have been an iron age beachhead, similar to Bindon Hill and Hengistbury Head on the south coast. [L. V. Grinsell, *Archaeology of Exmoor* (1970), 83.]

16 CRANBROOK CASTLE, Moretonhampstead   sx:738890
This is a hillfort of two periods. The first consists of a roughly circular banked and ditched enclosure of about 4 ha. It is badly damaged and the bank is only 1 m high. It is best seen on the south when the scrub is low. It has an oblique entrance outside the field wall on the west and another on the south-east. The northern side is little more than a scarp. At a later stage a second line of rampart and ditch was begun, inside the first, enclosing 2·8 ha. It is unfinished, and would seem to have been planned to overlie the earlier fort on the northern side. However

no construction took place there. Instead the bank rises about 2 m on the east, south and west sides only. There are entrances, on the east and south-west. which do not line up with the earlier ones and they too appear to be unfinished. [J. Collis, *PDAS*, 30 (1972), 216.]

17 DRIZZLECOMBE, Sheepstor   sx:592670

There is a wealth of monuments close together here. The main feature is a large bracken-covered barrow 3 m high and 21 m in diameter, with a hollow in the top called the Giant's Basin. North-east of this are three smaller barrows in a row. From the centre one a single line of stones runs south-west for 150 m ending in a larger stone 2·4 m high. To the south a second line of stones 84 m long terminates at a menhir 4·2 m high. This line seems to start again at a small barrow north-west of the Giant's Basin. It is double in places and runs for 150 m until it ends at an upright stone 3·1 m high. A barrow 270 m north of the Giant's Basin contains a stone cist, and 135 m east of that are two pounds with ruined walls about 1·5 m thick, one containing two hut circles, the other three. [R. H. Worth, *Dartmoor* (1967), 209.]

18 DUMPDON GREAT CAMP, Luppitt   st:176040

High above the river Otter are the bracken-covered ramparts of a kite-shaped fort 1·2 ha in area. There is a widely spaced double rampart and ditch on the north; elsewhere the defences are single with traces of a counterscarp. There is an inturned entrance 30 m long on the north-east with additional terracework outside which made direct access difficult.

19 FERNWORTHY   sx:655841

This circle in a clearing in the plantation is 18 m in diameter and is composed of some thirty blocks of local granite, which are graded in size from the largest, 1·2 m high on the south side. A damaged double row of stones approaches from the south. The floor of the circle was covered with charcoal but nothing else was found when the circle was excavated in 1897. [*VCH Devon*, 1, (1906), 356.]

20 FIVE BARROWS, North Molton   ss:732368 (centre)

Lying roughly from east to west, these nine barrows vary in height from 0·4 m to 3 m and in width from 12 m to 34 m. Amongst them is the only well-preserved bell-barrow on Exmoor with a clearly visible surrounding berm and ditch. No records of excavations in any of the barrows are known to exist.

21 FOALE'S ARRISHES, Widecombe   sx:737758

A group of six circular huts between 5·5 m and 9 m in diameter are scattered amongst a group of Celtic fields, which in turn are overlain by the long narrow strips of medieval systems. The hut roofs were supported on central poles, and cooking holes were found in some of them. The whole settlement was once surrounded by a wall like Grimspound, but this has long since vanished. [C. A. R. Radford, *PPS*, 18 (1952), 71.]

22   GREY WETHERS, Lydford   sx:638832

Situated on a saddle east of Sittaford Tor are two stone circles restored in the late nineteenth century. The northern is 31 m in diameter and the southern 35·5 m. A hundred years ago only nine stones were standing at the north and seven at the south, but today almost all the stones are standing again, each about 3 m from the next, and all around 1 m high. [R. H. Worth, *Dartmoor* (1967), 258.]

23   GRIMSPOUND, Manaton   sx:701809

This is an enclosure or pound of 1·6 ha, defined by a strong wall 3 m wide and 1·2 m to 1·5 m high, partly the result of reconstruction. There is a single original paved entrance on the eastern side facing uphill. A small stream passes under the wall on the west and runs through the enclosure, but this has a seasonal flow and could not have been relied on all the year round. Inside the pound were about two dozen huts, of which sixteen seem to have been built for permanent habitation with fireplaces, porches and benches. The others may have been store huts and animal sheds. Traces can also be seen of three or four cattle pens. Excavations have failed to date this site, but it is probably of the late bronze age, its inhabitants being pastoralists relying on the moors for the livelihood of their flocks. [A. Fox, *Arch. J*, 114 (1957), 158.]

24   HAMELDOWN, Widecombe   sx:706791 (centre)

A group of round barrows following the ridgeway include at the northern end Broad Barrow, then Single Barrow and further south Two Barrows. A cremation was found in the northernmost of the Two Barrows in 1872 accompanied by a grooved bronze ogival dagger with an amber pommel decorated with gold pointillé pins arranged in a cross pattern. Sadly the dagger was destroyed by enemy action in April 1941. The cremation was not at the centre of the barrow but may nevertheless have been primary, perhaps placed clear of the middle to deceive tomb robbers. The barrow had an outer kerb of stones, separated from a central cairn by a mound of peaty earth. [L. V. Grinsell, *PDAS*, 36 (1978), 112. *Dagger:* T. D. Kendrick, *Ant. J*, 17 (1937), 313.]

25   HEMBURY, Payhembury   st:113031

Hembury can offer a quiet retreat after queuing in a traffic jam on the A30 at Honiton. It is a beautiful hillfort with a long and important history. This began in the neolithic period when a causewayed camp was dug on the hill. Eight sections of neolithic ditch, each about 1·8 m deep and between 8 and 17 m long lay in a curved line from east to west across the middle of the later iron age fort, with traces of a rampart on their southern side. At the west end under the iron age entrance were found traces of a neolithic gate and an almost perfect circular hut site. At the eastern iron age entrance another section of neolithic ditch was uncovered with a line of palisade holes outside it. Finds included more than 1600 flints, fifteen greenstone axes, pottery and quite a lot of charred wheat. A corrected radiocarbon date of between 4200 and 3900 BC has subsequently been obtained for charcoal from the neolithic ditch.

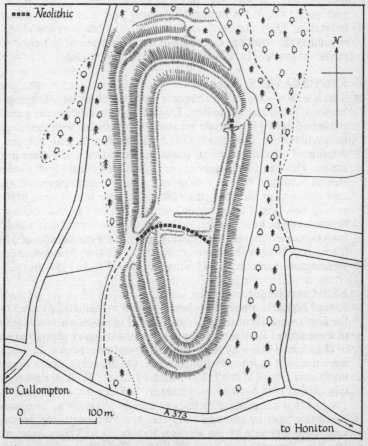

Fig 10. Hembury hillfort, Devonshire

The fort was next occupied in the iron age. Reinterpreting the excavations of 1930–35 it is probable that a single rampart surrounded the hill, built of material from an internal quarry ditch and faced with a palisade. The entrances midway along the west side and at the north-east seems to have had outworks whose precise form is uncertain. Later two ditches were dug producing an outer bank and counterscarp, and the inner bank was enlarged. The outermost bank on the north is unfinished. The entrances with short inturns were faced with timbers and probably bridged over. They were probably rebuilt a number of times. All this happened before the mid second century BC and may have been the work of the Dumnoni. In the Belgic period, perhaps about 50 BC, two banks were built midway across the fort with ditches on the south. The southern end of the fort was probably used as a stock enclosure, whilst the stronger northern part was used for human habitation. Only a trace of one rectangular hut has been found. A low mound at the southern extremity of the hillfort seems to have been a medieval motte. [D. Liddell, *PDAES*, 2 (1935), 135.]

26   KENT'S CAVERN, Torquay   sx:934641
This is a show-cave with a chequered excavation history. Digging was begun in the 1820s by the Rev. J. MacEnery, but the results were not published during his lifetime because they conflicted with the religious beliefs of the day. Between 1865 and 1880 William Pengelly stripped the interior of all archaeological strata and found over 1200 flint implements. These included early upper palaeolithic 'laurel-leaf' blades of British Solutrean type as well as later Creswellian implements. Bone and antler tools included three harpoons, one with double barbs, a sewing needle and an ivory rod. Amongst extinct animal bones were the cave hyena, bear and lion. There are display cases of material at the cave entrance, but the best impression of the site can be obtained from the finds in Torquay Museum or the Natural History Museum in South Kensington, London. [E. H. Rogers, *PDAES*, 5 (1954–5), 68.]

27   KESTOR, Chagford   sx:665867
Round Pound is a walled enclosure 33·5 m in diameter entered from the north-west. It contained a single hut 11 m across with wall footings of stone and a free-standing ring of posts inside, which supported a turf or thatch roof that may have been partly open to the sky. In the floor were traces of an iron-smelting furnace. On the north, north-west and north-east slopes of the hill crowned by Kestor Rock are more than two dozen huts 6–10 m in diameter, linked with rectangular field systems that are marked by lines of upright stone slabs. Two sunken roads that may be contemporary also run from north-east to south-west on either side of the modern Batworthy to Teigncombe road. [A. Fox, *Trans. Devon. Assn*, 86 (1954), 21.]

28 LAKEHEAD HILL, Lydford sx:644774
On an unplanted part of the hilltop are three stone cists. The most interesting is at sx:645776 where a great stone box stands above ground level, surrounded by a cairn circle of six stones with a row of eleven stones curving downhill on the eastern side. It was restored in 1895 and the cist is almost certainly now too large. At sx:643777 is a rectangular cist almost level with the ground, whilst the third, at sx:643774, lies at the centre of a kerb circle almost 6 m in diameter.
There is a pound containing hut circles at the northern end of the woodland clearing (sx:644782). [R. H. Worth, *Dartmoor* (1967), 229.]

29 LEGIS TOR, Sheepstor sx:570654
Four pounds butt on to each other here. The earliest is subrectangular and in the middle of the southern side. A second pound was built on to it on the west, then a much larger one on the east. Finally a small enclosure was constructed in the eastern corner of the largest pound. The walls are all about 1 m thick with inner and outer facing blocks packed with rubble. Traces of at least eleven huts can be found inside or close to the pounds. Their walls are of stone, about a metre high, and they were probably roofed with thatch or turf. Excavation has dated the site to the middle bronze age, about 1200–1000 bc. [C. A. R. Radford, *PPS,* 18 (1952), 61.]

30 MERRIVALE, Walkhampton sx:553746
A stone circle, three stone rows and a number of cairns are easily accessible. The circle is in fact oval, 18 m by 20 m, with a single standing stone outside to the south. About 180 m north-east is a large stone cist which may have contained a single burial destroyed by the acid soil; the covering slab was broken in 1860. North of the cist are two almost parallel double stone rows running east to west. The southern, 238 m long, has a round barrow at its centre; the northern is 78 m long. Both are blocked by triangular stones at the eastern end. There is also a single stone row running south-west towards the stone circle from a cairn which is close to the southern stone row.

31 MILBER DOWN, Haccombe sx:884699
On the western slope of Milber Down are four approximately concentric rectangular enclosures, bounded by banks and external ditches. Their position on the side of the hill makes it unlikely that they were defensive and they probably belong to the type of earthwork found in south-west Britain called a hill-slope fort (considered to have been connected with cattle ranching). Most such sites are close to the coast, and may have been involved in the export of cattle from Britain to the classical world. There was an entrance in the outer enclosure on the

north-west side, but the modern road has destroyed the entrances to the other enclosures. Excavation has shown that the site was built in the first century BC and abandoned early in the first century AD. A fine group of small bronze sculptures from the site is now in Torquay Museum. They were probably associated with a Romano-British farming site east of the fort. [A. Fox and others, *PDAES*, 4 (1949–50), 27.]

32   PRESTONBURY CASTLE, Drewsteignton   sx:746900
This multiple-enclosure fort stands on the steep north bank of the river Teign looking across the gorge to Cranbrook Castle. Its inner enclosure is oval in shape and is surrounded by a rampart but no ditch. The gorge to the south-west is sufficiently steep to require no extra protection. There is an entrance on the east. On the east and north is the first of the enclosures, marked by a bank and ditch. Well outside lies a second enclosure, also with bank and external ditch stretching round to the steep gorge sides. It is broken by a fine inturned entrance. Like Milber Down this must be yet another example of the enclosures used in the distribution of cattle in the south-west.

33   RIDERS RINGS, South Brent   sx:678644
There are two pounds adjoining one another. The earlier is roughly square in plan and encloses 1·2 ha. An entrance leads north out of it into the slightly later oval extension which covers 1·4 ha and is 213 m long. There are about fifteen circular huts in each pound, mostly against the north-western wall. Also against the wall are small rectangular enclosures which may have served as gardens or pens for flocks and herds. The pound walls are made of double rows of large stones packed with turf and small rubble. When new it was probably about 2 m high. The site is unexcavated. [R. H. Worth, *Dartmoor* (1967), 147.]

34   SCORHILL STONE CIRCLE, Gidleigh   sk:655874
It is well worth the effort to visit this jagged circle 27 m in diameter with twenty-three – of about seventy – of its stones still standing. Most of the stones are pointed in shape and the tallest is over 2 m high. This is undoubtedly among the finest circles on Dartmoor. [R. H. Worth, *Dartmoor* (1967), 248.]

35   SETTA BARROW, High Bray   ss:726381
Setta barrow is noticeable for its kerb of retaining stones; it lies astride the county boundary and measures 30 m in diameter and 2 m high. There are other barrows to the north and south, and a row of four standing stones to the south-west.

36   SHOULSBURY CASTLE, Challacombe   ss:706391
Probably a subrectangular hillfort, this site is surrounded by a bank and

ditch, with a second line on the north-west, north and east. Steep slopes on the south and south-west add to the protection. The entrances in the middle of the west side and at the south-east corner may be original. A hollow mound in the north-east corner may be on the site of a hut or a signal tower. It has been suggested that the regular plan of the fort makes it more likely to be Roman than prehistoric. [L. V. Grinsell, *Archaeology of Exmoor* (1970), 84.]

37   SHOVEL DOWN, Gidleigh   sx:660860
On the north facing slope of Shovel Down, west of Kestor rock, are three double stone rows. Two of the rows start from small cairns. The individual stones are about half a metre high. One row, 168 m long, ends in a cairn, which contains four concentric settings of stones and traces of a central cist. Between the cairn and the stone row are two fallen menhirs, 3·5 m and 2·2 m long respectively. A second row begins north-west of the cairn circle and stretches for 145 m. The third alignment runs south for 115 m and ends in a ruined cairn near the crest of the ridge. There is another single row of stones over the ridge, as well as a double row that ends at the *Longstone,* a menhir 3·2 m high. [A. Fox, *Arch. J,* 114 (1957), 155.]

38   SIDBURY CASTLE, Sidbury   sy:128913
A narrow pear-shaped contour fort of 4·4 ha surrounded by a double rampart and ditch. There is an inner quarry ditch in the south-eastern quadrant of the fort. The main entrance is at the north where the rampart ends turn out together forming an entrance passageway about 60 m long. The north and south ends of the fort are tree-covered.

39   SOUSSONS PLANTATION, Manaton   sx:676785
The retaining circle of a destroyed round cairn is well preserved in a clearing north of the road. It has a central stone burial cist measuring 1·5 m by 0·6 m.

40   SPINSTERS' ROCK, Drewsteignton   sx:700908
Three upright stones more than 2 m high support a capstone measuring 14·4 m by 3 m. The tomb collapsed in 1862 and was re-erected slightly inaccurately. Camera lucida drawings made in 1858 suggest that the entrance to a burial chamber faced north-eastwards. There are no traces of a surrounding barrow. [L. V. Grinsell, *PDAS*, 36 (1978) Drewsteignton 1, 132.]

41   STANBOROUGH CAMP, Halwell   sx:773517
This small circular fort commands wide views eastwards over Start Bay. It encloses 1·4 ha and is defended by a single rampart and ditch. It stands on a prehistoric ridgeway, and immediately to the north-east is a

fine group of round barrows. Only 2 km north-east is *Halwell Camp* (sx:784532), split in half by the Dartmouth road. The section north of the road is upstanding, but that to the south has been ploughed away. There is another barrow group 0·5 km north-east.

42   THREE BARROWS, Upton Pyne   sx:913993
The central barrow of the three lying south-east of Stevenstone Farm was opened in 1869. With a cremation was a small grooved bronze dagger, a bronze pin, a necklace of lignite and fossil beads and an incense cup. South-east of the Three Barrows is a large round barrow 40 m in diameter and nearly 2 m high (sx:915991). A ploughed-down barrow (sx:914989), now destroyed, was excavated in 1967 and produced a cremation in a collared urn and stone cist near its centre, as well as three other cremations in inverted urns. [S. H. M. Pollard and P. M. Russell, *PDAS,* 27 (1969), 44.]

43   TROWLESWORTHY WARREN, Shaugh Prior   sx:574645
All around this grid reference are at least seven walled pounds containing small groups of huts. They seem to be of early and middle bronze age date, though no excavations have taken place. To the south-east is a stone circle and two stone rows.

44   WRANGWORTHY CROSS, East Putford   ss:384174
A group of eight round barrows between 12 m and 36 m in diameter, and up to 1·8 m high, on pasture land. Two of the barrows were excavated in 1934. In one was a burial accompanied by a bronze dagger placed under a gabled timber mortuary house 1·5 m long and 0·9 m high, covered with a mound of turf and a small cairn of stones. A row of three posts had been erected in the other barrow with a sloping roof laid against them and the burials underneath. The excavator suggested that perhaps as many as eight burials may have lain side by side, possibly in hollowed tree trunks, but the evidence was not particularly convincing. [C. A. R. Radford and E. H. Rogers, *PDAES,* 3 (1947), 156.]

45   YELLAND, Fremington   ss:491329
Difficult to find, but worth seeking out at low tide because of their unusual location at river level, are a pair of parallel stone rows, 34 m long and 1·8 m apart, which run roughly east to west and disappear into the Tay estuary. The stones are each about 0·3 m high and are spaced at 2·2 m intervals. Only nine stones survive in the northern row and six in the southern. It is assumed that the rows are of bronze age date. [E. H. Rogers, *PDAES,* 1 (1932), 201.]

46 YELLOWMEAD DOWN, Sheepstor   sx:575678

This was once a burial cairn, traces of which can still be seen by those who look for them. It was defined by four roughly concentric circles of kerb stones (restored in 1921) with diameters of 6 m, 12 m, 15 m and 20 m. There are twenty-one stones still standing and almost touching each other in the central circle. The stones in the other circles are graded in size, the largest being in the outer ring. An avenue of stones may have led up to the cairn. [L. V. Grinsell, *PDAS*, 36 (1978), 'Sheepstor', 4, 166.]

DORSET

1 ABBOTSBURY CASTLE, Dorset   SY:555866

This is a triangular hillfort of nearly 2 ha. It is surrounded by two ramparts and ditches on all sides except the south-east corner where they have been increased to four, probably as part of an attempt to enlarge the fortified area. There seems only to have been one original entrance, at the south-east end of the north-east rampart. There is a gap in the north-west side which might represent a postern gate.

A squarish enclosure in the western corner has often been identified as a Roman signal station, particularly in view of its commanding position along the Chesil Beach, but recent excavation has failed to confirm this idea. There are a number of hollows inside the camp which may be hut circles, and traces of walling can be detected. The camp also contains a round barrow inside the southern rampart. [RCHM, *Dorset*, I (1952), 9.]

2 BADBURY RINGS, Shapwick   ST:964030

Badbury forms a conspicuous tree-clad monument, sadly scarred by the worn pathways made by too many visitors in recent years. Two strong inner ramparts and a weaker outer third enclose 7·3 ha within their massive fortifications. The site is unexcavated so it is impossible to be sure that they are of different periods of the iron age, as seems likely. There are entrances at the east and west. At the former the inner rampart turns inwards, whilst the latter is protected by a rectangular enclosure formed by the central rampart turning outwards. Two gateways cut the outer and central ramparts on the western side. There are traces of field systems, bronze age barrows and four Roman roads beside or very near this fort. [O. G. S. Crawford and A. Keiller, *Wessex from the Air* (1928), 58.]

3 BINDON HILL, Lulworth   SY:835803

This is one of the largest hillforts in Britain, enclosing some 114 ha, including Lulworth Cove, the relatively flat coastal strip and the hogs-back to the north. Along the ridge runs a rampart 2375 m long, with an inturned entrance 1800 m from the eastern end. Although partial excavation failed to find guard chambers at the entrance, the curving ends strongly suggest that they may have been present. Another section of rampart curved down the hillside to the miniature golf course and was partly destroyed by the village of Lulworth. A north-south cross-ridge dyke cuts off about 5 ha directly above Lulworth Cove at the western end of the fort. This may have been an attempt to reduce the area of the earthwork, which was certainly unfinished. Only this area of the fort is accessible to the public. Sir Mortimer Wheeler suggested that Bindon was a beachhead planned for an iron age invasion centred on the Cove. Others have suggested that it was protection for a trading post. [R. E. M. Wheeler, *Ant. J*, 33 (1953), 1.]

4 BLACK DOWN BARROWS, Portesham   SY:613876 (centre)
Of ten barrows close to the Hardy Monument, only one (SY:612874) has been excavated in modern times. It is badly disturbed and failed to produce a primary burial, though four middle bronze age urns were found in the barrow mound, three holding cremations.

5 BRONKHAM HILL, Winterborne St Martin   SY:623873
A long line of barrows stretches for 1·6 km along the ridge; there are at least thirty barrows, amongst them four bell-barrows and a double bowl-barrow. Although most of them have been dug into no records of their contents are known to survive. Three kilometres further west, at SY:663866, is a massive bell-disc-barrow with a mound 2·4 m high and 24 m in diameter, encircled by a bank 76 m across. [L. V. Grinsell, *Dorset Barrows* (1959), various.]

6 BUZBURY RINGS, Tarrant Keyneston   ST:919060
This earthwork belongs to the group known as hill-slope forts, commonly found in south-west England, associated with cattle husbandry. It lies on the hillside rather than at the top. The outer enclosure of 5 ha is kidney-shaped and consists of a bank and internal V-shaped ditch. Within it and to the south side is a roughly circular enclosure of 1 ha. There are traces of a third line of defence on the south-west, but this is incomplete, though it may once have swung round to join the north side of the camp at the point where it is cut by the B3082. This would have created two paddocks for livestock and a central living area for the inhabitants. There was an entrance on the south-west giving direct access to fields, traces of which can still be seen, especially from the air. One ditch on the west seems to have led from the fort to the river Stour and may mark an iron age trackway. [J. Forde-Johnston, *Proc. Dorset NHAS*, 80 (1958), 107.]

7 CAME WOOD, Whitcombe, etc.   SY:699855
The key to this group of barrows seems to be a bank barrow (SY:702853) 183 m long running from north-west to south-east. Most of the other barrows seem to be aligned on it. These include bowl-,

pond- and bell-barrows which extend from Came Wood for a kilometre eastwards beside the ridgeway. The Culliford Tree barrow (SY:698855) is the only one known to have been excavated. In 1858 it was found to contain four secondary burials, one with an amber necklace and two gold-plated beads, and a cremation in a collared urn. From the ridgeway fine views can be obtained of other barrow groups to the south and south-west. [RCHM, *Dorset*, II, 3 (1970), 458 (plan).]

8 CERNE GIANT, Cerne Abbas   ST:667016
(National Trust). A splendidly obscene male figure is cut into the turf of the steep escarpment to produce a chalk outline 55 m high and 51 m wide. Although the evidence is inadequate there is reason to consider that the figure may have been cut in Roman times during the reign of Commodus (AD 180–93) when attempts were made to revive the cult of Hercules. Above it on the hillside are numerous earthworks, including a rectangular banked enclosure called the Frying Pan, which are likely to be of late iron age date, and that sort of date should not be ruled out for the figure. The Frying Pan was the scene of maypole dancing, significantly connected with phallic worship. [RCHM, *Dorset*, I (1952), 82; L. V. Grinsell, *Antiquity*, 54 (1980), 29.]

9 CHALBURY, Bincombe   SY:695838
Prehistoric field systems surround this triangular hillfort of 4 ha, which is protected by a single rampart and ditch, with a well-marked quarry ditch inside on the east and west. The rampart was revetted with blocks of limestone at the front and back and the ditch was 5·5 m deep and 7 m wide. On the south-east is a simple entrance with a terraceway leading up to it. About seventy shallow depressions inside the fort represent storage pits and huts. Two circular huts have been excavated. One was of wood with human remains scattered on its floor. The other had stone walls and a paved floor. Pottery was of the earliest iron age types, and other finds included an iron knife, ornaments and milling equipment. Also on the hilltop within the fort are two round barrows. [M. Whitley, *Ant. J*, 23 (1943), 98.]

10 COMBS DITCH, Winterborne Whitchurch   ST:851021 to 890000
Stretching across the chalk ridge from Winterborne brook to the Stour is a line of rampart and ditch 6·4 km long. It has been built with its rampart on the south-west, presumably to resist attack from the north-east. Excavation suggests that it may have been an iron age field boundary, enlarged in the Roman period to form a defensive work. RCHM, *Dorset*, III, 2 (1970), 313.]

11 DEVEREL BARROW, Milborne St Andrew   SY:820990
This bowl-barrow is covered by bushes and hides behind a stone wall.

It is about 1 m high and 12 m in diameter. W. A. Miles cut a trench through it in 1824. Near the centre was a collared urn containing a cremation. Around it, and later in date, were twenty other cremations, mostly in globular and bucket-shaped urns. An inscribed slab on the site records that 'Sir Ricd. Colt Hoare considers it to be more antient and more curious than any barrow ever yet discovered in the island.' The site gave its name to the Deverel-Rimbury culture of the late middle bronze age, about 1400 BC. [W. A. Miles, *The Deverel Barrow* (1826).]

12 DORSET CURSUS   SU:040193 to ST:970124

Stretching for 9·6 km from Bokerley Down to Thickthorn Down, this is one of the longest, though least impressive, prehistoric monuments. Two parallel banks with outer ditches lie 90 m apart and the ends are closed by transverse banks and ditches. At the south-western end are the two Thickthorn long barrows, and similar mounds lie near to the north-eastern end; others are incorporated in it along its course. The cursus seems to have been constructed in two sections, the one from Thickthorn to Bottlebush Down being possibly earlier than that from Bottlebush to Bokerley. Today much of the monument has been ploughed out, but it can still be seen to the east and west from the B3081 road at Bottlebush. It has been suggested that its alignment has astronomical significance. That it was connected with the cult of the dead seems certain, but exactly what its role was is unlikely ever to be known. [R. J. C. Atkinson, *Antiquity*, 29 (1955), 4.]

13 EGGARDON CAMP, Askerswell   SY:541948

The spur of Eggardon Hill juts out north-westwards from the main chalk ridge. On it is sited one of the most impressive of British hillforts. Three ramparts with ditches between them enclose 8 ha. On the east, north-east and north-west the outer rampart is separated from the rest by a wide flat berm which may have formed a cattle enclosure. On the south-west the ramparts were destroyed in iron age times by a landslide, and a new line had to be cut in the loose material lower down the slope. The defences are particularly widely spaced on the ridge to the north-west and the entrances are staggered so that they do not face one another. On the south-east is an inturned entrance in the outer bank, which is oblique to the inner rampart. There are some five hundred hollows inside the fort that probably represent storage pits. Five were excavated in 1900 and found to be about 1·8 m deep. They produced flint knives and scrapers, but no pottery. An octagonal ditched enclosure inside the fort on the south-west side is of recent date. There are also two probable bronze age round barrows, one a metre high and both 12 m in diameter. [RCHM, *Dorset*, I (1952), 13.]

14 FIVE MARYS, Chaldon Herring   SY:790842

These are the Five Meers or boundary marks shown on a map of 1765.
This line of six barrows contains two bell-barrows. All have been dug
into in the past, two of them by the exiled Duchess of Berry before
1866. She found crouched male skeletons with stag antlers at their
shoulders. Today the barrows are overgrown and frequented by rabbits. [RCHM, *Dorset*, II, 3 (1970), 441.]

15 GREY MARE AND HER COLTS, Long Bredy   SY:584871

An untidy pile of stones which can be sorted into the remains of a
rectangular burial chamber with three wallstones and a slipped capstone. At the south-eastern end of the barrow it is possible to make out
a crescent-shaped forecourt. The mound is approximately 24 m long
and 1 m high with traces of a peristalith wall around it. Excavations in
the early nineteenth century revealed human bones and some pottery.
[RCHM, *Dorset*, I (1952), 42.]

16 HAMBLEDON HILL, Child Okeford   ST:849122

The southern crest of Hambledon Hill, outside the great iron age
hillfort, is ringed by a neolithic enclosure of about 8 ha. Along the
three spurs leading from the enclosure are more massive outer earthworks. Excavation of the inner enclosure reveals that the ditches were
re-cut many times and frequently filled with deposits of human skeletal
remains, including crouched infant burials, that were dug into time and
time again. Associated with the remains are pieces of neolithic pottery,
leaf-shaped arrowheads, stone axes and animal bones. The outer
earthworks were constructed on a quite massive scale with timber
revetting suggesting that they were of a defensive nature. There is a
small long barrow 26 m long just outside the southern outer defence.
The barrow and enclosure probably date from about 3500 BC.

The dominant feature of this splendid chalk ridge is the massive
earthwork of the iron age hillfort (ST:845125) which encloses 12·5 ha.
Two banks and ditches with a counterscarp enclose the long narrow
sweep of the hill-top. In places the ramparts still rise 15 m high. The
material for them was derived from inner quarry scoops and by dump-
ing the chalk from the ditches downhill. The defences are doubled on
the south-east where the fort adjoins the main hill mass.

Although it was unexcavated it is possible to detect three phases of
expansion with some certainty. At first only the northern area was
defended, and traces of a bank cutting off 3 ha can still be seen across
the ridge. Later the fort was extended south, past the long barrow, and
a further 2·2 ha were enclosed. Finally it was enlarged to its present
size of 12·5 ha. Traces of hut circles can be detected in each of the three
sections, indicating at least two hundred houses, though it is unlikely
that they were all contemporary. The fort had three entrances, on the

north, south-east and south-west. The latter is protected by a horn-work about 100 m long, very similar to that at neighbouring Hod Hill. This has prompted James Forde-Johnston to suggest that they are both the work of a single mind. Only excavation can hope to tell us what part the fort played in the affairs of the local iron age tribe, the Durotriges, who dominated this area at the time of the Roman conquest. Hamble-don Hill is one of the finest forts in Britain, and should certainly be a priority for any tour of the south-west. [*Neolithic enclosure:* R. J. Mercer, *Hambledon Hill, a Neolithic Landscape* (1980). *Hillfort:* RCHM, *Dorset*, III, 1 (1970), 82.]

17 HAMPTON STONE CIRCLE, Portesham   sy:596865
This sarsen circle was excavated in 1964 and shown to be a recent reconstruction of one which still lay buried to the west. The true circle is 6 m in diameter and consists of nine stones set in two arcs on the north and south sides. An old track led to the north-east entrance and was marked by stakes and two sections of ditch. [G. J. Wainwright; *Proc. Dorset NHAS*, 88 (1967), 122.]

18 HELL STONE, Portesham   sy:606867
It is possible to make out a barrow mound 27 m long and about 12 m wide. At the eastern end is a stone chamber with nine wallstones wrongly restored by Martin Tupper in 1866. There are traces of a peristalith wall close to the chamber; it probably did not enclose the whole barrow. Early drawings show the burial chamber with only three uprights and a sloping capstone, making a favourite shelter for shepherds. [RCHM, *Dorset*, II, 3 (1970), 432.]

19 HENGISTBURY HEAD, Bournemouth   sz:164910
This gravel headland juts westwards across the southern side of Christ-church Harbour. Its seaward side has been greatly eroded throughout the past two thousand years, whilst the harbour side has gradually silted up. Today the iron age promontory fort encloses about 70 ha. It must once have been almost twice as big. The western end of the spur is cut off by two close-set lines of rampart and ditch, the former still standing 7 m high above the ditch bottom. Although three entrances were recorded in 1777, the only gap that can probably be considered original is the one immediately opposite the cottage. Here the rampart ends turn inwards, and tumbled stonework was observed in 1973. The northern end of the inner defence originally swung round to the east, almost at right angles, to end on the harbour shores; eighteenth-century plans suggest that the southern end also turned eastwards along the cliff edge above the sea. Extensive but intermittent digging in the early years of this century indicates that the site was occupied throughout the whole of the iron age and into the Roman period. A

number of continental pottery types support the theory that Hengistbury was a major port in later prehistoric times, and that imports of wine, perhaps directly from Italy, were common. Trade with north-west France is demonstrated by imported coins from Normandy and Brittany. More than three thousand coins have been excavated at Hengistbury, certainly demonstrating that it was a major market and perhaps also the mint of the Durotriges.

There are thirteen round barrows on the Hengistbury headland, two west of the ramparts and eleven within. Most have been excavated and produced cremations in collared urns. The one due south of the cottage near the rampart produced an incense cup, two gold cones, a halberd pendant, amber beads and flint work, as well as a cremation in an inverted urn. [B. Cunliffe, *Hengistbury Head* (1978).]

20   **HOD HILL, Stourpaine**   ST:857106
A pleasant climb leads up to this great rectangular hillfort of 22 ha on the chalk downland above Stourpaine. Two massive ramparts and ditches surround it on all but the west side, where a single defence suffices above the steep drop to the river Stour 100 m below. Two of its five gates are of prehistoric origin: the Steepleton Gate at the north-east corner with its massive hornwork, and the Water Gate at the south-east where the outworks are unfinished. The north-west and east gate are Roman, and that at the south-east is medieval. Excavations between 1951 and 1958 helped to sort out the complex history of the defences, which seem to have developed in four phases from the early iron age. At first a box-like rampart filled with chalk from an external ditch surrounded the hill. Then quarry ditches were dug behind the rampart and chalk was piled over the box rampart to form a glacis, a scree of loose chalk rubble. It was topped with a wall and a palisade was set up on the outer edge of the ditch. This palisade was soon buried when a rampart of chalk was piled over it. In its final phase the main rampart was topped by a paved flint walk, raising its height to 4·6 m and its width to 13·7 m. Its ditch had already been re-dug and was now nearly 5 m deep and 13 m wide. A new, outer ditch was also under construction but never finished.

The hollows of many huts were visible inside the fort prior to ploughing in 1940. At least forty-four still survive in the south-east quarter. These average 3·5 m in diameter. The walls of those excavated were of daub, and no central post or porch was present. Piles of sling-stones by the doors testify to the method of defence. One of the houses stood in its own enclosure and careful examination revealed that it and its neighbour had been subjected to attack by iron ballista bolts, fired no doubt from a lofty Roman siege tower outside the south-east corner of the fort. The hostility is historically documented, for we know that in the first years of the conquest Vespasian captured over twenty oppida – the Roman name for such large hillforts – in south-western Britain and Hod Hill was clearly one of those attacked. No slaughter cemetery was found at the Steepleton Gate when it was excavated and we may imagine negotiation following attack on the probable chieftain's hut, with the subsequent removal of the inhabitants to a lowland site nearby. The Romans then took the unusual step of establishing their own fort in the north-west corner where it can still be clearly seen. [I. Richmond, *Hod Hill,* 2 (1968).]

21 KINGSTON RUSSELL STONE CIRCLE   SY:577878
The eighteen stones of this ring all lie flat in the grass and are difficult to see. They are arranged in an oval 27 m by 20 m with the longest stones at the north side.

22 KNOWLTON CIRCLES, Woodlands   SU:025100
Three circular earthworks form a line of henge monuments. The largest, the southern circle, is 244 m in diameter, and is not very accessible, lying on either side of the B3078 and containing farm buildings. The central circle is the most clearly defined, being in the custody of the Department of the Environment. It is about 96 m in diameter, with two entrances, of which that at the south-west is most likely to be original. A ruined twelfth-century church with fifteenth-century tower stands at the centre. The northern circle is in fact D-shaped in plan and 84 m across. It is not accessible. Due east of the central circle is the Great Barrow, a tree-covered round barrow 6 m high with a buried surrounding ditch and bank, making it about 150 m across in overall diameter. There are other barrows in the vicinity suggesting that this was a religious centre during the late neolithic and earlier bronze age.

An earthwork called the Old Churchyard, beside the lane near the northern circle, has an external ditch and is unlikely to be prehistoric. [N. H. Field, *Proc. Dorset NHAS,* 84 (1962), 117.]

23 MAIDEN CASTLE, Winterborne St Martin   SY:669885
An east-west ridge is dominated by the massive earthworks of this magnificent hillfort. Four periods of occupation on the hill can be detected and for convenience are described in chronological order.

The hill takes the shape of a saddle with prominent knolls at the east and west. It was the eastern knoll that was first occupied, around 3000 BC, when two concentric rings of ditches of a neolithic causewayed camp were dug. The ditches were steep-sided and flat-bottomed and those sections excavated were about 1·5 m deep. The neolithic banks have disappeared, probably thrown back into the ditches.

When the neolithic ditches were three-quarters full of chalk and the site had passed out of use, an unusual bank barrow was constructed along the northern crest of the hill. The mound was 546 m long, with parallel side ditches 18 m apart. It had stood about 1·5 m high, though today it is practically invisible due to destruction in antiquity and more recent ploughing. There was a concave setting of posts at the eastern end of the mound with the burials of two young children just inside it.

Some 2500 years passed before the hill was again occupied, around 350 BC, when a single rampart and ditch hillfort ringed the eastern knoll following the approximate course of the causewayed camp. It had entrances at the east and west sides. After a hundred years the fort had probably fallen into disrepair and the ramparts had collapsed into the ditches. Suddenly a new need for defence arose and hundreds of men reoccupied the fort and began to extend its size to 19 ha by enclosing the whole hill, including its western knoll. A heaped bank of chalk rubble formed a glacis rampart. At the southern point where the new rampart departed from the old, a human burial, perhaps a dedication, was found by Sir Mortimer Wheeler, the excavator. Elaborate entrances were constructed at both the east and west ends of the hill.

About 150 BC the defences were again in disrepair and had to be rebuilt. Double ramparts were constructed on the north and treble on the south. The inner rampart became an enormous affair, the drop from the rampart crest to ditch bottom being 15 m in vertical height. The back of the rampart was reinforced with blocks of limestone. The material for the construction came from great internal quarry ditches 21 m wide and 2·5 m deep. At the east and west entrances elaborate barbicans were constructed, whilst inside circular huts were built in the shelter provided by the quarry ditches.

By 100 BC it was necessary to remodel all the defences on the scale of the inner rampart and the entrances became the complex structures visible today, with platforms for slingers and sentry boxes at the excavated eastern entrance. Beside one of the sentry boxes was a pit containing 22,260 sling-stones gathered from the Chesil Beach 13 km away. The sling was ideal for the defence of the fort with an effective downhill range of 140 m. This would clear the defences from within, but make the returned fire uphill very inaccurate.

Further repairs took place from time to time until about AD 44 when the Legio II Augusta under the command of Vespasian attacked the eastern gate and slaughtered thirty-eight of the defenders. Their remains were buried at the gate and the walls of the fort were slighted. The inhabitants seem to have remained living there for a further twenty years, before they abandoned it in favour of Durnovaria, modern-day Dorchester.

This was not quite the end, for late in the fourth century AD a temple and adjoining house were built on the hilltop and a priest may have continued the worship of the iron age god there. The foundations of these buildings can still be seen today. The objects from Sir Mortimer

Wheeler's excavations between 1934 and 1938 are displayed at Dorchester Museum. [R. E. M. Wheeler, *Maiden Castle, Dorset* (1943).]

24   MAUMBURY RINGS, Dorchester   SY:690899
A Roman amphitheatre and Civil War gun emplacement make this an impressive site, but excavation by H. St George Gray between 1908 and 1913 showed that there was more to it than that. In the late neolithic period it had been a henge monument with a bank about 100 m in diameter and an internal ditch. There had been a single entrance at the north-east under the modern entrance. In the bottom of the ditch about forty-five shafts had been cut into the chalk rock, some more than 10 m deep and between 2 m and 4 m in diameter. Into these, deliberate deposits of bones and tools had been placed and carefully buried, whilst the shafts themselves seem also to have been deliberately refilled. The only datable find was a sherd of neolithic grooved ware, the usual pottery associated with henge monuments. The site was considerably altered when the Romans turned it into an amphitheatre. [R. Bradley, *Archaeologia*, 105 (1976), 1.]

25   MARTIN'S DOWN, Long Bredy   SY:571911
This extraordinarily long bank barrow is 197 m in length and about 2 m high. Along each side are the ditches from which it was constructed. It is broken at one point by a gap giving it the appearance of an elongated long barrow with a shorter one at the north-eastern end. About 180 m south-east is a long barrow 35 m long and 1·5 m high, apparently unexcavated. Seven round barrows can also be seen on the hillside. [RCHM, *Dorset*, I (1952), 41.]

26   NINE BARROWS, Corfe Castle   SY:995816
A linear cemetery of seventeen round barrows and a long barrow. The round barrows vary considerably in size. Only the second from the western end is particularly noticeable, with four causeways across its surrounding ditch suggesting a survival of a neolithic tradition. There is a record of a cremation from one of the group. The long barrow is 34 m long and 3 m high. Its ditch seems to be broken by causeways. [RCHM, *Dorset*, II, 3 (1970), 443 (Ailwood Down).]

27   NINE STONES, Winterborne Abbas   SY:610904
(Department of the Environment) Encaged within iron railings, this little circle 8·5 m in diameter contains nine stones, the largest nearly 2 m high.

28   OAKLEY DOWN, Wimborne St Giles   SU:018173
The finest group of round barrows on Cranborne Chase lies in a triangle between the A354, the B3081 and the Ackling Dyke Roman

road. They are best visited in the spring when the grass is short. Most of them were opened by William Cunnington in 1803 and 1804 and were numbered by Sir Richard Colt Hoare in the first volume of *Ancient Wiltshire*. Barrows 1–3 and 5 are bowl-barrows. No. 4 is a bell-barrow 3 m high. Under it lay three skeletons, one above the other with a four-footed handled clay cup and a bronze dagger. No. 6, a disc-barrow had three small burial mounds. Under the central one was a cremation in an urn with amber and faience beads. Both the other mounds also covered cremations. There were two mounds in the next disc-barrow (7), which covered cremations and amber beads. To the east is an oval disc-barrow (8) with two burial mounds, cut by Ackling

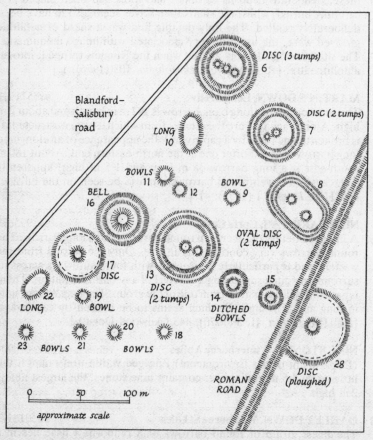

Fig 11. Oakley Down barrow cemetery, Dorset

128

Dyke, a Roman road. The western mound covered a cremation with a bronze awl and more than a hundred amber beads and spacer plates for a necklace. The eastern mound contained an Aldbourne cup with a cremation. A bowl-barrow (9) was built over a crouched burial with a gilt-bronze four-riveted dagger and four barbed and tanged arrowheads. At its feet was a 'drinking cup'. Two small oval barrows (10 and 22) contained cremations, the former with an incense cup, the other with amber beads. No. 11, a bowl-barrow, covered a cremation; of no. 12 we know nothing. Only one mound of the next disc-barrow (13) was dug. It, too, produced a cremation with a V-bored amber button. The adjacent bowl-barrow (14) covered two cremations, one under an inverted urn. Of no. 15 nothing is known and the bell-barrow (16) appeared empty. No. 17 is a disc-barrow. At its centre was a cremation wrapped in cloth 'lying like cobwebs on the calcined bones'. It was covered by a large collared urn and wood ash. Nos. 18–23 are bowl-barrows, some of which produced cremations, and no. 28 is a disc-barrow. Nos. 24–27 are some distance from the rest of the group. It was at Oakley Down that Cunnington came to the conclusion that disc-barrows seemed to be reserved for females, an idea now generally accepted. Many of the barrows show the scars of his digging; not altogether surprising, since some were left open for six months so that Sir Richard Colt Hoare could inspect them at his leisure. During that time the local folk took the opportunity of ransacking them further. [R. C. Hoare, *Ancient Wiltshire*, I (1812, 'Station VIII, Fovant'.]

29 PILSDON PEN, Pilsdon   ST:413013

This beautifully situated hilltop is crowned by an oval fort of some 3 ha. The defences consist of two lines of rampart and ditch with a counterscarp, broken by entrances at the northern corner and half way along the south-west side. There are pillow mounds and possible barrows inside the hillfort.

Excavations by Peter Gelling between 1964 and 1971 revealed a number of circular wooden hut foundations in the centre of the fort. One of the huts may have been a gold-worker's shop, since a crucible with traces of gold on it was found. These were replaced during the first century BC by an unusual large rectangular wooden building with an open courtyard at the centre. It was at least 32 m long and each wing was not less than 2 m wide. From the footing trenches it was impossible to decide how the building had looked or what its function had been, but one might suggest a cult centre as a possibility. When the building had ceased to function its foundations were covered with a low mound of earth, traces of which can still be seen on the surface today. Cobblestones were laid at the centre of the enclosure and there the excavators found the head of a Roman ballista bolt. [P. Gelling, *PPS*, (1977), 263.]

30 PIMPERNE LONG BARROW, Pimperne   ST:917105
This was probably the medieval meeting place of Longbarrow Hundred, which was named after a fine barrow 107 m long, 27 m wide and
2·4 m high. It has well-marked side ditches, which are separated from
the mound by a flat berm.

31 POOR LOT, Kingston Russell   SY:589907
A great Wessex cemetery of forty-four barrows, only two of which
have been excavated. The mounds form two lines, one close to the A35
and another 180 m south up the hillside. The groups include barrows of
bowl-, bell- and pond-type, as well as a local variant, intermediate
between bell and disc. The cemetery provides a good exercise for those
trying to identify barrow types. Particular notice should be taken of the
twin bell-barrow at SY:591906. Two pond-barrows contained flint
paving and small pits, but no sign of burials, when they were excavated. [L. V. Grinsell, *Dorset Barrows* (1959), various.]

32 POUNDBURY, Dorchester   SY:683912
Sited on a hill to the west of Dorchester, where a caravan park has been
allowed to encroach on the ramparts, is a rectangular hillfort of 5·5 ha.
Two banks and ditches surround the earthworks. Excavation has
shown that the inner bank is the oldest, perhaps as early as the sixth
century BC, having been built with a vertical timber face and an
accompanying ditch 9 m deep and 3 m wide. In the first century BC the
rampart was covered by a new glacis bank composed of material from
internal quarry ditches with a limestone parapet on its summit, and a
second bank and ditch were constructed outside the fort. The gap in
the eastern rampart seems to be the only original entrance. An extensive Roman cemetery has been excavated just outside this gate. The
fort has been damaged by a later Roman aqueduct on the north and by
a railway tunnel which passes under it. [RCHM, *Dorset*, II, 3 (1970),
487.]

33 POVINGTON HEATH, Tyneham   SY:876840
There are some two dozen barrows on the Heath but access is unfortunately restricted due to military use. Along the top of the ridge are six
barrows, three bowls and three bells, known as the Five Barrows
group. A twin bowl-barrow can be found at SY:880841. [RCHM,
Dorset, II, 3 (1970), 454.]

34 RAWLSBURY CAMP, Stoke Wake and Hilton   ST:767057
One of the most attractively situated contour forts in southern Britain,
enclosing only 1·6 ha. It is defended by two banks and ditches, though
the outer ditch is missing on the east. The ramparts bow out away from
each other on the north and south, forming enclosures 20 m wide. The

main entrance is at the east where the rampart turns outwards to create an elaborate entrance passage. Depressions near the centre of the fort probably indicate the presence of huts. The site is likely to have been occupied from the middle of the third century BC. A cross-dyke 36 m long and 152 m east of the fort must be related to the main work. [R. A. H. Farrar, *Proc. Dorset NHAS*, 76 (1954), 94.]

35 RINGMOOR SETTLEMENT, Turnworth   ST:809085
At the western end of the wood is a small oval enclosure surrounded by a bank and ditch. On the western side are traces of possible hut hollows. The entrance is on the east with an outer enclosure flanking it to the south. The settlement lies amongst Celtic fields visible from the air and it is approached by hollow ways on the north and west. [RCHM, *Dorset*, III, 2 (1970), 291.]

36 SHAPWICK, Sturminster Marshall   ST:934016
A round barrow about 25 m in diameter and 1·8 m high seems to have contained a primary cremation, buried in a large pit and covered with a flint cairn. Amongst the bones were several 'ruby-coloured barrel-shaped glass beads'. The barrow inspired the Rev. Charles Woolls to write a verse dialogue entitled The Barrow Diggers. An illustration in this book clearly shows the great gash through the barrow that was dug in 1838, and the poem sums up the attitude of the diggers:

> Clasps, Celts and Arrow-heads, I'll try
> To claw within my Clutch,
> And if a Shield I should espy,
> I'll vow there ne'er was such.

[L. V. Grinsell, *Dorset Barrows* (1959), 12.]

37 SMACAM DOWN, Cerne Abbas   SY:657994
This is a well-preserved bronze age settlement with a good field system in the adjoining valley to the south. A kite-shaped enclosure 46 m by 37 m contains a hut circle 11 m in diameter. There is a long barrow to the west of the enclosure, 30 m long and 1·5 m high. [RCHM, *Dorset*, I (1952), 83.]

38 SPETISBURY RINGS, Spetisbury   ST:915020
This relatively weak hillfort is on a sloping spur overlooking the river Stour. It is roughly oval in shape, enclosing 2 ha with a rampart and V-shaped ditch. The rampart ends turn outwards to form a horn at the entrance on the north-west. The hummocky nature of the defences suggests that they are unfinished, particularly on the north-east near the railway. When the railway was being constructed a great pit was found, dug into the hillfort ditch, containing about 120 burials as well

as iron age grave goods and Roman weapons. The skeletons were probably victims of the local Roman advance, and may have been engaged in strengthening the fort when the end came. [J. Forde-Johnston, *Proc. Dorset NHAS*, 80 (1958), 108.]

39 THICKTHORN, Gussage St Michael   ST:971123

Two long barrows lie parallel to the road, at the south-western end of the Dorset Cursus. The northern barrow is 46 m long, 20 m wide and 2 m high, and is enclosed by a U-shaped ditch. It seems to be un-opened. The southern barrow was totally excavated in 1933. Before opening it was 30 m long, 18 m wide and 2 m high and also had a U-shaped ditch. No primary burials were found in the excavation, but traces of a turf structure suggest that some sort of mortuary enclosure existed at the eastern end. Outside it was a large post-hole, with two others nearby. Pottery of neolithic Windmill Hill type was found in the barrow. Three secondary burials were later added to the mound, two of them with beakers. [C. P. Drew and S. Piggott, *PPS*, 2 (1936), 77.]

40 UPWEY RIDGEWAY DISC BARROW, Weymouth   SY:663866

This is an enormous disc-barrow with an outer diameter of about 80 m. At the centre is a mound 24 m in diameter and 2 m high. It is separated by a broad berm from the outer ditch and bank, which are each about 6 m wide. Attention has been drawn to the similarity between the site and a henge monument with a barrow at its centre.

41 VALLEY OF STONES, Littlebredy   SY:597877

This is likely to have been the source of stone for most of the megalithic monuments of southern Dorset. The blocks seem to have been left behind as the result of glacial action in the ice age. The valley sides are covered by a fine series of Celtic fields about half a hectare in area, marked by lynchets 2–3 m high. [RCHM, *Dorset*, II, 3 (1970) 64.]

42 WOR BARROW, Handley   SU:012173

The scene of Pitt-Rivers's classic excavation of 1893–4, this is the only permanently exposed long barrow ditch in southern England, since the site was not back-filled. The barrow was apparently built in two stages. First a rectangular wooden mortuary enclosure measuring 27·4 m by 10·7 m was built, with a narrow entrance at the south-east end. Outside, a shallow ditch was dug as a series of connected pits. A large post was erected inside the enclosure, and beside it six male burials were laid. Turves were placed over the bodies, forming a kind of hut. An enlarged ditch was next cut destroying most of the earlier one. The material derived from it was piled over the mortuary enclosure to make a long barrow 46 m long and about 6 m high. This was all cleared away by Pitt-Rivers and now stands in piles on three sides of the site. [A. L. Pitt-Rivers, *Excavations in Cranborne Chase*, 4 (1899), 58.]

DURHAM

1 **BATTER LAW, Cold Hesledon**   NZ:406460
A sadly mutilated barrow, once about 18 m across and 1 m high. The
primary burial has not been found, but a secondary grave was uncovered in 1911, containing a crouched middle-aged man with a flint
knife. [*Arch. Ael.,* 11 (1914), 158.]

2 **HEMPSTONE KNOLL, Eggleston**   NY:984251
A large round barrow, 30 m in diameter and 2 m high, sited near the
confluence of the Bell Sike and Eggleston Burn. Nothing is known of
its contents.

3 **LOW HILLS, Shotton**   NZ:413415
There were two burials in this oval cairn. The primary one had decayed
in the acid soil of a cist below ground level. Above it a roughly built
grave contained a cremation and a flint knife.

4 **MAIDEN CASTLE, Durham**   NZ:283417
An apparent promontory fort of 0·8 ha above the river Wear, with
steep, wooded slopes on all sides except the west. There is a slight bank
all round the edge of the escarpment, whilst the neck of the promontory has been cut off by a strong bank, now reduced to a scarp, with a
ditch separated from it some 20 m to the west. The bank still stands
about 2 m high and is 5·5 m wide. It is possible that there was an
entrance at the northern end of this bank where the footpath crosses
into the camp. Limited excavation has produced only medieval material. [*VCH Durham,* I (1905), 348.]

5 **MURTON MOOR, South Hetton**   NZ:382460
A ploughed-down round barrow still nearly 1 m high covered a cremation burial placed in a hole a little south of the barrow's centre. It was
accompanied by a burnt flint knife and scraper. [*Arch. Ael.,* 11 (1914),
167.]

6 **RANTHERLEY HILL, Eastgate**   NY:950379
A cairn of limestone 20 m in diameter and 3·6 m high may be of
prehistoric origin. It is prominently sited above the river Wear.

7 SWINKLEY KNOLL, Eggleston   NY:983242

This barrow is composed of stones and soil, and seems to be retained
by a kerb. It is about 15 m in diameter and 1 m high. It is sited in a low
position on the flood plain of the river Tees. On the west side of the hill
are traces of former cultivation.

ESSEX

1   AMBRESBURY BANKS, Epping Forest   TL:438004
This plateau fort is shield-shaped in plan, and encloses 4·5 ha. It is surrounded by a single rampart and ditch with traces of a counterscarp bank. The main rampart is between 1 m and 2 m high with a V-shaped ditch, shown by excavation to be 3 m deep and 6·7 m wide. There is an original entrance in the centre of the western side; that on the south-east is medieval. A stream rises inside the fort, providing it with a water supply. [R. T. Brooks and A. E. Fulcher, *Archaeological Guide to Epping Forest* (1979), 5.]

2   COLCHESTER DYKES   TL:995253 (centre)
Camulodunum was the oppidum of Addedomaros, ruler of the iron age tribe called the Trinovantes. Shortly after 10 BC the capital was captured by the neighbouring Catuvellauni under their leader, Tasciovanus, who minted coins there marked C A M V. The conquest was short lived and Addedomaros reappeared, followed by Dubnovellaunus. However, by about AD 10, Cunobelin, son of Tasciovanus, had acquired the Trinovantian throne and ruled the whole of south-eastern England from Camulodunum until his death in about AD 42.

The iron age capital was contained within a large promontory enclosing some 34 square kilometres, bounded on the north, south and east by the Roman river and the river Colne. The western defences were supplied by a series of dykes spanning the 5 km between the rivers. These dykes are extremely complex and a sequence of at least six phases has been proposed for their construction. The earliest Heath Farm Dyke curves around Gosbecks Farm (at TL:964218). It is now largely destroyed. Of the dykes still visible are the westernmost, called Gryme's Dyke, between TL:956267 and 956214; the Shrub End Triple Dykes (D of E) in Lexden Straight Road; and at TL:974246 the Blue Bottle Grove length of the Lexden Dyke (D of E). [W. Rodwell, in Cunliffe, B. W. and Rowley, T., eds., *Oppida in Barbarian Europe* (1976), 339.]

3   DANBURY, Chelmsford   TL:779052
This is a small oval fort in a poor state of preservation. Its single bank

and ditch is best seen on the west near the rectory, though most of its course is just visible. It is unexcavated and the position of the entrance is unknown.

4   LEXDEN TUMULUS, Colchester   TL:975247
In the gardens of numbers 30 and 36 Fitzwalter Road is a barrow about 23 m in diameter with a hedge running over it. This mound was excavated in 1924 and produced the burnt remains of splendid bronzes, a robe embroidered with gold threads, some decorative silver ears of wheat, pieces of chain mail, a funeral bier, wine jars and a portrait medallion with a coin of Augustus (minted in 17 BC) at its centre. There has been much discussion as to who might have been buried in the tumulus. Current opinion suggests Addedomaros, king of the local iron age tribe, the Trinovantes. The objects found are in the Colchester and Essex Museum. [P. Laver, *Archaeologia*, 76 (1927), 241.]

5   LOUGHTON CAMP, Epping Forest   TQ:418975
This hillfort is roughly oval in shape, with extensive views southwards from the end of a spur. It encloses about 2·6 ha with a single bank and ditch. The latter, which varies from 2·7 to 2·1 m deep, has been destroyed by a road on the west. There are numerous gaps, but no original entrance has been identified. Inconclusive excavations were carried out in 1882 by General Pitt-Rivers. A stream rises in marshy ground in the south-east corner. This is an unusual feature, found again at Ambresbury Banks 3 km to the north-east. [R. T. Brooks and E. A. Fulcher, *Archaeological Guide to Epping Forest* (1979), 19.]

6   PITCHBURY RAMPARTS, Great Horkesley   TL:966290
Originally enclosing about 2 ha, only the north-western rampart and ditch with a counterscarp survives. It still stands some 3 m high with the ditch 15 m wide. The gap may be an original entrance. The rest of the fort has long been ploughed away. Pottery of the early iron age and Belgic periods has been found. [RCHM, *Essex*, 3 (1922), 128.]

7   RING HILL, Littlebury   TL:515382
An oval fort of 6·7 ha defended by a bank, ditch and counterscarp. Both banks have been levelled by path construction, so that the ditch remains the prominent feature. It is about 15 m wide and 4·6 m deep. Of four gaps through the ramparts one on the north-west might be an original entrance. The site is completely covered by trees. [RCHM, *Essex*, 1 (1916), 191.]

8   WALLBURY CAMP, Great Hallingbury   TL:493178
Two tree-covered banks and ditches surround a pear-shaped hillfort,

which encloses 12·5 ha. On the east the inner rampart is still 3 m high and the ditch 3 m deep. Excavation has shown that the ditch was originally 6 m deep. On the west, above the steep slope down to the river Stort, the defence was single, presumably because the natural defence was strong enough. There are a number of gaps in the ramparts, but only that on the eastern side, about 100 m north of the modern entrance drive, is likely to be ancient. That on the south-east is recent. [RCHM, *Essex*, 2 (1921), 93.]

GLOUCESTERSHIRE

1 AVENING BURIAL CHAMBERS   ST:879983

In 1806 the Rev. Nathaniel Thornbury, Rector of Avening, excavated
a long barrow which lay to the south-east of Nag's Head hamlet,
(probably the long barrow at ST:895978). In it he found three stone
chambers, one containing eight skeletons and another three. After the
dig the clergyman had the chambers taken out of the barrow and
removed to a field adjoining the rectory gardens, where they stand
today. The chambers are best described from west to east. The westernmost is rectangular in plan and measures 1·5 m long by 0·9 m wide.
It has no capstone. The central chamber is rectangular, 1·7 m long and
0·9 m wide, walled with five upright stones and covered by a single
capstone. A notched stone at the front may be part of a porthole
entrance. The eastern chamber is also rectangular. It measures 1·8 m
long and 2 m wide, has six wallstones and is covered by a large
roofstone. Its main interest lies in its porthole entrance, a hole created
by semicircular cuts made into adjoining faces of two upright stones,
and just large enough for a corpse to be passed through. [E. Clifford
and G. Daniel, *PPS*, 6 (1940), 146.]

2 BAGENDON   SP:018064

This important but unimpressive site may have been the pre-Roman
oppidum of the Dobunni and Ptolemy's Corinion. It is low lying, and
therefore does not strictly speaking qualify as a hillfort. An area of
about 81 ha is defended by earthworks on three sides and forest on the
fourth.

The main earthworks run for 580 m south-east of Bagendon beside
Welsh Way near Perrot's Brook, and 0·8 km in a ploughed state
further north in the field east of Cutham Lane. The ditch has been
shown by excavation to be V-shaped, 3·2 m wide and 1·8 m deep. A
second line of ditches lies 75 m east of those in Cutham Lane. About
1·5 km north of the main system on either side of Scrubditch Farm is
another earthwork, facing south, called the Scrubditch. Its bank still
stands 2 m high, and it is probably part of the Bagendon system.

Elsie Clifford's limited excavations in 1954–6 produced many coins
and coin moulds, suggesting that the Dobunni had a mint at Bagendon
about 20–30 AD. Imported Italian pottery and brooches of continental

type indicate that trade was flourishing from about AD 15 to AD 60. [E. M. Clifford, *Bagendon* (1961).]

3   BELAS KNAP, Charlton Abbots   SP:021254
(Department of the Environment). It is amazing that anything remains of this remarkable barrow, for it has been vandalized and dug into on many occasions, so that by the beginning of this century it was an overgrown pile of stones with a deep trench running from north to south. Careful restoration in 1928 has produced the tomb we see today. The barrow is 52 m long, 18 m wide at the north end and 3·7 m high. It is enclosed by an original revetment wall. The most attractive feature of the long barrow is the false entrance between convex horns at the north end. The lintel of the door and much of the walling of the horns is of recent date. The skull of a man and the bones of five children were found in the rubble blocking behind the false door when excavations took place between 1928 and 1931. The area was already much disturbed and their original position is uncertain. There are a pair of burial chambers halfway along the barrow, a third chamber on the south-east side and a cist, somewhat dubiously restored, at the southern end. All the entrance passages to these chambers were originally sealed off, but since restoration they have been made accessible. There is doubt as to the shape of their original roofs, but they were probably corbelled. The remains of about thirty people were found in the excavations, together with a few pieces of neolithic pottery and flint work. The name Belas Knap means Beacon Mound. [W. J. Hemp and J. Berry, *TBGAS*, 51 (1929), 261.]

4   BERKBURY CAMP, Hailes Abbey   SP:064299
Steep slopes on the north and west makes defences unnecessary there. Only the south and east are protected by a bank nearly 2 m high and a silted ditch. There may have been an entrance at the south-west corner, or by means of the hollow way up the north-western slope. A length of drystone outer wall face and fire-reddened stones are visible on the eastern side of the fort. [RCHM, *Gloucs.*, I (1976), 116.]

5   BRACKENBURY DITCHES, North Nibley   ST:747949
This small triangular hillfort encloses 1·6 ha. Today it is completely covered by trees, which makes viewing difficult. The end of a south-west-facing spur is surrounded by a single rampart, ditch and counterscarp bank. The rampart stands 3 m high and the ditch is about 13·5 m wide. It is broken on the south by an oblique entrance passage 3 m wide and approached up the hill slope by a hollow way. Where the camp faces the flat hilltop on the north-east is a second weaker rampart and ditch, separated from the main camp defences by a space wide enough

for stock penning. This outer rampart has a simple entrance gap at its southern end. [RCHM, *Gloucs.*, I (1976), 86.]

6 CLEEVE CLOUD, Southam   so:985255
Two widely spaced sets of banks and ditches cut off 0·8 ha of this small promontory. On the west it is defended by the cliff-like escarpment. No entrances are now visible and access may have been gained round the ends of the rampart before they eroded away. Part of the outer rampart and ditch has been damaged on the north side by a golf course and visitors should be wary of attacking golfers. Hut circles about 8 m across can be seen in the grass of the interior. Pottery of the earlier iron age was found in the adjoining quarry.
About half a kilometre north of the fort (so:985263) is a linear dyke running east to west just south of the trigonometrical station on the hill. It has a ditch on its south side facing the fort, and it may mark a territorial boundary with nearby Nottingham Hill fort.
Also on the hill and close to the A46 road is a circular banked and ditched enclosure called The Ring (so:984266). Although it has been utilized by the golf course it is almost certainly of ancient construction. It has an entrance on the south-west. [RCHM, *Gloucs.*, I (1976), 106.]

7 COW COMMON CEMETERY, Swell   sp:135264
The overgrown and mutilated long barrow is of the false entrance type, 45 m long, 23 m wide and 1·5 m high. Two stone chambers held the remains of ten adults and an infant, as well as neolithic pottery and pieces of clay spoons.
The round barrows, too, have suffered from the plough. On the edge of the field west of the long barrow are the remains of five round barrows in an overlapping row. Opened by Canon Greenwell, they contained crouched and cremated burials. The second barrow from the south covered a circular beehive-shaped chamber, entered by a passage 6 m long from the west. Its contents had been robbed, but it is of a type not uncommon in Gloucestershire. [W. Greenwell, *British Barrows* (1877), 513, 445.]

8 CRICKLEY HILL, Coberley   so:928161
A beautiful spur of the Cotswolds is cut off by a rampart and ditch to form an iron age promontory fort of 3·6 ha, but this represents only the final stage in a site with a long and fascinating history. Annual excavations by Philip Dixon since 1969 are slowly revealing the full story.
Around 3500 BC two arcs of neolithic causewayed ditches with internal stone banks were built. Over many years the ditches were filled in and re-cut a number of times. Much later the whole site was remodelled with new deeper quarry ditches and a rampart faced with drystone walling at the front and a timber stockade at the rear, the

whole crowned by a wooden fence. Two gateways pierced the wall, 3 m and 5 m wide respectively, with post-holes indicating that they were closed by substantial gates. Clear evidence of burning and more than 200 arrowheads strongly indicate that Crickley was attacked and burnt down around 2500 BC, thus providing us with a glimpse of warlike conditions in the late neolithic period.

For many centuries Crickley was deserted and then, perhaps about 700 BC, the first iron age fortifications were set up, enclosing about double the area of the causewayed camps. A ditch was cut in the limestone 2 m deep and the excavated stone was piled into a drystone wall that must have been at least 3 m high. Entry was by a gate passage lined with wood and closed by two pairs of gates. Inside a roadway ran between long rectangular dwelling houses and smaller square store huts (indicated by blue markers). Like its neolithic predecessor the gates and houses were burnt down and the defences slighted.

Not long afterwards the fort walls were repaired and a massive new gate was designed with a claw-like stone barbican jutting out in front, protected by two gates. A large new round house was built, perhaps for a chieftain, whilst around it smaller circular huts were grouped (indicated by yellow markers). More small square huts were also built, probably as granaries, and other post-holes indicate a wealth of farm and domestic structures. The rebuilders not only changed their house style, but their pottery as well, and this suggests that they were new-

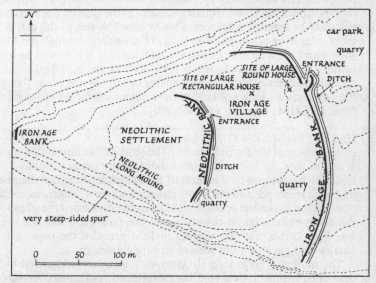

Fig 12. Crickley Hill, Gloucestershire

comers from south-eastern Britain. About 500 BC the site was burned down once more and abandoned, not to be reoccupied. [P. Dixon and P. Borne, *Crickley Hill and Gloucestershire Prehistory* (1977).]

9 GATCOMBE LODGE BARROW, Minchinhampton   ST:884997

At the beginning of the nineteenth century a poor woman known as Molly Dreamer dug into this long barrow in search of treasure of which she had a premonition. Whether she found any is not recorded. In 1870 Samuel Lysons opened the mound. At its eastern end was a false doorway between stone horns, with a low, thin drystone wall surrounding the rest of the mound. In front of the false entrance Lysons found a human skull and some ancient pottery. He failed to find a burial chamber, but one was accidentally discovered the following year on the northern side. This is overgrown but still visible. An entrance 1 m high leads into a chamber 2·4 m long, 1·2 m wide and 1·7 m high. Five stones form the walls of the chamber which is capped by an enormous block of stone measuring 3 m by 1·5 m. At the end of the chamber a crouched skeleton was found. A large slab of stone 10 m from the west end of the barrow may cover another chamber. [H. O'Neil and L. V. Grinsell, *TBGAS,* 79 (1961), 1.]

10 HARESFIELD BEACON, Haresfield   SO:823090

The western end of this promontory is occupied by a fort of 4 ha called Ring Hill. It is surrounded by a rampart but no external ditch. Instead there are traces of internal quarry scoops. Three gaps on the northern side may be original entrances. Five hundred metres to the east is a cross-ridge dyke called The Bulwarks. This is a bank 2 m high and 14 m wide with a ditch on the east away from Ring Hill. It is broken by four possible entrance gaps. Together the Bulwarks and Ring Hill make a formidable defence and should probably be seen as one work, though the two sections were unlikely to have been constructed at the same time. [RCHM, *Gloucs.,* I (1976), 62.]

11 HETTY PEGGLER'S TUMP, Uley   SO:789000

(Department of the Environment). The story of this fascinating tomb is one of woe. In 1888 it had been damaged by vandals, 'injured by mischievous persons . . . several of the stones forming the chamber had been removed, and the whole structure was in a dangerous condition'. When it was first opened in 1821 workmen smashed the stones of the north-eastern burial chamber, and the excavation that followed was little better. Further digging in 1854 revealed the plan of the barrow and gave us a fair idea of its original design.

The mound is 36 m long by 25 m wide and was surrounded by a drystone revetment, double at the eastern end, and today covered by the barrow turf. The entrance with its massive lintel stone is of recent origin. The genuine tomb begins at the second stone inside the doorway. On the left are two chambers or transepts. The end of the entrance passage forms a third. Two other chambers on the right have been sealed off as they are considered unsafe. The gaps between the wall-slabs are of drystone walling. The various excavations have between them revealed at least two dozen skeletons in the tomb, and two more in the forecourt outside the entrance. Hidden walls cross the barrow at its western end and must have been connected with the building ritual.

Visitors are advised to take a torch with them. The key can be obtained from the house 0·8 km along the road south to Uley. [E. Clifford, *Antiquity,* 40 (1966), 129.]

12 LAMBOROUGH BANKS, Bibury   SP:107094

Overgrown and very mutilated, this long barrow is 85 m long, 30 m wide and 4 m high. It is surrounded by a double wall of drystone which curves inwards to form horns at the southern end, where there is a slab of stone 1·5 m wide and 1·4 high forming a simple false entrance. Thurnam found a long, narrow burial chamber containing a single skeleton in 1854. [H. O'Neil and L. V. Grinsell, *TBGAS,* 79 (1961), 70.]

13 LECKHAMPTON HILL   SO:948184

This is a semicircular promontory fort enclosing about 3·2 ha. The western side has been so extensively quarried that it is not possible to tell if the fort once completed a circuit of the hill. It is protected by a rampart about 2 m high, with an external ditch 3 m deep. Recent excavations have shown that the rampart was drystone, faced with timber lacing, and was badly burnt on the eastern side where the wall was reduced to quicklime. Traces of this burning can still be seen in the reddened stones sticking out from the surface. The entrance is also on the east side and was protected by two semicircular guard chambers on either side of a 3 m entrance passage. No huts have been found inside the fort, but the discovery of a well is recorded in the last century.

Outside the fort to the north of the road is an overgrown square enclosure containing a barrow. Excavations in 1925 revealed a pit in the centre; it remains undated and may be contemporary with the fort. [S. T. Champion, *TBGAS,* 90 (1971), 5.]

14 LEIGHTERTON BARROW   ST:819913

This is one of the highest long barrows in Britain, standing almost 6 m tall. It is covered with trees and is enclosed by a modern stone wall. Measuring about 66 m long, it was opened around 1700 by Matthew Huntley, who found three arched chambers, at the mouth of each of which were urns containing cremations, though the skulls and thigh bones were unburnt. Huntley did not fill in his excavations, which were mainly at the eastern end, and the barrow has fallen into decay. It is impossible to identify any of the original walling with certainty, though Crawford thought he could trace some on the south side in 1920. John Aubrey recorded a stone at the eastern end which may have been a false portal. [O. G. S. Crawford, *Long Barrows of the Cotswolds* (1925), 136.]

15 LODGE PARK, Farmington   SP:143125
A very fine and typical long barrow which appears to be unexcavated. It is 46 m long, 23 m wide and 2·4 m high. At the south-east end can be seen two parallel stones and a collapsed roofing stone. Debate continues as to whether they represent a false entrance or a burial chamber. Other large stones protrude from the surface of the mound. [O. G. S. Crawford, *Long Barrows of the Costwolds* (1925), 112.]

16 THE LONGSTONE, Minchinhampton   ST:886999
This standing stone, 2·5 m high, is pierced by two large holes and several smaller ones, almost certainly the result of weathering. A second stone, less than 1 m high, forms a stile in the wall 10 m away. Both may once have formed part of a burial chamber. Early references suggest that they once stood on a barrow, but there are no traces of this today. It is recorded that superstitious mothers used to pass babies through the holes in the larger stone in the hope of preventing rickets. [O. G. S. Crawford, *Long Barrows of the Cotswolds* (1925), 113.]

17 LOWER SWELL, Swell   SP:170258
A barrow 46 m long, 15 m wide and 3 m high planted with trees is enclosed by a drystone wall. At the eastern end is a trench which suggests a collapsed side chamber or an early excavation.

18 LYDNEY PARK, Lydney   SO:616027
A steep-sided spur in a private deer park juts southwards to the river Severn. A bank with external ditch was cut across the spur in the first century BC to create a promontory fort of 1·8 ha. The bank stood 1·5 m high and was 6 m wide, with a V-shaped ditch 2·4 m deep. Late in the Roman period the rampart was heightened and two others were built in front of it. The entrance may have been at the south-east end of the promontory.

In the second and third centuries AD the site became important because of iron-mining inside the enclosure. Two shafts are still visible today: one (inaccessible) on the west where the later Roman baths were built and a second on the east beside the rampart and 37 m north of the Adam and Eve statues. This latter example is 15 m long and can still be explored (protective clothing and a torch are essential). Roman pick marks can still be seen on the mine walls.

Soon after 364 AD four Roman buildings were erected inside the fort, enclosed within a stone wall, with a gate at the south-east, where the hillfort gate had probably stood. There was a temple 26 m by 20 m, still visible, and dedicated to the Celtic god Nodens. To the north was a large guest house (not visible), baths on the west (visible) and a long dormitory. The whole sanctuary seems to have catered for the sick and to have been connected with healing. All may have been a survival of an earlier Celtic deity worshipped at the hillfort.

Finds from the site are in a private museum in Lydney Park house. [R. E. M. Wheeler, *Excavations in Lydney Park, Gloucestershire* (1932).]

19 MINCHINHAMPTON COMMON EARTHWORKS   so:858010
This is one of the most enigmatic groups of earthworks in Britain, and is difficult to categorize with accuracy. Consequently they are all considered as a group.

The Bulwarks (so:857004 to 870012). This is the most prominent earthwork, curving for 2·5 km across the Common from the Halfway House Inn to the north-west corner of Minchinhampton Park. Although it is continuous, it varies in size from place to place, the bank varying from 0·5 to 1·5 m in height. It is faced on the south-eastern side by a revetment wall and in front of it is a ditch, shown by excavation

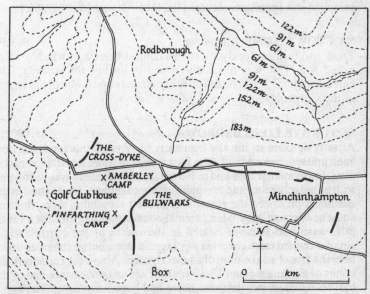

Fig 13. Minchinhampton Common earthworks, Gloucestershire

to be 7 m wide and 2·4 m deep. It had a flat bottom 1·5 m across. Two extensions of the Bulwarks at so:862013 and so:855007 may represent earlier courses of the earthwork, or later unfinished changes of alignment. If the ditch is on the outside of the rampart then the Bulwarks are facing east, giving protection to some 240 ha of land. This is a vast area, and perhaps we should therefore consider the ditch as being on the inside of an 80 ha enclosure containing the modern town of Minchinhampton. In 1853 there was a reference to an earthwork enclosing the whole of the town. The site has produced late iron age B pottery.

The Cross-dyke (so:852012 to 853014). Iron age pottery found when this earthwork was excavated suggests that it was contemporary with the Bulwarks. It is 240 m long and runs north-east from the edge of the escarpment. It comes to a sudden halt about a third of the way across the Common. The excavation showed the ditch to be 7 m wide and 2·5 m deep. The bank on the north-west is just over 1 m high. There is an entrance about halfway along it.

The Low Banks. Between the Bulwarks and the Cross-dyke are a series of low and irregular banks without ditches which could possibly be iron age. They seem to divide the Common into areas that may have been specifically for sheep or cattle.

Amberley Camp (so:852009 to 851016) and **Pinfarthing Camp** (so:856003 to 852008) are both recent constructions and certainly not camps in the prehistoric sense. [RCHM, *Gloucs.*, (1976), 81.]

20 NAN TOW'S TUMP, Didmarton   st:803893
Trees and bushes thickly cover this conical barrow in which a witch called Nan Tow was reputedly buried in an upright position. The barrow stands 2·7 m high and 30 m in diameter and is one of the largest in the Cotswolds.

21 NOTGROVE LONG BARROW   sp:096212
After lying open to the sky for nearly forty years this tomb has now been grassed over. About 49 m long and 24 m wide, it is trapezoidal in plan. Excavated in 1881 and in 1934–5, a central gallery was uncovered with an antechamber and two pairs of side chambers. Excavation in the chambers produced the remains of at least six adults, three children and a newly born baby. Many animal bones, including those of a young calf, were also present. Sealed in the centre of the barrow was a circular domed cairn covering a polygonal stone burial chamber which held the crouched skeleton of an elderly man. Above the cairn were the bones of a young woman 17–19 years of age. At the eastern end of the barrow between two drystone horns had been a forecourt. Here considerable evidence survived of fires, scattered animal bones and the

skeletons of two young people. [E. M. Clifford, *Archaeologia* 86 (1936), 119.]

22 NOTTINGHAM HILL, Gotherington   so:984284

In spite of its considerable size, 49 ha, this is a rather unimpressive site. A single small bank and ditch runs round the three sides of a steep promontory, with the stronger protection of two massive banks and ditches on the south-eastern side only. The inner bank is 3 m high, the outer 2 m. There is little else to see except for wide views across the Vale of Gloucester. No entrance is visible, probably because it has been quarried away at the south-west corner. Another entrance may have existed at the northern tip of the fort, but this is unproven. Coffins and coins are reputed to have been found inside the camp. More recently three leaf-shaped bronze swords have been found inside the camp. [RCHM, *Gloucs.*, I (1976), 59.]

23 NYMPSFIELD LONG BARROW, Frocester   so:794013

Sited in what is now a public picnic area, Nympsfield is likely to get many visitors. It has been excavated at least three times, in 1862, 1937 and 1974; it has recently been consolidated and now lies open to the sky for all to see. The plan is rectangular, 27 m long and 18 m broad, with drystone walls curving round the east end to form horns on either side of the central entrance. Here a short antechamber leads into a small gallery with chambers on the north and south sides and an end chamber. In 1937 Elsie Clifford found evidence of burning and a small pit in the forecourt at the east end of the barrow. Elaborate funeral rituals were probably carried out there. Between twenty and thirty burials came from the tomb during the various excavations as well as neolithic pottery and a leaf-shaped flint arrowhead. Some of the finds are in Stroud Museum. [E. M. Clifford, *PPS*, 4 (1938), 188.]

24 PAINSWICK BEACON, Painswick   so:869121

From the outside this hillfort looks most impressive against the sky-line. Sadly the interior has been mutilated by large-scale quarrying and by a golf course. Massive double ramparts and ditches as well as a counterscarp surround the west, south-east and east sides of the hill. A steep natural escarpment makes a defence on the north-west almost unnecessary. There is an entrance at the north-west corner, strongly inturned, the northern arm curving east to make entry even more difficult. At the west there may have been an entrance beside the escarpment, but this is less certain. There is a circular hollow 6 m in diameter and 2·4 m deep in the centre of the fort. It is unlikely to have been a well and may represent a shaft connected with Celtic religious practices. [RCHM, *Gloucs.*, I (1976), 91.]

25 POLES WOOD EAST, Swell   SP:172265
The barrow is about 37 m long, 12 m wide and 1·5 m high, and
trapezoidal in shape. It has a horned forecourt without a false entrance
at the northern end. Across the centre a trench-like burial chamber,
entered by a narrow passage from either side of the barrow, seems to
have cut into the subsoil. Finds include nineteen skeletons, animal
bones, neolithic pottery and worked flints. It was excavated a hundred
years ago, and the chamber can no longer be seen. [O. G. S. Crawford,
Long Barrows of the Cotswolds (1925), 124.]

26 POLES WOOD SOUTH, Swell   SP:167264
Excavated in 1874, this tree-covered barrow is still about 55 m long,
21 m wide and 3 m high. Its eastern end was horned, with a forecourt,
but there is now no sign of a chamber or false entrance opening on to it.
On the north side near the west end a rectangular burial chamber can
still be seen. An overgrown passage 1·8 m long leads into the chamber,
which is a further 2 m long. Six skeletons, animal bones and two pieces
of neolithic pottery were found in it. In the entrance passage lay two
more burials. [O. G. S. Crawford, *Long Barrows of the Cotswolds*
(1925), 125.]

27 RANDWICK BARROW, Randwick   SO:825069
This long barrow lies between two old quarries in Standish Wood.
Today it is about 35 m long, though before quarrying it was considerably longer. G. B. Witts excavated in 1883 and found it to be trapezoidal in shape, surrounded by a drystone wall. At the larger north-eastern
end, between two horns, was a smaller rectangular burial chamber
some 1·5 m square. It had clearly been open in Roman times, but on
the floor was found 'a confused mass of human bones, broken up into
very small pieces'. Witts noted a complete lack of femurs and few
pieces of skull. There was also some 'very old British' pottery and three
flint flakes. Outside the barrow but close to the wall on the south side
were several crouched skeletons, which seem to have been broadly
contemporary with it. The excavator considered that these were
slaves and retainers buried as near as possible to their chiefs 'and if
they were unable to get leave to place them in the barrow, they placed
them as near as possible to the external wall, just as we found them'.
When the excavation was over, the owner, Mrs Barrow, directed that
the site be covered over again for protection. There are a cross-ridge
dyke and round barrows in the woods to the north-east. [O. G. S.
Crawford, *Long Barrows of the Cotswolds* (1925), 131.]

28 SALMONSBURY, Bourton-on-the-Water   SP:175208
An unimpressive lowland camp, rectangular in plan, enclosing about
23 ha. The banks are double with external ditches. Both the banks are

present on the north-east and south-east sides. On the north-west only the inner rampart remains, along Harp Lane; ramparts have almost totally disappeared on the south-west. There were originally two entrances; that in the middle of the north-east side is in good condition, but the western gate has almost disappeared (it was on the site of Camp House). There is a stream that runs across the fort from north-west to south-east.

The ramparts were of gravel revetted with drystone walls, separated from each other by an inner ditch 10 m wide and 3·6 m deep. The outer ditch was smaller – 6 m wide and 2·7 m deep. The entrance had originally been 9 m wide with two sets of gates at the inner rampart. Later this was blocked by six posts placed across the centre of the passage, leaving only gaps 2 m and 1·6 m wide at either side. A bridge may have passed over the top. Late in the Roman period a wall was built across the entrance in much the same position as the six posts. Storage pits under the ramparts show that the site was occupied before the fort was built. They date to the third and second century BC. A number of circular huts and storage pits can be dated to the first occupation of the fort in the first century BC. The pits contained human remains, including the burials of two infants. Early in the first century AD a Belgic presence was apparent on the site; new huts were built and imported pottery made an appearance.

A hoard of 147 iron currency bars was found on the north-west side of the camp in 1860. [G. C. Dunning, in D. W. Harding, *Hillforts* (1976), 75.]

29   TINGLESTONE BARROW, Avening   ST: 882990
In spite of being planted with beech trees and encroached upon by ploughing, this is a remarkably well-preserved long barrow, still about 40 m long. It gets its name from a slab of oolite 1·8 m high which stands on the highest northern end. According to folklore this stone runs across the field when it hears the church clock strike twelve. [O. G. S. Crawford, *Long Barrows of the Cotswolds* (1925), 134.]

30   TOOTS BARROW, Kings Stanley   ST: 827031
This long barrow lies on the western side of Selsey Common overlooking the Vale of Gloucester and the Severn Valley. It is one of the largest in the county, being 64 m long, 27 m wide and 3 m high. It has been dug into on at least three occasions without record. One of these digs cuts the barrow into two parts, giving it the appearance of two separate barrows. It is probably chambered, but there is no sign of this now.

31   ULEY BURY, Uley   ST: 784989
Although ploughed inside, there is a footpath all round the finest

promontory fort in the Cotswolds. At all points except the north corner the ground falls steeply to the valley 100 m below. A quarry ditch, denuded rampart and silted ditch enclose some 13 ha. Lower down the hillside is a slighter ditch about 2 m wide with a low rampart on the outside. Traces of drystone walling can be seen on the south side. The main entrance at the north corner is defended by a deep inturn. Other original entrances include an outurned postern gate at the south and an oblique entrance on the east which has been recently shown to date from the earlier, pre-Roman, iron age. The entrance passage had been lined with turf and timber. The site is largely unexcavated, but an uninscribed gold stater of the Dobunni is amongst the finds from the fort which are now in Gloucester Museum. A crouched burial, a rubbish pit and two iron age currency bars were found prior to pipe-laying across the fort in 1976. [RCHM, *Gloucs.*, I (1976), 121.]

32   WEST TUMP, Brimpsfield   so:912133
This barrow in the centre of Buckle Wood was discovered and excavated by G. B. Witts in 1880. He was able to show that the barrow had been surrounded by a drystone wall and was horned at the eastern end, where two upright stones marked a false portal. It is still 45 m long and 20 m wide. Witts's excavation revealed a burial chamber 25 m from the horn along the south side. A passage 0·9 m wide and 2·1 m long led into the chamber, which had small upright wallstones. This vault was 4·5 m long and 1·2 m wide. Here were the disordered remains of at least twenty skeletons, only one of which, probably the first burial made in the chamber, seems to have been articulated. It was the skeleton of a young woman with the remains of a baby close by. Four skeletons were found by Witts in front of the false portal. Beech trees grow over the barrow today and the surrounding wallstones are no longer visible. [O. G. S. Crawford, *Long Barrows of the Cotswolds* (1925), 137.]

33   WHITFIELD'S TUMP, Minchinhampton   so:854017
This much-disturbed long barrow lies amongst the other earthworks on Minchinhampton Common. It measures 23 m long and 11 m wide and is orientated east to west. Its main claim to fame is that it was used as a preaching platform in March 1743 by George Whitfield, one of the founders of Methodism. It appears to be unexcavated.

34   WINDMILL TUMP, Rodmarton   st:932973
This is another of the Cotswold tombs with a false entrance at its eastern end, inset between horns of drystone walling. The site was excavated by Samuel Lysons in 1863 and again by Elsie Clifford in 1939. Drystone walling once surrounded the whole barrow. The entrance consisted of two upright slabs, each 2·4 m high, with a leaning door slab between them. In front of this entrance were animal bones

and traces of burning. Two burial chambers were discovered, one on either side. That at the south was entered by descending three steps and crawling through a 'porthole' cut into two upright slabs. Beyond was a chamber, 2·4 m by 1·2 m, which contained fragments of skeletons and pieces of neolithic pottery. The northern chamber also had three steps and a porthole entrance and measured 2·1 m by 1·07 m. It was covered by an enormous capstone that was estimated to weigh 8 tonnes. Beneath it were about thirteen crouched skeletons, six or seven men, three or four women and three children of about two, three and twelve years. With them were two leaf-shaped arrowheads. The barrow is overgrown with beech trees, and is enclosed within a drystone wall. The burial chambers are no longer visible. [H. O'Neil and L. V. Grinsell, *TBGAS*, 79 (1961), 1.]

35   WINDRUSH CAMP, Windrush   SP:182123
A roughly circular fort enclosing about 2·6 ha, sited on level ground above the Windrush valley. Of the single bank and ditch only the bank is now visible, the ditch having silted up and long been ploughed over. The entrance is a 7·5 m gap on the west. [RCHM, *Gloucs.*, I (1976), 130.]

1 CAESAR'S CAMP, Holwood   TQ:421640

This fort, sometimes called Holwood Camp, seems to have originally been oval in shape, enclosing about 17 ha, but the southern side was destroyed in landscaping for William Pitt in the nineteenth century, at which time much of the eastern sector was reduced. On the west a double bank and ditch still exist together with a counterscarp. Near the northern end of this section is an entrance with a slightly inturned rampart sited in a small valley. The entrance passage was 26 m long and was composed of flint walling between timber uprights. This seems to have been destroyed by a massive fire. Unpublished excavations indicate that the ramparts were strengthened three times and date to the second century BC. A slight enclosure on Keston Common nearby (TQ:418642) forms a simple promontory fort, most probably used as an annexe to Caesar's Camp. [N. Piercy Fox, *Arch. Cantiana*, 71 (1957), 243.]

2 CAESAR'S CAMP, Wimbledon   TQ:224711

Roughly circular and enclosing 4·3 ha, this site is now a golf course. Attempts were made to level its defences early in this century, but they were fortunately stopped before too much damage was done. Although not scientifically excavated, a water-pipe trench cut in 1937 showed a bank 9 m wide revetted with posts at front and rear, and a ditch 10 m wide and at least 3 m deep. A storage pit produced pottery of the third century BC. The entrance on the west may be original. [A. W. G. Lowther, *Arch. J*, 102 (1945), 15.]

3 PARLIAMENT HILL BARROW, Hampstead Heath   TQ:274865

High on the Heath above the lakes and football pitches is a bush-covered barrow 41 m wide and 2·4 m high, enclosed by iron railings. Nothing was found when it was dug into in 1894, but a sketch by William Stukeley in May 1725 strongly suggests that it is an authentic barrow: the drawing shows a causeway across the ditch on the north and another is reputed to have crossed the south side. [F. Celoria, *TLMAS*, 22 (1968), 23.]

1 WHITELOW, Bury   SD:805163

This damaged cairn stands above the river Irwell. Originally about 8 m across, only a small part of the central mound now survives, together with a segment of the kerb on the north side. Seven cremations were found when the barrow was excavated between 1960 and 1962, some in inverted collared urns, another with an incense cup and one with a cordoned urn. A burnt flint knife and a clay ear stud were also found. A broken bronze awl had been placed with the primary burial.

HAMPSHIRE and the ISLE OF WIGHT

1   AFTON DOWN, Freshwater (I of W)   sz:352857
A cemetery of two dozen round barrows runs along the ridge of the
Downs. It includes seventeen bowl-barrows, four bell-barrows and
two disc-barrows, as well as a long barrow 37 m long and 1 m high.
Excavations in 1817 by the Rev. J. Skinner produced a few cremations
in the round barrows, but nothing from the long barrow. [L. V.
Grinsell and G. A. Sherwin, *PIWNHS*, 3 (1941), various.]

2   BEACON HILL, Kingsclere   su:458573
A superbly situated contour fort in one of Hampshire's country parks.
A single rampart, ditch and counterscarp bank enclose 3·6 ha. The
entrance at the south-east has a pronounced inturn and semicircular
outworks, which are probably later. About twenty hut circles can be
recognized within the fort, together with lesser hollows that are probably storage pits. Two slight banks within the enclosure, clearly
visible on aerial photographs, may indicate the presence of a neolithic
causewayed camp. Within a railed enclosure on the south-west is the
tomb of Lord Carnarvon, patron of the Tutankhamun excavations. In
the valley to the south are traces of Celtic fields.

3   BUCKLAND RINGS, Lymington   sz:315968
Buckland Rings stands on a small spur about 25 m above Lymington
river. It is rectangular in shape, enclosing 3 ha, and is strongly defended
by two banks and ditches, with a counterscarp bank on the north and
south sides. The ramparts were lined with timbers both inside and out.
The eastern side has been partially damaged. Here was the only
original entrance, a long inturned passageway with a gate at the western end. In his excavations Christopher Hawkes revealed the hollow-
ing of the passage due to use by constant traffic. He also showed that
the site had probably been built in the first century BC, and deliberately
dismantled, perhaps on instructions from the Romans in about AD 45.
   A small fort called Ampress Camp once lay about 360 m to the east
(under the modern factory), beside the river. It may have formed a
beachhead for the inhabitants of Buckland Rings. [C. F. C. Hawkes,
P Hants. FC, 13 (1935–7), 131.]

4 BULLSDOWN, Bramley   su:671583

Bullsdown fort stands on a flat, low-lying site beside a stream. It is oval in shape, enclosing 4 ha, and the interior is tree-covered. The defences consist of an inner bank and ditch with small counterscarp, and a second minor bank, ditch and outer counterscarp bank. The banks are of no great height, though the ditches are still 1·5 m deep. An entrance on the north-east has been totally destroyed. [J. Forde-Johnston, *Hillforts* (1976), 91.]

5 BURY HILL, Upper Clatford   su:345435

This is one of the hillforts excavated by Christopher Hawkes in the 1930s. He was able to show two distinct periods of occupation. At first an oval enclosure of 9 ha was defined by a single rampart and U-shaped ditch, which today survives as a scarp stretching to the wood to the north-west of the main fortifications. This probably dates to the sixth or fifth century BC.

Later the fort was reduced in size to 5 ha, and a new bank, ditch and counterscarp bank were constructed, overlying the south-eastern part of the earlier site. The new banks were both more than 2 m high and were separated by a V-shaped ditch 6 m deep. Both earthworks had a common entrance 9 m wide on the eastern side, still in use today. The excavations showed that neither fort had timbered ramparts, but were of dumped chalk. This second period of the fort probably began about 250 BC, when settlement down on the valley bottom at the destroyed fort of Baulksbury near Andover came to an end, and lasted until the Roman conquest at best. [C. F. C. Hawkes, *P Hants. FC*, 14 (1939), 291.]

6 BUTSER HILL, Petersfield   su:712201

'A great green hill like the overturned hull of some gigantic ship', wrote Stuart Piggott of Butser Hill in 1929, a large flat-topped expanse of 32 ha of downland that is now a Country Park run by the Hampshire County Council. It is separated from the main mass of the South Downs to the south-west by a narrow neck of land cut by three cross-dykes. The first of these is badly damaged (su:709195), but the second is still reasonably upstanding, and consists of a double line of banks 500 m north-east of the first. The third dyke, behind a modern fence, is more substantial; it is bow-shaped in plan, being concave on the outer south-western side. There are lines of dykes on three other spurs of the hill, each following approximately the edge of the clay-with-flints on the hilltop. It has been suggested that they define an area of pasture on the hilltop, rather than an attempt at fortification.

The north-east spur of the hill, known as Little Butser, is the site of the Butser Ancient Farm Project (su:719207), where an attempt has been made to reconstruct a working farm using iron age methods as far as possible. The Butser Ancient Farm demonstration area is situated some 4·8 km south of Petersfield on the A3 Petersfield–Portsmouth Road, adjacent to the Queen Elizabeth Country Park Centre (SU:716189). It is open daily (except Mondays) during the summer season from 2 pm to 5 pm and on Sundays from 11 am to 1 pm and 2 pm to 5 pm. (There is a small admission charge.)

CAESAR'S CAMP, Farnham, see under Surrey.

7 CASTLE DITCHES, Whitsbury   SU:128197
Three banks and two ditches surround this roughly oval fort. The inner bank is of considerable strength – 6 m in height on the southern side – and the outer bank is almost as high. The fort encloses 7 ha. Its entrance, on the west, has been destroyed by farm buildings. There is an earthwork in the wood to the south-east, which may be connected with the considerable length of Grim's Ditch to the north. Perhaps all are connected with cattle ranching based on the fort. [H. Sumner, *Ancient Earthworks of Cranborne Chase* (1913), 20.]

CHILLERTON DOWN CAMP, Gatcombe, see Five Barrows Camp.

8 DANEBURY LONG BARROWS, Nether Wallop
Three once ploughed long barrows are still clearly visible and unexcavated. The first (SU:323387) is at the north-eastern end of the belt of fir trees, opposite Down Farm. Length 34 m, width 24 m, height 1·2 m. Still ploughed. The second (SU:320383) is midway along the south-east side of the fir-trees, behind the farm. Length 50 m, width 18 m, 1·2 m high, with side ditches. No longer ploughed. The third is 50 m west of the others. Length 60 m, width 20 m and height 1·5 m. No longer ploughed. [RCHM, *Long Barrows in Hampshire and the Isle of Wight* (1979), 35.]

9 DANEBURY RING, Nether Wallop   SU:323377
This tree-covered hillfort consists of an oval enclosure of 5·3 ha protected by a rampart, ditch and counterscarp bank. Outside is a later and weaker rampart and ditch containing 11 ha. Between the two, on the south side, is a semicircular annexe, probably built to hold cattle. An entrance to the inner fort on the west has been blocked, whilst a more imposing one has been constructed at the east.

Excavations at the site since 1969 are revealing a complex history. The earliest feature so far uncovered is a beaker period burial (2500–2300 BC) found in a shallow pit on top of the hill and probably originally placed under a barrow. In the later bronze age (1000 BC) ritual pits 2 m deep were dug on the hillside. In three of them the disarticulated remains of dogs were buried and then large wooden posts were set

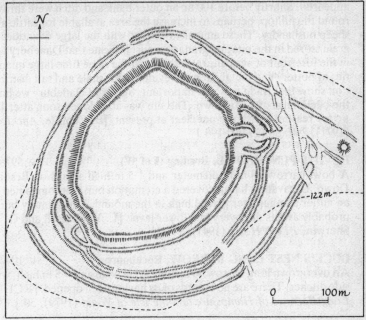

Fig 14. Danebury Ring, Hampshire (after Cunliffe)

above them. We can only guess at the meaning behind the posts; perhaps they were carved and painted like totem poles. The first hillfort may have been built in the fifth century BC. It had a box-type Hollingbury rampart and ditch and simple entrances on the east and west, with single gates. Inside there seem to have been small square huts, each with four corner posts, and probably raised floors; they may have been used as granaries. Over the next two hundred years these huts proliferated, some increasing in size and many standing beside streets in the southern part of the fort; the northern area was occupied by about five thousand pits.

Excavation of the eastern entrance revealed at least ten periods of rebuilding. About 400 BC the simple gateway was made into a double gateway with guard chambers to protect it. Some time later it was remodelled on a massive scale with semicircular claw-like outworks that provided increased defence and a slinging platform with an effective range of 60 m. During the third century the defences were strengthened with glacis slopes and V-shaped ditches, and the cattle annexe was added on the south. Inside the fort, circular huts with wattle and daub walls and thatched roofs were built, and at a later date rectangular buildings, which may have had a religious function,

157

appeared. Shortly before 100 BC an outer bank and ditch were thrown round the hilltop, perhaps to increase the area available for cattle and sheep husbandry. These animals, together with the large quantities of grain stored in the pits and granaries must indicate that Danebury was in the forefront of agricultural activity. At the same time large quantities of pottery and metalwork and evidence for shale and salt distribution show that trade was also important. Surely in Danebury we have the beginnings of a true town. The site was abandoned soon after 100 BC for reasons which are not clear at present. [B. Cunliffe, *Ant. J*, 51 (1971), 240; 56 (1976), 198.]

10   DEVIL'S PUNCHBOWL, Brading (I of W)   SZ:597869
A bowl-barrow 18 m in diameter and 1·5 m high stands on Brading Down. Excavation has uncovered a cremation burial accompanied by an antler axe-hammer placed high in the mound. The primary burial probably awaits discovery at a lower level. [L. V. Grinsell and G. A. Sherwin, *PIWNHS*, 3 (1941), 179.]

11   DUCK'S NEST LONG BARROW, Rockbourne   SU:104204
An overgrown long barrow 40 m long, 20 m wide and 4·5 m high, with side ditches. There are no records of its having been opened. [RCHM, *Long Barrows of Hampshire and the Isle of Wight* (1979), 50.]

12   FIVE BARROWS, Brook Down (I of W)   SZ:390852
A linear cemetery of eight barrows, with a bell-barrow at the western end 2·7 m high, and a disc barrow at the east 35 m across. Between the two are six bowl-barrows, the most easterly of which has a causeway across the ditch, clearly giving access to the central area before the mound was erected. The barrows all show signs of unrecorded antiquarian openings. [L. V. Grinsell and G. A. Sherwin, *PIWNHS*, 3 (1941), 179.]

13   FIVE BARROWS CAMP, Gatcombe (I of W)   SZ:483842
Cutting off a promontory above Gatcombe are what appear to be five mounds of earth. On closer inspection they are seen to be the rather irregular rampart of a promontory fort of about 10 ha. The bank stands 3 m high in places with a ditch on the south-western side. There is an entrance at the north-western end of the rampart, approached by a track from the south-west. The defences, which have every appearance of being unfinished, represent the only iron age defensive work so far recognized on the island. [G. C. Dunning, *PIWNHS*, 4 (1947), 51.]

14   FLOWER DOWN, Littleton   SU:458318
On the edge of the common is a very fine disc-barrow with two tumps

or burial mounds, one in the centre and the other to the south-west. The barrow is 55 m in diameter, with a surrounding ditch and outer bank. Disc-barrows usually cover female burials; this one is unopened.

15 GALLIBURY HUMP, Calbourne and Newport (I of W)   sz:441854
Possibly the largest round barrow on the island, it was described in 1640 as 'where yo ffrench weare buried, being overcome theyre in a battayle'. It stands 3 m high and 30 m in diameter. Other barrows can be seen nearby, including a disc-barrow. [L. V. Grinsell and G. A. Sherwin, *PIWNHS,* 3 (1941), 179.]

16 GIANT'S GRAVE, Breamore   su:139200
Although its western end had been damaged, this long barrow still stands 3 m high at the east, and is 50 m long and 24 m wide. Its contents remain unknown. There is a maze cut into the turf in the woods nearby, probably created by monks in the twelfth century. It is known locally as the Mizmaze.

17 GRANS BARROW, Rockbourne   su:090198
Lying north to south, this long barrow is 58 m in length, 18 m wide and 2 m high. Ditches surrounding the barrow are visible only from the air. Knap Barrow lies 100 m north-west.

18 HOUGHTON DOWN, Broughton   su:330357
This long barrow is 50 m long and 12 m wide, but only 0·3 m high. During the last century crouched skeletons and a bronze age cremation were uncovered.

19 KNAP LONG BARROW, Martin   su:089199
This long barrow lies close to a bridle track across Toyd Down. It is nearly 100 m in length and about 30 m wide. Its side ditches have been destroyed by ploughing, though the mound still stands 2 m high. It is unexcavated. [RCHM, *Long Barrows of Hampshire and the Isle of Wight* (1979), 31.]

20 LADLE HILL, Sydmonton   su:478568
The importance of Ladle Hill lies in the fact that it was unfinished, and consequently it is possible to work out the building sequence. A small agricultural boundary ditch already marked out part of the circuit. Joining on to this a small circular ditch, about 3 m wide and 0·5 m deep, was dug, marking out a circular area of 3·3 ha. Gaps were left for entrances on the south-west and east. Next, gangs of workmen began to deepen the ditch, and the topsoil and chalk rubble that they removed was dumped well back inside the fort. The lower, harder chalk was kept back to build the rampart. At this point the scare which necessi-

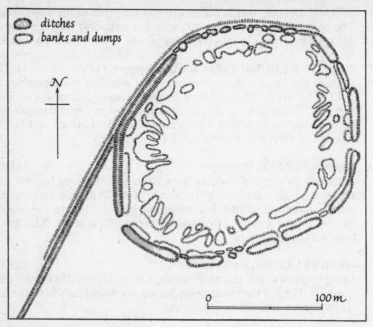

ditches
banks and dumps

N

0   100 m

Fig 15. Ladle Hill, Hampshire

tated the construction of the fort diminished and the earthwork was left unfinished, frozen for posterity.

There is a fine disc-barrow due north of the fort, 52 m in diameter and scarred by a robbers' hollow. Inside the northern half of the earthwork is a smaller disc-barrow, whilst to the south-east are a damaged bell-barrow and a ploughed-down saucer-barrow. [S. Piggott, *Antiquity*, 5 (1931), 474.]

21 LAMBOROUGH LONG BARROW, Bramdean   su:593284
This long barrow, lying east to west, is 67 m long and 33 m wide. A section cut across the side ditches produced one piece of late neolithic pottery in 1932. The ditches were 6 m wide and between 2·5 m and 3·5 m deep. The mound remains unopened. (RCHM, *Long Barrows of Hampshire and the Isle of Wight* (1979), 8.]

22 THE LONGSTONE, Mottistone (I of W)   sz:408843
This pear-shaped mound in a plantation is 21 m long and about 9 m wide, and was probably a long barrow. Limited excavation has revealed a kerb on the north side but no trace of burials. East of the

mound stands a large block of sandstone 4 m high, with another lying at its base. Both have always probably stood free of the barrow. [J. Hawkes, *Antiquity,* 31 (1957), 147.]

23   MARTIN DOWN, Martin   su:043201
A rectangular enclosure of 0·8 ha is surrounded by a V-shaped ditch 2–3 m deep, with the excavated material piled into an internal bank which may have supported a wooden stockade. There are entrance gaps in the south and east sides and a broad gap on the north which may have been filled by a hedge or portable fence. The enclosure lies amongst Celtic fields and was clearly withdrawn from ploughing to act as a cattle pound. Pitt-Rivers, excavating in 1895–6, found nothing to suggest that the site was permanently occupied, but more recent excavations on similar sites that he dug suggest that he may have missed a great deal. [A. Pitt-Rivers, *Excavations in Cranborne Chase,* 4 (1898), 185.]

24   MICHAEL MOOREY'S HUMP, South Arreton (I of W)   sz:536874
The last of a group of four round barrows, standing 1·8 m high and 18 m in diameter. Secondary Saxon burials were found in the mound in 1815, though the primary burial was not reached. The barrow is named after a man who was hanged on a gallows that stood on the summit in 1730. The socket for the gibbet was found in 1815 and the original timber is said to form a beam in the Hare and Hounds public house at Downend. [L. V. Grinsell and G. A. Sherwin, *PIWNHS,* 3 (1941), 179.]

25   MOODY'S DOWN, Barton Stacey and Chilbolton   su:426387
Three long barrows, none of which appear to have been excavated, lie on the downs. One (su:426387) is oval in shape, 38 m long, 27 m wide and 1·5 m high. Another (su:417383) in the fields to the south-west measures 46 m by 24 m. The last (su:435388) lies east of the farm and is 67 m in length by 23 m. It is ploughed but has clear side ditches 8 m wide.

26   OLD WINCHESTER HILL, Meonstoke   su:641206
This attractively sited hillfort commands wide views as far as the Isle of Wight. It is oval in plan and encloses 5 ha. Defences are a single bank and ditch with counterscarp, the rampart still standing 6 m high. There are inturned entrances at the eastern and western ends. Outside the eastern entrance, one either side, are two pits whose original function is uncertain. Barrows that used to stand in front of this entrance have been destroyed. There are five bowl-barrows and a saucer-barrow outside the west entrance, four more bowl-barrows on the crest of the ridge inside the fort, and there seem to be three incorporated in the

counterscarp bank on the southern side. (L. V. Grinsell, *Archaeology of Wessex* (1958), 181.]

27   PETERSFIELD HEATH, Petersfield   su:758232
An ideal site for barrow spotting. There are twenty-one barrows on the Heath, which is now covered by a golf course and clumps of fir trees and bracken. The diligent searcher can find fifteen bowl-barrows, four saucer-barrows, a disc-barrow with two tumps and a bell-barrow. No excavation records exist. [L. V. Grinsell, *P Hants. FC*, 14 (1940), 210.]

28   POPHAM BEACONS, Overton   su:525439
A few fir trees stand on this linear cemetery of five barrows. From south to north can be seen a bell, bowl, saucer, bell and bowl. Nothing is known of their contents. [L. V. Grinsell, *P Hants. FC*, 14 (1940), 210.]

29   QUARLEY HILL, Quarley   su:262423
A number of boundary ditches of bronze or early iron age date meet on top of Quarley Hill and were still clearly visible when the iron age fort was constructed. The fort started life as a timber-palisaded enclosure, but was soon replaced by the bank, ditch and counterscarp visible today. Excavation has shown that the rampart was 2 m high and 8 m wide at its base, and that it was built of chalk blocks without any timber revetting. The V-shaped ditch was 4 m deep and 7·6 m wide. The rampart was never completed and gaps on the north and south show this. Only at the north-east and south-west were original entrances constructed. The former has been excavated. It seems that a complicated gate surmounted by a bridge was planned but never built. [C. F. C. Hawkes, *P Hants. FC*, 14 (1939), 136.]

30   ROUNDWOOD BARROWS, Laverstoke   su:507444
The badly damaged remains of a linear barrow cemetery lie behind a wood. There are two almost flattened disc-barrows at the western end of the line, one of which was partially excavated in 1920 but failed to produce a central burial. There is a twin barrow, possibly a double bell, whose western mound was empty and whose eastern one had been robbed, leaving only wood ash under a pile of flints at the centre. At the east is the remnant of a single bell-barrow. At its centre a man had been cremated and placed in a pit cut through the funeral pyre, after which the surrounding ditch had been dug, its excavated chalk piled up to make the barrow mound. [O. G. S. Crawford, *P Hants. FC*, 9 (1922), 189.]

31   ST CATHERINE'S HILL, Winchester   su:484276
One of the classic excavations of the 1920s was carried out on this rounded, tree-clad summit, south of Winchester.

Oval in shape, the hillfort encloses 9 ha, with a rampart, ditch and small counterscarp. It has a single entrance on the north-east. Inside are the remains of a medieval chapel and a miz-maze traditionally cut by the boys of Winchester School.

In the early iron age the hilltop had been occupied by an open settlement that produced pottery and storage pits of perhaps 500 BC. The excavations showed that the fort rampart was built about 400 BC using dumped soil with no revetment timbers. It was separated by a berm 2 m wide from a V-shaped ditch 8 m wide and originally 3·5 m deep. The entrance is strongly inturned and the excavation showed a road causeway 12 m wide passing between squared ditch ends. The gate had been of the two-leaf-type hung across an oblique timber-lined passage. After a period of decay the entrance passage was reduced to one gate width with flint walls. At the same time the rampart height was increased and the ditches deepened.

Eventually, about 50 BC, the entrance was burnt, perhaps following a raid, and the site ceased to be occupied. The excavation concentrated on the rampart history of the site, and we know nothing of the occupation of the fort between the initial settlement and its final destruction. [C. F. C. Hawkes, in D. W. Harding, *Hillforts* (1976), 59.]

32   SETLEY PLAIN DISC-BARROWS, Sway   SU: 296000
On the south side of the road are two overlapping disc-barrows. The earlier one lies to the north-west and has a central mound 14·6 m in diameter. Its outer bank is slightly damaged by the later southern barrow, 43 m across. Both are overgrown. A late eighteenth-century report says that one of the barrows covered a cremation.

There is another disc-barrow 0·4 km to the south-east. It is 28 m in diameter and has a central mound 9 m across and nearly a metre high. This, too, contained a cremation and traces of the funeral fire. [L. V. Grinsell, *P Hants. FC*, 14 (1940), 224.]

33   SEVEN BARROWS, Burghclere   SU: 463555
Cremations, flints and a bronze pin have been found in this linear cemetery of round barrows. Unfortunately the row has suffered badly from ploughing. South-west of the A34 are a bell-barrow (furthest from the road), four bowl-barrows and a disc-barrow. Between the road and the railway are two ploughed bowl-barrows, and another bowl-barrow lies beyond the embankment. [L. V. Grinsell, *P Hants. FC*, 14 (1940).]

34   SHALCOMBE DOWN, Shalfleet (I of W)   SZ: 391855
A fine bell-barrow 46 m wide and 2 m high dominates this group of barrows in a wood on the side of the hill. There are also five bowl-barrows, one of which was opened by J. Dennett in 1816. It contained a

cremation with a bronze axe, two boar tusks and a bronze knife-dagger with a pommel carved from bone. These are now in Carisbrooke Castle Museum. [L. V. Grinsell and G. A. Sherwin, *PIWNHS*, 3 (1941), 179.]

35 STOCKBRIDGE DOWN, Stockbridge   SU:375347
A group of about sixteen low and inconspicuous round barrows, of which one, at SU:378351, was excavated in 1938. It was built almost entirely of flint nodules, and was surrounded by five causewayed ditch segments. At the centre was a crouched female skeleton with a bell beaker and copper awl. Three cremations in urns were found in the barrow mound, one accompanied by beads of faience, calcite, lignite, jet and shale, as well as two awls of copper and bronze. [J. F. S. Stone, *Ant. J*, 20 (1940), 39.]

36 WHITESHOOT PLANTATION, Broughton   SU:290329
Between the plantation and the line of trees to the south are two saucer-barrows and a bell-barrow. One of the saucer-barrows is 7 m in diameter and is surrounded by a shallow ditch and bank. South-east of it is the bell-barrow 20 m in diameter and nearly 2 m high. On its eastern side is the second saucer-barrow, 8 m in diameter, with a surrounding ditch and outer bank. The bell is spoilt by a robber's trench; there is no record of the contents of any of the barrows. [L. V. Grinsell, *P Hants. FC*, 14 (1940), 210.]

37 WINCHESTER   SU:475297
A Belgic coin mould found close to Winchester Cathedral seems to confirm that the town was once the oppidum of the local Belgic Tribe, the Venta Belgarum. Nearly a kilometre to the west between Clifton Road and Clifton Terrace parts of an iron age earthwork have been excavated. Called Oram's Arbour, it is a rectangular enclosure of about 18 ha surrounded by a V-shaped ditch, and entered through an inturned gateway on the western side. Sections cut in the Castle Yard and beneath the new assize courts have helped to date it to the mid first century BC. Few traces of the earthwork can be seen on the surface today. [M. Biddle, *Ant. J*, 48 (1968), 250; 50 (1970), 279; 55 (1975), 98.]

38 WOOLBURY RING, Little Somborne   SU:381353
A roughly circular fort of 8·1 ha with a cultivated interior, defined by a single rampart and ditch and slight counterscarp bank. The rampart is about 3 m high in places, but on the east it has been destroyed. There is an entrance gap on the south-west.
    The fort is notable for its associated field and ranch systems, marked

by three dykes which run up to it on the west and south-west, presumably separating grazing grounds from the cultivated Celtic fields which run down the valley to the south. [J. P. Williams-Freeman, *Field Archaeology as Illustrated by Hampshire* (1915), 234.]

1 ACONBURY HILL, Kingsthorne   so:504331

This oval-shaped fort of 6·9 ha encloses a steep-sided, tree-covered hill. A single rampart and ditch with traces of a counterscarp bank encircle the hill. The entrance at the east end is strongly inturned, another at the west is inturned only on the south side. Only minimal excavation has been undertaken, suggesting that the rampart is stone revetted, and that the fort was occupied from the first century BC until well into the Roman period. [K. Kenyon, *Arch. J*, 110 (1953), 25.]

2 ARTHUR'S STONE, Dorstone   so:318431

A massive capstone boulder weighing about 25 tonnes is supported by nine low wallstones to form a polygonal burial chamber lying west of north. The entrance passage approaches at an angle from the west and leads into a small antechamber. Direct approach to the burial chamber is blocked by a sill stone. Although there are traces of the surrounding burial mound its shape is not clear, though records from 1881 suggest an oval mound 18 m long and 9 m wide. [G. E. Daniel, *Prehistoric Chamber Tombs* (1950), 217.]

3 BREDON HILL, Bredon's Norton   so:958402

This is a roughly square-shaped promontory fort with north-east and north-west sides naturally protected by strong cliff-like slopes. On the south-east and south-west are two widely spaced lines of ramparts and ditches. The outer defences consist of a drystone wall, separated by a berm from a V-shaped rock-cut ditch 10 m wide and 4·5 m deep. The entrances at either end of the rampart have been largely destroyed by landslides, but traces of their long inturns can still be found. The inner rampart stands 3 m high in places and is of glacis type, built of dumped clay, without revetting of any kind, though it may have had a timber breastwork. Its ditch was 2·5 m deep and 9 m wide. At its centre was a single entrance which showed three periods of construction when it was excavated in 1935–7. At first it had been a simple overlapping entrance, but this was remodelled to form an inturned passage 40 m long and 7·5 m wide. At its inner end was a strong gateway, whilst about halfway along the passage a bridge carried a rampart walk over it.

The excavator considered the inner rampart was the earliest, but recently A. H. A Hogg has demonstrated that the outer defence was probably built first, about 300 BC, the inner rampart about 150 BC, and the inturned entrance around 100 BC, remodelled perhaps fifty years later.

The fort was destroyed early in the first century AD; it was attacked, the gateway burnt down and the bodies of more than sixty young men left hacked to pieces on either side of the inner entrance. A row of skulls set on poles above the gate lay where they had fallen. When this grotesque episode took place and who the attackers were is not clear; they may have been a Belgic war party prior to the Roman invasion. [A. H. A. Hogg, *Hill-forts* (1975), 141.]

4 CAPLER CAMP, Fownhope SO:593329

This is a narrow oval hillfort enclosing 4 ha just above the Wye. Surrounded by trees on most sides, it is protected by double banks and ditches on the south and west, but only by a steep-scarped slope on the north. The entrance is close to the house at the eastern end and is marked by a heaped-up rampart on the south side, whilst the northern defence curves round it to make an approach passage.

5 CONDERTON CAMP, Conderton SO:972384

This small oval fort is set on a south-facing spur of Bredon Hill with steep slopes on all sides except the north and with magnificent views of the Cotswolds to the south-east. Excavation has shown two phases of occupation. At first an area of 1·2 ha was bounded by a single stone rampart and ditch, with traces of a counterscarp on the east and west, and broken by entrances at the north and south. It was probably a cattle enclosure, datable to about 300 BC.

In the first century BC a wall was built across the spur inside the original earthwork, isolating 0·8 ha to the north. The neatly built drystone wall had a rubble and soil core and no accompanying ditch. It had a central inturned entrance with double gates halfway along its passage. The northern area became the site of a village with about a dozen circular huts, storage pits and working hollows. The simple northern entrance was reconstructed, its inturns being lined with drystone walling. Later it was blocked off with another drystone wall. The lower enclosure probably continued as a cattle corral. Finds from the site indicate that it was abandoned before the Roman occupation. The iron age pottery is identical to that from rescue excavations at the nearby unprotected village site of Beckford, and it is conceivable that Conderton acted as the citadel to which the Beckford folk turned for protection in times of stress. [N. Thomas, *Proceedings of the Cotteswold Naturalists Field Club,* 33 (1959), 100.]

6   COXALL KNOLL, Buckton and Bucknell   so:366734
This tree-covered fort of almost 5 ha occupies an elongated hilltop
which rises steeply from the plain of the Teme to the south. The badly
damaged earthworks can be divided into three sections. First an oval
enclosure of 3·4 ha on the west is defended by two banks and ditches,
though these are reduced to scarps on the steeper south side. The
western entrance is inturned and protected by a hornwork. There is an
oblique passage through the eastern defence. To the east and north-
east is a univallate enclosure of 1 ha with an inner quarry ditch. This is
presumably a later extension to the first enclosure. An entrance gap on
the north leads into a second annexe of about 0·4 ha defended by a
bank, a ditch and, in parts, a counterscarp bank. A straight-through gap
in the northern side forms the only certain entrance. [RCHM,
Herefordshire, III (1934), 27.]

7   CREDENHILL CAMP, Credenhill   so:451445
This fine contour fort covers 20 ha and is one of the largest in Britain.
Unfortunately its interior is forested. It is surrounded by a single
rampart and ditch, and more material was obtained from internal
quarry ditches. Two ancient entrances survive, one in the centre of the
eastern side and one at the south-east corner, both with long inturns
and, possibly, guard chambers.
   Limited excavations in 1963 south of the eastern gateway found
traces of nine square (2·5 m) or rectangular (2·5 by 3·5 m) huts set in
rows, and each had been rebuilt a number of times. The excavator
showed that, as dwellings, the buildings must have had raised floors.
Assuming that the whole of the fort was covered with houses a population of about four thousand has been suggested, but this seems to be
assuming too much from a very small excavation and must be treated
with caution. [S. C. Stanford, *Arch. J*, 127 (1970), 82.]

8   CROFT AMBREY, Croft   so:444668
(National Trust). This is a triangular fort north of Croft Castle. Extensive excavations have made its history reasonably clear. It began life
about 550 BC as an enclosure of 2·2 ha, protected on the north by the
very steep escarpment of Leinthall Common and on the south and west
by a small dumped rampart and ditch. Inside were rows of four-post
buildings.
   About 390 BC a quarry ditch was dug outside these defences and the
material obtained thrown up into a massive rampart now enclosing
3·6 ha. Gates were made at the south-west and east and later guard
chambers were added to both. The huts of the old fort continued to be
used and rebuilt and new structures extended into the quarry ditches.
By 80 BC the guard chambers had passed out of use and bridges were
built above the gateways. An annexe of 4·8 ha had been added by this

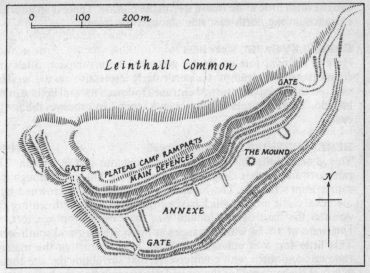

Fig 16. Croft Ambrey, Hereford

time, probably used for animal storage, and by the early Roman period a circular mound identified as a sanctuary had appeared. The occupation of the fort seems to have come to an end about AD 48 when the people, identified by the excavator as the Decangi, were conquered by Ostorius Scapula.

Dr Stanford's excavations revealed that twenty sets of gateposts had been replaced at the inturned south-west gate, and that some huts had been rebuilt at least six times. It was also worked out that the population was probably between 500 and 900. [S. C. Stanford, *Croft Ambrey* (1974).]

9   DINEDOR CAMP, Dinedor   so:524364
This rectangular hillfort of almost 5 ha is best preserved on the eastern side, where the rampart stands up prominently. On the west it has been flattened and the ditch only shows as a terrace at the rampart foot. The entrance at the east is of a simple straight-through type. Limited excavation suggests that the rampart was stone-faced, both inside and out. Occupation, in the small area examined, seems to have been dense. [K. Kenyon, *Arch. J,* 110 (1953), 23.]

10   GADBURY BANK, Eldersfield   so:793316
On a low hill between the Malverns and the river Severn is this small contour fort of 4 ha. The sides of the hill are not very steep, but the only protection is afforded by a single bank and ditch. The bank is now low

and the ditch little more than a step in the hillside. There is an inturned entrance on the north-east side amongst the trees.

11 GARMSLEY CAMP, Stoke Bliss   SO:620618
Here is an oval fort of 3·6 ha protected by a rampart, ditch and counterscarp. The rampart is particularly impressive on the western side. At this point an inturned entrance follows a natural hollow in the hillside. There appears to have been a second entrance on the north-east.

12 HEREFORDSHIRE BEACON, Colwall   SO:760399
This is one of the finest examples of a contour fort in Britain. The ramparts and ditches cling to the shape of the hill, even though it is rather impracticable. The highest point of the hill is crowned by a medieval castle mound which has been dated to the twelfth century AD. Around the base of this mound was the earliest iron age fort, an enclosure of 3·2 ha with entrances at the north-east and south-west. This little fort was enlarged to 13 ha by constructing the massive ramparts and ditch with counterscarp that surrounds the site today. Much of the material for the main defence came from an inner quarry scoop which can be clearly seen, resembling an inner ditch, around most of the southern part of the fort. There are four entrances. That at the north has been damaged by the modern footpath, but it seems to be overlapped, as does the southern gate, which is approached by what might be a contemporary zigzag pathway. On the east the entrance is also overlapped, whilst its western counterpart is inturned. In the right light traces of many hut circles can be seen on the hill, and estimates for a population of 1500–2000 have been claimed, though this seems excessive.

Clutter's Cave, which lies about 160 m south-east of the camp beside the footpath, may have been used as a hermitage in the middle ages. It has no obvious prehistoric connections. Similarly, the Shire Ditch, which runs east from the southern tip of the fort, was probably constructed as a boundary in 1290 AD. [S. C. Stanford, *The Malvern Hill-forts* (1973).]

13 IVINGTON CAMP, Leominster Out   SO:484547
Steep slopes almost surround this triangular fort of 9 ha. Only at the east where the hill joins the spur are the double rampart and ditch massed up to present an even stronger aspect. The rampart has a pronounced terrace on the inside. At the south-west corner the entrance rampart is strongly inturned and approached by a steep hollow way which is flanked by two ramparts on its right-hand side. Between these two banks is a massive cruciform earthwork which must have supported some kind of watch-tower. At the north-east corner there is

a simpler entrance of inturn/out-turn type, which was protected by outworks, now ploughed down. The gap for the farm drive must be modern.

In the north-west corner of the fort is an earlier earthwork of 3 ha. It has a single bank and ditch with a gap on the east which is probably recent. The original entrance may have been under the farm buildings. [RCHM, *Hereford,* III (1934), 131.]

14 KING ARTHUR'S CAVE, Whitchurch   so:545155
Situated in light woodland above the river Wye, this small cave has a wide entrance which opens into two small chambers. It was first dug in 1871 by the Rev. W. S. Symonds, who found the remains of numerous extinct animals, including mammoths, woolly rhinoceros, lion and cave bear, all beneath a thick layer of stalagmite. Flint tools show that the earliest inhabitants belonged to the upper palaeolithic and meso-lithic periods. At first they lived inside the cave, but later moved to the mouth and the ledge outside where the ashes of their fires and the bones of the animals they hunted have been found in deposits 2 m thick. [T. F. Hewer and H. Taylor, *PUBSS,* 2 (1925), 221; 3 (1927), 59.]

15 MIDSUMMER HILL, Eastnor   so:761375
(National Trust). Two hilltops are enclosed by a bank and ditch and in places a counterscarp, containing an area of 12 ha. The fort is irregular in shape with a long narrow spur jutting to the south and an oval area to the north-west. The rampart is stone-faced and there are traces of shallow internal quarry ditches. At the north-west is an entrance, originally inturned, and there is another at the south-west. Excavation of the latter has shown at least seventeen rebuilds, during which time it had guard chambers of both wood and stone. Hollows in the interior suggest the presence of about 250 huts, and those excavated seem to have been rectangular in shape and about 3·5 m by 4·5 m across. The buildings seems to have been laid out on a regular plan with streets between them. A radiocarbon date suggests that occupation of the fort began about 400 BC and ended when it was burnt down by Ostorius Scapula when he attacked the Decangi in AD 48. The low mound 49 m long and 12 m wide on the east side of the fort is probably a pillow mound, an artificial rabbit warren of medieval construction. [S. C. Stanford, *The Malvern Hill-forts* (1973), 11.]

16 PYON WOOD, Aymestry   so:424664
This is a steep hill covered with trees. On top is a triangular escarpment of 3·6 ha protected by a bank, ditch and counterscarp. There are traces of a quarry ditch inside the rampart. At the south-east is an inturned entrance approached by a hollow way.

17 RISBURY CAMP, Humber   so:542553
Massive banks between 7·6 m and 9 m high surround this low-lying fort
of 3·6 ha. The camp is rectangular in shape with a double rampart and
ditch on the west side and triple defences elsewhere. A modern cut
through the eastern ramparts shows that they are made of dumped
clay, and a stone facing can be seen on top of the northern rampart.
The most likely original entrance is in the middle of the west side where
banks funnel the approach road, although the entrance itself is only
slightly inturned. On the south-east and south-west are a number of
low cross-banks and ditches whose purpose is obscure. They resemble
the hollows by the entrance at Old Oswestry, Shropshire. [RCHM,
Herefordshire, III (1934), 73.]

18 SUTTON WALLS, Sutton St Nicholas   so:525464
This is a long narrow oval-shaped hillfort of 12 ha. It is also one of the
biggest disgraces in the history of British archaeology. About half the
interior has been removed for gravel and the resultant quarry is now
used as a tip for toxic waste.
     The hill was first occupied in the early iron age without any defence.
About 100 BC a rampart revetted with timber and drystone walling was
set up inside a V-shaped ditch. Material was also scraped from shallow
quarry ditches, in which huts were later built. About AD 25 the ditch
was widened and the material used to enlarge the rampart. The next
major event was the slaughter of at least two dozen inhabitants,
perhaps by the Romans in AD 48. Skeletons were found thrown casually into the ditch at the inturned eastern entrance: some had battle
wounds, others were decapitated. Doubtless many others remain to be
found. The ramparts were slighted and pushed over the slaughter
victims. In spite of this the fort continued in use until at least the third
century AD. [K. Kenyon, *Arch. J,* 110 (1953), 1.]

19 WAPLEY CAMP, Staunton-on-Avon   so:345625
This is a triangular fort of 10 ha with a very steep northern escarpment
overlooking the valley of the river Lugg. On the south it is protected by
four ramparts and ditches and on the west by five sets of defences, with
quite a large gap between the second and third row. There is an oblique
entrance halfway along the south side with a long inturn, which curves
to the left on the inside. The gap at the south-east corner may be
modern and that at the north-east is more likely to be original. The
ramparts are covered with pine trees, but the interior is unplanted.
Here, just to the west of the entrance, is what appears to be a well or
'ritual shaft' and at least four low pillow mounds. [RCHM, *Herefordshire,* III (1934), 184.]

20 WOODBURY HILL, Great Witley   so:749645
This fort is kidney-shaped and encloses about 10 ha. Its strong ram-

part, ditch and counterscarp follow the contour of the hill on the east, south and west, but plunge down into a combe on the north. There are three breaks in the northern rampart, of which that at the north-west is deeply inturned and so most probably original.

21 WYCHBURY HILL CAMP, Hagley   so:920818
Situated on a north-west-facing spur of the Clent Hills overlooking the Stour valley, Wychbury is a triangular-shaped fort with an annexe on the south-west side. There is no need for defence on the west and there is only a slight bank on the north, but on the south-west are two lines of rampart and ditch with a counterscarp. The inner rampart is most pronounced. At the eastern and western ends are inturned entrances. A causeway runs for about 100 m from the western entrance with a bank and ditch on either side of it. It then meets another bank and ditch running south-west from close to the eastern entrance and defining the annexe, which seems to be late in the fort's history and may have acted as a cattle pen. Excavation in 1884 produced an early iron age knobbed terret, an iron dagger and a bronze ring.

HERTFORDSHIRE

1 ARBURY BANKS, Ashwell   TL:262387
This oval plateau fort crowns a low hill to the south-west of Ashwell. It
encloses about 5 ha and is surrounded by a single damaged bank and
filled-in ditch. The latter was excavated in 1856 by Joseph Beldam,
who found it to be V-shaped, 4·6 m deep and 6·1 m wide. In the fort he
found storage pits and gullies, quantities of pottery and the bones of
domestic animals. Aerial photographs show the fort to be dominated
by a single large circular hut, so perhaps we should see Arbury Banks
as a fortified farming establishment not far off the Icknield Way.

2 THE AUBREYS, Redbourn   TL:095113
This circular plateau fort enclosing 7·3 ha is defended by a double bank
and ditch, except for a short length on the west where a single bank
suffices. It has been suggested that the earthwork is unfinished. There
appear to be two entrances where the double ramparts end on the west
and north-west. The site is on clay land, which would probably have
been forested, suggesting that it was used for cattle and pig husbandry.
Unpublished excavations by Sir Mortimer Wheeler produced a few
pieces of hand-made late iron age pottery. [RCHM, *Hertfordshire*
(1910), 166.]

3 BEECH BOTTOM DYKE, St Albans   TL:155093
This consists of a massive ditch with banks on the north and south
sides. It is 27 m wide and about 9 m deep and looks in every respect like
the Devil's Dyke at Wheathampstead, 4·5 km to the north-east.
Although the two dykes are not continuous there seems no reason to
imagine that they were not originally related, made by the same
builders in order to cut off the area between the Ver and Lea valleys. It
appears likely that they were connected with the Catuvellaunian oppidum at Prae Wood. [R. E. M. and T. E. Wheeler, *Verulamium, a
Belgic and Two Roman Cities* (1936), 16.]

4 DEVIL'S DITCH, St Albans   TL:123084
This ditch lies close to Mayne Farm on the Gorhambury Estate. The
ditch is still 15 m wide and its original depth is unknown. It seems to
have run from the Ver into wooded land on the west, perhaps making a

174

northern boundary to land directly connected with the Catuvellaunian oppidum at Prae Wood 1·5 km to the south. [R. E. M. and T. E. Wheeler, *Verulamium, a Belgic and Two Roman Cities* (1936), 15.]

5   DEVIL'S DYKE, Wheathampstead   TL:186133
This enormous dyke was created by deepening a natural valley. It is 460 m long, 12 m deep and 40 m wide at the top. On its eastern side is a bank 2·5 m high and another, 2 m high, on its western edge. It seems to be part of a discontinuous dyke system running north-east to south-west between the Lea at Wheathampstead and the Ver at St Albans.

In the 1930s Sir Mortimer Wheeler related the Devil's Dyke to a natural valley to the south called The Slad and suggested that together they had formed the boundaries of a massive hillfort of about 36 ha that might have formed the headquarters of Cassivellaunus when his tribe was attacked by Caesar in 54 BC. There now seems to be little to support this theory and it is more logical to see the Dyke as an extension eastwards of the Beech Bottom Dyke at St Albans. [R. E. M. Wheeler, *Antiquity*, 7 (1933), 21.]

6   PRAE WOOD, St Albans   TL:123068
A substantial semicircular earthwork with upstanding banks and ditches still survives in Prae Wood. It is very overgrown and visitors are seldom admitted, so it is not described in detail. The north-eastern end of the earthwork is only 150 m north-west of the gamekeeper's cottage, and there are many minor banks in the undergrowth close by. These all form part of the Belgic 'town' of Verulamium excavated by Sir Mortimer Wheeler in the 1930s; they were found to extend parallel with the western wall of the later Roman town for about 1 km, though much of the site has now been built on. Masses of pottery and ovens, as well as two cemeteries, have been found associated with the Prae Wood site. Baked clay coin moulds indicate that coins were minted on the site, bearing the inscriptions VER or VERL and TASC, being shortened forms of the name of Verulamium, the tribal capital, and of Tasciovanus, leader of the tribe of the Catuvellauni. [R. E. M. and T. E. Wheeler, *Verulamium, a Belgic and Two Roman Cities* (1936), 10.]

7   RAVENSBURGH CASTLE, Hexton   TL:099295
This tree-covered fort of 9 ha is rectangular in plan, with very deep, steep-sided, dry valleys on three sides. It is surrounded by a single bank and ditch, which is doubled on the western side. Excavation has shown the ditch to be 3·6 m deep and 6 m wide, and the rampart on the east still reaches a height of 6 m. At first, about 400 BC, this rampart was constructed with stout posts at the front and rear tied together with horizontal cross-bars, but in the middle of the first century, after it had been deserted for many years, the bank was rebuilt in glacis fashion

with material from a re-dug ditch. The earliest fort had only one entrance, of oblique type, at the north-west corner, but the later fort included a new entrance of straight-through type at the south-east corner, which presumably gave access to a nearby spring. Excavation has suggested that the fort was used mainly for cattle herding and penning. Being the largest hillfort in eastern England, it is possible that Ravensburgh was the oppidum defended by Cassivellaunus against Caesar in 54 BC. [J. Dyer, in D. W. Harding, *Hillforts* (1976), 153.]

8 **THERFIELD HEATH, Royston**   TL:342402
A relatively small long barrow opened by Edmund Nunn in 1855 and excavated by C. W. Phillips in 1935 crowns the golf course. It is 33 m long, 17 m wide and 1·8 m high. A heap of human bones was found near the lower, west end (though more burials may still await discovery). A stack of turves had been placed over this, perhaps as a primitive mortuary house. A ditch had been dug all round the stack and chalk from it piled up to form the barrow. There is no record of any other primary contents, though a Saxon burial with a spear was found near the eastern end. [C. W. Phillips, *PPS,* 1 (1935), 101.]

    There are eight round barrows on the Heath a few metres north of the long barrow. Six of these barrows are known as the Five Hills and were opened by Edmund Nunn between 1854 and 1856. One of them contained the disarticulated remains of nine corpses, others held cremations and collared urns. On the summit above the cricket pavilion is an unexcavated barrow called Earl's Hill. Finds from the barrows are in the Museum of Archaeology and Ethnology at Cambridge. [J. Dyer, *Arch. J,* 116 (1961), 6.]

HUMBERSIDE

1 ARRAS, Market Weighton   SE:930413

This cemetery of small mid-second-century-BC barrows originally contained at least a hundred graves. Today only three are still visible. Most of the barrows were opened around 1815 by E. W. Stillingfleet and Barnard Clarkson and many of the finds have been lost. Three of the barrows contained chariots. One is known as the King's Barrow. In it were found the skeleton of an elderly man, two horses and the wheels of a chariot. The Charioteer's Barrow covered a skeleton and chariot wheels, though no horses. The Lady's Barrow also contained a skeleton and chariot, and an iron mirror as well. Another mound, called the Queen's Barrow, produced a female skeleton accompanied by much jewellery, including a necklace of about a hundred blue and white glass beads, an amber ring and a gold finger ring, two bronze bracelets and a bronze brooch and pendant decorated with white coral. Pig bones have been found in almost all the barrows. These burials are peculiar to the tribe called the Parisi who lived in the Yorkshire Wolds at this time; they are not found in other parts of Britain. [I. M. Stead, *The Arras Culture* (1979), various.]

2 CALLIS WOLD BARROW CEMETERY, Bishop Wilton
SE:830554 (centre)

This group of at least eighteen barrows were dug between 1860 and 1892 by J. R. Mortimer. His published plans make it difficult to correlate his discoveries with existing barrow mounds, but this can to some extent be achieved, bearing in mind that in numerous cases barrows have been totally destroyed. In March 1865 Mortimer opened the barrow at SE:829556. At the centre was an oval grave containing a crouched burial with a food vessel and stone battle-axe. Around this were two almost concentric circles of stakes and posts at diameters of 6·5 m and 8·5 m. Some of the stakes could be seen still standing 1 m high in the barrow mound. Whether they formed a fence or free-standing ring of posts around the barrow is open to speculation. Mortimer suggested a wooden hut, but this would have been very difficult to roof. A barrow in the wood by Callis Wold Farm produced a number of crouched and cremated burials, but at the base, on a limestone pavement 3·6 m and 0·9 m, lay ten crouched adult skeletons, two with arrowheads. The primary burial was a cremation in a wood-covered pit. [J. R. Mortimer, *Forty Years' Researches* (1905), 153.]

3 DANE'S DYKE, Flamborough   SE:216694
An area of 8 sq. km is cut off by this massive dyke that runs north to south across the headland from coast to coast. A bank stands nearly 6 m high with a ditch on its western side 18 m across, with traces of a counterscarp bank. This is the sort of earthwork associated with tribal oppida in the south of England and we can only speculate on the presence of such a site on this part of the east coast.

4 DANES GRAVES, Driffield   TA:018633
Only a few of these barrows on the edge of the Yorkshire Wolds remain, but originally there were about five hundred. Many were dug into by J. R. Mortimer and others in the nineteenth century, and Mortimer recorded that the poorer burials seemed to be in the north of the cemetery, whilst those with richer grave goods were to the south. Surviving barrows are seldom more than 1 m high and between 3 m and 9 m in diameter, occasionally with a surrounding ditch. Examination of the contents of more than a hundred barrows shows that the burials were usually crouched in rectangular graves with food offerings, usually of pork, pots, brooches and bracelets, pins and beads. In 1897 Mortimer uncovered a chariot burial containing 'the iron hoops of the wheels and naves, and rings of bronze and iron belonging to the chariot and trappings of the horses. In the grave with these were two adult skeletons, probably the remains of the owner of the chariot and his charioteer.' The Danes Graves belong to the middle of the second century BC and seem to indicate an immigrant population, the Parisi, from France. [I. M. Stead, *The Arras Culture* (1979), 99.]

5 KILHAM LONG BARROW, Kilham   TA:056674
Lying west of the Kilham–Thwing road this long barrow was opened by Canon Greenwell in the autumn of 1868 and by T. G. Manby between 1965 and 1969. It is now very ploughed. The recent excavations located two parallel ditches some 40 m long and 6·5 m apart. They may have marked the outline of an earlier barrow whose mound was destroyed. Next a rectangular bedding trench was dug to hold upright timbers. This structure was about 55 m long and from 7·5 m to 9 m wide, and lay south-west to north-east. It had entrances at either end and an avenue of posts led north-east for an uncertain distance. Inside the enclosure was a burial chamber of earth and timber in which Greenwell seems to have found two burials. Outside the enclosure quarry ditches were dug, at first only at the south-western end, but after the burial chamber was destroyed by fire they were extended right along both sides and the

whole mound was covered with chalk. The barrow has been dated by radiocarbon to 2880 bc.

In the bronze age two burials with food vessels were inserted into the long barrow, and what may be a round barrow was constructed over the line of the avenue at the north-eastern end. [T. G. Manby, *PPS,* 42 (1976), 111.]

6 RUDSTON TA:097677

Reputed to be the tallest standing stone in Britain, this monolith, 7·7 m high, 1·8 m wide and 0·8 m thick, stands in the churchyard. It is made of gritstone and must have been brought from Cayton or Carnelian Bay, more than 16 km away. There is a smaller stone on the north-east side of the churchyard, also of grit, and close to it a cist constructed of sandstone slabs, which appear to be ancient. The whole area around Rudston was important in neolithic times, and aerial photographs show the crop marks of three cursuses. Part of one of these can be seen on the ground at TA:099658, where the squared-off end is still visible as a bank a metre high. [D. P. Dymond, *PPS,* 32 (1966), 86.]

7 SCORBOROUGH, Leconfield TA:017453

On damp clay land in a field south-east of Scorborough Hall survives the finest cemetery of the iron age Arras culture barrows in Britain. At least 120 barrows survive, though most of them are only 4–5 m in diameter and 15–30 cm high. The largest is 15 m in diameter, and two others, 10 m across, are square in plan. Only a few of the barrows have been opened. Mortimer found poorly preserved contracted burials with no grave goods in 1895, and one of the smallest barrows dug in 1970 covered a grave only 40 cm deep, also containing a contracted burial, with the skull at the south-east end. [I. M. Stead, *The Arras Culture* (1979), 18.]

8 SOUTH SIDE MOUNT, Rudston TA:107665

Aerial photographs show that this barrow is surrounded by a square-ditched enclosure, with a circular ditch broken by an entrance cause-way inside it. The barrow mound itself has been badly damaged by ploughing. The skeletons of seventeen men, women and children have been found, together with beakers and food vessels. All must be secondary, suggesting that the primary burial remains to be found.

9 TOWTHORPE PLANTATION, Fimber SE:879638

A linear cemetery in the line of trees stretching to the east. The barrow at the grid reference was opened by J. R. Mortimer in 1870 at a cost of £30. At the time it was 40 m in diameter and more than 3 m high. At the centre of the barrow was a grave containing an extended male skeleton buried with a Wessex-type bronze dagger, a bored stone hammer-head and a flint knife. The burnt bones of a child in a wooden box were also found.

It is difficult to follow Mortimer's numbering, but the barrow at approximately SE:884641 seems to have had traces of a wooden burial chamber. West of the centre was a grave containing a crouched male burial with a bronze dagger at its hip. Altogether Mortimer opened twenty barrows along the ridge, most of them producing burials with beakers, food vessels and flint implements. [J. R. Mortimer, *Forty Years' Researches* (1905), 1.]

10 WILLY HOWE, Thwing   TA:063724

A huge and irregular tree-covered round barrow, reminiscent of Duggleby Howe; it measures 40 m in diameter and is 7 m high. In 1857 Lord Londesborough failed to find a burial or reach the centre. Thirty years later it was trenched by Canon Greenwell, who found a central grave pit, but no burials. [W. Greenwell, *Archaeologia*, 52 (1890), 22.]

KENT

1   ADDINGTON PARK, Addington   TQ:653591
This site, cut in half by a road, is rectangular, its edges marked by a
kerb of sarsen stones 1 m to 1·5 m high. At the north-east end are the
remains of a burial chamber that collapsed in the nineteenth century.
The barrow is 61 m long and 11 m wide and urgently needs conserva-
tion. There are reports of 'rough pottery' having been found there in
1845. [R. Jessup, *South-East England* (1970), 103.]

2   BIGBURY, Harbledown   TR:116576
Caesar was almost certainly describing Bigbury when he wrote of 'a
well-fortified post of great strength . . . all the entrances blocked by
felled trees laid close together' which the seventh legion attacked in
54 BC. It is a large rectangular contour fort of some 10 ha, easily
approached from the south-west and protected on all sides by a single
bank and ditch. On the northern side is a large indentation that is
protected by a semicircular outlying cattle enclosure of 2·5 ha. It is not
a particularly strong fort, the main rampart being only 2·5 m high, with
a ditch 5 m wide and 1·8 m deep. There is an original eastern entrance
into the main enclosure, from which there is no direct access to the
annexe.
   Bigbury has been badly damaged by extensive woods, gravel digging
and roads, and the southern section is planted with orchards, all of
which makes it a difficult site to understand on the ground. The gravel
pits have produced early iron age and Belgic pottery and a variety of
metalwork, including chariot fittings, iron firedogs and an iron slave-
chain 5·5 m long, fitted with a barrel padlock. [R. F. Jessup. *Arch.
Cantiana,* 48 (1936), 151.]

3   THE CHESTNUTS, Addington   TQ:652592
Recently partly restored, this chambered barrow is now quite devoid
of its covering mound, which appears to have been D-shaped. The
entrance on the straight side led into a gallery 3·7 m long, 2·3 m wide
and 2·1 m high, divided into two by a septal stone. Two large facade
stones stand on either side of the entrance. Excavation in 1957 revealed traces of nine cremations and one or two infant burials together
with Windmill Hill and late neolithic pottery, three barbed and tanged

arrowheads and a baked clay pendant. Excavation also showed that the site had been occupied in mesolithic and Romano-British times. [J. Alexander, *Arch. Cantiana*, 76 (1961), 1.]

4 COFFIN STONE, Aylesford TQ:739605
This is a large block of sarsen stone 4·4 m long and 2·4 m wide, with others lying near it. In 1836 searchers found two human skulls under the stone, and this suggests that it was once a chambered long barrow. [R. Jessup, *South-East England* (1970), 100.]

5 COLDRUM, Trottiscliffe TQ:654607
(National Trust). A short rectangular barrow 21 m by 17 m, outlined by a peristalith of fallen sarsen stones which would have supported the earth of the barrow. On the east, above the artificial slope created by chalk digging, is a burial chamber measuring 4 m by 1·5 m. This was once divided into two compartments by a stone with a porthole opening in it. Excavation in 1910 revealed twenty-two skeletons, neolithic pottery and flint work. The skeletons showed physical similarities suggesting close relationships. The tomb itself shows closer affinities with chambered barrows in north-west Europe than with the rest of Britain. In July 1926 the barrow was given to the National Trust in memory of Benjamin Harrison, the grocer and archaeologist of nearby Ightham. [R. Jessup, *South-East England* (1970), 108.]

6 FREE DOWN, Ringwould TR:365471
Only two bowl-barrows survive, from what was once a much more extensive group. Both are about 22 m in diameter and 1 m high, and were excavated by the Rev. C. H. Woodruff in 1872. The western mound covered four inverted cremation urns, accompanied by incense cups and faience beads. The eastern barrow produced only a part of a collared urn. [R. Jessup, *South-East England* (1970), 116.]

HIGH ROCKS, Frant, see under Sussex, East.

7 IFFIN WOOD, Thanington TR:133541
This overgrown bowl-barrow, 45 m in diameter, covered five inverted bronze age cinerary urns, their mouths blocked with clay. It was dug early in the nineteenth century. [J. Y. Akerman, *Archaeologia*, 30 (1844), 57.]

8 JULLIBERRIE'S GRAVE, Chilham TR:077532
This is the only known earthen long barrow in Kent; it is 44 m long, 15 m wide and 2 m high. The northern end has been damaged by a chalk pit. When excavated in the 1930s no burials were found, though

it was observed that the barrow was built of turf covered with chalk. Four Romano-British burials dating from about AD 50 lay in the upper filling of the southern side ditch. A neolithic axe from the core of the barrow confirms its early date. [R. Jessup, *Ant. J,* 19 (1939), 260.]

9   **KITS COTY HOUSE, Aylesford**   TQ:745608
A well-known site in the south-east of England, Kits Coty House consists of three upright stones in an H-shaped plan, about 2·4 m high covered by a large capstone 4 m by 2·7 m. These may represent a false entrance, or part of a burial chamber. A sketch by Stukeley in 1722 shows a further large stone, The General's Tomb, but this was blown up in 1867. The sketch also shows a long mound which is now almost invisible. Air photographs have revealed side ditches and digging has shown these to be 3·8 m deep. [R. Jessup, *South-East England* (1970), 98.]

10   **LOWER KITS COTY, Aylesford**   TQ:744604
Demolished in the eighteenth century for use as road material, this site now consists of a jumble of twenty sarsen stones that may once have formed a burial chamber. Only excavation is likely to solve the problem. Meanwhile, it is worth noting that a reconstruction drawing by Stukeley in 1722 bears striking similarities with Coldrum, a site that he did not know. [R. Jessup, *South-East England* (1970), 100.]

11   **OLDBURY HILL FORT, Ightham**   TQ:582562
Here is a large fort of 50 ha protected on the east by steep natural cliffs. A single rampart and ditch surround the north, west and south, and where necessary this is doubled. Excavation showed that the defences were of two periods; the first, about 100 BC, had a large bank of dump construction, apparently without any supporting timbers, and a V-shaped ditch. Perhaps half a century later the bank was enlarged by adding loose material to form a glacis, and the ditch was enlarged to give a wide, flat bottom of the type known from France as Fécamp. At the north-eastern entrance a stone revetment was built with a probable wooden breastwork above and beside a heavy wooden gate, whilst some kind of protective outwork was constructed. This gate was eventually destroyed by burning, and a large hoard of sling-stones was found nearby. Another gate at the south was inturned, but has been damaged by a modern road. There is no clear evidence of buildings from the interior, although plenty of pottery was recovered in the excavations of 1938. [J. B. Ward Perkins, *Archaeologia,* 90 (1944), 128.]

12   **OLDBURY HILL ROCK SHELTERS, Ightham**   TQ:584565
(National Trust). Beneath the iron age hillfort are two small rock

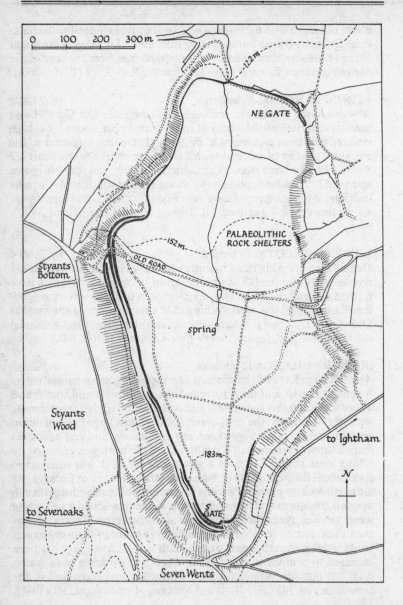

Fig 17. Oldbury, Kent

shelters caused by the erosion of softer sandstone below a capping of greenstone. Excavations in 1890 and 1968 have produced middle palaeolithic flint implements of Mousterian type. [D. and A. Collins, *Univ. London Inst. Arch. Bulletin,* 8 (1970), 151.]

13 **SQUERRYES PARK, Westerham**   TQ:443522
This is a triangular fort, its apex pointing north. On the east and west the sides are steeply scarped and protected only by a V-shaped ditch and counterscarp. Across the southern neck are a bank, ditch and counterscarp. Both banks stand 1·5 m high. The original entrance seems to be at the south-east corner where there is an outlying defensive bank. Excavation has revealed later iron age material, from about 100 BC, but no sign of Belgic occupation. [N. Piercy Fox, *Arch. Cantiana,* 86 (1971), 29.]

14 **STOWTING**   TR:127426
The centre of this round barrow exhibited a large burnt area with a 'roughly baked urn' above it. Other urns are also recorded from the mound.

15 **SWANSCOMBE, Barnfield Pit**   TQ:596746
(Nature Conservancy – restricted access). In this pit on a former terrace of the river Thames three pieces of the skull of Swanscombe Man have been found. This skull, probably belonging to a young adult, dates back about 250,000 years. It is reported that some sixty thousand hand axes have come from the Swanscombe gravels, mainly of Acheulean date, although Clactonian material has also been found there. The remains of at least twenty-six different species of mammals, mostly extinct, have also been unearthed. Most of the finds are in the Natural History Museum in London. [J. Wymer, *Lower Palaeolithic Archaeology in Britain* (1968), 334.]

16 **UPPER WHITE HORSE STONE, Aylesford**   TQ:753603
A large block of sarsen stone, 2·4 m long and 1·5 m high, superficially resembling a horse, is claimed to have once formed part of a burial chamber. Fragments of other stones scattered around it help to support the theory. [R. Jessup, *South-East England* (1970), 101.]

1 BLEASDALE, Bleasdale   SD:577460

Sited in a plantation, this site consists of a turf barrow 11 m across and nearly 1 m high, surrounded by a ditch lined with birch poles. Sticking out of the barrow mound was a ring of eleven oak posts (now marked by concrete pillars). At the centre was a grave 1·2 m long and 0·5 m deep. In this had been buried two inverted collared urns containing cremations, the larger also holding an incense cup. There was a break in the barrow ditch on the east side through which passed a double avenue with three posts on either side, stopping abruptly at an outer palisade circle to which the barrow was eccentric. This circle was 45 m in diameter and was made up of a continuous circle of closely spaced posts with larger ones about every 4·5 m. An entrance on the south-east was marked by two much larger posts. A radiocarbon date for one of the oak posts suggests a date between 1900 and 1720 BC. [W. J. Varley, *Ant. J,* 18 (1938), 154.]

2 CASTERCLIFFE CAMP, Nelson   SD:885384

This oval hillfort encloses 0·8 ha and is probably of two periods. Its first phase is represented by a slight inner bank only about 30 cm high and without a ditch. This was supplemented by a new bank, ditch and counterscarp of more massive form, though with clear indications that it was never completed on the north side where a series of unconnected short lengths of ditch survive. There are entrances on the east and west. At the latter are a series of outworks. Many of the stones of the bank show signs of burning, though whether this represents the destruction of the fort or an attempt at vitrification only excavation will tell. [J. Forde-Johnston, *Hillforts* (1976), 101, 106.]

3 CHAPELTOWN (Cheetham Close), Turton   SD:716159

At a height of 320 m above sea-level are two small stone circles. The northern one contains six or seven stones all less than 1 m in height. The circle has a diameter of 15 m. About 12 m to the south-west is an outlying stone.

Some 20 m south-west is a second, smaller circle made up of two concentric rings of stones, the outer 11 m in diameter, the inner 9·6 m across. Between them is a packing of rubble. More stones in the centre suggest that this is a ruined ring cairn, probably covering a burial. [*TLCAS,* 12 (1894), 42.]

4   FAIRY HOLES, Bowland with Leagram   SD:651467
Situated on the southern slope of New Laund Hill, this small cave, 3 m high, 1·8 m wide and 20 m long, is important for its use in the bronze age, when pottery, including pieces of collared urn, was deposited on the flat platform in front of the cave mouth.

5   PIKESTONES, Anglezarke   SD:627172
This is a long cairn, 45 m in length and 18 m wide, with a burial chamber of five stones at its northern end. The chamber is long and narrow and may once have been divided into two parts. A drystone-walled circular structure stood south of the chamber. At the northern end of the cairn are the remains of a double drystone revetment wall.

6   PORTFIELD CAMP, Whalley   SD:745355
A triangular fort of 1·5 ha protected by natural escarpments on the south-east and south-west. A single rampart surrounds the whole camp with extra defence along the south-east. The main fortifications, a triple bank and ditch, are visible on the north-west. When the site was excavated the base of a single wall built of clay with a stone face was found. This had been levelled and replaced by the present earthworks. [*TLCAS,* 67 (1957), 115.]

7   WARTON CRAG, Warton   SD:492727
Situated on the southern end of Warton Crag, with precipitous drops on the south-west and south-east, this roughly triangular fort encloses a total of some 6 ha, and is defended by three widely spaced ramparts. The inner defence is the best preserved. It has no ditch, but seems to have an entrance near its eastern end. The middle rampart is ill-defined and lies 45 m north of the inner, whilst the outer one is very overgrown and difficult to see. It runs 60 m north of the middle defence. [J. Forde-Johnston, *TLCAS*, 72 (1962), 9.]

LEICESTERSHIRE

1 **BULWARKS, Breedon-on-the-Hill**   SK:406234

High above the valley of the Trent this pear-shaped hillfort once
enclosed 9·2 ha. Sadly more than half has been quarried away on the
south and east sides in recent years. At least three excavations have
attempted to retrieve some of the history of the site. A single rampart
and ditch survive on the west side, and a badly disturbed inturned
entrance also lies on the west, partly under the churchyard wall.

The excavations show that the fort was of two periods of construction.
At first a wall of limestone was reinforced with timbers at the back and
front. Later, when the timbers had decayed, a new wall was built in
front and the bank was stabilized with turf. The ditch was broad and
flat bottomed, 8 m wide and 2 m deep. Pottery in large quantities is of
iron age A type. [J. S. Wacher, *Ant. J*, 44 (1964), 122.]

2 **BURROUGH HILL, Burrough-on-the-Hill**   SK:761119

This is a fine trapezoidal hillfort of nearly 5 ha, protected on three sides
by very steep slopes as well as a rampart and ditch. The fourth side is
defended by a formidable rampart, faced with a drystone wall. There is
a massive inturned entrance at the south-east corner, 45 m long, which
has been shown by excavation to be of two periods, and was possibly
enlarged by the Coritani who built stone guard chambers at its inner
ends. Trial excavations within the camp found many storage pits but no
huts. The pits contained pottery ranging from the second century BC
well into the Roman period, and pig, sheep, cow and horse bones. A
number of fine rotary querns indicated that grain was ground on the
site. [J. Dyer, *Hillforts of England and Wales* (1981).]

LINCOLNSHIRE

1 ASH HILL LONG BARROW, Binbrook   TF:209962
Once considered the best preserved of the Lincolnshire long barrows,
Ash Hill is now a sorry mess, having had a wartime dugout cut into one
end. It is 38 m long and 15 m wide at its broadest, east end and still
stands 2 m high. Its side ditches are no longer visible, though a cart
track seems to run along one of them. There are no records of its being
opened. [C. W. Phillips, *Arch. J*, 89 (1933), 174.]

2 ASH HOLT, Cuxwold   TA:190012
This long barrow, lying on the side of a small wood and overgrown with
trees and bushes, has been damaged on its southern end by having a pit
dug into it. It is one of the smallest of the Lincolnshire barrows,
measuring only 24 m by 12 m at its widest end. Its side ditches are no
longer visible. [C. W. Phillips, *Arch. J*, 89 (1933), 174.]

3 BULLY HILLS, Tathwell   TF:330827
Here is a linear cemetery of seven bowl-barrows with one standing
slightly apart from the rest. Their heights vary between 1·5 m and 3 m
and their diameters between 15 m and 24 m. The mounds appear to be
unopened.

4 BURGH ON BAIN   TA:213849
This long barrow is oval in shape; it measures 27 m long by 14 m wide
and 2 m high. It is covered by a clump of beech trees and has been
damaged by burrowing animals. Its oval shape resembles a shorter
type of barrow found in Yorkshire.

5 BUTTERBUMP BARROWS, Willoughby   TF:493724
There are twelve barrows in this group and were once probably more.
Only one has been excavated in modern times. It covered a cremation
in a pit beneath wooden planks, which may have formed a bier. Nearby
was a perforated whetstone and a bronze ogival dagger with its wooden
sheath. The burial deposit had been surrounded by a ring of turves
before the barrow was erected. Later seven secondary burials were
added to the mound. A radiocarbon date for the original burial lies
between 1930 and 1570 BC. [J. May, *Prehistoric Lincolnshire* (1976),
81.]

6 CAREBY CAMP, Careby   TF:040157

This oval fort is hidden in a wood and is a very slight affair. Its inner
bank measures 0·9 m high and its outer one seldom more than 0·3 m.
There is a gap of 36 m between the two banks and no clear sign of an
original entrance. The fort measures 225 m by 255 m. The possibility of
the site being of pre iron age date should not be discounted. [C. W.
Phillips, *Arch. J,* 91 (1934), 97.]

7 DEADMEN'S GRAVES, Claxby   TF:444720

Two long barrows can be clearly seen on the skyline from the road near
the farmhouse at TF:443716. They lie above a narrow, steep-sided
valley with lynchets on its southern side. The western barrow is 48 m
long, 17 m wide and 1·8 m high. It lies east to west and is apparently
unexcavated. The south-eastern barrow is 52 m long, 18 m wide and
1·8 m high. It lies in a similar position. Neither barrow shows signs
of any side ditches. [C. W. Phillips, *Arch. J,* 89 (1933), 174.]

8 FORDINGTON, Ulceby   TF:417714

These two circular mounds are surrounded by the banks and ditches of
a deserted medieval village with a disused churchyard close by. While
they are probably bronze age barrows, they could be the bases for
medieval windmills or dovecotes.

9 GIANTS' HILLS, Skendleby   TF:429712

Although ploughed, the low mound of this barrow is still visible and is
a classic in the history of barrow excavation. Built of chalk, it was 65 m
long and 23 m high, being slightly higher on the south-west. The
material came from a ditch which totally enclosed the barrow except
for a narrow causeway on the north-west. A trench at the south-east
end indicated a continuous facade of split timbers, with rows of posts
extending down either side of the barrow for 49 m. These seem to have
retained the barrow material and to have covered a platform of chalk
blocks on which lay the remains of eight people, seven adults and a
child. At the north-west end of the barrow stood a line of eight
apparently free-standing posts, perhaps symbolizing the eight burials.
The body of the barrow mound had been divided up into segments by
short lengths of hurdling. This feature is not uncommon in long barrows, but has not been satisfactorily explained. A radiocarbon date for
deer antler from the barrow ditch suggests that it was in use between
3500 and 2700 BC.

There is a second ploughed-down barrow 225 m to the south. [C. W.
Phillips, *Archaeologia*, 85 (1936), 37.]

10 HOE HILL, Binbrook   TF:215953

This well preserved long barrow lies in a small wood visible from the road. It measures 54 m long and 18 m wide at its eastern end, and must be 4 m high. It has suffered some damage near its centre. [C. W. Phillips, *Arch. J,* 89 (1933), 174.]

11   HONINGTON CAMP, Honington   SK:954424
Roughly rectangular, this fort of 0·6 m is rather low-lying, on a limestone plateau above the river Witham. Its defences consist of two strong banks and ditches and a counterscarp bank on all sides. The entrance, on the eastern side, is quite simple. No excavations have taken place to date it securely, and information from Camden and Stukeley relating to 'bits of weapons and bridles' found in 1691 is of little help. [J. May, *Prehistoric Lincolnshire* (1976), 141.]

12   REVESBY BARROWS, Revesby   TF:303616
Both round barrows are about 2·5 m high and 20 m in diameter. They are surrounded by well-marked ditches. One is reported to have covered a pit containing burnt bones. Nothing certain is known of their date.

13   ROUND HILLS, Ingoldsby   SK:992308
Lying on the flat limestone upland, this circular fort encloses about 1 ha. It consists of a bank a metre high and an external ditch, all covered with dense bushes, though the interior is open and ploughed.

14   SPELLOWS HILL, Partney   TF:402723
At first sight this long barrow will be mistaken for a row of three round barrows, having been cut through in two places. It is in fact 55 m long, 12 m wide and 2 m high. There is no record of its opening but many human bones are reported to have been found in the neighbourhood. This may be why the barrow is sometimes known as the Hills of the Slain. [C. W. Phillips, *Arch. J*, 89 (1933), 174.]

15   TATHWELL LONG BARROW   TF:294822
A single large tree grows on this extremely overgrown long barrow. Badly disturbed by rabbits, it is still 32 m long, 16 m wide and 2 m high at its south-eastern end. [C. W. Phillips, *Arch. J*, 89 (1933), 174.]

NORFOLK

1 ARMINGHALL, Bixley   TG:240060

Woodhenge and Arminghall were both discovered from the air by
Wing-Commander Insall in the 1920s. Both were settings of wooden
posts surrounded by a bank and ditch. At Arminghall two concentric
ditches are present, 36 m and 66 m in diameter, separated by a low
bank 15 m across and with an entrance facing south-west. The outer
ditch was 3·7 m wide and 1·5 m deep, the inner was 8·5 m across and
2·4 m in depth. In the central area was a horseshoe-shaped arrangement of eight massive oaken posts, set into holes 2 m deep and almost
1 m in diameter. Charcoal from the posts has been radiocarbon dated to
about 3350 BC. Complete tree trunks stood in the holes. How high they
reached cannot be told, and one can only contemplate that they may
have been carved or painted with neolithic designs. Little is visible of
this site today, but it is included because of its importance. [J. G. D.
Clark, *PPS*, 2 (1936), 1.]

2 BIRCHAM COMMON, Great Bircham   TF:775310 (centre)

A group of five round barrows opened in 1842 by F. C. Lukis. Two are
bell-barrows. That at TF:774315 is 1·8 m high and overgrown with
bushes; it produced only a fragment of pottery. The other, at
TF:776308, covered a pile of flints, at the centre of which was an
inverted urn containing a cremation, a small copper awl and six or
seven gold-covered beads, now lost. Nothing was found in two of the
bowl-barrows, and the third at TF:772310, has been almost ploughed
away. It contained a cremation in an urn. [F. C. Lukis, *A Brief
Account of the Barrows near Bircham Magna, Norfolk* (1843).]

3 BROOME HEATH, Ditchingham   TM:344913

This long barrow, unusual in East Anglia, is 35 m long and 2 m high,
lying roughly north-east to south-west. At this latter end is a low tail
mound about 40 m long. The barrow is unexcavated. East of it is a
round barrow 30 m in diameter, and further east still are traces of a
horseshoe-shaped enclosure of neolithic date, excavated in 1970–71.
The enclosure bank and outer ditch can be seen beside the village hall,
and further south beside Green Lane. The bank was held in position by
a timber palisade with a second fence on its summit. A wide scatter of

1 Victoria Cave near Settle in North Yorkshire was occupied by man in the upper palaeolithic period

2 The Cheddar Gorge in Somerset contains at least three caves occupied by man in the upper palaeolithic period

3 At least five of the caves in the limestone gorge at Creswell Crags in Derbyshire were occupied by stone age man

4 A cup-and-ring marked stone near Lordenshaws hillfort in Northumberland

5 *(above right)* An aerial view of native settlements of iron age and Roman date at Crosby Garrett in Cumbria

6 *(below right)* Iron age courtyard houses at Chysauster in Cornwall

7 The plateau fort of Uffington Castle beside the Ridgeway in Oxfordshire
8 In this aerial view, part of the excavations can be seen at Danebury Ring in Hampshire
9 (*above right*) The contour fort of Caer Caradoc, strongly sited above Church Stretton in Shropshire
10 (*below right*) Tre'r Ceiri hillfort with massive stone walls and groups of huts stands high above the Gwynedd countryside

11 The entrance to Yarnbury hillfort in Wiltshire
12 The rampart and ditch of Stanwick fort in North Yorkshire, which was attacked by the Romans around AD 70

13 The multiple ramparts of Maiden Castle, Dorset, possibly built as a defence against sling warfare

14 Three lines of rampart and ditch isolate the Rumps promontory fort in Cornwall

15 Lanyon Quoit in Cornwall, the remains of a much higher burial chamber, was restored in 1815

16 Dyffryn Ardudwy chambered cairn, Gwynedd, contains two burial chambers

17 The massive chamber of Plas Newydd in Anglesey has long since lost its covering mound of earth

18 The weathered stones of Maesyfelin, Glamorgan, stand over two metres high

19   An aerial view of Belas Knap chambered barrow, Gloucestershire, with its false
      entrance at the northern (left) end
20   The horned forecourt and transepts of Parc-le-Breos chambered barrow, Glamorgan,
      are clearly visible from above

21 The entrance to the passage grave of Bryn-Celli-Ddu on Anglesey
22 Excavation of one of the bronze age cairns at Brenig, Clwyd

23 The Chestnuts chambered tomb in Kent has only been partially restored since its excavation in 1957

24 Silbury Hill, Wiltshire, the largest prehistoric man-made hill in Europe, is probably a large chambered barrow

25 Stonehenge, isolated and majestic on Salisbury Plain, Wiltshire

26 Avebury henge monument and stone circles, Wiltshire, with the Kennet Avenue running into the distance

27 The tiny Yockenthwaite stone cirle in North Yorkshire probably marks the edge of a burial cairn

28 The entrance to the stone circle called Long Meg and her Daughters in Cumbria

29 The Devil's Arrows, more than six metres high, march across a field beside the A1 near Boroughbridge in North Yorkshire

30 In Gwent, Harold's Stones stand in a line outside the village of Trellech

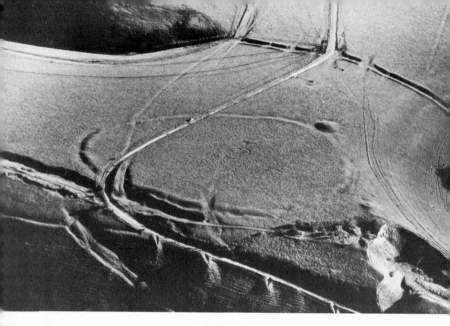

31 The neolithic causewayed camp of White Sheet Hill in Wiltshire, with a bowl-barrow clearly overlying its south-eastern side

32 The ruined bank of the central circle of the Thornborough henge monuments in North Yorkshire

post-holes inside the enclosure produced no coherent plan. Fragments of at least 418 pots were uncovered and there were more than 22,000 flint artefacts. The site was dated from the mid fourth to the late third millenium BC. Another round barrow can be seen on the south of the Heath cut by a garden fence. [G. J. Wainwright, *PPS*, 38 (1972), 1.]

4 GRIMES GRAVES, Weeting (Fig 18, p. 194)   TL:817898

In the middle of extensive conifer plantations is an area of some 7 ha of bracken-covered Breckland, its surface pock-marked by at least 360 craters. These mark the tops of buried flint mines, each separated from its neighbour by piles of flint debris, now grassed over. More shafts lie buried beneath the flatter ground to the north.

There were two types of mines at Grimes Graves. On the north exposures of flint were quarried opencast on the surface or by means of simple bell-shaped pits up to 4 m deep. Where the seam of flint dipped deeper into the chalk, hour-glass shaped shafts up to 12 m deep were dug, with three or four galleries opening off the bottoms. The galleries could be up to 9 m long, and then usually ran into the neighbouring worked-out mines. It has been estimated that some twenty men might work a mine, with ten in the galleries, and the rest carrying the flint to the surface and trimming it there. The shaft would take about four months to dig and the galleries a further two months. Once completed the mine was almost immediately back-filled with the material from a new shaft.

There are three layers of flint in the mines. The top-stone and wall-stone layers are of inferior quality, and the lowest floorstone was the material most sought. The chalk was cleared away above it, and then large slabs were removed with the aid of red-deer antlers as picks, wedges and rakes. The blocks were dragged to the bottom of the shaft and hauled to the surface with ropes and baskets. The men themselves probably reached ground level by one or two ladders fixed to the side of the shaft. Tallies of the amounts of flint removed were scratched on to the chalk walls. A single pit might produce about fifty tons of material.

Only one shaft is open to visitors at present. It is 9 m deep and the visitor climbs down an iron ladder to inspect the entrances to the galleries. Other pits not accessible to the general public include one in which the supply of flint seems to have run out. A crude statuette of the Earth Mother was set on a ledge, faced by a chalk phallus standing on a pile of flint nodules and antler picks, presumably acting as an offering to the deity in the hope of increasing the fertility of future mines. The shafts have been dated by radiocarbon to between 3000 and 2500 BC. [A. L. Armstrong, *PPSEA*, 5 (1927), 91 (outdated); R. Mercer, *BAR*, 33 (1976), 'Settlement and Economy', 101.]

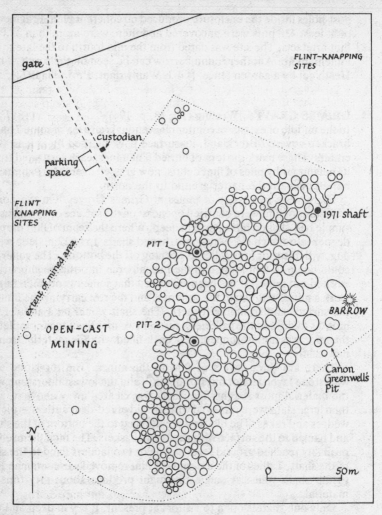

Fig 18. Grimes Graves, Norfolk

5 HARPLEY COMMON, Harpley   TF:765280

Six round barrows remain of a linear cemetery that stretches beside the
road to Harpley. Some are overgrown but all are very upstanding,
particularly one at TF:768279, which has been deliberately set on a
low ridge to give it extra height. Nothing is known of their contents,
though one barrow in the group (now destroyed) excavated in 1973
produced sherds of a collared urn and cremated bones. The barrow

194

was dated by radiocarbon to 1770 bc. [A. Lawson, *East Anglian Arch.*, 2 (1976), 45.]

6 HOLKHAM CAMP, Holkham   TF:875447
Until 1722 this fort of about 2·4 ha was separated from the mainland by a tidal marsh. It is protected on the south and east by a rampart and ditch, with traces of a second bank on the south. A steep scarp and water afford natural protection on the north and west. The only probable entrance is of the straight-through type in the southern side. The site is unexcavated and the only finds have been sherds of pottery – possibly iron age – and mesolithic flints. Holkham may well have been a beachhead for trade with north-west Europe. [A. Lawson, *Prehistoric Earthworks in Norfolk* (1978).]

7 LITTLE CRESSINGHAM   TL:861986
The round barrow west of the plantation is known locally as Bell Hill. It is the largest in Norfolk, 65 m in diameter and 4 m high. Two others lie east of the plantation and another north of the road at TL:858990. A ploughed-out barrow close to the crossroads at TL:864989 was excavated in 1977 but only two concentric ditches were found. The most important barrow in the group was destroyed some years ago, and contained the only rich Wessex culture material from East Anglia (TL:867990). At the centre was the crouched skeleton of a man. According to a phrenological report his skull showed 'a large development of the animal passions, caution and love of approbation'. Buried with him was a grooved bronze dagger with a wooden hilt, a flat bronze dagger and an elaborate amber necklace. Sheet-gold mountings were sewn to the clothing on his chest. [T. Barton, *Norfolk Archaeology*, 3 (1852), 1.]

8 SALTHOUSE HEATH, Clay and Salthouse   TG:069421 to 077423
An extensive group of about half a dozen barrows range over the Heath and are best visited when the bracken is low. Search will reveal a good Wessex-type disc-barrow and a series of small mounds, 2 or 3 m in diameter, which cover late bronze age bucket-shaped urns.

9 SEVEN HILLS, Brettenham   TL:904814
This area was badly used by the military during the two World Wars. Now only six of the Seven Hills barrows survive: two bowl-barrows and a bell-barrow in a group on the west and three bowl-barrows in an eastern group. The largest barrows are about 2 m high and 30 m in diameter. The barrows are unexcavated but damage shows that they are constructed of sand capped with chalk dug from the surrounding ditches. Large bowl-barrows can also be seen west of the A1088 on Elder Hill and Tutt Hill.

10   TASBURGH   TM:200960
Not an impressive site, but hillforts are so rare in East Anglia that it is
worth including. It is situated on a low spur of the river Tas. About
10 ha are enclosed by a single rampart and ditch, slight traces of which
can still be seen north of the church, although much of the site has been
mutilated by roads and buildings. In view of its large size it must have
been a tribal capital. [R. R. Clarke, *Arch. J,* 96 (1939), 1.]

11   WARHAM CAMP, Warham St Mary   TF:944409
Positioned on the hillside sloping down to the river Stiffkey, this is the
finest fort in Norfolk and notable for its remarkably circular plan,
which suggests that it was laid out mathematically. Its ramparts stand
3 m high and ditches 3 m deep. It is claimed that it was originally a
complete circle covering 3·6 ha, and that when the river was canalized
in the eighteenth century the south-eastern side was levelled and the
only certain original entrance, which faced east, destroyed. The site
has failed to produce iron age dating evidence, though excavation by
H. St George Gray in 1914 produced Roman material, and Rainbird
Clarke in 1959 found evidence to suggest that the inner rampart was
crowned by a palisade. Clarke also dug a rectangular enclosure with
rounded corners in the field to the north-east. It was unfinished and
seemed to date to the late first century BC. [H. St G. Gray, *Ant. J,* 13
(1933), 399.]

12   WEASENHAM PLANTATION, Weasenham All Saints   TF:853198
There were at least fifteen barrows in this group, but about half have
been destroyed by cultivation. Four, consisting of two saucers, a bowl
and a bell, are hidden in the wood north-west of the crossroads
(TF:848201). The best example is the overgrown bell-barrow in the
arable field (TF:853198). Its mound is 30 m in diameter and 2·2 m high
with a berm, inner bank, ditch and outer bank, the whole being 57 m in
diameter. Two barrows south of the bell were excavated in 1972 and are
no longer visible. One contained an unaccompanied cremation as well
as 350 beaker sherds. Further east along the minor road to Litcham
Heath is a good bowl-barrow 1·5 m high, just inside a wood
(TF:863201). Traces of two ploughed-down bowl-barrows can just be
made out in the field to the south. [L. V. Grinsell, *Ancient Burial
Mounds of England* (1953), 201.]

13   WEST RUDHAM, West Rudham and Harpley   TF:810253
This overgrown long barrow situated in a plantation is 66 m long, 18 m
wide and 2 m high. It lies north-south and is surrounded by a ditch,
shown on excavation to be 3·7 m wide and 1·2 m deep, with an
additional forecourt at the south end. A small pit was found in the
forecourt, the whole of which was covered by the barrow mound. At

Norfolk · West Rudham

the southern end of the main barrow was a platform on which a body
had been cremated. The northern end of the mound was not examined
and further burials may await discovery.

Beside the road at TF:809252 is the grass-covered Harpley long
barrow. Until recently it was ploughed and it is now very low. Its
surrounding ditch is no longer visible. A sherd of Windmill Hill pottery
has been found on the surface.

A little further east is what may be a third long barrow (at
TF:817249). It is now a large irregular mound damaged by sand
quarrying. Close by (at TF:814249) is a bell-barrow, 4 m high and 36 m
in diameter, with a shallow outer ditch and slight surrounding bank.
[A. H. A. Hogg, *Norfolk Archaeology,* 27 (1940), 315.]

NORTHAMPTONSHIRE

1 ARBURY CAMP, Chipping Warden   SP:494486

This small circular fort is probably iron age in date. It is surrounded by
a single rampart and ditch and has an entrance at the south-east. It is
overlain by a fine medieval field system.

2 BOROUGH HILL, Daventry   SP:588626

Much of the hillfort has been made inaccessible by the erection of a
wireless station on the hilltop. On the golf course at the northern end is
a very strongly defended enclosure of 1·8 ha, surrounded by a rampart,
ditch and counterscarp bank. An extra ditch was added on its weaker
southern side. This defence is cut through by an overlapping entrance.
Later in the iron age a large but weaker enclosure of 6·5 ha was added
to the fort on the south side of the hill. The only parts of this that can be
seen are on the west beside the golf course. A linear cemetery of
Romano-British barrows originally crowned the hill. These were
opened in the early nineteenth century and have since been destroyed.
A Roman bath suite, also recorded from the hill, may indicate that it
was a cult centre like Lydney, before the inhabitants were persuaded to
move north-east to Bannaventa (Whilton Lodge).

3 HUNSBURY, Hardingstone   SP:737584

Hunsbury was badly damaged by ironstone working between 1880 and
1886, when practically the whole of the interior of the fort was lowered
by about 2·4 m, giving the ramparts a more imposing appearance than
they deserve. These are now covered with trees and bushes, and
encircle 1·6 ha with a rampart, ditch and counterscarp. A gap at the
south-east seems to have been the only prehistoric entrance. A line of
defence 72 m north of the fort and now destroyed may represent the
original extent of occupation dated to the earliest iron age. This area
was perhaps later reduced to the present circuit, with its V-shaped
ditch 12 m wide and 7·5 m deep and rubble wall with timbered inner
face. This wall was partly rebuilt in glacis style by removing the timbers
and coating it with clay in the first century BC. The quarrying revealed
some 300 storage pits, but these may have been connected with as few
as half a dozen huts. They produced evidence of agriculture, metal-
working and weaving, and curvilinear decorated pottery of Glastonbury type.

On the slope of the hill 1 km to the north a neolithic causewayed camp has recently been excavated at Briar Hill. Nothing of it is now visible. [C. Fell, *Arch. J*, 110 (1953), 212.]

4   RAINSBOROUGH CAMP, Newbottle   SP:526348

Rainsborough was the site of one of the most important excavations of recent times. It is a roughly oval hillfort enclosing 2·5 ha. It has a double bank and ditches, although the outer ditch is completely silted. The inner bank stands some 3 m high and the ditch is still 1·5 m deep in places. The only certain original entrance is in the middle of the west side. The excavations of 1961–5 showed this to be strong and complex, with stone-built semicircular guard chambers beside an entrance passage 18 m long. A double gate was hung between three posts and a bridge carried a rampart walk over the top.

The hill was occupied prior to the first period of building at the fort. This took place some time towards the end of the fifth century BC, when the inner bank was built in three tiers, each narrower than the one below, and faced with drystone walling and turves. In front was a V-shaped ditch 4 m deep and 6 m wide. The outer rampart was also stone-faced, but consisted of a single drystone wall backed with rubble and a V-shaped ditch some 4 m deep.

After about a century the site was given a thorough clean-up, the gates were rebuilt and the ditches cleaned out. Whatever the reason, it was not sufficient to stop the gateway and part of the rampart from being burned down. The skeleton of a defender was found in the guard chamber.

The fort was then deserted until the second century, when glacis ramparts were made by cleaning out the ditches and piling the material on top of the existing mounds. Plans were made to rehang the gates but everything suggests that the work was not completed. Perhaps the scare had passed.

Late in the fourth century AD a Roman building was set up outside the gate. In 1772 the site was landscaped, which involved building a drystone wall on top of the ramparts, often nowadays mistaken for iron age work. [M. Avery, *PPS,* 33 (1967), 207.]

5   THREE HILLS, Woodford   SP:961760 (centre)

Three unploughed bowl-barrows form a linear cemetery lying north-west to south-east. They touch each other and are pitted with rabbit and fox holes. Each is about 20 m in diameter and 2 m high. Nothing is known of their contents. [RCHM, *Northants,* 1 (1975), 111.]

NORTHUMBERLAND

1 ALNHAM CASTLE HILL, Alnham   NT:980109
A multivallate fort typical for this part of England, with an internal
area of about 0·3 ha. There are triple ramparts with broad ditches in
between enclosing an oval area, which contains traces of three or four
possible huts. The entrance is on the east, with the remains of a later
settlement outside it.

2 BELLSHIEL LAW, Rochester   NT:813014
Excavation has shown that this barrow is surrounded by a kerb of stone
retaining a mound of boulders. The mound projects forward into slight
horns at the eastern end. Inside this end an empty grave was found,
probably dug for the primary burial. The barrow, which lies west of a
plantation on the south side of Bellshiel Law, measures 110 m long and
18 m wide at its widest, eastern end. [A. J. W. Newbigin, *Arch. Ael.*,
13 (1936), 293.]

3 BLAWEARIE, Eglingham   NU:082223
A stone circle 11 m in diameter is all that remains of a retaining wall
around a burial cairn. The mound material had already been removed
when it was excavated by Canon Greenwell. Inside it were four grave
cists; no trace of burials remained, but one cist contained a food vessel,
another a necklace of jet beads and a flint knife. Two cists are still
visible, one with its capstone still in place. [W. Greenwell, *British
Barrows* (1877), 418.]

4 CARTINGTON, Rothbury   NU:056046
A small stone circle 4·5 m in diameter marked with eight stones. Canon
Greenwell excavated in the centre and found a hollow 50 cm square
which contained a cremation.

5 COUPLAND, Ewart   NT:940330
A few metres above the flood plain of the river Till is a plough-
damaged henge monument, 100 m in diameter with the usual bank and
internal ditch. There are wide entrances on both the north and south
sides. The site, which is in a classic position for its kind, is at present
unexcavated.

6 DEVIL'S LAPFUL, Kielder   NY:642928
Deep in the forest on the side of Castle Hill, this 60 m long cairn has
been badly damaged by sheepfolds along its north-west side and three
modern cairns on its summit. There may be horns at the northern end
marking the entrance to a burial chamber but the damage obscures
them.
   At NY:638923 is a ruined round cairn 18 m in diameter called the
Deadman. It has been opened but its contents are unknown.

7 DOD LAW, Doddington   NU:004317 (centre)
Some of the finest rock carvings in the country occur on Doddington
Moor. Many rock outcrops bear carvings and the enthusiast will have a
lengthy but rewarding search. It is not possible to describe exact
locations in a book such as this. It is best to begin your search at the
Shepherd's House. There are carvings on the rocks to the east beside
the ramparts of the hillfort. Others occur at NU:009313 and some as far
north-east as The Ringses (NU:013328). Beckensall's book gives more
detailed local information. [S. Beckensall, *Prehistoric Carved Rocks
of Northumberland* (1974), 21.]

8 DOD LAW CAMPS, Doddington
Western Camp (NU:004317), a D-shaped enclosure, is surrounded by
double ramparts 4·5 m to 6 m wide and up to 3 m high in places. There
is an entrance on the south-east and another on the north-west that
leads into a semicircular annexe protected by a single rampart. It has a
possible entrance on the west. The main camp contains a number of
huts 4–6 m across.
Middle Dod Law (NU:006317) is much the same shape, with a single
bank and ditch and traces of an additional inner bank at the north. An
entrance at the south-west is out-turned. No huts have been found,
suggesting that this was a stock enclosure.
East Dod Law (NU:008316) is an oval enclosure with a single rampart
and ditch.
   Many of the carved rocks mentioned in the previous entry lie
amongst these camps.

9 DUDDO STONE CIRCLE   NT:931437
This circle, which is nearly 10 m in diameter, stands on a low knoll.
Five stones remain, one of which has possible cup marks on it.
[*T Berwick FC*, 28 (1932), 84.]

10 FENTONHILL CAMP, Wooler   NT:979354
A palisaded enclosure, dated by radiocarbon to the ninth century BC,
has been excavated underlying the ramparts of this small oval hillfort

of 0·4 ha. Ploughing has damaged the three later ramparts which are separated by two ditches. There is a staggered entrance on the west.

11   FIVE BARROWS, Holystone   NT:953020
Traces of fourteen cairns, nine of them well preserved, can be found on Holystone Common overlooking the river Coquet. They vary in size from 0·3 m to 1 m high and from 3 m to 18 m across. The British Museum contains a number of food vessels, collared urns, bone pins and flint tools that were found here with inhumation and cremation burials.

12   FIVE KINGS, Holystone   NT:955015
In spite of their name there are only four stones on Dues Hill, spread out along a distance of 18 m and varying in height from 1·5 m to 2 m. One stone is lying on the ground.

13   GOATSTONES CIRCLE, Simonburn   NY:829748
This circle belongs to the type known by specialists as a four-poster, since a rectangular area is marked out by four stones, in this case 4·9 m apart. A turf-covered ring cairn may lie within the stones. The top of the eastern stone is carved with thirteen cup markings.

14   GREAT HETHA CAMP, Hethpool   NT:885274
A small oval fort with two massive stone ramparts that are roughly concentric, except on the east where they widen out. At this point is a slightly inturned oblique entrance, partly obscured by a building of much later date. There are numerous hollows inside the fort indicating the sites of wooden huts.

   The site overlooks a fort on Little Hetha, 0·5 km to the north; at the foot of the hill is the **Hethpool stone circle** (NT:892278). The circle is really a horseshoe of eight stones, most of which have fallen, and none of which is more than 2 m in length. There are three additional stones north-east of the circle, one of which is ring marked.

15   GREAVES ASH, Ingram   NT:965164
On a south-facing slope above the river Breamish is the most extensive group of hut circles in Northumberland, spread over something like 8 ha. At the west is a large double-walled enclosure, of which the inner wall seems to be the earlier. This is broken by a single entrance on the east, whereas the outer wall has three entrances and paddocks attached. There is a second, smaller, group of huts lying in courtyards about 30 m to the east. Altogether the two enclosures contain about forty huts. Around them are field and paddock boundaries indicating a small agricultural settlement. Some 90 m to the north-east is another nucleated settlement with about a dozen circular huts in it. The settle-

ment lasted from the iron age into the Roman period. Rectangular foundations in the vicinity seem to be part of a medieval farmstead. [G. Jobey, *Arch. Ael.,* 42 (1964), 41.]

16   HAREHAUGH CAMP, Holystone   NY:969998
This fort occupies a commanding position looking down Coquetdale. It lies on a steep-sided east-west ridge and is defended on the east by two ramparts and ditches, and on the west by three ramparts and ditches. There is an inturned entrance on the eastern side and that on the west probably passed round the northern end of the ramparts. There is a trace of a curving bank across the camp from north to south that seems to be part of an earlier phase of occupation. [G. Jobey in A. L. F. Rivet, ed., *The Iron Age in Northern Britain* (1966), 96.]

17   HEPBURN MOOR, Bewick   NU:083231
A cemetery of at least twenty-seven ditchless cairns, averaging 50 cm high and between 3 m and 6 m in diameter. The only record of contents is from the cairn with two burial cists. In the larger of these a crouched burial was found accompanied by a beaker. Its cover stone lies close by.

18   HETHA BURN, Kirknewton   NT:881275 and NT:878276
On the north-west slope of the hill below the fort are two separate rectangular settlements, unusual in that they have been scooped out of the hillside, thus constructing a series of level platforms on which huts have been built. These are visible as low walls of turf and stone. There are gardens or paddocks associated with the huts. The site probably dates from the end of the iron age.

19   HETHPOOL STONE CIRCLE   NT:892278
This untidy horseshoe-shaped setting of stones on a level knoll measures 61 m by 42 m and contains eight stones averaging 1·6 m high. There are three further stones to the north-east, one of which is ring marked. [*PSAN,* 6 (1935), 116.]

20   HUMBLETON HILL, Wooler   NT:967283
Steep slopes surround most sides of this fort, which overlooks the Till and the Glen. It has a stoutly walled central enclosure with an entrance on the north-east, leading into a less strongly walled semicircular annexe on its eastern side. One gate on the east of the annexe leads out of the fort and another on the north leads into a much larger annexe that encircles the north and west. All the enclosures contain hut circles. [G. Jobey, in A. L. F. Rivet, ed., *The Iron Age in Northern Britain* (1966), 98.]

21 KIRKHAUGH, Knaresdale with Kirkhaugh   NY:704494
A small barrow 7 m in diameter and less than 1 m high produced traces
of an inhumation burial with a gold basket-shaped earring of beaker
type. The barrow was built with an earthen core covered with rubble
and stood on a small knoll that gave it greater height. [H. Maryon,
Arch. Ael., 13 (1936), 207.]

22 LORDENSHAWS, Hesleyhurst   NZ:054993
Lordenshaws, one of a number of hillforts that border the Coquet
river, lies on a moorland spur. It has three ramparts and ditches as well
as a counterscarp bank. The inner bank is 2 m high in places and
encloses 0·3 ha. There are entrance passages through the ramparts at
the east and west. Inside are circular houses of Romano-British date,
some of which overlie the defences on the south-east. About 60 m to
the south-west is a slight bank and ditch cutting across the spur.
  About 270 m south-west of the centre of the fort are two stones with
cup-and-ring marks, one on either side of the collapsed deer park wall.
There are also six cairns (NZ:056993), one with a stone cist, and two with
retaining walls, north-east of the fort.

23 OLD BEWICK, Bewick   NU:075216
This strongly defended fort lies on the southern side of a west-facing
spur above the river Breamish. It seems to have begun as a circular
enclosure with a double rampart and ditch on the escarpment edge.
Soon a second enclosure of similar formation was added to the east in
hour-glass plan. Then the whole was enclosed with a rampart and ditch
60 m to the northern side. On the escarpment edge at the south is a
slight bank. A little excavation has taken place showing that the
ramparts are of rubble over a clay core. There are traces of possible
huts in the western enclosure, but they should not be confused with old
quarry workings for millstone.
  Between 30 m and 90 m east of the fort are half a dozen rocks bearing
cup-and-ring markings (NU:078216).

24 RAYHEUGH MOOR, Adderstone   NU:118268
Three round barrows, one of which was opened by Major Luard-
Selby in 1862. The north-western is 18 m in diameter and was once 3 m
high. At its centre was a shale sandstone cist containing a skeleton
buried with a beaker. The barrow had been carefully constructed of
sandstone and traces of a kerb were found. A second barrow of similar
size 70 m south-east of the last covered an empty grave, and a third
60 m south-east of that contained an empty stone cist. The acid soil had
probably destroyed both burials. [W. Greenwell, *British Barrows*
(1877), 413.]

25 RINGSES CAMP, Doddington   NU:013328
At the north-eastern end of Doddington Moor is a small oval fort of
about 0·3 ha enclosed by three widely spaced ramparts, with room
perhaps for a stock compound. There is an entrance at the south-east
and possibly another at the south. A search of the centre will reveal
four huts, and there are outworks of uncertain purpose to the north.

26 ROUGHTING LINN, Doddington   NT:984368
The largest inscribed rock in the county lies close to the defences of the
iron age fort. The rock measures some 18 m long and 3 m high, and is
covered with carvings which include cup marks, concentric circles and
flower-like figures. The rock is visible for some distance and must
always have been a landmark. [S. Beckensall, *Prehistoric Carved
Rocks of Northumberland* (1974), 15.]

27 ROUGHTING LINN FORT, Doddington   NT:984367
The Linn, or waterfall, lies just outside the north-east corner of this
fort. It is a roughly rectangular camp on a promontory between
streams on the north, west and south. The easier eastern approach is
guarded by at least three banks and ditches with a counterscarp. These
features are increased at the southern side. The only entrance is
inturned at the north-east corner.

28 SWINBURN CASTLE, Chollerton   NY:935753
In the grounds of the Castle is a standing stone 3·6 m high, deeply
grooved by the weather down each of the sides. On its faces are a series
of cup markings.

29 THREE KINGS, Redesdale   NT:774009
This stone circle in Redesdale Forest is 3·4 m in diameter and belongs
to the type with four stones known as 'four-poster'. It had an internal
ring cairn which had already been robbed when excavated in 1971.
[A. Burl, *Arch. Ael.*, 49 (1971), 37.]

30 THREE STONE BURN, Ilderton   NT:972205
An oval ring of thirteen stones, measuring 36 m by 29 m, with only five
of them still standing. The surviving stones range up to 1·7 m high on
the northern side. The excavators in the nineteenth century found
spreads of charcoal on the inside, suggesting ritual fires or funeral
pyres.

31 WEETWOOD MOOR, Chatton   NU:024282
Following the track beside North Plantation a barrow is passed between the footpath and the road. There are three groups of carvings on
the ridge of sandstone north of the path consisting of concentric circles

around cup marks and grooves. Other carvings are in the south-western end of the plantation, just inside the gate, on the right, leading to Fowberry Moor Farm. [S. Beckensall, *Prehistoric Carved Rocks in Northumberland* (1974), 32.]

32   WEST HILL, Kirknewton   NT:909295
On a knoll overlooking the junction of the College Burn with the river Glen are two concentric, widely spaced, oval enclosures defined by stone walls. Both have entrances on the east. There are the foundations of eight stone huts within them. At the north-west is a rectangular enclosure, also with an eastern entrance, containing four circular huts.

33   WOOLER FORT   NT:984274
A roughly oval fort divided into two halves by triple ramparts running east to west. The south-western half is surrounded by two banks with a ditch between them and an entrance on the south-east side. There is a single wall round the north-west half, but this is tripled at the northern end, where there is an entrance. The central triple rampart is breached by an entrance which has an inturn on the north-west side. Slight walls divide up the fort, but definite huts have not been recognized.

34   YEAVERING BELL, Old Yeavering   NT:928293
This hillfort of 5·2 ha encloses the two summits and the saddle between of a hill that rises to a height of 360 m above sea level. The single stone rampart is 4 m wide, with entrances midway along the north and south sides, and a third on the north-east. At the east and west ends are small crescentic annexes, the latter with an entrance at its mid-point. The centre of the fort is riddled with hollows and scoops which mark the sites of about 130 circular huts. The eastern summit is ringed by a trench which held a wooden palisade nearly 50 m in diameter, and earlier than some of the house platforms. It was excavated in the nineteenth century. More recent excavations produced scraps of Roman Samian ware and coins, and showed that two rectangular huts overlay circular ones. It is not known whether there is any relationship between the hillfort and the Anglo-Saxon royal town of Ad Gefrin at the foot of the Bell. [G. Jobey, *Arch. Ael.*, 43 (1965), 35.]

NOTTINGHAMSHIRE

1   OXTON CAMP, Oxton   sk:634532

Only 0·6 ha in extent, this small fort on Robin Hood Hill has a single rampart, ditch and counterscarp on the west, and three banks and ditches on the east. There is an entrance through the centre of the north-west side and another at the south-east. A large mound outside the north-west entrance some 6 m high is called Robin Hood's Pot. It seems to have been a round barrow and has produced a pot of Roman coins and a Saxon burial.

OXFORDSHIRE

1 ALFRED'S CASTLE, Ashbury SU:277822

This is said to be the meeting place of King Alfred's army before the battle of Ashdown in AD 871 and there may well be some truth in the tradition, for Saxon material has been found at the site, together with iron age and Romano-British pottery. The fort is roughly hexagonal in shape, and a single rampart and ditch enclose 0·8 ha. Only on the south-east is there an extra defensive ditch together with an original entrance. The entrance on the north-west may also be original. The ramparts seem to have been stone-faced and John Aubrey (1670) records their being 'spoil'd and defac'd by digging for the Sarsden-Stones to build my Lord Craven's house in the Park'. Aerial photographs show that the fort is on the south side of a 3 ha enclosure, which is now visible only from the air. [M. A. Cotton and P. Wood, *Berks. AJ*, 58 (1960), 44.]

2 BLEWBURTON HILL, Blewbury SU:547862

Blewburton, situated on a low outlier of the chalk downs, is not an impressive fort. The eastern half has been badly damaged by ploughing and the western ramparts are not particularly upstanding; the importance of the site lies in the extensive excavations that have taken place there. The site began as a stockaded camp of 2 ha at the western end of the hill, probably dating from the sixth or fifth century BC. Inside were storage pits and huts. The fort proper, enclosing 4 ha, was built about 400 BC. Its rampart was faced with timber at the front and back, tied together with cross-beams and filled with chalk rubble. Outside was a deep V-shaped ditch. A gate on the west side was 11 m wide and may have had a bridge over it. It was given extra strength by the presence of a defensive ditch 2 m deep inside the entrance and later filled in.

After being deserted for a period, Blewburton was reoccupied about 100 BC and the rampart rebuilt in 'dump' style; the ditch was re-dug and a counterscarp bank topped with a palisade added. The entrance was remodelled and faced with drystone walling. The fort was abandoned, perhaps by the middle of the first century BC, possibly as a result of Belgic expansion. The skeletons of ten horses were found in the fort, mainly in an apparent ritual deposit at the entrance. [D. W. Harding, *The Iron Age in the Upper Thames Basin* (1972), 45.]

3   BOZEDOWN CAMP, Whitchurch   su:643783

Some 22 ha in extent and circular in shape, this fort is situated in a commanding position which overlooks the Thames valley on its southern side. It has been extensively damaged by cultivation, but where it is best preserved, in the 'Wilderness' to the north of Bozedown House, a strong rampart and ditch are visible, with traces of a counterscarp bank. There seems to have been an angular entrance on the northwestern side, but this is far from certain, and looks rather out of keeping with the rounded plan of the rest of the fort. A trial excavation in 1953 produced a few scraps of iron age A pottery and part of a shale bracelet. [P. Wood, *Oxoniensia*, 19 (1954), 10.]

4   CHASTLETON CAMP, Chastleton   sp:259283

This is a circular fort, 125 m in diameter and enclosing 1·2 ha. It has substantial walls 6 m wide and in places 3·6 m high, which are overgrown and tree-clad. Minor excavations in 1928–9 showed that the inner face of the wall was of large blocks of stone, probably supporting a rubble core. The outer face was not seen, nor was a surrounding ditch detected. There are two entrances, one on the east and the other on the north-west. Although lots of iron age pottery was recovered, and hearths and paving were found, the excavation failed to recognize any buildings. The camp may have been designed as a cattle corral. [E. T. Leeds, *Ant. J,* 11 (1931), 382.]

5   CHERBURY CAMP, Kingston Bagpuize   su:374963

This iron age site of 3·6 ha was once on a low-lying island surrounded by marshy ground. Today the area has been drained and provides good farmland. The island was approached from the north-east where an entrance penetrated the three ramparts and ditches and minor counterscarp bank that surrounded this oval fort. Excavations in 1939 showed that the ditches were broad, but fairly shallow, and that the inner rampart was faced with drystone walling both inside and out. The other ramparts were of simple (though probably later) dump construction. A rutted metalled roadway approached the gate which had post-holes at its outer end. The entrance passageway had also been drystone lined. Pottery, now in the Ashmolean Museum, Oxford, suggested occupation from the first century BC to the first century AD. [J. S. P. Bradford, *Oxoniensia*, 5 (1940), 13.]

6   CHURN FARM, Blewbury   su:515837

East of Churn Farm are three barrows in a row, measuring respectively 27 m, 38 m and 24 m in diameter and all 1 m high. A cremation was found in one of them in 1848. To the south-east of the farm (SU:520833) are two bell-barrows that have been dug into on a number of occasions. The larger produced a cremation accompanied by a riveted bronze dagger. **Churn Knob** (SU:522847) and **Fox Barrow** (SU:506831) are also worth seeking out. [L. V. Grinsell, *Berks. A J*, 40 (1936), 42.]

7 **DYKE HILLS, Dorchester-on-Thames**   SU:574937
On low-lying ground between the Thames and the Thame, this great enclosure contains 46 ha. Two banks and a broad intervening ditch run east-west and cut off the promontory formed by a loop in the rivers. The earthworks were partly levelled in the last century, but still stand 3 m high in places. The entrance was probably on the east side where the earthworks curve south, parallel to the Thame. Aerial photographs show that the interior of the site is packed with huts, pits and gullies. The only excavation, by Pitt-Rivers in 1870, produced hand-made pottery as well as a wheel-turned sherd. This suggests that the site may have been an earlier iron age defended enclosure occupied during the Belgic period. [D. W. Harding, *The Iron Age in the Upper Thames Basin* (1972), 54.]

8 **GRIM'S DITCH, East and West Hendred**   SU:423845 to 542833
Although this earthwork was probably once more or less continuous, it is now broken into a number of sections, largely as a result of agriculture. Its antiquity is demonstrated by the fact that a number of parish boundaries run along it. Its date is not known, but such earthworks are generally considered to be of the iron age, often defining boundaries rather than defences. The greatest height of the earthwork from the crest of the bank to the ditch bottom is 1·8 m.

9 **GRIM'S DITCH, Mongewell**
An 8 km length of dyke runs east from the river Thames and ends south-east of Nuffield Common. It seems to be part of the Chiltern Grim's Ditch, but the wide gap before the next section to the east starts is difficult to explain. It is provisionally dated to the iron age. Good viewing points are at SU:636606 and SU:669869. [R. Bradley, *Oxoniensia*, 33 (1968), 1.]

10 **GRIM'S DITCH, North Oxfordshire**   (various)
During the first century BC Belgic iron age people expanding westwards from Hertfordshire decided to isolate an area between the rivers Evenlode on the west and Glyme on the east with north-facing dykes. At least five sections seem to have been constructed across stretches of open country, in between areas of woodland. The best sections to view are as follows:

Blenheim Great Park (SP:427183). The ditch crosses the drive 0·8 m south of the Ditchling Gate. A gap in the dyke seems to have been used by the Romans as a crossing place for their road, Akerman Street.
Glympton Farm (SP:423197). Approached along a cart track off the A34, it runs parallel to the main road.
Out Wood and **Berrings Wood** (SP:413208). Footpath through Berrings Wood from the A34 (at SP:419209). Both butt-ends of this section of the dyke can be clearly seen.
Home Farm (SP:402215). Beside the minor road from Over Kiddington to Charlbury, through Ditchley Park.
Model Farm (SP:383209). Approach from minor road to Model Farm and follow the path east beside the dyke. The east butt-end of this section is clearly visible. [N. Thomas, *Oxoniensia,* 22 (1957), 11.]

11 **HOAR STONE, Enstone** SP:378237
Here are the ruined remains of a chambered long barrow. Three rough stones, the longest 2·7 m high, form a roofless U-shaped chamber with an opening facing east. It is just possible that these were once the portals and door slab of the type of monument more common in Wales called a portal dolmen. Three other stones lie in front of the chamber and must once have been part of it. The mound of the barrow, which was 1 m high in 1824, has now disappeared. [O. G. S. Crawford, *Long Barrows of the Cotswolds* (1925), 159.]

12 **HOAR STONE, Steeple Barton** SP:458241
A long barrow at least 15 m in length, with a pile of broken stones at its east end; it seems to be the remains of a chambered barrow, probably with a false entrance, described in 1845. [O. G. S. Crawford, *Long Barrows of the Cotswold* (1925), 162.]

13 **KNIGHTON BUSHES, Compton Beauchamp** SU:300830 (centre)
On the hillside to the west of Knighton Bushes are the ploughed-down remains of something like 800 ha of Celtic fields, together with at least three Romano-British settlements and a cross-dyke. The fields stretch almost from the Ridgeway in the north to Ashdown Park on the west. Of the settlements little remains. One lies due west of Knighton Bushes Plantation (at SU:298831). A second rectangular settlement lies between Woolstone Down and Uffington Down. It is on the northern edge of the fields (SU:302853) but is separated from them by a massive cross-ridge dyke. The third settlement is polygonal in shape and encloses 0·8 ha. It lies east of the small wood at Compton Bottom (SU:286843) and produced a quantity of Romano-British material when excavated in 1950. Ancient trackways pass through the Celtic fields and meet south of the Knighton Bushes Plantation site. [P. P. Rhodes, *Oxoniensia,* 15 (1950), 1.]

14 LYNEHAM BARROW   sp:297211
A single upright stone 1·8 m high and 1·5 m broad stands at the
north-east end of this long barrow and may once have formed a false
entrance. The remains of two burial chambers were found on the south
side in 1894 and skulls and animal and human bones were found
scattered through the mound. Two Saxon graves were also uncovered
at this time. The mound is still 50 m long but has been severely
damaged by ploughing, as can be seen from the numerous stones and
bones lying on the field surface today. [O. G. S. Crawford, *Long
Barrows of the Cotswolds* (1925), 163.]

15 LYNEHAM CAMP, Lyneham   sp:299214
A small circular enclosure of 2·6 ha surrounded by a single stone-built
rampart and ditch. The rampart is still 1·8 m high and is faced with
stone inside and out. The ditch has been filled in almost everywhere,
but can still be seen in the wood to the west. It is U-shaped, 2·1 m deep
and 5·5 m wide. The gap on the north is probably the original entrance.
This Oxfordshire fort, like Chastleton and Windrush, should probably
be seen as a cattle corral rather than as a defensive monument.
[B. Bayne, *Oxoniensia*, 22 (1957), 1.]

16 MADMARSTON, Swalcliffe   sp:386389
This important site has been virtually destroyed by ploughing, but can
be clearly seen from the Swalcliffe–Tadmarton road, 1 km south,
especially in winter. Madmarston was 2 ha in extent, and was surrounded by double ramparts and ditches, except on the south and west
where they were trebled. There was a gate in the centre of the south
side. Pottery indicates occupation in the third century BC, and again in
the fourth century AD, both connected with agriculture. [P. J. Fowler,
Oxoniensia, 25 (1960), 3.]

17 ROLLRIGHT STONES, Little Rollright   sp:296308
'Corroded like wormeaten wood by the harsh jaws of time,' wrote
William Stukeley in the eighteenth century. This is one of the best
preserved and most dramatic British stone circles, spoilt only by its
situation beside a busy road. The circle, known as the King's Men, is
31 m in diameter (38 megalithic yards) and contains about seventy-
seven blocks of gnarled and weathered limestone. There is a possible
entrance on the north. About 73 m north-east of the circle is a single
eroded outlying stone called the King Stone, 2·4 m high and 1·5 m
wide. Professor Thom has suggested that it is aligned on the rising of
the star Capella in 1790 BC, but that date is rather late. Three hundred
and sixty metres east-south-east are the ruins of a burial chamber
called the Whispering Knights. Folklore has it that the Rollright
Stones are a king and his army, turned to stone by a witch; the knights

were petrified whilst plotting together in the distance. [L. V. Grinsell, *The Rollright Stones and their Folklore* (1977).]

18   SEGSBURY CAMP, Letcombe Regis   SU:385845
One of the larger Oxfordshire hillforts, Segsbury has an area of 10·5 ha. It has a single bank and ditch defence, with a counterscarp on the north-west side. The bank seems to have been stone faced, sarsen stones having been 'placed in the Banks of the Dike or Trench in form of a Wall'. These were 'vast stones, being a red flint, some of which a cart will hardly draw'. Thomas Hearne, who wrote this at the beginning of the eighteenth century, described cartloads of stones being removed for local building purposes. The main entrance on the east connects the fort to good pasture land and springs. This entrance is flanked by an out-turned rampart. The other breaks in the rampart are almost certainly modern. In 1871 excavations by Dr Phené revealed a small stone 'cist' in the southern rampart, containing human bones, flint scrapers, pieces of pottery and what seems to have been the *umbo* of a shield. Whilst this sounds like a later Saxon burial, there is a possibility that it was an iron age dedicatory burial as at Maiden Castle. [M. A. Cotton, *Berks. AJ*, 60 (1962), 43.]

19   SINODUN CAMP, Little Wittenham   SU:570924
This fort is magnificently sited on a steep-sided hill, with wide views in all directions, especially along the Thames valley. It is kidney-shaped, encloses about 4 ha and is defended by a deep ditch, the material from which has been thrown downhill to make an outer rampart. There is little trace of an inner bank, though this could easily have become buried by soil creeping down the hill from above. The entrance on the west is a simple gap. Finds of iron age pottery have been made inside the camp and outside the entrance. The **Brightwell Barrow** is clearly visible about 1 km to the east. It has produced iron age pottery. [P. P. Rhodes, *Oxoniensia*, 13 (1948), 18.]

20   SLATEPITS COPSE, Wychwood   SP:329165
This chambered long barrow is 30 m long, 14 m wide and nearly 2 m high. It has a much ruined burial chamber at the eastern end, composed of three upright stones, but no capstone. A gamekeeper found three human skulls in the chamber in the 1850s. [O. G. S. Crawford, *Long Barrows of the Cotswolds* (1925), 164.]

21   UFFINGTON CASTLE, Uffington   SU:299864
Two banks and an intervening ditch surround about 3·2 ha of land. They are broken by an entrance facing north-west. At this point the bank curves outwards along both sides of the entrance causeway and runs along the outside of the ditch for some distance. Digging by Martin

Atkins about 1850 showed that the inner bank seemed to be faced with sarsen stones and also contained two rows of post-holes, but it is not clear how they relate to each other. [M. A. Cotton, *Berks. AJ*, 60 (1962), 48.]

22 UFFINGTON WHITE HORSE   su:302866

Although a case has recently been made out for a Saxon date for the White Horse, most prehistorians still prefer to see it as a relic of the late iron age, probably a tribal emblem of the Dobunni or Atrebates, who may have occupied the nearby Uffington Castle hillfort. The design of the horse is similar to pictures that occur on iron age coins. The curious beaked animal measures 112 m from tip of tail to ear and has been carved through the turf into the chalk. In the past the outline of the horse was scoured every few years by local villagers who celebrated the event with festivities that lasted several days. Nowadays the Department of the Environment undertakes the work in a less romantic way.

There are numerous legends connected with the horse. It was, for example, considered lucky to wish when standing on the eye of the beast. The flat-topped hill immediately below the horse is known as Dragon Hill. It was here, according to tradition, that St George slew the dragon. In spite of its curious shape the hill seems to be natural. [L. V. Grinsell, *White Horse Hill* (1939).]

23 WAYLAND'S SMITHY, Ashbury   su:281854

Situated in a clump of beech trees beside the Ridgeway, this long barrow has been proved by excavations in 1962–3 to be of two periods of construction. In Period I a wooden mortuary chamber had been built with a sarsen stone floor. On this the bodies of fourteen persons had been laid. Some of the bones lay in piles, suggesting that they had been stored elsewhere before being brought to the tomb. When the mortuary chamber was considered full sarsen boulders were placed around it, and chalk from two flanking ditches was piled over the top, the whole being kept in position by a kerb of boulders. This was all covered over in Period II and cannot be seen today.

The Period II barrow was a trapezoidal mound of chalk 55 m long, 14·5 m wide at the southern end, tapering to 6 m at the north. Great ditches on either side 1·8 m deep and 4·6 m wide provided the chalk, which was held in place by a continuous kerb of stones. At the southern end of the barrow stood six large sarsen stones averaging 3 m high and flanking the entrance to the burial chamber. Cross-shaped in plan, this consisted of a passage 6·7 m long with a single chamber on either side. Where the passage roof still exists it is 1·8 m high and each chamber is 1·4 m high. Excavations in the western chamber in 1919 revealed the

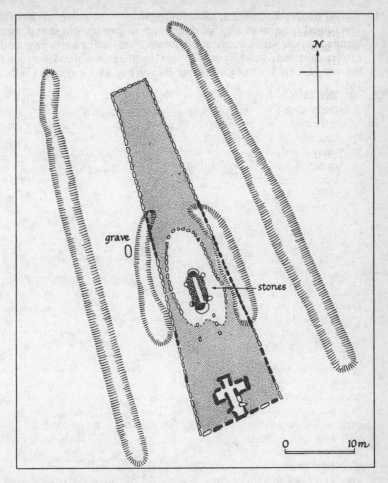

Fig 19. Wayland's Smithy, Oxfordshire

skeletons of eight people including a child. The barrows can be dated by radiocarbon to between 3700 and 3400 BC.

The stories of Wayland Smith have been told by many writers, including Scott and Kipling. In 1758 Anna Stukeley wrote 'the country people have a notion of an invisible smith living there; and if a traveller's horse happens to loose a shoe, leave him there, and a penny, and your horse will be well shoed'. [R. J. C. Atkinson, *Antiquity*, 39 (1965), 126.]

24 **WHISPERING KNIGHTS, Little Rollright**   SP:299308
The ruined remains of a burial chamber with four upright stones, two
forming portals with a doorstone between them, facing south-east, and
a fallen capstone. Stukeley in 1746 says that the stones stood in a round
barrow. [O. G. S. Crawford, *Long Barrows of the Cotswolds* (1925),
165.]

SHROPSHIRE

1 THE BERTH, Baschurch   sj:429237

A single bank and ditch enclose an area of 2·5 ha around a low hill. On the east is a strongly inturned entrance, which is approached from the south by an artificial causeway. The causeway continues north-eastwards to a second smaller enclosure, perhaps used for stock or as a dam to trap water coming down the hillside. Excavation has shown that the rampart was a slight affair, faced on the outside with large stones. Finds include iron age pottery, a La Tène III brooch and some Roman ware.

2 BURROW CAMP, Hopesay   so:382831

This oval fort of 2 ha, high above Hopesay, is surrounded by forest. It is encircled by a double ring of defences composed of bank, ditch and counterscarp bank, with an additional bank and ditch on the south and west. Four entrances cut the ramparts, each forming a passageway. The one at the south-west is protected by converging ramparts; at the south there is an elaborate inturn; at the south-east is a direct passage 60 m long, whilst at the pointed north-east end a direct approach is deflected by the oblique inturn of the inner rampart. Inside the main defences on the south side air photographs show clear traces of an abandoned earlier univallate defence.

3 BURY DITCHES, Lydbury North   so:327837

There is a steep climb through thick woodland up to this fine little fort of 2·5 ha. Although not proven by excavation this fort seems to be of at least two periods. At first the hill was surrounded by two banks, with an intermediate ditch only on the south side. On the north there is a gap of 3–15 m between these banks, which may have provided an area for animal pens. Later the north-western side was strengthened by adding two further banks with an intermediate ditch. There are two complex entrances. On the north-east a slightly oblique approach gives way to a long inturned passage 60 m long. The innermost ends are stepped outwards for 6 m in such a way as to suggest the presence of guard chambers. At the southern entrance the outer western rampart curves round the inturned inner eastern end providing an oblique passage nearly 80 m long in which the attacker exposed his right flank before facing a final gate with another hint of a guard chamber on the northern side. [J. Forde-Johnston, *Hillforts* (1976), 162.]

4 BURY WALLS, Weston-under-Redcastle   SJ:576275
Set well back above the headwaters of the river Roden, this superb promontory fort encloses 5·5 ha, with steep, tree-covered, univallate defences on all sides except the north. Here, as one approaches along the gentle slope from Bury Farm are two banks and ditches, the inner being one of the most enormous hillfort ramparts in the country, at least 11 m high above the ditch. The entrance has cut a deep passage through the natural rock at the north-east corner, and was probably inturned southwards between the rampart and rock outcrop to the left inside the fort. There is a spring at the north-west corner of the interior, and another outside the gate on the north-east. Traces of an internal road and huts were found in the 1930s. [*T Shrop. AS,* 46 (1931), 35.]

5 CAER CARADOC, Church Stretton   SO:477953
Visible for many miles, Caer Caradoc clings to a rocky windswept ridge, making one wonder how on earth the Cornovii could have existed in it. It is a long, narrow fort of 2·5 ha, not only relying on its natural slope for defence, but being protected also by an inner quarry ditch and bank of stone or natural rock outcrops, then 20 m of natural hillslope before an outer ditch and counterscarp bank appear. The inner quarry ditch is missing at the south end of the fort; instead an extra line of wall is present. An artificial trackway leads up the eastern face of the hill to an entrance at the south-east. This is inturned with clear indications of a guard chamber on the south. For sheer impressiveness and tenacity on the part of the builders Caer Caradoc takes a lot of beating. [*VCH Shropshire,* I (1908), 361.]

6 CAER CARADOC, Clun   SO:310758
Almost every hilltop in this part of Shropshire carries a hillfort. Caer Caradoc, though only 1 ha in extent, is one of the finest, with commanding views in all directions. On the steep south-east side is a single rampart, ditch and counterscarp. On both sides there are extensive and deep internal quarry ditches, which have led to their interpretation partly as hut platforms, but this is unlikely. Entrances at the east and west are inturned, and that at the west may have had guard chambers. Outside the easily accessible west entrance an extra bank and ditch lies across the direct approach, acting as a kind of hornwork. Opposite, on the northern side of the entrance, the outer bank rises up higher than elsewhere, as though to complement the hornwork in the form of a slinging platform.

There are three forts all assigned to Caratacus, but there is no reason for associating him with any of them. [*VCH Shropshire,* I (1908), 362.]

7   CAYNHAM CAMP, Caynham   SO:545737

This is a rectangular hillfort of 4 ha sited on a ridge above a tributary of the Teme. On the north, steep hill slopes make only a single line of rampart and ditch necessary. On the other sides these are doubled, the inner rampart being of considerable size. Excavations by Peter Gelling show that there were four phases in the history of the fort's defences. At first the rampart was timber-laced with a rock-cut ditch about 3 m deep, but this was refashioned as a small, crude, dumped-stone rampart. Later this was enlarged and given a better stone facing, before it was finally altered by raising its height. There is a strongly inturned entrance at the eastern end of the fort whilst at the west is an annexe within the main rampart. There are signs of outworks at both the east and west ends of Caynham. Storage pits and post-holes have been revealed by aerial photography and confirmed by excavations. Although very little occupational material was found, making dating difficult, considerable quantities of carbonized wheat were recovered. A large semicircular building was also located. [P. Gelling, *T Shrop. AS*, 57 (1962–3), 91.]

8   THE DITCHES, Shipton   SO:563943

Situated in Mogg Forest above Wenlock Edge School, this is an oval fort of 2 ha protected by three ramparts and ditches. The rampart stands 4·5 m high in places. There are two gaps in the earthworks. The antiquity of that on the south-west is uncertain, but the entrance on the north-east is protected by a strong passageway and is obviously of iron age date.

9   EARL'S HILL, Pontesbury   SJ:408046

A rocky escarpment marks the eastern edge of this steep-sided hillfort and a bank, ditch and occasional counterscarp surround the remaining sides, enclosing 1·2 ha. Lying roughly north-south, it is oval in shape with a simple but strongly inturned entrance at the northern end. The entrance at the south seems to be modern, but it provides the only access to an annexe of 1·6 ha which continues south-west along the ridge. North of the main fort entrance is a cross-dyke with a central entrance, and 120 m north of that again is another dyke, with an inturned entrance clearly relating it to the main site. There is a small oval earthwork 550 m north of the main fort entrance. Although it encloses only 0·3 ha it has an inner and outer rampart and ditches and a counterscarp bank. [J. Forde-Johnston, *Arch. J*, 119 (1962), 66.]

10   HOARSTONE CIRCLE, Chirbury   SO:324999

This circle, 23 m in diameter, is situated on a dry island amidst boggy peatland. All of its thirty-eight stones are less than 1 m in height, except for one at the centre which is just 1 m high. There are two small mounds on the north-west of the circle which are probably barrows. [W. F. Grimes in I. Ll. Foster and L. Alcock, eds., *Culture and Environment* (1963), 127.]

11 MITCHELL'S FOLD, Chirbury   so:304983
This circle is about 27 m in diameter and contained sixteen stones of which ten are still standing, the tallest being 1·85 m high. The stones are very irregularly spaced and it is clear that there were once may more. It is possible that there was once a central stone. The circle is visible for some distance. On a cairn 70 m to the south-west is an outlying block of stone known locally as 'the altar'. [W. F. Grimes in I. Ll. Foster and L. Alcock, eds., *Culture and Environment* (1963), 125.]

12 NORDY BANK, Clee   so:576847
A small D-shaped fort of 1·6 ha on a low west-facing spur of Brown Clee Hill. The defences consist of a rampart, ditch and counterscarp, the former rising nearly 2 m above the interior. On the north and north-west are traces of an outer rampart. There are a number of breaks in the defence, but only that with obvious inturns on the south-west can be safely identified as original.
    The twin summits of Brown Clee Hills are crowned by two other forts: **Abdon Burf** to the north (so:595866) is 6·5 ha in extent and enclosed by stone walls with opposing single-gap entrances, whilst to the south **Clee Burf** (so:593844) is difficult to sort out from the natural irregularities of the hilltop. [*VCH Shropshire* (1908), 371.]

13 NORTON CAMP, Culmington   so:447819
A circular fort, wooded on the north and west, enclosing about 5·2 ha. The northern side is very steep and protected only by a single massive rampart with inner quarry ditch. There are two banks and ditches on the other sides and, on the south-west, a short third line. There are entrances at the east and south-east, where the inner rampart ends turn outwards. The south-eastern entrance is slightly oblique and forms a passage 46 m long.

14 OLD OSWESTRY, Selattyn   so:296310
This is one of the more complex of England's hillforts; it encloses 5·3 ha and in parts has as many as seven ramparts. It was excavated by Professor W. J. Varley in 1939, who has suggested the chronological sequence of the earthworks.
    An undefended group of circular timber-built huts was at first constructed on the hilltop. These had been deserted for some time before two ramparts were built, encircling the hill. They were faced with stone at front and back and had accompanying ditches and inturned en-

trances at the east and west. Circular stone huts stood inside the enclosure.

Next, two further banks and ditches were built round the circuit and the inner rampart was enlarged. Yet further changes took place when two massive banks were constructed round the base of the hill, making most of the other defences obsolete. On either side of the long western entrance are a series of deep hollows and ridges, which seem to act as buttresses to the upper rampart, which is built of unstable gravel. They could not have been cattle pens, for they have no entrances; nor were they ponds, since they slope downhill. The sides of the western entrance were walled in stone. The results of the excavations have not yet been published, but the fort is likely to date from between the third century BC to the first century AD. [W. J. Varley, *Arch. J*, 105 (1948), 41.]

15   ROBIN HOOD'S BUTT, Bromfield   SO:490779
A round barrow about 4 m high and 27 m in diameter covered the remains of a child of about twelve to fourteen and a bronze knife. The body may have been burnt under the mound. Four barrows on the race course (SO:495776) have been flattened since they were dug in 1884, revealing cremations. [*T Shrop. AS,* 8 (1884–5), 445.]

16   THE ROVERIES, Lydham   SO:325925
A kidney-shaped fort of 4 ha protected by a single wall with an outer vertical drystone face and no accompanying ditch. At the north-eastern corner is a long inturned entrance with rectangular guard chambers and the holes for a massive gate with a bridge over the top. This can still be seen as left by the pre-war excavators. Opposite the entrance, across the valley, was a tiny bivallate fort of 0·4 ha. This has now been destroyed by forestry clearance. It must have been an outpost observing dead ground and preventing surprise attack. At the south-west corner of the Roveries is a simple entrance gap. The site has produced no iron age pottery, though fragments of neolithic wares have been found.

17   TITTERSTONE CLEE, Bitterley   SO:592779
At 533 m above sea-level this is not only one of the highest, but also one of the larger of British hillforts, enclosing 28·8 ha. It is defended by an earth and rubble bank without a ditch. There are two entrances, of which the southern is the more important and inturned; the other is at the north. Excavations in 1932 suggested that the fort was built in two phases. In the first the rampart was revetted with timber, and the southern entrance was timber lined with a bridge over the top. Later trapezoidal stone guard chambers were inserted behind the gate. The only finds from the excavations were one flint flake and two pebbles.

There are traces of hut circles on the eastern side of the fort. The south-western side has been badly damaged by quarrying. The present radar installation does not prevent visitors from viewing the fort. [B. St J. O'Neil, *Arch. Camb.*, 89 (1934), 83.]

18 THE WREKIN, Wellington Rural   SO:630083

A long, narrow, craggy ridge is crowned by this fort of some 8 ha. There is a small inner enclosure of only 2·8 ha. This was protected by a flat-topped bank some 6 m wide with conspicuous inturned entrances through it at the north-east and south-west. The larger outer rampart is in places single, in others double, depending on the local topography. It also has a long inturned entrance at the north-east. Later the inner rampart was enlarged in 'dump' style, possibly with a stone rampart walk. The south-western entrance was extended inwards and poorly built stone guard chambers were constructed. Rows of small square buildings have been found between the outer and inner walls. Storage pits have produced pottery from as early as 300 BC. [K. M. Kenyon, *Arch. J*, 99 (1942), 99.]

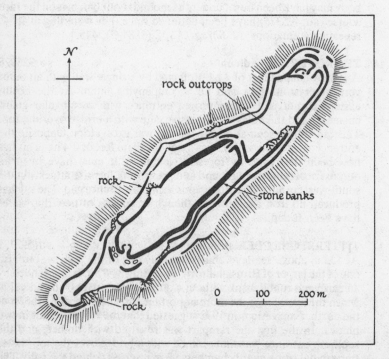

Fig 20. The Wrekin, Shropshire (after K. M. Kenyon)

SOMERSET

1 ALDERMAN'S BARROW, Exford ss:837423
A round barrow 27·4 m in diameter and 1·2 m high marks the boundaries of three parishes. It is covered with heather and seems to be unopened.

2 ASHEN HILL, Chewton Mendip st:539520
A cemetery of eight round barrows between 1·5 m and 2·5 m high. All were opened by the Rev. John Skinner in 1815, who found cremations in each, often in a cinerary urn. The second from the east also held five amber beads and a blue glass bead, a grape cup and a bronze knife dagger with traces of a wooden sheath. [L. V. Grinsell, *Somerset Barrows*, 2 (1971), 98.]

3 BEACON BATCH, Burrington st:485571
On the summit of Black Down Heath are ten barrows, of which two are possible bell-barrows. They are mostly between 1 and 2 m high and about 6 m in diameter. Most have diggers' hollows in the summits, but nothing is known of their contents. [L. V. Grinsell, *Somerset Barrows*, 2 (1971), 81, 93.]

4 BEACON HILL BARROWS, Ashwick st:635462
A group of about a dozen barrows averaging a metre high, of which five are in a field, the rest in a wood. There is a possible long barrow, but this could be a number of round barrows ploughed together. At the west is a doubtful bell-barrow. Most of the mounds were opened in the nineteenth century, when cremations and urns were found. [L. V. Grinsell, *Somerset Barrows*, 2 (1971), 88.]

5 BRENT KNOLL, Brent Knoll st:341510
This sub-triangular hillfort of 1·6 ha crowns an isolated hill above the Somerset Levels. It is surrounded by a single rampart and ditch, and has in addition been scarped on the west and south sides to make it more difficult to gain entry. The entrance seems to have been in the middle of the east side where there are traces of outworks. Roman pottery and coins have been found in the ploughed central area, which has been damaged by quarrying. (National Trust)

6 CHEDDAR CAVES   ST:466539

There are at least three caves in the Cheddar Gorge which were inhabited by upper palaeolithic man. The most famous and easily accessible is Gough's Cave, discovered by R. C. Gough in 1893. The outer part of the cave was first occupied between 12,000 and 8000 BC, and it was re-used in iron age and Romano-British times. More than 7000 flint blades belonging to what is called the Creswellian or Cheddarian cultures have been recovered, together with carved bone and antler objects, which included two 'bâtons-de-commandement'. One of these lay beside a human burial, whilst the other was made from a human arm bone. There is an excellent little museum on the site.

At the south-west end of the Gorge is **Flint Jack's Cave** (ST:463538) which has produced a quantity of flint work. About 180 m east of Gough's Cave, and above it, is the **Soldier's Cave.** Difficult of access, it has produced flint work of the earlier Solutrean period of the upper palaeolithic, perhaps as early as 30,000 BC. [L. V. Grinsell, *The Cheddar Caves Museum* (1969).]

7 COW CASTLE, Simonsbath   SS:795374

Splendidly isolated, this little fort lies close to the junction of the White Water and the Barle. It is an oval fortification of 1·2 ha surrounded by a single stone rampart 2 m high, built in part of stone from an internal quarry ditch. There are entrances at the north-east and south-west, the latter with a small standing stone that may have been part of the doorway.

8 DEVIL'S BED AND BOLSTER, Beckington   ST:815533

A ruined long barrow lying east to west and measuring 26 m by 20 m. Its surface is scattered with stones whilst others stand at the ends. It is difficult to suggest the original form without excavation. [G. E. Daniel, *Prehistoric Chamber Tombs* (1950), 231.]

9 DOWSBOROUGH, Holford   ST:160392

At 333 m above sea-level this is one of Somerset's highest hillforts, with magnificent views across Holford and Bridgwater Bay. Unfortunately it is almost completely covered by scrub oak except along the north side, where it is clear. Oval in shape, and enclosing almost 3 ha, it is surrounded by a rampart, ditch and counterscarp. The entrance at the east end is of the simple straight-through type. There is a possible round barrow inside the fort at the west end. A little under a kilometre to the south (ST:161381) lies the **Dead Woman's Ditch,** a rampart some 1·7 m high with a ditch on the west, almost certainly forming a ranch boundary connected with Dowsborough. [L. V. Grinsell, *Prehistoric Sites in the Quantock Country* (1976), 17.]

10   ELWORTHY BARROWS, Brompton Ralph   ST:070338
On a summit of the Brendon Hills is a small fort fossilized in an incomplete state. The eastern side with its inturned entrance is more or less finished. The southern sector has a ditch and rampart mound in places, but the north has had much less work done on it. The quarry ditch has been started, and the top soil and chalk have been dumped well inside the earthwork so as not to get in the way of rampart construction. Clearly the fort was being constructed by gangs of workmen, each digging their own sector. No marking-out ditch is now visible, but later ploughing may have destroyed it. The fort is unexcavated and we have no idea why it was never finished. [R. W. Feachem, in M. Jesson and D. Hill, eds., *The Iron Age and its Hillforts* (1971), 25.]

11   GLASTONBURY and MEARE   ST:492409 and ST:446423
Nothing is visible on the surface at these two famous iron age marsh village sites except for a few humps in the fields. The best information is available in the museums in Glastonbury and Taunton and it is to these that the visitor is referred.

12   GORSEY BIGBURY, Cheddar   ST:484558
This rather inconspicuous henge monument overgrown with bracken has a bank 70 m in diameter and in places 1·5 m high, with an inner ditch originally cut into five segments. There is an entrance on the north that leads to the flat central area, some 23 m in diameter.
    The site dates from the late neolithic period but was temporarily abandoned before being used by beaker folk who left fragments of nearly 100 beakers in the ditch. Just to the west of the entrance the ditch had been dug deeper, and here in a stone cist the bodies of a man, woman and child had been buried. These were later disinterred, leaving only the man's skull in the cist, the rest of the bones being scattered in the ditch, save for the skulls of the woman and child, which were re-buried east of the entrance. [A. M. ApSimon, *PUBSS,* 14 (2) (1976), 155.]

13   HAM HILL, Stoke-sub-Hamdon   ST:484164
One of the largest forts in England, the perimeter measures 4·8 km and it encloses 85 ha. On this information alone the site must surely qualify as an oppidum of the Durotriges. It dominates an outcrop of oolitic limestone, the source of the famous Ham Stone used in thousands of buildings throughout southern Britain. This stone has been the undoing of the fort, for it has been badly mauled by quarrying, particularly on the west, but the quarrying has also revealed many archaeological finds from time to time. The site is L-shaped, consisting of a large rectangular area on the south and a triangular extension to the north. The defences are double ramparts and ditches, except on the north-

west and south-west, where they are tripled. There is no certainty about original entrances. There seems to be inturning on the south-east where the Stoke–Odcombe road cuts the ramparts, and at the point where the north-west spur meets the northern face of Stroud Hill above The Combe. Other gaps, probably the result of quarrying, are more confusing.

From accidental discoveries it is clear that the fort was in use throughout most of the iron age. Of particular interest are a probable Belgic cremation burial in a pit and an infant burial in a stone-lined cist with a ring-headed iron pin. A wide range of pottery, chariot fittings and a splendid stylized bull's head of bronze all belong to the iron age occupation, as do currency bars and silvered bronze coins of the Durotriges. Traces of a large Roman villa have been found in the south-east of the fort. [W. A. Seaby, *Arch. J,* 107 (1950), 90.]

14   HYENA DEN, Wookey   st:533478
This small cave is 55 m south-east of the large Wookey Hole show-cave. It was explored in 1852 by Boyd Dawkins, who found a large central cavern with a narrow passage at the back. It was clearly used as a den by hyenas and other wild creatures, and the gnawed bones of innumerable ice age animals have been found, including mammoth, woolly rhinoceros and cave bear. Man also used the cave, and the remains of his fires, food and tools show that he occupied it during the Solutrean phase of the middle and upper palaeolithic. Finds can be seen in the museums at Wells, Bristol, Manchester and the Pitt Rivers Museum, Oxford. [D. T. Donovan, *PUBSS*, 7 (1954), 23.]

15   JOANEY HOW, ROBIN HOW, Luccombe   ss:908426
Three stone cairns stand on a moorland summit. To the north is Joaney How, a ditched barrow 24 m in diameter and 1·5 m high. In the centre is Robin How, 22 m across and 3 m high. The southern mound is called the Beacon and is 23 m in diameter and nearly 2 m high. Quarrying has taken place around the barrows. Nothing is recorded of their contents. [L. V. Grinsell, *Somerset Barrows*, 1 (1969), 35.]

16   MAESBURY CASTLE, Dinder and Croscombe   st:610472
This oval fort covers 6 ha. It is surrounded by a rampart and a U-shaped ditch. On the north there are traces of two minor banks and an outer ditch. On the south side the outer ditch has almost disappeared. There is a wide gap on the south-east which must be modern, while that on the north-west is probably original, with traces of outworks. There are suggestions that the rampart covers a stone wall, and that the site is of Belgic construction. [E. K. Tratman, *PUBSS*, 8 (1959), 172.]

17 OLD DOWN FIELD, Cranmore   ST: 658427
There are half a dozen round barrows beside the railway line, including
two fine bell-barrows. These latter seem to have been dug in 1827 by
Rev. J. Skinner and one again in 1869 by J. W. Flower, who found in it
a cremation with a grooved bronze dagger and knife. [L. V. Grinsell,
Somerset Barrows, 2 (1971), 103.]

18 PONTER'S BALL DYKE, Glastonbury   ST: 533377
The ridge that connects the 'island' of Glastonbury to the mainland is
cut by a dyke called Ponter's Ball. Lying at right angles to the Shepton
Mallet road it runs from marsh to marsh for a distance of 1·6 km. Its
rampart is 3·7 m high and 9 m wide, with a ditch of comparable size on
the east. Excavation has produced iron age pottery, suggesting that it
was once the boundary of the local tribe, perhaps the tribe who lived in
the Glastonbury marsh village. It may have been later adapted to suit
the dark age occupation of Glastonbury Tor. [C. A. R. Radford, in
G. Ashe, ed., *Quest for Arthur's Britain* (1968), 102.]

19 POOL FARM, West Harptree   ST: 537541
The mound of this round barrow was destroyed in 1930. Today only a
rectangular cist survives. It originally contained the cremated remains
of an adult and child. In 1956 L. V. Grinsell observed a series of
carvings on its inner (north-facing) side. These consisted of seven
human feet, ten cup-mark hollows and a horned device. The original
stone is now displayed in the City Museum, Bristol, and a reinforced
concrete copy replaces it on the site. [L. V. Grinsell, *PPS*, 23 (1957),
231.]

20 PORLOCK COMMON, Porlock   SS: 846446
Hidden behind a wall is a low stone circle of forty-three stones damaged during the last war, of which ten are still standing. Originally the
circle would have been impressive, with stones about 2 m high, but
today in their flattened state they are a sorry sight. The circle is about
24 m in diameter. [L. V. Grinsell, *Archaeology of Exmoor* (1970), 39.]

21 PRIDDY CIRCLES, East Harptree   ST: 540530 (centre)
There are four henges in a line; the three southernmost are 82 m apart,
but the northern circle is 458 m beyond. From the excavation of the
southern circle it is reasonable to assume that they each consisted of
banks of stones and turf, dug from an external U-shaped ditch, and
were retained by a double line of posts and stakes. The excavated ditch
was 1·2 m deep and 3·7 m wide. All the henges seem to have had single
entrances; in the southern two they faced north, the third faced south
and that in the fourth, northern circle has been destroyed. This northern circle is unfinished. It is noteworthy that henges are often arranged

in lines, as at Knowlton, Thornborough and Hutton Moor. [E. K. Tratman, *PUBSS*, 11 (1967), 97.]

22   PRIDDY NINE BARROWS, Priddy   ST:538516
A linear cemetery of seven large barrows, with two outliers to the north. They average 3 m high and 45 m in diameter, but little more can be said of them. The north-west mound was dug by John Skinner in 1815 and produced cremated remains. [L. V. Grinsell, *Somerset Barrows*, 2 (1971), 113.]

23   READ'S CAVERN, Churchill   ST:468584
South of the footpath from Dolebury hillfort to Burrington is a natural amphitheatre at the base of which a small entrance leads into a single large chamber, which seems to have been occupied during the late iron age. A number of people were killed when a massive roof-fall occured. Amongst the contents of the cave were a set of shackles and bronze bands from a tankard.

24   ROBIN HOOD'S BUTTS, Otterford
                    ST:230143 (north); ST:237128 (south)
Robin Hood and Little John used to throw their quoits from one to the other: you can still see the hollow where the quoits fell. That is the legend, and the hollows of former openings still show in these two groups of barrows on Brown Down. The northern cemetery lies under beech trees near a farm, where the barrows have merged into one another as a result of ploughing. Most of them are about 1·8 m high. The second group lie 1·6 km to the south. Of these only four survive. One of them had a surrounding kerb of stones and covered a cremation when it was opened in 1818. [L. V. Grinsell, *Somerset Barrows*, 1 (1969), 37.]

25   SMALL DOWN, Evercreech   ST:666406
A roughly oval fort on a limestone outcrop occupying about 2 ha. It has a single rampart, ditch and counterscarp except on the flatter, eastern side where a second rampart and ditch appears. The original entrance, 10·7 m wide, occurs in the centre of the eastern defence, and there is another original entrance to the south-east. Iron age pottery dates the camp, and burials were found inside it at the beginning of the century.
    There is a linear cemetery of fourteen round barrows in the fort. None are more than a metre high and most are 3–4 m in diameter. The Rev. John Skinner dug into a number of the barrows early in the nineteenth century and found cremations. Barrow 12 at the centre of the fort contained a fine collared urn half-full of ashes, resting on a stone slab. It is now in Taunton Museum. [*Fort*: H. St George Gray,

P Somerset A S, 50 (1905), 32. *Barrows*: L. V. Grinsell, *Somerset Barrows*, 2 (1971), 81, 106.]

26   SOUTH CADBURY CASTLE, South Cadbury   ST: 628252
South Cadbury is a steep-sided hill, trapezoidal in shape, surrounded by four sets of ramparts and ditches enclosing about 8 ha. The site has entrances at the south-west, the north-east and possibly the east. Extensive excavations from 1966 to 1970 have untangled some of its history. The earliest occupation on the hill dated from the neolithic, around 3300 B C, from which pottery, pits and a ditch have survived. In the later bronze age the people living on the hill left behind a gold bracelet, bronze objects, loom weights and more pottery. Two bronze razors and yet more pottery were contributed by the first iron age people, who lived there in an undefended settlement early in the sixth century BC.

The earliest iron age defence consisted of a small bank revetted with timber and with a small ditch in front. This dated from the middle of the fifth century BC. A period of neglect separated it from a new rampart, built about 400 BC, composed of rubble between rows of upright posts at the front and rear, and held in place by a revetment of limestone slabs along the front. The ditch had been re-cut deep into the rock.

All the four existing ramparts had been built by 200 B C, each with its ditch – except for the outer bank, which was in effect a massive counterscarp. The gateway on the south-west by this time had a pair of semi-circular guard chambers. Inside the defences round and rectangular timber buildings jostled together in what can best be described as a defended town. Everywhere there were storage pits filled with everyday refuse, including a wide range of iron age pottery.

The first century AD saw the fort defences rebuilt after a period of decay. In the centre a wooden shrine with a wide veranda was built, and in front of it twenty sacrificial animals were buried. The fort's end came in the Roman period, but not at the hands of Vespasian, as might have been expected. Evidence showed that between AD 70 and 80 a violent end overcame men, women and children whose bones were found scattered in the entrance passage, gnawed by scavenging animals. The reason for the attack is unknown, but the gateway was rapidly demolished by Roman troops and the hill deserted.

The hill was occupied again between AD 400 and 600 during the Arthurian period, thus suggesting a foundation for the tradition that the fort was Arthur's Camelot. [L. Alcock, '*By South Cadbury is that Camelot*' (1972).]

27   TRENDLE RING, Bicknoller   ST: 118394
One of the group of hill-slope enclosures, the Trendle Ring is 0·8 ha in

area and, as its name suggests, is roughly circular in plan. There is an entrance on the north-east side. About 0·4 km higher up the hill is a linear bank with ditch on the upper north-east side. It seems to have been an outwork of the main enclosure, which was probably connected with stock rearing. [L. V. Grinsell, *Prehistoric Sites in the Quantock Country* (1976), 18.]

28 WAMBARROWS, Winsford   ss:876343
Just north of the road are three closely spaced round barrows. A little over a metre in height, they rise above the heathland, but still retain their secrets, although cavities in their surface show that they have been dug into at some time. There is another example to the southeast. [L. V. Grinsell, *Somerset Barrows*, (1969), 41.]

29 WICK BARROW, Stogursey   st:209456
This is a round barrow 24 m in diameter and about 3 m high, which was excavated by H. St George Gray in 1907.

At the centre of the site was a drum-shaped mound 9 m in diameter revetted by a drystone wall, a feature reminiscent of the fence at Silbury Hill. Over this a cairn of lias blocks had been built. The whole feature had been robbed in Roman times. Three secondary crouched burials high in the mound, each with a beaker and one with a fine flint knife, had been missed by the Romans. [H. St George Gray, *P Somerset AS*, 54 (1908), 1.]

30 WITHYPOOL STONE CIRCLE   ss:838343
A good circle of thirty-seven small stones, each about 1 m apart, 36 m in diameter, and 0·5 m high. There were perhaps about a hundred stones originally. [L. V. Grinsell, *Archaeology of Exmoor* (1970), 39.]

STAFFORDSHIRE

1 BERRY RING, Bradley   SJ:887212
Ringing the northern end of a spur this oval contour fort of 2·8 ha has
its ramparts, which may be double on the northern side, covered with
trees. The interior is ploughed and can be reached from entrances on
the east and south; the latter is more likely to be original, but it has
been widened in modern times.

2 BERTH HILL, Maer   SJ:788391
On a tree-covered spur immediately above the A51 is a small roughly
triangular fort of about 3·6 ha. It is surrounded by a bank, ditch and
counterscarp bank, which is strengthened by a second bank and ditch
on the more vulnerable north-north-east side. A hollow way leads
uphill to a fine inturned entrance on the west, and a second track leads
to a simple entrance on the north-east. This is one of the few hillforts
with its own water supply, for a spring rises inside it on the north-east
side. [*VCH Staffs.* (1908), 339.]

3 BRIDESTONES, Congleton   SJ:906622
This burial chamber has lost its covering mound, though it was once
90 m long. The chamber is 5·5 m long and 1·5 m wide. Halfway along its
length is a broken porthole stone: an upright with a hole in it wide
enough to allow the passage of a corpse, a feature normally found in
the Cotswolds. It is recorded that two small side chambers were
destroyed in the eighteenth century. At the eastern end of the chamber
was a semicircular forecourt, traces of which can still be seen today,
marked by large stones, although bushes have grown over most of it.
There is no record of the barrow's contents. [M. Dunlop, *TLCAS*, 53
(1939), 14.]

4 BURY BANK, Stone Rural   SJ:883359
This is an oval, tree-covered semi-contour fort of 1·5 ha, overlooking
the river Trent. It is defended by a rampart, ditch and counterscarp
bank. Unfortunately the soft nature of the soil has allowed the
earthwork to weather badly, and it is no longer very upstanding.
However, the inturned entrance on the north-west can be clearly seen.
It has not been dated by excavation. [*VCH Staffs.* (1908), 342.]

5 CASTLE RING, Cannock   SK:045128
In a commanding position overlooking Cannock Chase, this fort is
roughly oval in shape and encloses 3·5 ha. On the north and south-west
it is defended by two banks and ditches, but these have been doubled
on the eastern side where the fort faces flatter ground. There is an
original entrance at the north-east corner, which is very slightly inturned. The entrances on the south and south-east are recent. [*VCH
Staffs*. (1908), 336.]

6 DEVIL'S RING AND FINGER, Mucklestone   SJ:707379
Two stones are built into the wall of Oakley Park. One, the Ring, is
1·8 m wide and 1·2 m high, and has a porthole cut into it. The other, the
Finger, is 1·8 m high and 0·9 m wide and leans against the first.
Although it is probable that the stones were part of a burial chamber,
they are unlikely to be in their original positions. [G. E. Daniel,
Prehistoric Chamber Tombs (1950), 184.]

7 ILAM MOOR, Ilam and Alstonefield
On the southern edge of the Peak District National Park and on the
high ridge west of Dovedale are a number of interesting round cairns.
Beside a track from Stanshope is a cairn (SK:132542), 30 m in diameter
and 1 m high. The central hollow was made by Samuel Carrington in
1849 when he uncovered three rock-cut graves, all containing
skeletons and two with necked beakers. Another grave on the east
held a crouched skeleton with a bronze round-heeled dagger. Two
hundred and seventy metres further east (SK:135542) is another cairn
excavated by Thomas Bateman and Samuel Carrington, which produced both skeletons and cremations. South-west of Damgate (at
SK:124532) is an oval cairn nearly 2 m high, in which Bateman found a
crouched skeleton in 1845 buried with a necked beaker. North of the
track to Castern Hall is a cairn (SK:128529) in which Carrington found
a crouched skeleton with a food vessel. Just to the west are two further
cairns (SK:126528) but no record of their contents exists. The most
prominent cairn is **Ilam Tops Low** (SK:136527). Alternate layers of
earth and stones covered a rock-cut pit in which the remains of a bull
were found on a bed of charcoal. Above this were a mixture of adult
and child bones, a bronze awl and the crushed remains of a bell beaker.
[T. Bateman, *Vestiges* (1848), 82).]

8 KINVER HILLFORT   SO:835832
(National Trust). Sited on a north-east-facing spur above the Stour,
Kinver is protected by steep slopes on all sides except the south-west
and south-east. Here the site is protected by a strong bank rising
3 – 4·5 m above the interior and an external ditch. The western end of
the rampart curves along the north-western scarp for some 40 m,

suggesting an eroded inturned entrance, but access was more likely to be at the eastern end, where it was subsequently blocked by a shallow ditch.

9   LONG LOW, Wetton   SK:122539
Two limestone cairns are joined together by a low, broad bank faced with upright limestone slabs. The much denuded northern mound is about 22 m in diameter and 2·4 m high. The southern mound is smaller, 20 m in diameter and 1 m high. A modern field wall runs along it. Samuel Carrington dug into the northern mound in 1849 and found a large stone chamber in which were buried thirteen skeletons with three leaf-shaped arrowheads. There were traces of a cremation in the southern mound and in the adjoining bank. [C. W. Phillips, *Map of the Trent Basin* (1933), 9.]

10   MUSDEN LOW, Waterhouses   SK:118501
Four cairns on the hill were excavated by Samuel Carrington in 1849. They stretch over 0·4 km, from north-west to south-east:
1   A cairn 20 m across and 1 m high covering a primary skeleton with a bronze round-heeled dagger and a flint scraper. There were five other secondary burials, two with food vessels, as well as a cremation in an urn. The barrow was also used for two Saxon burials.
2   This cairn was 18 m across and 1·5 m high. It contained a single prehistoric cremation, as well as a skeleton with two Saxon urns.
3   The largest cairn, 25 m across and 1 m high; it covered a skeleton and two cremations.
4   Carrington found nothing in the fourth cairn.
Also in the area are a number of other prominent barrows. Beside the road (at SK:113495) is a large cairn that covered a crouched skeleton with a bronze round-heeled dagger. No finds are recorded from **Dun Low** (SK:119494). Ten skeletons were found in **Top Low** (SK:129491) together with a beaker and bronze clasp. In the same barrow were three cremations: one with a collared urn. **Lady Low** (SK:138497) housed a cremation accompanied by a flint arrowhead and a bone pin.

11   THOR'S CAVE, Wetton   SK:098549
It was not only in the stone ages that cave mouths were occupied. Although used in the upper palaeolithic, Thor's Cave seems to have been mainly in use during the iron age and Roman periods, perhaps from about 200 BC to AD 300. The cave is sited high up in a jagged peak above the eastern bank of the Manifold river, with an enormous entrance facing north-west. Inside are a number of small passages, as well as a second entrance facing west, which would have created problems for keeping the cave warm.

SUFFOLK

1 CLARE CAMP, Clare   TL:768458
This site overlooks a tributary of the river Stour. It has been identified
as an iron age hillfort, but this has been disputed. However, forts are so
rare in this area that it may be Trinovantian in origin. A double
rampart and ditch surround a rectangular area 2·6 ha in extent. It has
been damaged by houses on the south and east and the entrances are
by no means certain, though gaps in the north and south sides may be
original. [R. R. Clarke, *Arch. J*, 96 (1939), 1.]

2 POLE HILL BARROW, Foxhall   TM:236442
The last surviving barrow in a once extensive cemetery largely
destroyed to make way for a wartime airfield. About 25 m in diameter
and 1 m high, it is surrounded by a clump of fir trees. Close by, the
Devil's Ring saucer-barrow has been flattened. A carbon-14 sample
from one of its companions gave a date somewhere between 1900 and
1640 BC. [R. R. Clarke, *East Anglia* (1960), 78.]

SURREY

1 ABINGER COMMON TQ:112459
A shallow pit, 0·9 m deep, 4·3 m long and 3·1 m wide, seems to have been a working and sleeping place for mesolithic man 8000 years ago. Louis Leakey, excavating in 1950, observed that the pit, which had been dug into the greensand, had a ledge along its eastern side, opposite which were indications of a hearth. Above the fire were a couple of post-holes that may have supported some kind of screen or windbreak of branches. Leakey found more than a thousand microlithic implements, which suggests that the site was occupied for a considerable length of time. It is now covered by a wooden hut and may be visited on application to the Manor House. [L. S. B. Leakey, *Surrey Archaeological Society Report No. 3* (1951).]

2 ANSTIEBURY, Capel TQ:153440
This strongly fortified circular hillfort encloses 4 ha. It is surrounded by two banks and ditches and a counterscarp bank, except on the steep south and west sides, where none are present. The inner rampart is 10·7 m wide and 1·8 m high, and has a strongly revetted stone face. The middle rampart is little more than a broad platform 15 m wide and less than 1 m high. The counterscarp bank is also less than 1 m high. Between the banks are two V-shaped ditches 2 m deep and 4·5 m wide. There is an entrance on the east with a simple gate between the inner ramparts. Hugh Thompson's excavations suggest that the fort was of one period, built in the second half of the first century BC and perhaps never finished. The inner rampart face was deliberately destroyed not long after its construction. Pebbles from the site suggest that it was subjected to sling warfare. The fort was reoccupied in the middle of the first century AD. [*VCH Surrey* (1912), 381.]

3 BANSTEAD GOLF COURSE, Banstead TQ:249607
There are four mutilated barrows on the golf course, one of which is now used as a bunker, making it difficult to recognize. Two others are 12 m in diameter and 1·5 m high, each dimpled by a robbers' pit on their summits. The fourth stands 0·6 m high and 9 m across. It, too, has been dug into, but no record of the contents has survived. [L. V. Grinsell, *Surrey AC*, 42 (1934), 43.]

4 CAESAR'S CAMP, Farnham   SU:825500
A level platform of 10·2 ha is cut off on the south-west side by a strong
ditch, bank and counterscarp, with a lesser bank and ditch outside.
There is also a weak single bank, ditch and counterscarp on the
south-east side of the hill. The rest of the fort is defended only by the
natural strength of the hill slopes, though there is a double bank along
part of the north side opposite an isolated knoll. The only entrance is
through the centre of the south-west rampart. There is a spring at Jock
and Jenny's Stones on the hill slope at the north-east corner, and a
pond inside the fort. [J. P. Williams-Freeman, *Field Archaeology as
Illustrated by Hants.* (1915), 366.]

5 CROOKSBURY COMMON, Elstead   SU:894449
This appears to be a triple bell-barrow, and consists of three mounds
enclosed within a single ditch and external bank. The mounds vary in
size, being 9 m in diameter and 2 m high at the north, 14·6 m across and
2·4 m high in the centre, and 18 m in diameter and nearly 3 m high on
the southern side. We have no knowledge of the barrow's contents.
[L. V. Grinsell, *Surrey A C,* 40 (1932), 58.]

6 DEERLEAP WOOD, Wotton   TQ:118480
This bell-barrow is very overgrown. The mound is a little over 2 m high
and about 18 m in diameter. It is surrounded by a berm 6 m wide and
a ditch 1·5 m deep. When excavated in 1960 a turf mound was found at
the centre covered with a rubble pile. No burial had survived, probably
due to the acid nature of the soil. [J. X. W. P. Corcoran, *Surrey A C,* 60
(1963), 1.]

7 DRY HILL, Lingfield   TQ:432417
'With five spades regularly, and six or seven occasionally, at work, we
catechized the place, in spite of its large area, somewhat severely; its
answers were few and grudging.' 'We may claim that we have shown
that money [£30] and time [three weeks] need not again be expended
on Dry Hill.' So much for the excavations of 1932. This Wealden fort is
oval in shape, enclosing 10 ha of fruit trees. It has strong double
ramparts and ditches with counterscarps on the south-west and north-
east. On the south-east it becomes a single rampart, ditch and counterscarp, and on the north only the rampart has survived. There is an
oblique entrance on the south-west by the reservoir, and others at the
south and north-west. No dating material was found in 1932 but there
is little doubt of the fort's iron age origin. Iron smelting may have taken
place in the interior. [S. E. Winbolt and I. D. Margary, *Surrey A C,* 41
(1933), 79.]

8 FRENSHAM COMMON, Frensham   SU:854407
Four bowl-barrows form a linear cemetery, each a little under 2 m high

and around 20 m in diameter. The southern one has certainly been opened at some time, though nothing is known of any of their contents. [L. V. Grinsell, *Surrey AC*, 42 (1934), 59.]

9 **FROWSBARROW, Puttenham**   su:939476
Archaeology seldom seems to have amused Queen Victoria, but according to a stone on this barrow, she visited it in 1857. It is a bowl-barrow 2·3 m high and 41 m in diameter, with a golf-tee on the summit. It is surrounded by a well-marked ditch. [L. V. Grinsell, *Surrey AC*, 42 (1934), 56.]

10 **HASCOMBE HILL, Hascombe**   TQ:004386
A wooded south-west-facing promontory is an excellent setting for this little 2·4 ha hillfort. The sides are very steep and they have been artificially scarped at the top to make them almost unassailable. In addition, a ditch 1·5 m deep was dug 4·5 m below the crest of the hill. Only on the north-east, where the fort faces the main hill mass, is there a strong line of rampart and ditch, broken by a single entrance where the rampart ends turn outwards at right angles and form an entrance passage about 24 m long. Slight excavation in 1931 showed that the fort was occupied during the first century BC. [S. E. Winbolt, *Surrey AC*, 40 (1932), 78.]

11 **HOLMBURY, Shere**   TQ:105430
Holmbury is defended on the west and north by double ramparts and ditches, and on the south and east by natural slopes which have been scarped. The outer ditch was originally about 2·4 m deep and 6 m wide and the inner one was considerably larger, 4 m deep and 9 m wide. The original entrance was probably in the north-west corner. Excavation indicates a Belgic date in the first century BC for the fort. [S. E. Winbolt, *Surrey AC*, 38 (1929–30), 156.]

12 **HORSELL COMMON BARROWS, Horsell** TQ:014598 and TQ:016598
Two bell-barrows stand one on either side of the road. The western barrow is larger, with a mound 30 m in diameter and 1·5 m high. It has a berm 6 m wide separating it from a ditch and outer bank. The eastern barrow is about the same height, but has a mound only 24 m across. It, too, has the traditional berm and ditch. No finds are recorded from either barrow, though the eastern mound was damaged for military purposes in the First World War. [L. V. Grinsell, *Surrey AC*, 40 (1932), 62.]

13 **MILTON HEATH, Dorking**   TQ:153489
On the north side of the A25 is a bowl-barrow 20 m in diameter and 1.5 m high. It is covered with trees and nothing is known of its contents.

14 NEWLANDS CORNER, Guildford   TQ:045492

In the woods at Newlands Corner is a round barrow 18 m in diameter and a little over a metre high. From the indentation on its summit it is clear that it has been dug into at some time, but no record remains of what was found.

15 REIGATE HEATH BARROWS   TQ:237504

There are seven barrows on Reigate Heath, four of which were opened in 1809. Two of these produced cremations, one in a cinerary urn. The other two failed to provide the diggers with any trophies. The barrows, which are spread out in a rough line, vary in diameter between 8 m and 33 m, and in height between 0·3 m and 2·5 m. [L. V. Grinsell, *Surrey AC*, 42 (1934), 52.]

16 ST ANN'S HILL, Chertsey   TQ:026676

This steep-sided wooded hill is a public park, and contains a possible hillfort of 5 ha. A ditch and counterscarp bank are prominent on the west and run southwards towards the Dingle, but are not visible on the other sides of the hill. [*VCH Surrey*, 4 (1912), 384.]

17 ST GEORGE'S HILL, Walton-on-Thames   TQ:085618

Hidden amongst woods and houses which have sprawled over it, this fort of 5·7 ha is in a poor state of preservation. It is roughly rectangular in shape and is surrounded by a single rampart and ditch, which has been doubled on the north-west side. Here there is a single entrance. On the north-east side is a semicircular enclosure, which seems a little later than the original site and may have acted as a stock enclosure. The site seems to have been occupied during the third century BC and early in the first century AD. [*VCH Surrey*, 4 (1912), 388.]

18 SUNNINGDALE, Chobham   SU:952665

In a private garden in Heathside is a large bowl-barrow 23 m in diameter and 1·5 m high. It was trenched in 1901, when twenty-five cremations were discovered, twenty-three of them in Deverel-Rimbury urns. The burials were close to the surface of the barrow mound and were almost certainly secondary. They lay in shallow holes, in which slabs of sandstone had been placed, and were covered with pieces of conglomerate. Since the urns can be dated to about 1600 BC, the barrow itself is likely to be about five hundred years older. [L. V. Grinsell, *Surrey AC*, 42 (1934), 36.]

19 THURSLEY COMMON, Thursley   SU:909409

On the north side of the road across the Common are two bowl-barrows. One on the west is 1·8 m high and 24 m wide; the other, which lies 180 m to the east, is nearly 3 m high and 23 m across. It is best to search for them when the bracken is low. [L. V. Grinsell, *Surrey AC*, 42 (1934), 59.]

20 WEST END COMMON BARROWS, Worplesden   su:934616
There are four round barrows in a row. At either end are ditched bowl-barrows, with two smaller overlapping barrows in between. They are all a little under 2 m high. [L. V. Grinsell, *Surrey AC*, 42 (1934), 39.]

21 WHITMOOR COMMON, Worplesden   su:997537
In a wood on the eastern side of the Common is a barrow of a type intermediate between bell and disc. It is about 30 m wide with a central mound only 0·6 m high. Pitt-Rivers dug into it and found an empty hole at the centre. Close by were two bucket-type cinerary urns. A little over 1 km south-west (at su:987534) is a small round barrow 14 m in diameter and 0·3 m high with a shallow surrounding ditch. The hollow at the centre is probably the result of another dig by Pitt-Rivers in which three bucket urns containing burnt bones were found. [L. V. Grinsell, *Surrey AC*, 42 (1934), 48.]

22 WISLEY COMMON, Wisley   TQ:079592
A large bell-barrow which is 44 m in diameter and 3 m high. Ploughing around it seems to have left it isolated on a kind of platform, and it has been damaged by a parish boundary and iron working on its east and north-east sides. Excavation produced a cremation high in the mound, but no primary burial has yet been found. [L. V. Grinsell, *Surrey AC*, 42 (1934), 59.]

1 THE CABURN, Glynde   TQ:444089

The history of hillfort excavation in Britain is closely linked with the history of the Caburn. In 1877–8 Pitt-Rivers dug forty storage pits inside the fort and in 1925 the Curwens, father and son, dug a further ninety-nine; Christopher Hawkes has studied the pottery found. Finally in 1937–8 A. E. Wilson examined the entrance and ramparts, thus making it possible to reconstruct the history of this 1·5 ha site with reasonable accuracy.

The fort crowns the summit of Mount Caburn. On its northern side is a double line of rampart and ditch, broken at the north-east corner by an entrance with clubbed inturned ends. Around the rest of the fort the inner rampart and outer ditch disappear and leave a terrace where the inner ditch and outer merge.

The hilltop was first settled about 500 BC and seems to have been lightly defended with a palisade and entrance at the north-east. Around 150 BC the fort was constructed, with a V-shaped ditch 1·5 m deep and a high internal bank for protection. Inside, at least 150 storage pits were dug, and huts must have been constructed, though only two doubtful examples have been found. One pit, north of the centre, may have held a water supply.

By AD 43 the threat of a Roman invasion had reached Sussex and the Caburn was hastily refortified. A new box rampart with stout posts at back and front was filled with chalk, partly from the old ditch, but mainly by digging a massive new ditch in front of it along the north side. This new ditch was 2·5 m deep and 9 m wide, of a type common in France, known as Fécamp. The entrance was remodelled and strengthened, but to no avail. The fort was attacked, the gate was burnt to the ground and the camp was hastily abandoned. In the twelfth century AD an adulterine castle was established on the hilltop. [A. E. Wilson, *Sussex AC,* 80 (1939), 193.]

2 CLIFFE HILL, South Malling   TQ:432110

This long barrow, sometimes known as the Warrior's Grave, is 36 m long, 15 m wide and 2 m high. The side ditches are visible and there are signs of disturbance in the barrow mound.

240

3 COMBE HILL, Jevington   TQ:574021

Two concentric arcs of causewayed ditches and banks butt on to the north-facing Combe and enclose about 0·6 ha. The inner arc of ditches is broken by at least sixteen causeways. Excavation in 1949 showed that the ditch is U-shaped, about 3·7 m wide and 1 m deep, and that it contained many pieces of local neolithic Ebbsfleet ware. No post-holes were found to suggest either a stockade or interior buildings. The other arc of ditches has not been examined or fully traced.

There is a large ring barrow to the east of the camp. [R. Musson, *Sussex AC,* 89 (1950), 105.]

4 EAST HILL, Hastings   TQ:833099

A. H. A. Hogg has suggested that this important promontory fort may have been a pre-Roman invasion base. The sea-cliffs to the south and steep natural slopes to the north isolate a peninsula which is defined by a strong bank running north-south and cutting off about 14 ha. There was probably an entrance at the south end of the rampart where a second line of bank lies west of the main defence, and where there may have been a long inturn. Sadly, it is much eroded by the sea. [A. H. A. Hogg, *Hill-forts* (1975), 203.]

5 FIRLE BEACON, West Firle   TQ:486058

This long barrow lies east to west, 33 m long, 20 m wide and 2·5 m high. A hollow at the eastern end suggests a collapsed wooden burial chamber. The side ditches turn inwards at the end.

There are numerous bowl-barrows on either side of the long barrow along the ridge, including one to the west, 18 m in diameter, once used as a beacon. [L. V. Grinsell, *Sussex AC,* 75 (1934), 220.]

6 FIVE LORDS BURGH, South Heighton   TQ:486036

The main interest of this plundered barrow is its name, which indicates that it was formerly the meeting place of five parishes. It is a little over 14 m in diameter and 1 m high. [L. V. Grinsell, *Sussex AC,* 75 (1934), 269.]

7 HIGH ROCKS, Frant   TQ:561382

There are two archaeological sites to explore. At the wooded foot of the High Downs Rocks escarpment (TQ:560383) are a series of rock shelters beneath the overhanging Tunbridge Wells sand where mesolithic and neolithic man sheltered close to a stream in the valley bottom. A dozen sites have been excavated at the foot of the rocks, producing flints of Wealden type. Neolithic pottery of Windmill Hill and Ebbsfleet types was also found in association with hearths, whose charcoal has produced a calibrated radiocarbon date of 4500 BC.

Above the escarpment are the damaged remains of a 10 ha promontory fort. On the south, east and north-east of the promontory a rampart of dumped earth and a steep-sided U-shaped ditch were constructed, probably in the first century BC. Later, in the first century AD, the area was refortified by building a new rampart and ditch inside the earlier one and heightening the first rampart as a counterscarp. The new ditch was wide and irregular in shape and of Fécamp type, as at the Caburn and Oldbury. On the north and east a second rampart was constructed. This was pierced at the south end by an entrance with elaborate outworks. Another possible entrance may have existed on the north-east where the rampart meets the escarpment cliffs. The whole of the north-west side of the fort is protected by these cliffs, though occasional gaps may have been blocked with masonry. [*Rock shelters:* J. H. Money, *Sussex AC,* 98 (1960), 173. *Hillfort:* J. H. Money, *Sussex AC,* 106 (1968), 158.]

8 HOLLINGBURY, Brighton   TQ:322078

A wilderness at the centre of a golf course and surrounded by Brighton's hideous suburbia, Hollingbury is a classic site in the British iron age, excavated by E. Cecil Curwen in 1931. Square in shape, but with rounded corners, it is a hillfort of 3·5 ha. It is defended by a rampart and ditch with traces of a counterscarp on the south side. Curwen showed that the rampart was composed of two rows of posts 2·1 m apart running along the rampart, and the same distance apart at back and front. These were tied together with cross-beams and filled with chalk rubble forming what is now known as a Hollingbury-type rampart. The posts were 15 cm in diameter and the position of some of them is marked on the site with modern metal posts. The gate on the west has inturned rampart ends; that on the east is a simple straight-through one. The latter had holes a metre deep for two massive oak gateposts. The fort ditch was flat bottomed, 1·8 m deep and 3 m wide.

A slight bank 30 m inside the fort and parallel to the east side indicates the presence of an earlier enclosure, which still shows as a slight ridge. There are four mounds inside the camp which seem to be bowl-barrows. One contained bronze axes and jewellery now in the British Museum. [E. C. Curwen, *Ant. J,* 12 (1932), 1.]

9 HUNTER'S BURGH, Wilmington   TQ:550036

Lying north to south and measuring 56 m long, 22 m wide and 2 m high, this long barrow is quite well preserved. Side ditches can be clearly seen, as can an attempt to open it at the southern end. [E. C. Curwen, *Sussex AC,* 69 (1928), 93.]

10 ITFORD HILL, Beddingham   TQ:447053

A climb up a hollow way from the west leads to the humps and bumps of a small middle bronze age village active for a short period around

Fig. 21 Itford Hill, Sussex: probable original appearance of the settlement (after Patrick Burke)

1400 BC. Only a few banks show today where once eleven huts stood surrounded by wooden fences which separated individual gardens and paddocks. Excavation has shown that the huts ranged from 4·5 m to 6·5 m in diameter, the largest built with a circle of eight posts around a central one. It had a porch on its south-east side, and was probably constructed with wattle-and-daub walls and a thatched roof. None of the huts had fireplaces. Outside the village are the low lynchet banks that mark the edges of fields, whilst above the settlement to the north was a burial mound surrounded by a ring of posts; it contained seventeen cremations and thousands of flint chippings, showing that this was a favourite flint-working spot. [G. P. Burstow and G. A. Holleyman, *PPS*, 23 (1957), 167; E. W. Holden, *Sussex AC*, 110 (1972), 70.]

11   LEWES PLATFORM-BARROW, Lewes   TQ:402110
This round barrow 28 m in diameter has a flat top 0·9 m high. Around it are a ditch and external bank. This is an example of a rare type of barrow known as a platform-barrow. Since it is unexcavated nothing is known abouts its contents. Close by are two bowl-barrows, [L. V. Grinsell, *Sussex AC*, 75 (1934), 226.]

12 LITLINGTON LONG BARROW, Litlington TQ:535006
There are a number of oval barrows in Sussex and Wiltshire that may be a form of long barrow. This example is 25 m long and 14 m wide. Its greatest height is 1·2 m, and it shows no sign of side ditches.

13 LONG BURGH, Alfriston TQ:510034
This long barrow is 46 m long and 18 m wide and reaches a height of 2·4 m at its north-eastern end. On either side were ditches, which produced the material for the barrow mound. It is unexcavated.

Just over 300 m to the north was a barrow, now almost totally obliterated by the plough. This oval-shaped barrow once stood 2 m high, 46 m long and 18 m wide. Excavation in 1974 showed that material from the side ditches had produced a simple mound of dumped chalk covering a pit that contained a crouched female burial without any grave goods. Attempts had been made to rob the barrow in the nineteenth century, but without success. [P. Drewett, *PPS*, 41 (1975), 119.]

14 LONG MAN, Wilmington TQ:543095
Although we have no idea of his date I have included the Long Man as a likely survival from iron age times, though the outline we see today is the result of restoration by the Rev. de Ste Croix in 1874. The outline figure stands 69 m high with staffs in either hand 1·2 m higher. The figure may once have held spears in his hands and might at one time have represented Woden, before he was demilitarized when Christianity reached Sussex. [C. F. C. Hawkes, *Antiquity,* 39 (1965), 27.]

15 MONEY BURGH, Piddinghoe TQ:425037
A skeleton, probably secondary, is the only find recorded from this long barrow. The mound is 37 m long, 18 m wide and 2 m high. [L. V. Grinsell, *Sussex A C*, 75 (1934), 219.]

16 OXTEDDLE BOTTOM, Glynde TQ:444104
There are about a dozen very low barrows on Saxon Down of which five occur at the above grid point. Dr Gideon Mantell dug two cinerary urns from one of them in 1820. One of the urns held a faience ring pendant, beads of jet and amber and a bronze spiral finger ring. The skeleton Mantell found was probably of Saxon date. There is another group of barrows at TQ:447096.

17 PLUMPTON PLAIN, Plumpton TQ:358122
A thickly overgrown area amongst cornfields is all that is visible of a very important bronze age settlement slightly excavated in 1934. Four rectangular enclosures containing huts were linked together by hollow roads. Deverel-Rimbury pottery from one of the enclosures suggests a

middle bronze age date around 1400 BC. [G. A. Holleyman and E. C. Curwen, *PPS*, 1 (1935), 16.]

18 RANSCOMBE CAMP, South Malling   TQ:438092

What at first sight appears to be a cross-ridge dyke 450 m west of the Caburn is probably an unfinished hillfort. It consists of a curving length of rampart and ditch 440 m long which excavation has shown to be laced with horizontal as well as vertical timbers. The ditch is shallow and U-shaped and lies east of the rampart. Only 30 m from the northern end of the earthwork is a gateway, though no gateposts are present. The site has produced early iron age pottery and Roman wares of the second and third centuries. [G. P. Burstow and G. A. Holleyman, *Sussex AC*, 102 (1964), 55.]

19 SEAFORD HEAD, Seaford   TV:495978

Triangular in shape, largely as a result of erosion which has removed the southern side, this is now a fort of 4·6 ha. The south-east and north-west sides are defended by a rampart 2 m high, with traces of a V-shaped ditch at the western end, 2 m deep. There are three gaps in the earthwork of which those at the north-west and north-east are most likely to be original. An excavation in 1876 by Pitt-Rivers was unable to establish the date, but it is almost certainly iron age.

There is a bowl-barrow midway along the north-west side some 12 m in diameter and 0·6 m high. Pitt-Rivers failed to find a burial, but he did uncover two small pits containing carpentry equipment: flint axes, scrapers, saw blades and hammer stones. [*Fort:* J. E. Price, *Sussex AC*, 32 (1882), 167. *Barrow:* A. H. Lane Fox, *J Anthrop. Inst.*, 6 (1877), 287.]

20 WHITEHAWK, Brighton   TQ:330048

In the area of Manor Hill Road on the Brighton racecourse are the last traces of a neolithic causewayed camp, originally 4·7 ha in extent, with four concentric enclosures. The third from the centre forms a distinct ridge along the almost precipitous slope above Whitehawk Bottom. South of the road towards the TV mast further traces of the third and fourth ditches can be found. When excavated in the 1930s the inner ditches were shown to be the shallowest, each about 1 m deep, whilst the third was the deepest, 2·5 m deep. Large quantities of pottery, flint work and animal bones were uncovered as well as numerous human remains, some deliberately buried and the rest casually thrown into the ditches: a pattern which is repeated elsewhere. [E. C. Curwen, *Sussex AC*, 71 (1930), 57; 77 (1936), 60.]

21 WINDOVER HILL, Arlington   TQ:542033

Above and to the south-east of the Long Man are a series of hollows

245

which have been identified as flint mines. They are unexcavated and lie between the large and fairly modern quarry hollow on the crest of Windover Hill and the terraceway to the north-west of it.

There are also a number of round barrows on the hill. A large bowl-barrow south of the Long Man on the edge of a small quarry is of interest. It is 40 m wide and 2 m high and was opened by Gideon Mantell in 1832. He found a cremation urn in a pit under a pile of flints. On the ridge between Wilmington Hill and Windover Hill is a small but good example of a platform barrow, 10 m in diameter and 0·6 m high. [E. C. Curwen, *Sussex AC*, 69 (1928), 93.]

SUSSEX, WEST

1 BARKHALE, Bignor Hill SU:976126
This oval enclosure is one of the largest discovered causewayed camps in Britain and encloses about 2·5 ha. Ploughing in the past has badly destroyed much of the earthwork, but sections of the causewayed ditches can still be seen on the north and north-east, together with the internal bank. Excavation about 1960 produced late neolithic pottery, confirming the antiquity of the site. [E. C. Curwen, *Archaeology of Sussex* (1954), 89.]

2 BEVIS'S THUMB, North Marden SU:789155
Lying just inside a ploughed field, this long barrow is 64 m in length, 21 m wide and nearly 2 m high. It is the longest of the known long barrows in Sussex. Its northern side ditch has been filled by a minor road, whilst ploughing has destroyed the southern one. [L. V. Grinsell, *Sussex A C*, 82 (1941), 122.]

3 BLACKPATCH, Patching TQ:094089
Low mounds and hollows on the hillside mark the site of about a hundred neolithic flint mines. Between 1922 and 1930 seven of the pits were excavated, showing that the miners were seeking a layer of flint 3·4 m below the surface. From a central shaft galleries radiated out for about 5 m, approximately to the limit of daylight. Once these had been exhausted a new shaft was dug and material thrown into the old one. This material included deer antler picks, one of which has given a radiocarbon date of about 4000 BC for the mines. Burials were also made in the shafts, and barrows were built over the filled-in mines. It seems likely that this group of pits was used for a long period of time, perhaps intermittently into the bronze age. North-east of the mining area traces of a village have been found, probably where the workers lived. [J. H. Pull, *Flint Miners of Blackpatch* (1932).]

4 CHANCTONBURY RING, Washington TQ:139120
This dominant wooded hilltop is the site of a small pear-shaped fort of 1·4 ha. It is protected by a single bank and ditch, broken by an entrance at the narrower south-western end. Excavation in 1977 showed the bank to be of simple dump construction and of early iron age date. To

east and west of the fort, at 0·4 km, are cross-dykes which guard the approaches. Excavation in the centre of the fort in 1909 revealed the foundations of a Romano-Celtic temple, rectangular in shape, measuring some 7·3 m by 5·2 m. Beside it was a curious oval foundation. Both structures were of flint and mortar. It seems to date from the first and second centuries AD. [G. S. Mitchell, *Sussex AC*, 53 (1910), 133.]

5 CHICHESTER DYKES

An area of many square kilometres between Bosham and Bognor and 3 km north of Chichester is cut off, either by streams on the east and west, or by a line of dykes 10 km long with additions that total 27 km in all. These dykes are still traceable in places, standing to a height of 3 m, with a rampart width of 6–8 m and the ditch 6 m wide. Good sections are visible at a number of places, especially at su:837080, su:847080 and between su:880085 and su:918086.

The dykes were probably constructed in the century or so before the Roman invasion in order to protect the territory around the capital of the Atrebates, which lay to the south. Precisely where this capital was is unknown; speculation suggests that it was either at Selsey and has been destroyed by erosion, or closer to the dykes near Chichester, in which case it still awaits discovery. [R. Bradley in B. W. Cunliffe, *Excavations at Fishbourne* (1971), 17.]

6 CHURCH HILL, Findon   TQ:112083

The chalk at Church Hill is too soft for flint mines with radiating galleries; instead the pits, almost 5 m deep, mushroom out at their bases to cover as large a floor space as possible. An antler pick from one of the shafts gave a radiocarbon date of 4300 BC. Amongst the hollows at the top of the mines were a number of working places where the raw flint had been worked into finished tools. There are not a lot of mines at Church Hill, but their use seems to have spanned a very long period of time. In the top of one shaft a beaker with 'barbed-wire' decoration datable to about 2100 BC was found with a cremation burial and two flint axes. [E. C. Curwen, *Archaeology of Sussex* (1954), 114.]

7 CISSBURY, Worthing   TQ:137079

More than two hundred depressions mark one of the most extensive groups of flint mines in Britain, lying both inside and out of the ramparts of the south-eastern section of Cissbury hillfort. Excavations more than a hundred years ago by General Pitt-Rivers and others showed that the mines extended down through six layers of flint and chalk to depths of about 12 m. At this point up to eight shafts radiated out, thus enabling the miners to win large quantities of stone. One shaft contained the skeleton of a young woman, who may have accidentally fallen into it head first; another contained the crouched

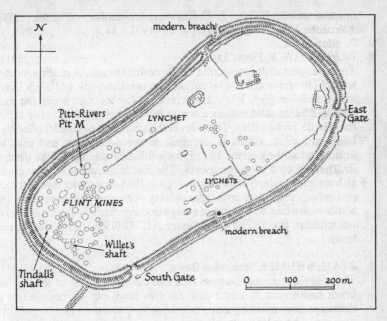

Fig 22. Cissbury, Sussex

burial of a young man deliberately surrounded by blocks of chalk. Pottery found in some of the mines belongs to the neolithic period and an antler pick from a shaft gives a corrected radiocarbon date of 3600 BC. The mines do not seem to have been worked in the bronze age, and their use was forgotten by the time the iron age fort was built.

The oval hillfort caps a prominent hill which is steep on all sides except the south and east where the two original entrances are sited. The fort encloses 26 ha with a strong rampart, 9 m wide at the base, ditch and counterscarp bank. Excavation has shown that the ditch is more than 3 m deep and has a curious central ridge on its flat bottom. On its inner edge the rampart was revetted with a continuous line of timber uprights. The two gates have not been excavated but appear to be simple straight-through affairs. The ramparts have been enlarged on either side of them, perhaps indicating the presence of bastions. Inside the fort pits containing iron age pottery were excavated, but the material remains unpublished. Late in the iron age the interior of the fort was ploughed and lynchets formed. Some ten enclosures and pits containing Romano-British pottery were constructed after the lynchets had developed. Finally the fort was refortified in late Roman times when the inner bank was heightened with chalk and turf, perhaps material from a slight inner ditch which can be seen on the north and north-west side. [*Mines:* E. C. Curwen, *Archaeology of Sussex* (1954), 106. *Fort:* E. C. Curwen, *Ant. J,* 11 (1931), 14.]

8 DEVIL'S DYKE, Poyntings   TQ:259111

This is a spectacular viewpoint of the South Downs. A chalk promontory 217 m above sea level is cut off by a massive bank and ditch 183 m long and 3·7 m high. It is cut by a modern gap through which the road passes. The original entrance was at the southern corner at the top of the Devil's Dyke valley. The sides of the spur are weakly defended by a bank and ditch, which is strongest at the north-east, and may be unfinished at the eastern end of the south-east side where the ditch is interrupted by undug causeways. The fort is undated by excavation, although a circular hut was uncovered in 1935 containing three storage pits which produced iron age pottery. On the golf course to the south-west of the fort traces of a large iron age farming settlement have been found. [G. P. Burstow, *Sussex AC,* 77 (1936), 195 (hut excavation).]

9 DEVIL'S HUMPS, Stoughton Down   SU:819111

There are five round barrows in a line along the crest of the downs. From south-west to north-east are two large bell-barrows 40 m in diameter, separated by a tiny pond-barrow, and then two large bowl-barrows. The most northerly barrow contained a cremation accompanied by a whetstone. Although the others have been opened nothing is known of their contents. There is a cross-ridge dyke immediately south of the south-western bell-barrow.

There is a twin-barrow (SU:807107) in the woods 1·2 km west of the Devil's Humps and on a south-easterly spur of Bow Hill is a group of possible neolithic flint mines (SU:825109). [L. V. Grinsell, *Sussex AC,* 75 (1934), 223; 82 (1941), 115.]

10 DEVIL'S JUMPS, Treyford   SU:825173

A splendid linear cemetery of six bell-barrows, five in a good state of preservation, the sixth at the south-east end almost destroyed. They have all been dug into and cremations are recorded from two of them. There is a ruined bowl-barrow a few metres to the west of the row. [L. V. Grinsell, *Sussex AC,* 75 (1934), 223.]

11 DIDLING HILL, Treyford   SU:828177

This rather damaged round barrow is interesting because it is surrounded by a square ditch with an entrance in its eastern side. The barrow mound is 0·6 m high and 5·5 m in diameter. Although it is undated, barrows surrounded by square ditches normally belong to the iron age, and are frequently found in south-east Yorkshire. [L. V. Grinsell, *Sussex AC,* 75 (1934), 245.]

12 GOOSEHILL CAMP, West Dean   SU:830127

A pleasant climb on the downs leads one to this overgrown site on the side of the hill. It is of the type with widely spaced ramparts probably used for cattle ranching and more commonly found in the west country. There is an oval enclosure of 0·2 ha defined by a rampart and V-shaped ditch, which was about 1·5 m deep when excavated. Surrounding this is a second rampart, now incomplete on the south-east side, enclosing an oval area of about 1 ha. The ramparts were only made of chalk and showed no signs of strengthening timbers when examined. There is an entrance in the inner ring on the south-east and in the outer on the west, with perhaps another on the north. There are at least two hut hollows inside the inner oval. Pottery dates the site to the end of the third century BC. [J. R. Boyden, *Sussex AC*, 94 (1956), 70.]

13 GRAFFHAM AND HEYSHOTT DOWNS SU:915163 and SU:895165

These barrows are spread out along the ridgeway in a tight linear cemetery on Heyshott Down, and a more widely dispersed group on Graffham Down. Few of the barrows are more than a metre high and nothing is known of their contents. It is just possible that one of the Graffham barrows is a bell, all the rest being bowls. [L. V. Grinsell, *Sussex AC*, 75 (1934), 246.]

14 HAMMER WOOD, Iping   SU:845240

This wooded promontory of 7 ha is cut off on its northern side by two widely spaced ramparts and ditches. A single rampart and ditch surrounds the other sides, though these again become double on the south. The inner rampart had a stone face and the ditch, which is V-shaped, was about 2·2 m deep. There is an oblique entrance through the northern ramparts. Pottery of a degenerate local early iron age type was found when the site was partially excavated. [J. R. Boyden, *Sussex AC*, 96 (1958), 149.]

15 HARROW HILL, Angmering   TQ:081100

A conspicuous hilltop with the hollows of 160 filled-in flint mines on its eastern side, many of them still as much as 4 m deep. One of these shafts, opened in 1924–5, reached a depth of 6·8 m. Roughly oval in plan, it cut through three seams of flint, the third determining the bottom of the pit. This lowest level was worked from several galleries, whilst the upper seams were dug into at a convenient point whilst the shaft was being cleared. The deepest galleries were lit by simple lamps that have left soot on the tunnel roofs. Deer antler picks, one giving a radiocarbon date of 3700 BC, were common in the mine, together with ox scapulae (shoulder blades), used as shovels. At the entrance to some of the galleries were a number of scratches, suggesting tallies of how much flint had been removed. The modern excavators estimated that they had dug out 350 tonnes of chalk from the pit.

Three small shafts that lay beneath the earthwork of a small iron age enclosure built on the hilltop were investigated in 1936. These mines were only 2·5–3 m deep with short galleries at the bottoms. The overlying enclosure was very small, only 60 m by 52 m, with entrances at the north-east and west. The western entrance was cleared and shown to have post-holes for a strong gateway and the footings of a stout surrounding fence. Dozens of ox skulls from the site suggest that cattle slaughtering was its main occupation, there being no signs of other permanent habitation. [*Mines:* E. Curwen, *Sussex AC,* 67 (1926), 103. *Enclosure:* G. Holleyman, *Sussex AC,* 78 (1937), 230.]

16   HARTING BEACON, Harting   su:806184
This is a slightly constructed rectangular fort of 10 ha. A rampart and ditch are broken on the west by an entrance – excavations there produced two gold penannular rings. The ditch was flat-bottomed and 1·2 m deep, and the bank was of dumped chalk retained by a wooden fence. Structures of four and six post-holes have been found in the south-east corner of the fort, together with storage pits. All were associated with early iron age pottery. The weakness of the fort makes it more likely to have been used as a stockade for cattle ranching than for defence. This may be supported by the presence of a linear earthwork running along the hill ridge from east to west, and a series of cross-dykes. A barrow excavated inside the fort had been robbed but contained traces of an adult male burial. [O. R. Bedwin, *Univ. London Inst. Arch. Bulletin*, 14 (1977), 57.]

17   HIGHDOWN, Ferring   TQ:093043
This hilltop has been used intermittently for fortification for 2500 years, most recently as a radar station in the Second World War, but originally about 500 BC when an iron age fort of 0·8 ha was constructed there. The first defence was a chalk and timber-faced rampart separated from a flat-bottomed ditch, 1·8 m deep, by a flat berm. A skeleton lay on the ditch bottom. The fort is rectangular in shape and additional strength was given to it by constructing an extra bank and ditch along its south and east sides. It has also been found on the west, filled in by ploughing. The entrance was on the east, just north of the quarry. About two centuries later the fort was remodelled with a new V-shaped ditch and a glacis-faced rampart. At the same time the entrance was moved 3 m to the south. In the interior a rectangular hut has been uncovered, as well as signs of bronze age occupation. The site was refortified by re-cutting the ditch and heightening the rampart in the third century AD. Later still it was used as a Saxon burial ground. [A. E. Wilson, *Sussex AC*, 89 (1950), 163.]

18 PARK BROW, Sompting   TQ:153086
This is one of the classic sites excavated in the 1920s, though little of it
remains visible today. Celtic field systems can be seen over the hillside,
ranging in date from the bronze age to the late Roman period. About
eight huts originally stood on the hill around 1000 BC, with conical
thatched roofs and small storage pits in their floors. In the early iron
age two huts were built 180 m north-east. These two had larger and
deeper storage pits, and spindle whorls and weaving combs indicated
that textiles were being manufactured. By 100 BC the settlement had
returned to its former position and the large wooden huts left few
recognizable traces except, yet again, for the storage pits, which were
abandoned and used for rubbish. The houses were rebuilt on a rectangular plan with plastered walls and glass in their windows once the
Romans had arrived in Britain. The settlement was eventually destroyed by fire in the third century AD. [W. Hawley, *Archaeologia*,
76 (1927), 30.]

19 STOUGHTON DOWN, Stoughton   SU:823121
Two overgrown long barrows on arable land. The north-western is
30 m long and 24 m wide and still stands 2 m high. To the south-east, on
slightly higher ground, is another, 23 m long and 14 m wide. The side
ditches of both barrows have been filled in by ploughing. [L. V.
Grinsell, *Sussex AC*, 75 (134), 219.]

20 THUNDERSBARROW HILL, Old Shoreham   TQ:229084
A small rectangular enclosure of about 0·5 ha, consisting of a low bank
and external ditch marked a small agricultural settlement of about 450
BC. Fairly soon after its establishment it was surrounded by a roughly
triangular hillfort of 1·2 ha, whose ramparts still stand 2 m high. It has
damaged entrances on the east and west, both of which are inturned.
By about 250 BC the fort was abandoned and was not used again.
Instead a small Romano-British farmstead was constructed outside the
eastern rampart of the fort and lasted until late Roman times. Many
Celtic fields lie on the hill and must be connected with the farm.
   The hill gets its name from a bowl-barrow close to the fort's southern
gate. **Thunder's Barrow** is 14 m in diameter and 1·8 m high. There is no
record of its contents. [E. C. Curwen, *Ant. J*, 13 (1933), 109.]

21 THE TRUNDLE, Singleton   SU:877110
Another beautifully sited hillfort with wide views over central Sussex
and the sea, somewhat spoilt by the presence of ugly radio masts. The
Trundle is a site dating from at least two periods.
   About 3000 BC it was a neolithic causewayed camp. The site was
excavated in 1929 and shown to consist of a spiral of banks and ditches
with an inner ring 122 m in diameter and an outer diameter of 300 m

between the gates of the later iron age hillfort. The causewayed ditch sections varied in depth between 1·5 m and 2·5 m. The material taken out formed an almost continuous bank on the inner side. One section of the neolithic ditch underlies the iron age rampart on the north side. There the skeleton of a woman was found under a pile of chalk blocks. Other neolithic finds included pottery, flint, bone and chalk objects.

The iron age site seems to have been unenclosed at first – perhaps about 500 BC. The rampart and ditch with counterscarp was constructed around 320 BC. The only part excavated is the inturned eastern entrance. This was complicated and was shown to have had at least three periods of development. One of these must have been connected with a massive bridge carrying a rampart-walk over the gate. The fort seems to have been abandoned when the Belgae reached the area, about 100 BC.

In the fifteenth century AD a chapel to St Roche stood on the top of the hill, and later a windmill, which was burnt down in 1773. [E. C. Curwen, *Sussex AC*, 70 (1929), 33; 72 (1931), 100.]

22 **WOLSTONBURY, Pyecombe**   TQ:284138
An unusual oval fort in which the main feature is a ditch with an external bank standing some 0·6 m high and clearly built by throwing the chalk outwards and downhill. No entrance can be recognized, but the rampart is destroyed on the north and south. A southern position is most probable. Inside the fort is an oval enclosure resembling those found at Yarnbury and the Trundle and possibly of neolithic date. Excavation in 1929 obtained iron age pottery from this feature, but its dating is not conclusive. To the south of the fort is a cross-ridge dyke defending an outer enclosure. [E. C. Curwen, *Sussex AC*, 71 (1930), 237.]

TYNE AND WEAR

1 COPT HILL, Houghton le Spring   NZ:353492

In neolithic times the builders of this barrow had collected together the remains of an unspecified number of disintegrated corpses, stacked up wood and limestone blocks over them into a pile about 10 m by 2 m, and then ignited the lot. Once they were well burnt a mound of limestone and sandstone chips was then erected over the whole thing. In the bronze age eight more burials were added to the barrow, four cremations and four inhumations, including a child in a stone-lined hollow, and another with a food vessel. Today the barrow is 18 m in diameter and 2·5 m high. [*Arch. Ael.*, 11 (1914), 123.]

2 HASTING HILL, Offerton   NZ:353544

This small round barrow was built for a crouched beaker burial, but two inhumations in stone cists were added later, as well as six cremations, four in cists and two in collared urns. At various places in the mound a food vessel and other pottery and animal bones were found. [*Arch. Ael.*, 11 (1914), 135.]

WARWICKSHIRE

1 BURROW HILL, Corley   SP:304850
This square fort of 3 ha lies on the south-eastern slope of Burrow Hill
overlooking Coventry. It is surrounded by a strong bank and ditch
which has been damaged on the west side. The entrance on the
south-west, which is slightly out-turned, has also been damaged. Excavation has shown that the fort was surrounded by a strong drystone
wall, backed by a timber-laced bank of earth and rubble. The site has
been dated to between 50 BC and AD 50. [P. Chatwin, *Trans. Birmingham
AS*, 52 (1927), 282.]

2 KING STONE, Long Compton   SP:297309
This gnarled stone is part of the Rollright group (see under Oxfordshire). It stands 2·5 m high and 1·5 m wide at its base. It has a
semicircular bite missing from one side which has led some people to
suggest that it once formed part of a porthole entrance to a chamber
tomb. There seems little doubt that it was really an outlier of the stone
circle, and may have had some astronomical significance.

3 MEON HILL, Quinton   SP:177454
A double rampart and ditches ring this hilltop except on the north-west
where the steep natural slope makes only a single bank necessary.
Ploughing has rendered the position of original entrances uncertain.
Parts of a drystone wall on the north may be an original feature. In
1824 a hoard of 394 currency bars was found in the centre. These
sword-shaped iron fore-runners to coinage have mostly been dispersed, though examples can still be seen in the museums at Gloucester
and Stratford-upon-Avon, and at the Ashmolean, Oxford.

4 NADBURY, Ratley and Upton   SJ:390482
A bank, ditch and counterscarp surround this oval fort of 7 ha. The
main road runs along the ditch for about half its length. The ramparts
are high but badly damaged. The original entrance faced west, with a
hollow way leading towards it, but this has been damaged by the
modern road. Air photographs show a large annexe on the south-east,
which has been destroyed by ploughing. [*VCH Warwickshire*, 1
(1904), 389.]

5 OLDBURY CAMP, Oldbury   SP:314947

A bank nearly 2 m high still encloses this rectangular fort of 2·8 ha. Only on the south-east is the rampart much denuded. There are a number of gaps which may have been entrances, but none are certain. Minor excavations suggest an early iron age date. [British Association, *Birmingham and its Regional Setting* (1950), 93.]

6 WAPPENBURY   SP:377694

The whole village lies within this mutilated rectangular earthwork. On the north, west and south are steep scarps, whilst to the east of the church there are low banks and ditches. There is a hollow way which cuts the southern scarp, west from the church, and this seems to be the only entrance. There are fords across the river opposite the south-east and south-west corners, which may explain why it is in this unexpected low-lying position. A cutting through the rampart showed that it was 12 m wide and composed of gravel held in place by clay. The site is dated to the first century BC and the early first century AD. [M. B. Stanley, *Trans. Birmingham AS*, 76 (1958), 1.]

1 BERRY MOUND, Solihull   SP:095778

Surrounded on three sides by water, this oval fort of 4·5 ha has been much reduced in recent times. Only a single bank and ditch remain on the southern side where once there were three. This part is tree-covered, and a boundary bank to the field shows where other earth-works stood. There may have been an entrance on the east facing the gravel pit. [L. S. Garrad, *Trans. Birmingham AS*, 75 (1957), 93).]

WILTSHIRE

1 ADAM'S GRAVE, Alton Priors
su:112634

A very prominent long barrow, 61 m long and 6 m high, on Nature Conservancy land. In a hollow at the south-east are traces of a sarsen stone burial chamber. Excavations by John Thurnam in 1860 revealed parts of three or four skeletons and a leaf-shaped arrowhead. He also found a kerb of sarsen and drystone walling. Side ditches are visible, still a metre deep. [J. Thurnam, *Archaeologia*, 38 (1860), 410.]

2 ALDBOURNE FOUR BARROWS
su:249773

A group of three bell-barrows and a bowl-barrow. At the southern end of the group is the bowl-barrow 1·5 m high and 18 m in diameter. It contained a cremated adult burial covered by four sarsen slabs and the bones of a pig. Slightly north is the first bell-barrow, 40 m across and 3 m high. Opened by William Greenwell a century ago it contained a cremated adult and a bone pin. There were pieces of beaker pottery in the covering mound. The second bell-barrow covered two skeletons, one with a grooved dagger and tanged flint arrowhead. The most northerly mound covered an adult cremation with a small pot, amber beads and a bone pin.

Two ploughed barrows beside the A419 were examined by Greenwell. One (su:247770) contained a cremation lying on a plank of wood. Beside it was a fine incense cup (the Aldbourne cup), parts of a bronze dagger, two bronze awls, amber beads, pendants and a V-bored button. North of the burial was another also accompanied by an Aldbourne cup and a flint arrowhead. [W. Greenwell, *Archaeologia*, 52 (1890), 46.]

3 AMESBURY DOWN, Amesbury
su:148394

A rare type of bell-barrow in which three mounds are enclosed by a single ditch and external bank. The mounds are under a metre high; the long axis of the barrow is 57 m, the narrow axis 42 m. There is no doubt that the mounds have been opened but no record exists of their contents.

4 AVEBURY
su:103699

There are few more impressive archaeological sites in Europe than the

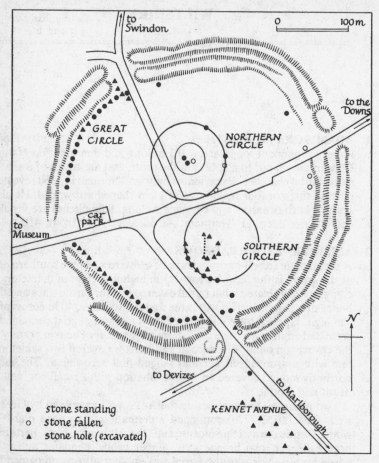

Fig 23. Plan of the Avebury circles and the Kennet Avenue, Wiltshire

great earthwork and stone circles at Avebury. Lying on low land at the
foot of the Marlborough Downs one comes upon them suddenly and
unexpectedly. The main road swings through the massive bank and
one is immediately inside an enclosure 427 m in diameter (11·5 ha) and
over 1 km in circumference. The material for the bank was derived
from an internal ditch, which averaged 9 m in depth and 21 m wide at
the top. The ditch seems to have been dug by gangs of workmen who
built the spoil into the great bank which still stands 5·5 m high in places.
Parts of the bank are held in position by an inner wall of chalk blocks.
The bank and ditch are broken by four entrances at the cardinal points,

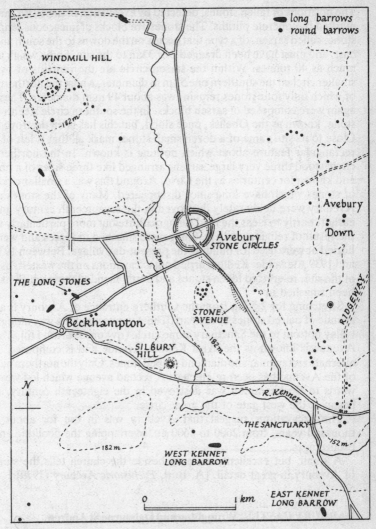

Fig 24. The Avebury region, Wiltshire

which seem to have been original features. All these components constitute one of the largest henge monuments in Britain.

Inside the henge are the remains of three stone circles. The largest and most impressive stands 7 m inside the inner lip of the ditch, and consisted of approximately ninety-eight stones, of which only twenty-seven remain standing today. This is the largest stone circle in Britain.

The positions of fallen stones, detected by excavation in the 1930s, are marked by concrete plinths. The stones are blocks of micaceous sandstone, called sarsen, of a type that occurs on the downs to the south and east, and must have been dragged 2 or 3 km to the site. Some weigh as much as 40 tonnes. Within the sarsen circle are the remains of two smaller circles, the southern one 52 m in diameter, whilst the northern, of which only four stones remain, was about 49 m in diameter. These again were composed of sarsen blocks. In the southern circle a central stone, known as the Obelisk, once stood, but this has been destroyed. Close to its site a line of a dozen small stones mark all that is left of a rectangular feature about which nothing is known. In the northern circle stood three very large sarsens arranged like three sides of a box and known for centuries as the Cove. Around this was a smaller circle of stones which have long since disappeared. Many of the stones at Avebury were deliberately destroyed in the seventeenth century and earlier, partly to clear the land for agriculture but more particularly as the result of religious beliefs. Some were smashed to pieces and were buried or were used for building the present-day village. Between 1936 and 1939 Alexander Keiller carried out excavations on the western half of the site, re-erected fallen stones and partly mended those which had been smashed up.

Stretching for 2·5 km from the southern entrance of Avebury is an avenue of paired stones 15 m apart. The Avenue winds its way along a valley bottom to the Sanctuary stone circle (qv) on Overton Hill. The Avenue is known as the West Kennet Avenue and is composed of alternate rectangular and diamond shaped stones. Only the northern half of the Avenue has been re-erected. A second avenue which led westwards to Beckhampton was destroyed in the eighteenth century. It began at the west gate of the great circle.

The excavations suggest that Avebury was in use for about a thousand years, from 2600 to 1600 BC, overlapping the neolithic and bronze ages.

A small, but excellent, museum beside the church tells the story of Avebury in great detail. [A. Burl, *Prehistoric Avebury* (1979).]

5   BARBURY CASTLE, Wroughton and Ogbourne St Andrew

SU:149763

This oval hillfort of 4·7 ha is strongly defended by two banks and ditches, and shows traces of sarsen stone facing in the ramparts. There are entrances on the east and west. Direct access is prevented on the east, where the ground levels out, by a semicircular barbican directing access from the north or south. The west entrance is inturned. Ploughing of the interior has enabled its crop-marks to be photographed from the air, revealing hut circles and storage pits. In the nineteenth century the fort produced iron age agricultural implements and weapons of iron as well as parts of harness and chariot fittings. The fort may have been refortified in the Saxon period – it is the traditional site of the battle of Beranbyrig in AD 556. [*VCH Wiltshire*, I, 1 (1957), 94.]

6 BATTLESBURY CAMP, Warminster ST:898456

Battlesbury is a pear-shaped hillfort above the river Wylye. It encloses 10 ha, and has double ramparts separated by a ditch, together with a massive inner quarry ditch and an extra line of rather weak rampart on the northern side. There are entrances on the north-west and south-east. The latter has outworks that may have provided a slinging platform. A barrow-like mound on the south-west may have been a medieval motte.

A rescue excavation in 1922 revealed nine pits containing iron age pottery, quernstones, iron work and part of a chariot wheel. In quarrying outside the north-west entrance a pit containing a mass iron age burial was found. This seems to have been a massacre, although whether by Roman legions or by a neighbouring tribe is uncertain. [*VCH Wiltshire*, I, 1 (1957), 118.]

7 BOTLEY COPSE, Shalbourne SU:293599

Between the track and the wood lies a fine disc-barrow 36 m in diameter. In 1910 Peake and Crawford found a cremation burial accompanied by a bronze awl and rivet under the central mound, which had its own surrounding ditch. A Saxon skeleton was also uncovered in the barrow. A dyke with its ditch on the downhill side cuts the barrow on the northern edge and runs westwards to join up with a prehistoric field system. Just inside the wood is a long barrow 64 m long and 3 m high at its southern end, where there is a rectangular-shaped robbers' pit. [H. Peake and O. G. S. Crawford, *WAM*, 46 (1934), 164.]

8 BRATTON CASTLE, Bratton ST:900516

Although surrounded by ploughing, a long barrow lies on grassland inside the hillfort. It is 70 m long and 20 m wide, and still stands 4 m high at its eastern end. It has been dug into at various times. William Cunnington examined the ditches and found 'black vegetable earth for 5 feet deep [1·5 m] intermixed with pottery, animal bones, etc.'. Near the top of the eastern end were three intrusive skeletons. John Thurnam found a 'heap of imperfectly burnt, or rather charred human bones, as many as would be left by the incineration of one or two adult bodies'. These appeared to be lying on a 'platform' at the higher eastern end of the barrow.

The single rampart and ditch which form the northern defence of

Bratton Castle hillfort follow the contours of the downs. On the east and south the ramparts are doubled by strong banks and ditches, thus giving extra protection to the more vulnerable part of the camp. There is a rectangular annexe outside the north-eastern entrance where the road passes into the camp. At the southern entrance there is also a rectangular outwork, similar to that at Badbury Rings. Nearly 200 years ago the local schoolmaster dug inside the camp and found a large number of querns (grinding-stones), some parched wheat and 'nearly a cart load of large pebbles' – presumably sling-stones.

The Westbury White Horse, below the rampart of the fort, was not cut until 1778. [*Long barrow: V C H Wiltshire*, I, 1 (1957), 138–9. *Hillfort: V C H Wiltshire*, I, 1 (1957), 263.]

9 BURY CAMP, Colerne   ST:818740
This is a triangular fort of 9 ha jutting out on to a spur, with a single line of rampart and ditch on the two steep tree-covered sides, and double defences on the level grounds facing south-west. The gap through this south-western defence is not ancient. There are two original entrances: one in the north-east corner has a long inturned passageway and was destroyed by fire; another on the north-west was also inturned. A small rectangular earthwork inside the fort is also of iron age date. The fort was finally destroyed perhaps by the Belgae or by the Roman second legion which assaulted the north-east gate and burnt parts of the interior at the same time. [D. Grant King, *WAM*, 64 (1969), 21.]

10 CASTERLEY CAMP, Upavon   SU:115535
This is a very large enclosure of about 27·5 ha, though it is not very well sited for defence, being overlooked from the west. There is evidence that the defences were never completed, though where they do exist There was a drop of 6·5 m between the top of the rampart and the bottom of the ditch. R. W. Feachem has suggested that the fort was incomplete on the northern side where a curious semi-circular salient seems to jut out of the more obvious line. Entrances existed on the north, west and south. The latter was 2·5 m wide between two pairs of posts 1·2 m apart. In the centre of the fort were two enclosures (destroyed by modern ploughing), one subrectangular and the other oval, which have been shown by excavation to date from the late pre-Roman iron age and extend into the Roman period. The oval enclosure contained a large pit in which a post, almost a metre in diameter, had stood. Around it were four human burials and fourteen red-deer antlers. There seems little doubt of the enclosure's ritual function. Such pits are not uncommonly connected with hillforts and seem to signify some inner sanctuary for Celtic worship, which may have pre-dated the hillfort; this would explain why it was built in such a

position. [R. W. Feachem, in M. Jesson and D. Hill, *The Iron Age and its Hillforts* (1971), 35.]

11 CASTLE DITCHES, Tisbury ST:963283
This tree-clad fort, on a lower escarpment of the downs overlooking the Nadder valley, is triangular in shape, and encloses about 10 ha within triple banks and ditches. There is a long oblique entrance on the west, whilst another at the east is also oblique, but more elaborate, with extra ramparts and ditches in front of the entrance passage to prevent a direct approach.

12 CLEY HILL, Corsley ST:839449
(National Trust). The Frome gap is guarded by an isolated chalk hill, the top of which is ringed by the single bank and ditch of a 7 ha hillfort. On the south-eastern side there is the scar of an enormous chalk quarry, which seems to have destroyed the entrance to the fort. On the north-west side of the enclosure are the hollows of many hut platforms, whilst the hill is crowned by two round barrows. [R. C. Hoare, *Ancient Wiltshire*, 1 (1812), 51.]

13 COLD KITCHEN HILL, Brixton Deverill ST:847389
A long barrow 70 m long and 3·7 m high at the south-eastern end. It has clearly defined side ditches, and appears to be unexcavated.

14 COW DOWN, Collingbourne Ducis SU:229515
A group of twelve badly damaged bowl-barrows and a disc-barrow form two linear cemeteries running parallel to each other from south-west to north-east across the northern end of the wood. Most of the barrows were dug by William Cunnington and later by Lukis. The southern line from west to east commences outside the wood. The third barrow from the west contained a secondary cremation burial in a Deverel-Rimbury urn, but the primary burial has not been found. The fourth barrow (the first in the wood) produced a crouched skeleton that lacked an arm and both hands. In the middle bronze age thirteen cremations were added, three in urns. Barrow 5 had held a tree-trunk coffin containing a cremation burial and an antler mace head. Only the impression of the coffin was left in the packed chalk. In barrow 6 a child of three or four years was buried at the centre together with a collared urn and food vessel. Later eighteen cremations and pieces of about forty-five Deverel-Rimbury urns were added. In the seventh barrow the dead were buried in tiers. At the bottom was a cremation. Above it on a plank was part of a male skeleton, and above that another cremation with shale beads. The last two barrows lie beyond the wood. There is no record of the contents of the eighth; the last in the line contained a cremation.

The second row of barrows from west to east consisted of a bowl-barrow with an empty central grave; a disc-barrow about 45 m across from bank to bank, in which neither Cunnington nor Lukis found a primary burial; a third mound covering a primary cremation and three later cremations; and a barrow containing the skeleton of a child with a shale bead and a handled cup 9 cm high. [L. V. Grinsell, *VCH Wiltshire*, I, 1 (1957), 167.]

15 CURSUS BARROWS, Amesbury (Fig 28, p. 281)   SU:115428
A significant linear cemetery of six round barrows lies north-west of Stonehenge and south of the Cursus. From east to west are a bell-barrow, a double bell-barrow, three more single bell-barrows and a bowl- (or possibly disc-) barrow. When William Stukeley examined the eastern mound of the double bell-barrow he found the cremated remains of a young woman in a collared urn. 'This person', he wrote, 'was a heroine, for we found the head of her javelin of brass.' Also with her was a flat bronze dagger, an awl, a gold-mounted amber disc and a variety of beads. Most of the other barrows contained cremations with beads of amber, faience, shale and bone. There are a scatter of bowl-barrows lying to the west of the group. [L. V. Grinsell, *Stonehenge Barrow Groups* (1979), 26.]

16 THE DEVIL'S DEN, Preshute   SU:152696
The mound of this long barrow had almost disappeared but a burial chamber at its south-east end consists of four partly collapsed sarsen wall-stones supporting a capstone re-erected in 1921. The chamber was complete and upright when Stukeley drew it in the eighteenth century. [A. D. Passmore, *WAM*, 41 (1922), 523.]

17 DURRINGTON WALLS, Durrington   SU:150437
A much ploughed bank can still be seen encircling the upper end of a dry valley which runs down to the river Avon. This is all that remains of a huge henge monument with a maximum diameter of 520 m, enclosing 12 ha. Although the bank is now only about a metre high, excavation has shown that it was originally 27 m wide and was separated from the inner ditch by a berm varying from 6 m to 36 m wide. The ditch was 6 m deep with a flat bottom and 18 m wide at the top. It is broken by two entrances, one at the north-west and the other at the south-east, 60 m from the river Avon.

In 1966–8 Geoffrey Wainwright conducted excavations under what is now the A345 road. Just inside the south-eastern entrance was a complex structure originally consisting of five concentric rings of wooden posts with a tight-packed timber facade facing south. The posts increased in size towards the centre of the structure, which is best

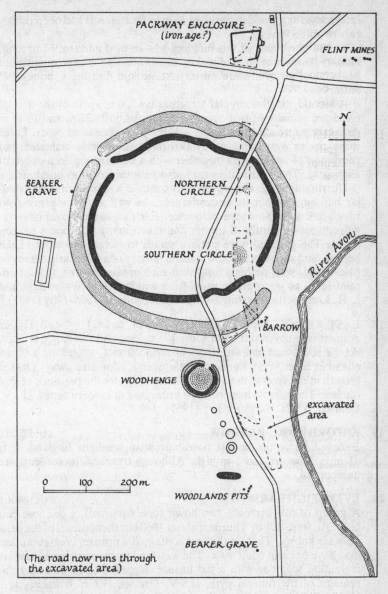

PACKWAY ENCLOSURE
(iron age?)

FLINT MINES

N

BEAKER
GRAVE

NORTHERN
CIRCLE

SOUTHERN CIRCLE

River Avon

BARROW

WOODHENGE

excavated
area

0   100   200 m

WOODLANDS PITS

BEAKER GRAVE

(The road now runs through
the excavated area)

Fig 25. Excavation plan of Durrington Walls, Woodhenge, Wiltshire (after
G. Wainright)

interpreted as a wooden building 38 m in diameter. It had been rebuilt two or three times.

To the north-east of this building was an oval midden, 12 m long, held in position by arcs of stakes and containing a large quantity of beaker and grooved-ware pottery, stone and flint tools, bones and antlers.

A second, smaller circular structure lay 120 m north of the first. It consisted initially of two concentric rings of posts 27 m and 19 m in diameter approached from the south by an avenue of posts. Later these circles were replaced by two more, smaller in diameter, but composed of larger posts, together with a new avenue on a different alignment. These structures may also be interpreted as buildings.

Durrington Walls almost certainly contains a number of other circular buildings within its circumference, as well as Woodhenge (qv) which lies on its southern perimeter. Each structure would have required vast quantities of timber and taken many man-hours to construct. The grooved-ware pottery seems to isolate the users of the henges, and suggests that this was the pottery of a select aristocracy or priesthood, who perhaps inhabited such monuments or at least administered an appropriate ritual from within. [G. J. Wainwright and I. H. Longworth, *Durrington Walls Excavations, 1966–1968* (1971).]

18 EAST KENNET LONG BARROW (Fig 24, p. 261) SU:116669
A great tree-covered mound some 105 m long and standing 6 m high. At the south-east end are traces of sarsen stones, suggesting a burial chamber as at West Kennet a little over a kilometre away. Darker growth in the crop of the adjacent fields indicates the presence of side ditches. The barrow has not been excavated in modern times. [L. V. Grinsell, *VCH Wiltshire*, I, 1 (1957), 140.]

19 ENFORD BOWL-BARROW SU:129516
Believed to be the largest bowl-barrow in southern England, it is 48 m in diameter and 5 m high. Although trenched, its contents are unrecorded.

· 20 EVERLEIGH BARROWS SU:184561
A group of five barrows, two bowls (one flattened), a disc and two bells. All were dug by Thurnam about 1860 but the contents of the bells only are known. That on the east contained a primary cremation that may have been an adult male. The western barrow contained a similar cremation together with a flat bronze dagger. Beside them lay the remains of the funeral pyre. [L. V. Grinsell, *VCH Wiltshire*, I, 1 (1957), 209.]

21 FIGSBURY RINGS, Winterbourne SU:188338
This circular fort is ringed by a bank 3·4 m high and 12·8 m wide,

enclosing 6 ha. There are entrances on the east and west. Excavations in 1924 showed that the external ditch had been V-shaped, 10·7 m wide and 4·3 m deep. Thirty metres inside the rampart is a second ditch without a bank. It is irregularly cut and more or less causewayed in places. The excavations failed to establish its date; it could be an earlier neolithic causewayed camp or henge monument, an iron age quarry ditch, an incomplete line of defence or a multiple enclosure for cattle ranching. A few storage pits and scraps of bronze age and early iron age pottery were found. [O. G. S. Crawford and A. Keiller, *Wessex from the Air* (1928), 84.]

22   FOSBURY CASTLE, Tidcombe and Fosbury   su:320565
A large oval fort of 12 ha within the ramparts, partly tree-covered on the north. It is defended by double ramparts and ditches. There are a number of gaps through the defences, but only that on the east side, which is inturned, seems to be original. Sherds of early iron age pottery have been found on the surface. [R. Hoare, *Ancient Wiltshire*, 1 (1812), 188.]

23   FYFIELD AND OVERTON DOWNS   su:142710 (centre)
This is probably the finest example of a prehistoric landscape in southern Britain, consisting of many examples of rectangular Celtic fields, some with banks 3 m high, and trackways between them. These grass-covered lynchets originated when soil piled up behind rows of boulders, stone walls, fences or ditches that marked the field edges. Excavation has shown that some of the Celtic fields were cross-ploughed with a simple ard. Farming seems to have been practised here continuously from about 700 BC into the Roman period, though the fields did not always follow the same shape. The Downs now form a Nature Reserve administered by the Nature Conservancy.
  Scattered over the Downs are thousands of sarsen stones, the grey wethers used for the building of Avebury and Stonehenge. The most accessible groups are at Piggle Dean beside the A4 (su:143688) and Lockeridge Dene (su:145674). A beaker settlement has been located on the north-west side of the Downs close to a large sarsen stone whose surface is deeply scoured with grooves resulting from the polishing of stone axes (around su:128715). Also on the Downs is the experimental earthwork (su:129706) constructed by the British Association in 1960 to study at fixed intervals the changes which have taken place over a known length of time in a carefully constructed bank and ditch in which selected materials have been deliberately buried. [P. A. Jewell, *The Experimental Earthwork on Overton Down* (1963).]

24   GIANT'S CAVE, Luckington   st:820829
This is a trapezoidal long barrow 37 m long and 15 m wide, constructed

of limestone. At the eastern end is a false entrance between horns revetted with drystone walling. There are four burial chambers at the sides, each with passages leading to them, two on the north side and two on the south. Some of these have been opened in the past making it difficult to assess the original number of burials. The north-west chamber (2·6 m by 1·4 m) held at least six skeletons, three men, two women and a child. The north-east (3·4 m by 1·2 m) chamber held five and there were more in the passage approaching it. The south-west grave was only partially excavated in 1960–62 when at least seven individuals were uncovered, an adult male, three women, and three infants. The south-eastern chamber (4 m by 0·8 m) was much disturbed and only the remains of one woman were found. A few flint implements and a sherd of neolithic pottery have also been exposed.

A second long barrow lies 225 m to the south-east at ST:821828. It is badly preserved and may have been chambered. [J. X. W. P. Corcoran, *WAM*, 65 (1970), 39.]

25 GIANT'S GRAVE, Milton Lilbourne   SU:189583
This is one of the many Wiltshire long barrows excavated in the nineteenth century by John Thurnam. Built of chalk, it is 90 m long, 20 m wide and 2 m high. At its eastern end it covered a pile of bones of three or four people, one of whom had died from a blow which had cleft his skull. A leaf-shaped arrowhead lay nearby. The barrow has ditches on either side. [J. Thurnam, *PSAL*, (2nd S), 3 (1867), 170.]

26 GOPHER WOOD, Wilcot   SU:139639
On the steep slope of the hill is a disc-barrow about 27 m in diameter. William Cunnington found an urn and incense cup, together with an awl and bone pin, at the beginning of the nineteenth century. There were two other cremations surrounded by a pile of flints. Extending north from the disc-barrow is a line of seven bowl-barrows, each about 9 m in diameter and 1 m high. Some of them have produced cremations. [L. V. Grinsell, *VCH Wiltshire* I, 1 (1957), 219.]

27 GRAFTON DISC-BARROWS   SU:271563
Here are two overlapping disc-barrows, each about 46 m in diameter with central mounds a metre high and 10 m across. There is no record of their contents.

28 KNAP HILL, Alton Priors   SU:121636
This was the first neolithic causewayed camp recognized in Britain. It is splendidly sited on a steep-sided scarp above the Vale of Pewsey, and is marked by an arc of six or seven ditch sections broken by a series of causeways, forming an enclosure of 1·6 ha. The ditch varied in depth between 1·2 m and 2·7 m but was usually about 3·5 m wide. The bank

inside the ditch is negligible in height. Windmill Hill pottery and bone from the ditches was scarce, but a radiocarbon date of about 3500 BC has been obtained. Later, when the ditches had silted up a little beaker pottery, which can be carbon-dated to about 2200 BC, was dropped. The site is very clearly visible from the road to the north, especially in midday light. [G. Connah, *WAM*, 60 (1965), 1.]

29   LAKE BARROW CEMETERY, Wilsford (Fig 28, p. 281)

SU:109402

This is one of the major barrow cemeteries around Stonehenge. At least fifteen bowl-barrows as well as four bell-barrows, two discs and a long barrow lie in the plantation and on the northern side of it, where they have been ploughed down. In the southern angle outside the wood are five more examples. Inside the beech wood one of the bowl-barrows midway along the northern side is known as the Prophet Barrow; 18 m in diameter and 1·8 m high, it contained a cremation in a wooden box buried in a chalk-cut grave, together with a grooved bronze dagger and a perforated slate pendant. Under another bowl-barrow, 3 m high, was the primary burial of a child with a beaker and two secondary bronze age skeletons, together with an inverted urn containing a cremation and bone pin. One of the bell-barrows contained a primary cremation with a bronze dagger, awl and some beads. Nothing is known of the contents of the disc-barrows, which are badly overgrown. A wedge-shaped long barrow, also apparently unopened, lies in the wood. It is 42 m long and 2·4 m high, and has deep side ditches. [L. V. Grinsell, *Stonehenge Barrow Groups* (1979), 37.]

30   LAKE DOWN, Wilsford (Fig 28, p. 281)   SU:117393

Another of the Stonehenge barrow cemeteries, containing at least ten scattered bowl-barrows, one disc-barrow and five pond-barrows. Most of the mounds were dug into by the Rev. Edward Duke at the beginning of the nineteenth century and few records survive of his findings. The pond-barrows are uncommon in such a large concentration. Two bowl-barrows that were opened produced cremations. The disc-barrow, 54 m in diameter, with a very low central mound, contained a cremation in a very small urn. [L. V. Grinsell, *Stonehenge Barrow Groups* (1979), 42.]

31   LANHILL, Chippenham Without   ST:877747

A badly mauled long barrow about 56 m in length and 27 m wide, lying east-west, with a false entrance at the east removed in 1909. Three side chambers are known; one still visible on the south opens out of a passage and measures 2·4 m by 1·2 m. It originally had a corbelled roof and contained eleven or twelve burials. On the north both chambers have been destroyed. One was entered through a roughly shaped porthole. When it was excavated in 1936 it held nine skeletons. The other was destroyed in the nineteenth century. Drystone revetment walls outlining the horns at the eastern end of the barrow have been destroyed in the past twenty years. [D. Grant King, *PPS*, 32 (1966), 73.]

32 LIDDINGTON CASTLE, Liddington   su:209797
For two hundred years Liddington has been associated with the site of the battle of Mons Badonicus, when King Arthur traditionally defeated the Saxons about AD 500. Recent excavations have not disproved the theory and have indeed produced pottery that could be as late as that date. The hillfort is oval in shape, with a single rampart, ditch and counterscarp enclosing about 3 ha. Excavation showed that at first the rampart was composed of turf revetted with blocks of chalk and flint. Later this was raised with a timber work behind and more chalk on the top. Most of the pottery is of the early iron age – the sixth or fifth centuries BC – and consisted of haematite-coated bowls and vases with incised decoration and white inlay. Romano-British grey ware was also present. The only obvious entrance is on the south-east, facing earthworks likely to be connected with cattle ranching and agriculture.

Pits about 0·8 km north-east (su:214799) may have been neolithic flint mines. [*VCH Wiltshire*, I, 1 (1957), 267.]

33 LUGBURY LONG BARROW, Nettleton   st:831786
This fine long barrow is 58 m long, 27 m wide and 2 m high. At the eastern end, according to John Aubrey, is 'a great Table stone of bastard freestone leaning on two pitched perpendicular stones'. These three large stones form a false entrance, the central one measuring 3·7 m by 1·8 m, with lesser stones on either side. Four sealed burial chambers were found on the south side, which contained twenty-six skeletons, ten of them children. None of these chambers are now visible. In 1821 Sir Richard Colt Hoare uncovered a crouched primary burial near the eastern end, and a further chamber was found in 1854. [O. G. S. Crawford, *Long Barrows of the Cotswolds* (1925), 230.]

34 MANTON LONG BARROW, Preshute   su:152714
In a poor state of preservation, this barrow is about 18 m long and 12 m wide. At the eastern end a forecourt leads into a single burial chamber with a capstone still in position. A kerb of sarsen stones surrounded the barrow, and excavation has revealed a large pit in the forecourt containing the skeleton of a pole-axed ox. Neolithic pottery suggests a date around 3000 BC. [S. Piggott, *WAM*, 52 (1947), 60.]

35 MARDEN HENGE   su:091584
The little village of Marden stands inside the largest known henge monument in Britain. Oval in shape, 14 ha is enclosed on the east,

north and north-west by a bank and internal ditch, whilst the meandering river Avon forms its south and western sides. Two entrances lie at right angles to one another on the north and east sides.

Excavations in 1969 at the northern entrance showed that the ditch was at least 15 m wide, but only 1·8 m deep. Pieces of neolithic grooved ware, antler picks, flint tools and fragments of animal bone had been dropped into this ditch by visitors to the site. Just inside the entrance was a timber circle 10·5 m in diameter, with three further posts for a roof support near its centre. The surrounding bank is badly ploughed away, but it can still be seen for much of its course.

A great mound, the Hatfield Barrow, once stood 6·8 m high inside the earthwork. It was excavated by William Cunnington in October 1807 using eight men for ten days, but they failed to find the primary contents. The barrow was totally destroyed shortly afterwards. [G. J. Wainwright, *Ant. J*, 51 (1971), 177.]

36 MARLBOROUGH MOUND   SU:183687

In the grounds of Marlborough College is one of the largest barrows in England, second only to Silbury Hill. Standing almost 100 m in diameter and 18 m high, this great mound was reshaped in 1650 with a path forming a spiral round it, rising in tiers like a wedding cake, and ending at a gazebo on the top. Today the mound is overgrown and tree-clad with a great water tank on top of it. Red-deer antlers were found buried in the side of the barrow in 1912. [H. C. Brentnall, *WAM*, 48 (1937–9), 133.]

37 MARTINSELL, Pewsey   SU:177639

This large rectangular fort of 13 ha overlooks the Vale of Pewsey. Its only defence is a single rampart and ditch with a probable entrance at the north-east corner. Protection on the south and east sides is aided by steep escarpment slopes. A Belgic rubbish pit was found in the copse to the north of the camp in 1907.

South-west along the escarpment is the little promontory fort called the **Giant's Grave**. It is protected by a main rampart and ditch with central entrance, and two outlying banks and ditches. Iron age pottery indicating two periods of occupation has been found inside. [L. V. Grinsell, *VCH Wiltshire*, I, 1 (1957), 268.]

38 MILSTON DOWN, Milston   SU:217463

Two long barrows lie side by side west of the road. Neither appears to have been excavated. One is 49 m long, 21 m wide and 2 m high; the other to the north is 27 m long, 15 m wide and 1 m high. Their side ditches are still visible. [L. V. Grinsell, *VCH Wiltshire,* I, 1 (1957), 142.]

39 NORMANTON DOWN, Wilsford (Fig 26, p. 274)   SU:118413

Perhaps the most important barrow cemetery in England, these monu-

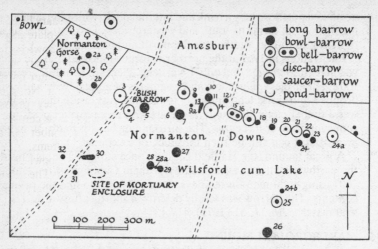

Fig 26. The Normanton group, Wiltshire (after L. V. Grinsell)

ments sweep across the horizon south of Stonehenge for more than a kilometre. Almost every type of barrow is represented here; most of them are protected but a number of outliers have been destroyed or are being damaged by ploughing. It is easiest to describe them from west to east. (The numbers are Grinsell's.)

At the northern end of the wood called Normanton Gorse is a bowl-barrow (1) 3 m high built to cover two burials, one a man, laid on a plank of wood with a grooved bronze dagger in a wooden scabbard, a beaker and deer antlers. A tripod arrangement of poles above the grave may represent a mortuary hut. Six infant burials with beakers were also included in the barrow. In the wood is a disc-barrow (2) and a bowl-barrow (2a). East of the wood and west of the cart track is a fine disc-barrow (3) opened in 1804 to reveal a cremation, with amber, shale and faience beads. The adjoining disc-barrow (4) was opened by William Stukeley in 1723 when he found a cremation. The most famous barrow in the group is a bowl-barrow called Bush Barrow (5) opened by William Cunnington in September 1808. The extended skeleton of a man was found, with two bronze daggers at his side. One of these had a wooden hilt decorated with hundreds of gold pins. In his right hand was a smaller dagger, and close by a wooden mace with stone head. At his shoulder lay an axe wrapped in fabric, and above his head was a wooden shield. Although his clothes had not survived, a lozenge-shaped sheet of gold had been sewn on to his chest, whilst a hook of gold hung at his waist. Barrow 6 is a plundered bowl-barrow. Another bowl-barrow (7) covered a skeleton buried with a grape cup, amber, shale and gold beads and a finely decorated collared urn. The bell-barrow (8) is 40 m in diameter and 3 m high. Its primary burial lay with an incense cup, a gold-plated shale cone, two gold-plated amber discs and other items of jewellery. The next three small bowl-barrows (9, 10, 11) were plundered without record. A small long barrow (13) may have formed the religious focus around which the later barrows were arranged. Colt Hoare found nothing of interest in it. Nor did he find the nearby bowl-barrow (12) productive. Stukeley probably opened the next disc-barrow (14) to find a cremation at its centre. An unusual twin bell-barrow (15, 16) was opened on a number of occasions. Both mounds covered cremations and minor items. A bell-barrow (17) was opened without result. Next are two bowl-barrows (18, 19), the second with a skeleton and bronze dagger. The group is completed with two good disc-barrows (20, 21), two bowl-barrows (23, 24), a saucer barrow (22) and a disc-barrow (24a).

Two hundred and seventy metres south of Bush Barrow, beside the cart track, is a long barrow (30), 36 m long and 1·8 m high, in which Cunnington found four skeletons 'curiously huddled together' at the eastern end. Immediately south of the long barrow a mortuary enclosure used for storing corpses before burial was discovered by aerial photography, and later excavated. [L. V. Grinsell, *Stonehenge Barrow Groups* (1979), 30.]

40 OGBURY CAMP, Durnford su:143383
Although enclosing 25 ha, this oval-shaped hillfort has little natural strength. Its rampart still stands 2·4 m high, though its ditch has long since been silted up. There are a number of gaps in the earthworks – that on the east is usually considered to be ancient. William Stukeley and Richard Colt Hoare have referred to internal enclosures and these have been seen on recent aerial photographs, all substantiating the claim that the camp was an agricultural enclosure rather than a defensive work. [O. G. S. Crawford and A. Keiller, *Wessex from the Air* (1928), 150.]

41 OLD AND NEW KING BARROWS, Amesbury (Fig 28, p. 281)
su:134426, su:135421
Two groups of seven barrows covered with trees and named by Stukeley in the eighteenth century. They have all been dug into at various times, but nothing is known of their contents.

42 OLDBURY CASTLE, Calne su:049693
This roughly rectangular fort encloses 4·8 ha. A bank cutting across it from north-west to south-east suggests that it originally had only a single rampart and ditch, but that this was doubled when the fort was enlarged on the western side. There is a strongly inturned entrance on the eastern side defended by an outlying bank and ditch. The gap at the

south may also be original, but the interior has been disturbed by flint digging in the nineteenth century, and it is now difficult to be certain. The digging produced iron age pottery and storage pits.

The White Horse dates from 1780 and was cut by Dr Christopher Alsop of Calne.

43 OLD SARUM, Stratford-sub-Castle   SU:137327
Old Sarum is best seen from the Avon valley to the west. Although today it is dominated by a Norman castle motte, it is the surrounding earthworks which formed an iron age hillfort that are of special interest. These were clearly enlarged in the middle ages, but in essence they form an oval enclosure of 11 ha with an entrance on the east where the later Norman gate was built, and probably another on the northeast, obscured by later work. Iron age material, including a storage pit, has been found incidentally during excavation of the medieval remains. [P. A. Rahtz and J. W. Musty, *WAM*, 57 (1960), 353.]

44 OLIVER'S CASTLE, Bromham   SU:001646
A pleasant little fort at the end of a spur overlooking Bloody Battle Ditch of Civil War fame. A single bank and ditch encloses 1·2 ha and is broken by an entrance on the east. When excavated this revealed two holes for gateposts on either side. The ditch was 4·3 m deep and of normal V-shape. Pits in the interior produced early iron age pottery.

Two bowl-barrows on the south-west have been excavated. The southern contained a cremation in a Cornish-type handled urn, together with a bronze dagger, and the northern, which also contained a cremation, produced part of an incense cup and a conical bone button. [L. V. Grinsell, *VCH Wiltshire*, I, 1 (1957), 162, 263.]

45 OVERTON HILL BARROWS, West Overton   SU:119682
The prehistoric Ridgeway crosses the A4 at this point. South of the main road is a bowl-barrow 18 m in diameter and 3·7 m high. Excavated by Colt Hoare, it contained a crouched burial in a tree-trunk coffin, together with a flat bronze dagger and axe and a crutch-headed pin of Germanic type.

The first barrow north of the A4 is a damaged bell-barrow, which covered a cremation and incense cup. The second bell-barrow also contained a cremation. Next is a small bowl-barrow that seems to overlie its neighbours. It held a cremation buried in a cloth once secured by a bone pin. The most northerly bell-barrow is 38 m in diameter and 3 m high. Under it was a cremation with a bronze dagger and bone belt hook. The last and most northerly barrow in the row is a bowl-barrow, which also covered a cremation. There are further barrows along the ridge, most of them ploughed low. A good bell-barrow survives at SU:117691 and a disc-barrow at su:116689. [L. V. Grinsell, *VCH Wiltshire*, I, 1 (1957) 195.]

46   PERTWOOD DOWN, Brixton Deverill   ST:872374
This long barrow, 76 m long and 2 m high, is unusual in having a flat berm to separate the mound from its clearly defined side ditches. It appears to be unopened.

47   RYBURY CAMP, All Cannings   su:083640
A small iron age fort of 1·5 ha overlies a neolithic causewayed camp. The neolithic camp consists of two concentric oval ditches, of which eight segments of the outer ring are visible on the east side of the hillfort. About 300 m south-east is a small knoll, Clifford's Hill, with seven more segments of causewayed ditch. Excavation of the main site has shown ditch segments 2 m deep and flat bottomed.

The iron age rampart is a slight affair with a possible entrance at the south-east. [S. Piggott, *VCH Wiltshire* I, 2 (1973), 296.]

48   THE SANCTUARY, Overton Hill, West Overton (Fig 24, p. 261)
                                                          su:118679
This circle lies at the end of the West Kennet Avenue, south-east of Avebury. Destroyed in the eighteenth century, it was rediscovered and excavated in 1930. The digging revealed two stone circles and six concentric rings of post-holes. It is now considered that the post-hole rings are not contemporary with each other, but represent a number of successive circular wooden buildings of which the last was surrounded by the two stone circles. The position of the stones and posts are marked today by concrete plinths. It is important that the Sanctuary be seen as part of the Avebury complex. [A. Burl, *Prehistoric Avebury* (1979), 124.]

49   SCRATCHBURY CAMP, Norton Bavant   ST:912443
Finely sited above the Wylye, this irregular-shaped contour fort of 15 ha has a single bank and ditch with a counterscarp. It has three entrances, two in the south-east side and one on the north-west. Inside is a smaller circular earthwork dated to about 350 BC, which indicates an earlier enclosure, as at Yarnbury. Low banks running south-west towards the north-eastern gate may also be of iron age date. A ditch running east-west across the southern portion of the fort is likely to be Romano-British or later.

Two small barrows lie inside the fort north of the north-east gate; that on the east has produced a cremation. In the south-west corner is a bowl-barrow 30 m in diameter and 3 m high. It was opened by William Cunnington in September 1802. Animal bones and burnt stones were found in it, but no burial. On the same day Cunnington dug another barrow in the centre of the fort, still a metre high. In it he found a small bronze dagger, a bronze pin, fifty amber beads and a large amber ring. [O. G. S. Crawford, *Air Survey and Archaeology* (1924), 36.]

50 SILBURY HILL, Avebury   su:100685

One cannot suppress a feeling of excitement on first seeing Silbury Hill, its great conical profile dominating the undulating landscape. It stands 40 m high and its base covers more than 2 ha. It was first dug into in 1776 when the Duke of Northumberland employed Cornish tin miners to dig down from the summit. Seventy years later in 1849 the incomparable Dean Merewether of Hereford opened thirty-five barrows in twenty-eight days, including the West Kennet long barrow and Silbury Hill! Silbury was 'opened' by driving a tunnel into the centre from the south side, but nothing was found. The work was terminated in a tremendous thunderstorm, which made 'Silbury . . . tremble to its base'. Although its entrance was sealed over, Merewether's tunnel was re-located and followed by Richard Atkinson when he dug into Silbury between 1968 and 1970. Although the Atkinson dig was equally un-lucky in failing to find a definite answer to the question 'What was Silbury Hill?', it did obtain a great deal of scientific information about the mound. It was possible to ascertain four building phases, which were as follows:

1 A drum-shaped clay and flint mound was constructed, 4·9 m in diameter and 0·9 m high. This was covered with a heap of turf and soil that spread outwards to a low wooden retaining fence 20 m in diameter. Over this four layers of chalk, gravel and subsoil were laid to complete a conical mound about 34 m in diameter and 5 m high. The centre of this structure had been completely destroyed by the digging of 1776.

2 Soon after Phase 1 was completed the mound was enlarged by commencing to dig a quarry ditch around it and piling up the chalk to make a mound with a diameter of 73 m.

3 Before Phase 2 could be completed a change of plan occurred. The ditch was abandoned and a much larger mound was commenced, built in a series of great steps, like a wedding cake, presumably for greater stability. The outline of the uppermost step is still visible. Chalk from a great new ditch 7–10 m deep and 26 m wide was piled between concentric retaining walls that were all part of a masterly engineering plan to counteract weathering and prevent the mound from slipping.

4 The final stage at Silbury was probably the westward extension of the ditch to obtain enough chalk to fill in the steps of the mound and give it its present smooth appearance.

A revised radiocarbon date for the first phase of Silbury suggests that it was constructed around 2500 BC, well into the neolithic period.

Most authorities regard Silbury Hill as a great neolithic barrow, built perhaps to cover the material remains of some prehistoric dignitary whose rank required such an elaborate tomb. If that was so, then his remains have not been found. Were they destroyed by Dean Merewether? Do they lie in a stone chamber off-centre awaiting discovery? Or is our interpretation quite wrong? Did Silbury have a major religious or astronomical significance? Speculation is idle – we do not know. [R. J. C. Atkinson in R. Sutcliffe, ed., *Chronicle* (1978).]

51 SNAIL DOWN, Collingbourne Ducis and Kingston SU:218522 (centre) One of the great Wessex barrow cemeteries about which much is known from modern excavations, but being on Ministry of Defence land it is virtually inaccessible. Almost thirty round barrows of every type are represented. Many were dug by William Cunnington for Colt Hoare in 1805, and ten were re-dug by Nicholas and Charles Thomas between 1953 and 1957.

It seems highly likely that a beaker period settlement existed at Snail Down before any of the barrows were constructed. In due course a neolithic round barrow (23) was built to cover a cremation encircled by a ring of posts. Soon afterwards five small bowl-barrows (9 to 13) were scraped up over cremations. Other barrows in a variety of Wessex types followed. A bell-barrow (4) covered the cremation of an adult male in an urn. A radiocarbon date of 1540 ± 70 bc has been obtained for it. A double bell-barrow (25) covered a loose cremation under one mound and a wooden coffin containing more burnt human bones, and a bronze dagger and pin, under the other. Both mounds had been

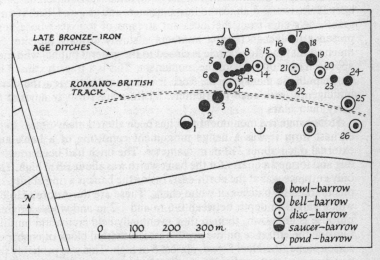

Fig 27. Snail Down, Wiltshire (after N. Thomas)

retained by circles of short wooden posts. No. 18 is a bowl-barrow, called 'Hunter's Barrow' by Cunnington because its cremation was surrounded by a circle of red-deer antlers, five flint arrowheads and the skeleton of a dog. 'Thus we most clearly see the profession of the Briton here interred. In the flint arrowheads we recognize his fatal implements of destruction; in the stags' horns we see the victims of his skill as a hunter; and the bones of the dog deposited in the same grave, and above those of his master, commemorate his faithful attendant in the chase, and perhaps his unfortunate victim in death' (Colt Hoare, *Ancient Wiltshire*, 1812). Over about two hundred years the cemetery slowly grew to its final shape. Almost at the centre of the cemetery is a disc-barrow (21) which had a small central mound and another off-centre. Under the central tump was a cremation pit that had been robbed even before Cunnington's time. The other mound covered a large empty pit that must have played some obscure part in funerary ritual. The barrow has been left open since it was totally excavated in 1953. In the later bronze age a Celtic field system spread around the barrows, probably connected with Sidbury hillfort to the south. Later still a V-shaped boundary ditch cut across the northern edge of the cemetery, perhaps indicating that arable farming was now being replaced by stock rearing. [N. and C. Thomas, *WAM*, 56 (1959), 127.]

52   STONEHENGE, Amesbury   su:122422

This most renowned and badly displayed archaeological site in Europe is something of an anticlimax to the uninitiated. Its isolation on Salisbury Plain dwarfs it almost to insignificance, and gasps of 'Isn't it tiny' greet one's ears from the incessant streams of tourists whose very presence in ever-increasing numbers is slowly eroding the site. So much so that the stone circle is closed to the general public, who may approach only one side of the monument. This is a tragedy caused by unsympathetic management, since it is impossible to view the circle intelligently with such restrictions. Visitors are strongly advised to carry binoculars.

Stonehenge is a monument that has been altered many times. In its earliest form it was a henge monument consisting of a bank and external ditch about 110 m in diameter. The ditch had been roughly dug and formed a quarry for the bank which was about 1·8 m high. The only entrance was at the north-east. Inside the bank is a ring of fifty-six pits marked by patches of white chalk. These are the Aubrey Holes, which varied in depth between 0·6 m and 1·2 m and whose original purpose is unknown, though they eventually held cremation burials. Outside the entrance on the north-east is a twisted block of unshaped sarsen stone, the Heel Stone, almost 5 m high. This was probably the first stone erected on the site. Around its base is a small circular ditch.

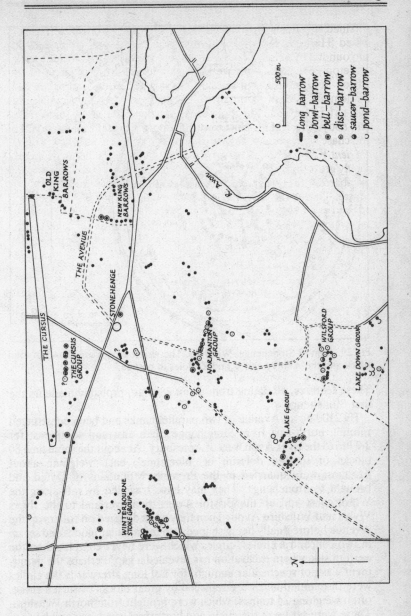

Fig 28. The environs of Stonehenge, Wiltshire

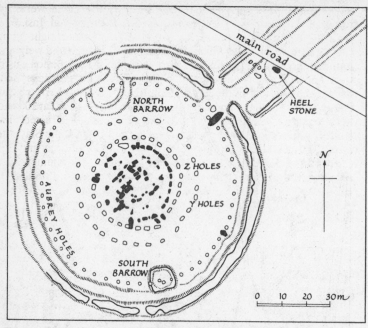

Fig 29. Plan of Stonehenge, Wiltshire. The visible stones are shown in solid black and the Aubrey and Y and Z Holes in outline

These features, all dating from about 2800 BC, probably made up the first Stonehenge.

By 2100 BC an Avenue of two parallel banks had been constructed running north-east from Stonehenge, then east and south-east for 2·7 km to the river Avon west of Amesbury. At about the same time 80 blocks of spotted dolerite or 'bluestone', each weighing about 4 tonnes, were quarried in the Prescelly Mountains of Dyfed and brought to Stonehenge. They may have travelled by raft along the Welsh coast and up the Bristol Avon, then overland to the rivers Wylye and Wiltshire Avon. Then they were dragged on rollers up the Avenue before finally being shaped into rectangular blocks and set up in two concentric circles, circles which were never completed on the western side where excavation has revealed a gap. Perhaps the monument was not spectacular enough, for not long afterwards the circles were dismantled and were replaced by great blocks of sarsen stone, often weighing 26 tonnes, which were brought from north Wiltshire. These were set up in the circle and horseshoe which can still be seen today. Each stone was carefully shaped, the lintels being dovetailed into each other and secured on the uprights with primitive mortice and tenon joints. The inner and outer faces of the circle were also smoothed and here and there carvings of axes were placed. Inside the circle in a horseshoe setting are five trilithons (two upright stones capped by one lintel) of which the tallest is 6·7 m high and weighs 45 tonnes. These stones increase in size up to the great trilithon on the west, and have also been carefully shaped. Carvings of more axes and a dagger can be seen on the left-hand upright of the southern trilithon (stone 53). It is worth remembering that this took place about 2000 BC, before many of the great pyramids of Egypt were constructed. Two stones were set up beside the entrance, of which one, the Slaughter Stone, though fallen, still survives. These formed a gateway and from the centre of the circle the sun could be viewed on midsummer morning apparently entering the circle above the Heel Stone; similarly at midwinter the sun set in the opposite direction.

The Welsh bluestones were next brought back into use. Twenty were set up in an oval inside the sarsen horseshoe, whilst the rest were to be arranged in a double circle outside the great sarsen circle. Although the holes were dug (Y and Z holes) these later circles were never erected and for some unknown reason the oval setting was removed.

By 150 BC changes had again taken place and the bluestones had now been placed in a circle of about sixty uprights between the main circle and the trilithons, with the rest in a horseshoe setting inside the five trilithons. A rectangular block of green sandstone, 3·7 m high, quarried near Milford Haven was set up as a pillar in front of the great trilithon; this is the so-called Altar Stone.

In time Stonehenge spans from the end of the neolithic period to the middle bronze age, yet in the popular imagination it was the Druids almost two thousand years later who were supposed to have built it. By their day it was almost certainly in ruins.

The purpose of the circle is obscure. There is little doubt that it was a place of worship and the presence of many axe carvings suggests that axe worship may have been involved. It has been observed that the circle is aligned on midsummer sunrise and midwinter sunset. Other astronomical observations may also have been possible, though probably far fewer than some modern astronomers would like to suggest. These astronomical details would help to establish a simple calendar with fixed feasts and ceremonial days, when tribal meetings for making laws or electing chiefs could be held.

The material from the excavations at Stonehenge is in the Salisbury and South Wiltshire Museum in Salisbury. [R. J. C. Atkinson, *Stonehenge* (1979).]

53 STONEHENGE CURSUS, Amesbury (Fig 28, p. 281)   SU:124430
Thought by William Stukeley to have been a prehistoric chariot course, this long narrow rectangular monument might have been

connected with funeral games of some kind. It is certainly aligned on a long barrow that contained the skeleton of a child. A bank and external ditch mark an enclosure 2·8 km long and about 90 m wide. Its closeness to Stonehenge emphasizes the part that religious or astronomical ritual may have played in the area. [J. F. S. Stone, *Arch. J*, 104 (1947), 7.]

54 THORNY DOWN, Winterbourne   su:203339
On top of the Downs and sheltered from the north by a wood is an uneven area of banks and hollows which on closer examination proves to be a rectangular enclosure of about 0·2 ha. On the north is a bank and ditch, on the west and south a bank only, and on the east a gap that must once have been marked by a hedge or fence. Excavation revealed nine circular or rectangular huts, together with storage pits, cooking holes and posts for corn-drying racks and granaries. Large quantities of globular Deverel-Rimbury cooking pots of the middle bronze age were found. [J. F. S. Stone, *PPS*, 7 (1941), 114.]

55 TIDCOMBE LONG BARROW, Tidcombe   su:292576
This upstanding long barrow 56 m long and 3 m high has been badly damaged in the past by the digging of a trench along it. Four sarsen stones in a hollow at the southern end are the remains of a burial chamber which contained a skeleton when ransacked in 1750 by local folk searching for treasure. A bank and ditch a few metres to the east may represent an iron age ranch boundary. [L. V. Grinsell, *VCH Wiltshire*, I, 1 (1957), 144.]

56 TILSHEAD OLD DITCH, Tilshead   su:023468
As it is on Ministry of Defence land this barrow is not directly accessible, but is clearly visible from the road to the north. It is almost certainly the longest true long barrow in England, measuring 120 m long, 30 m wide and 3·4 m high. It was dug into twice, by William Cunnington in 1802 and John Thurnam in 1865. At the base of the barrow was a layer of black soil and on this lay two burials. One was an adult that had been partially burnt, whilst the other was a small woman who had probably died from a blow on the skull. The burnt burial lay on a funeral pyre of burnt flint and ashes, and both ladies were covered by a cairn of flints. Three other burials found in the mound were probably added later.

Beside the road to the north at Tilshead Lodge (su:021475) is a second long barrow, which also contained two burials, one with a cleft skull. Beside them were the carcasses of two slaughtered cattle. [L. V. Grinsell, *VCH Wiltshire*, I, 1 (1957), 144.]

57 TILSHEAD WHITE BARROW, Tilshead   su:033468
Known as **Whiteburgh** since at least 1348, this fine long barrow is 78 m long, 46 m wide and 2 m high, with well-defined berms and side

ditches. It was excavated by William Cunnington for Sir Richard Colt
Hoare more than 150 years ago, but the only recorded finds are pieces
of an antler. [L. V. Grinsell, *VCH Wiltshire*, I, 1 (1957), 144.]

58 UPTON GREAT BARROW, Upton Lovell   ST:955423
A bell-barrow 53 m in diameter and 3 m high is almost all that remains
of a group of barrows opened by Cunnington and Colt Hoare in 1801.
Under the Great Barrow was a cremation with a fine necklace of
amber, shale and faience beads. [L. V. Grinsell, *VCH Wiltshire*, I, 1
(1957), 215.]

59 WEST KENNET LONG BARROW, Avebury (Fig 24, p. 261)
                                                             SU:104677
Visible as an undulating ridge on the hilltop to the south the West
Kennet long barrow can be clearly seen from the A4. This is hardly
surprising for the barrow mound is 100 m long and 2·5 m high. At its
eastern end is a burial chamber 12 m long and high enough to walk into
without stooping. Restoration after excavations in 1955–6 has revealed
a facade of large sarsen stones at the eastern end, with the great
entrance blocking stone replaced in its original position. Behind the
facade is a crescent-shaped forecourt and then the central gallery with
two pairs of chambers on either side and one at the end. The barrow
has been dug into from time to time, and in 1859 John Thurnam
cleared the end chamber in which he found five adult burials and a
child. The Piggott–Atkinson excavations of 1955–6 revealed the other
four side chambers, with their corbelled and capstoned roofs some
2·3 m high. The north-east chamber held a male and two female
burials, the south-east held single male and female burials together
with five infants and four babies. The north-west and south-west
chambers were smaller and lower. Amongst a mass of bones in the
north-west vault twelve individuals could be recognized, and in the
south-west nine adults, a youth, a child and two infants. Mixed with the
bones throughout the tomb were sherds of neolithic pottery, beads,
flints and animal bones. The pottery represented types in use for as
long as a thousand years, and this suggests that the tomb may have
been re-opened many times over such a period of time. We know of
forty-six burials from the tomb, and there is evidence that many more
were removed in the seventeenth century. Objects found at West
Kennet are on display in Devizes Museum. [S. Piggott, *The West
Kennet Long Barrow: Excavations 1955–56* (1962).]

60 WHITESHEET CASTLE, Stourton   ST:804346
Three widely spaced ramparts and ditches cut off this triangular promontory fort of 5·6 ha on its north-east side. The defences are broken
by a number of gaps, none of which can readily be recognized as an

original entrance. Above the steep chalk escarpment on the south and west is a single rampart and ditch. The site is unexcavated but it is clear that the fort is of several periods and the sequence of ramparts on the north-east was probably middle, followed by outer and then inner. The embanked circle in the fort is an eighteenth-century tree-ring enclosure. (There were banks built to protect newly planted trees from damage by animals.) Three barrows can also be traced. North-west and south-east of the fort are cross-dykes facing northwards. [R. C. Hoare, *Ancient Wiltshire*, 1 (1812), 43.]

61   WHITE SHEET HILL, Kilmington   ST:802352
This neolithic enclosure consists of an oval-shaped earthwork of about 1·6 ha, whose bank is interrupted at irregular intervals by twenty-one causeways of undug chalk. Excavation in 1951 showed that the ditch was about 3 m wide with a depth that varied from 0·3 m to 1·5 m. On the bottom were pieces of Windmill Hill pottery and the skull of an ox.
   A bronze age bowl-barrow overlies the ditch of the camp on the south-east side. It was opened in 1807 by William Cunnington who found a skeleton in it, although it had clearly been opened previously. [S. Piggott, *WAM,* 54 (1952), 404.]

62   WHITE SHEET HILL LONG BARROW, Ansty   ST:942242
An oblong barrow 41 m long, 23 m wide and nearly 2 m high at its eastern end, with well marked side ditches. It appears to be unexcavated.

63   WILSFORD BARROWS (Fig 28, p. 281)   SU:118398
Divided equally between a plantation and a field to the north are the remains of a group of (originally nineteen) barrows, which have been badly damaged by farming. There were eleven bowl-barrows, five discs, a pond-, saucer- and bell-barrow. Half a dozen of the bowls and a disc can be made out amongst a tangle of undergrowth in the wood. The bell-barrow at the western end of the group survives. It is 45 m in diameter with a central mound 3 m high. In it was found the skeleton of a man lying on his right side holding a greenstone battle-axe. Beside him was a flanged bronze axe and a bone musical instrument – a sort of flute – as well as the handle of a bronze cauldron. [L. V. Grinsell, *Stonehenge Barrow Groups* (1979), 40.]

64   WINDMILL HILL, Winterborne Monkton   SU:087714
Three approximately concentric ovals of causewayed ditches ring a low hilltop a little less than 2 km north-west of Avebury. This is the largest causewayed enclosure yet recognized in England. It has an area of 8·5 ha and its outer ditch has a diameter of some 360 m. The mean diameter of the middle ditch is 200 m whilst the inner measured about

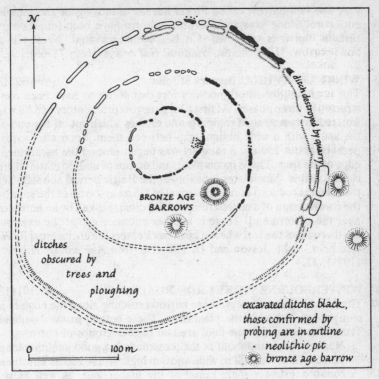

Fig 30. Windmill Hill, Wiltshire (after A. Keiller)

85 m. The ditches do not lie around the summit of the hill but tend to
hang lopsidedly down the steeper northern slope.

All the sections of the ditch are very irregular. Apart from having
flattish bottoms, there are no other similarities. Depth and width
varies from area to area and gives every appearance of having been the
work of separate groups of workmen. The causeway gaps between
ditch sections can vary from a few centimetres to 7·5 m. The inner ditch
tends to be shallower than the more massive outer ring. The ditches
acted as quarries for the inner banks, but these can be seen only on the
eastern side, the remainder having been thrown back into the ditches
in prehistory or by ploughing. More than 1300 neolithic pots have been
identified from the site, together with flint and stone objects and
animal bone. Many of these were found deliberately buried in the
ditches and it is clear that a ritual involving the frequent clearing and
burial of objects took place on the site. A corrected radiocarbon date
of 3350 BC sets the period when this took place.

A fine bell-barrow called **Picket Barrow** stands inside the middle enclosure. Stone axes and a bronze age urn have been found on its surface, but it is unknown if it has been excavated. Nearby is a bowl-barrow. [I. F. Smith, *Windmill Hill and Avebury* (1965).]

65 WINKELBURY HILL, Berwick St John   st:952218
This is an unfinished promontory fort that seems to have been constructed in three phases. At first a long narrow promontory of 5 ha was isolated by two straight ramparts and ditches which cut off the end of the spur, with a wide oblique gap between them. Soon afterwards, perhaps about 250 bc, a rampart was begun around the escarpment edge of the spur. This is incomplete, and dumps of unused material are clearly visible. Much later, possibly in the Belgic period about 50 bc, the fort was reduced in size to an oval of 1·8 ha at the tip of the spur by the construction of a curved rampart and ditch, broken by an entrance near the eastern end. There is another entrance gap at the extreme northern tip of the fort where a farm track enters the enclosure. [R. W. Feachem, in M. Jesson and D. Hill, *The Iron Age and its Hillforts* (1971), 32.]

66 WINTERBOURNE STOKE CROSSROADS   su:101417
There is a linear cemetery of ten barrows running along the edge of a ploughed field beside the plantation. These belong to the National Trust. Further out in the field are two further groups of barrows.
 1 Nearest the roundabout at the crossroads is a good neolithic long barrow 72 m long, 22 m wide and 3 m high. In 1863 John Thurnam found a primary male burial at the higher end, as well as six secondary skeletons of a man, woman and four children, buried with a food vessel and flint scraper.
    The contents of the linear cemetery from south-west to north-east were:
 2 A low bowl-barrow which contained a cremation.
 3 A pond-barrow – apparently unopened, it overlaps 4.
 4 A bell-barrow which took Colt Hoare four days to open. In it was a wooden box, perhaps with bronze fittings, which held a cremation, also two bronze daggers, a bone pin and tweezers.
 5 The King Barrow – another rich bell, contained a skeleton in a tree-trunk coffin, a five-handled Bretton-type urn, two bronze daggers and a bronze awl with a bone handle. There might have been a wreath above the coffin.
 6 to 10 are all bowl-barrows.
 8 In this was a skeleton with a grape cup, whetstones and jewellery.
 9 Covered a boat-shaped wooden coffin that held a skeleton, some shale and amber beads, a bronze dagger and awl, and a small pottery cup.

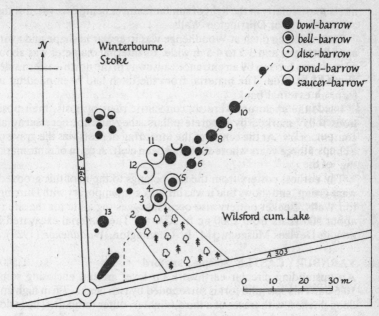

Fig. 31. Winterbourne Stoke crossroads, Wiltshire

10 Two skeletons in a large rectangular grave with a long-necked beaker. Six skeletons and an inverted cremation urn were added later.

Amongst the parallel row of barrows out in the field are seven bowls, two discs and a saucer. Noteworthy are:

11 A fine disc-barrow 53 m in diameter with three burial tumps. Under each mound was a cremation, and the centre tump also covered a small cup and some amber beads.

12 The second disc-barrow, 52 m across, covered a cremation.

13 A bowl-barrow near the road covering a cremation and small pot.

[L. V. Grinsell, *Stonehenge Barrow Groups* (1979), 18.]

67 WOODHENGE, Amesbury (Fig 25, p. 267)   SU:150434

This site was one of the first major discoveries by aerial photography in Britain. It was photographed by Squadron Leader Insall in 1925 and subsequently excavated by Mr and Mrs B. H. Cunnington in 1926–7. It consisted of six concentric circles of posts surrounded by a ditch with an outer bank. It is uncertain whether the structure formed a roofed building or stood open to the sky like a wooden Stonehenge, as the name given to it by the Cunningtons implies. The former seems more likely, particularly in the light of similar features being excavated at the adjoining site of Durrington Walls.

The enclosing ditch at Woodhenge was irregular in shape and averaged 2 m deep and 3·5 to 4·5 m wide. Its internal diameter was about 52 m. It was broken by an entrance causeway in the north-eastern side, about 10 m wide. The material from the ditch had been piled up to form an external bank.

Inside the enclosure were six concentric rings of posts, their positions today marked by concrete pillars; they are not necessarily all contemporary. At the centre of the inner ring of posts was the grave of a child of three years whose skull had been cleft. A cairn of flints marks the spot.

The earliest pottery from the site belongs to the neolithic grooved-ware group, and shows that it was broadly contemporary with Durrington Walls. Beaker pottery also occurs, suggesting a life for the site of about 500 years from 2500 BC to 2000 BC. The material excavated is now in Devizes Museum. [M. E. Cunnington, *Woodhenge* (1929).]

68 YARNBURY CASTLE, Steeple Langford   SU:035404
An upstanding circular earthwork on level ground enclosing some 10·5 ha. This splendid fort is surrounded by two banks, 7·6 m high and deep ditches, with traces of a third, slighter, outer rampart. The inside of the inner bank is pitted with what appear to be quarry scoops. There is a strongly inturned entrance on the east, 9 m wide, with elaborate outworks including a kidney-shaped enclosure which forces the entrance passage south and north-east. This work was possibly constructed by the Belgae about 50 BC.

Inside the fort are traces of an earlier 3·7 ha enclosure which has been shown by excavation to date from the seventh to the fifth centuries BC, and to have a V-shaped ditch 3 m deep and an entrance on its western side with a wooden gate.

A small triangular outwork on the western side of the fort is likely to be Roman in date. From the eighteenth century until 1916 an annual sheep fair was held inside the fort. The sheep-pens have left rectangular ridges on the eastern side of the enclosure. [C. F. C. Hawkes, *Arch. J*, 104 (1947), 29.]

YORKSHIRE, NORTH

1 ACKLAM WOLD CEMETERY, Acklam   SE:796621 (centre)
Some seventeen round barrows were recorded by J. R. Mortimer and dug by him in the 1860s and 70s. Many have been destroyed by ploughing, but some can still be identified. That at SE:799619 contained a cremation covered by an inverted collared urn and an incense cup. The contents of SE:797621 (east of the road) had been destroyed by the burial of animals that died in the cattle plague of 1865. The adjoining barrow on the west side of the road produced five burials, including a child with a beaker, a cremation with a food vessel and a child of six or seven. At SE:796621 was a barrow that produced six burials, all crouched, and one with a riveted bronze dagger blade. The barrow at SE:794624 contained four burials, two men, a woman and a child. One of the men clutched a fine white flint dagger 18·5 cm long, and wore a jet ring and an amber button. A crouched burial in a barrow east of Stone Sleights at SE: 807616 had two pairs of jet buttons near its feet, suggesting that it wore leggings or buttoned trousers. [J. R. Mortimer, *Forty Years' Researches* (1905), 83.]

2 ALLAN TOPS, Goathland   NZ:828028
About 2 km north-west of Goathland are a number of overgrown enclosures, field walls and long banks running north to south. Amongst these are about seventy small cairns whose purpose is unknown, but which may be of a different date to the enclosures, which are probably field boundaries of the bronze age.

3 AYTON EAST FIELD, East Ayton   TA:000864
This long barrow is about 26 m long and 15 m wide and lies north to south. It is only a metre high at the north end and slopes down to the south. It is built of stony material and has been disturbed by early diggers and a hedge. Digging shows that at its centre had been a cairn of limestone on which a large fire had burnt, reducing the stone to lime. Two masses of human bone were found together with a deposit of more bones, five leaf-shaped arrowheads, four partly polished flint axes, two flint knives, boar tusks and an antler axe handle. The original account does not make it clear if the bones were cremated, but this

seems likely, since cremation was not uncommon in this part of York-shire. [F. Elgee, *Early Man in North East Yorkshire* (1930), 40.]

4   BLAKEY TOPPING, Allerston   SE:873934
Only three stones remain in this circle 15 m in diameter. Each stands
2 m high, whilst the hollows of the other stone holes can be clearly seen.

5   BOLTBY SCAR, Boltby   SE:506857
This is a semicircular cliff-edge fort, defended by a single rampart and
ditch which has been badly damaged by bulldozing. It is about 1 ha in
size and has steep cliffs for protection on the west. No entrance has
been identified. Three barrows, also destroyed, once stood inside the
camp, where a pair of bronze age gold earrings were found. The
relationship of the fort to the Hesketh Dyke to the north (SE:515878)
and the Casten Dyke to the south (SE:520828), which effectively cut
off 20 sq km of upland leaving the hillfort at its centre, is worth
investigating in terms of iron age territorial divisions. [I. Longworth,
Yorkshire (1965), 78.]

6   BRANSDALE LONG CAIRN   SE:607967
A ruined long cairn 16 m long and 7 m wide.

7   BRIDESTONES, Bilsdale Midcable   SE:576978
On the crest of Nab Ridge is a circle of about forty small stones with a
diameter of 12 m, with many of the stones touching one another. This
was almost certainly the retaining wall of a barrow which is now
destroyed. Outside the circle are traces of an earthen bank.

8   BURTON HOWE, Ingleby Greenhow   NZ:607033
Beside the northern end of Rudland Rigg trackway are four cairns.
The southern one has a stone kerb around it. At its centre was a robbed
cremation in a cist with traces of an urn. Four post-holes around the
cist suggest that it was covered by some kind of small wooden mortuary
hut. The cairn to the north covered a cremation with pieces of urn. The
third had similar contents in a cist that was surrounded by a ring of
stones. Nothing was found in the northernmost.

CANA, Marton-le-Moor, see Hutton Moor.

9   CARPERBY, Aysgarth   SD:990904
Fallen stones up to a metre long lie round an embanked oval, 28 m by
24 m. There are slight traces of a barrow at the centre.

10 CASTLE DYKES, Aysgarth   SD:982873
On a spur above Wensleydale and Bishopdale is a slightly oval henge

monument, its bank measuring 60 m across, with an internal ditch. The original entrance faces east; the other gaps in the bank are almost certainly modern. [R. J. C. Atkinson, *Excavations at Dorchester, Oxon,* 1 (1951), 97.]

11   CASTLE STEADS, Gayles   NZ:112074
On a steep-sided north-facing spur at 285 m above sea level, and only a few kilometres south-west of Stanwick, this small Brigantian hillfort is protected by a stone rampart, ditch and, in places, a counterscarp bank. The fort encloses 1·6 ha, but is badly preserved; its original entrance has not been identified.

12   CASTLETON RIGG, Westerdale   NZ:682041
Two earthworks cut across this narrow spur at the above reference and at NZ:684048. The former has a few large stones standing on its crest which would once have made a continuous wall. Both walls are stone faced. Between the two are traces of circular huts, fields and barrows. They all probably date from the late bronze age or early iron age.

13   COMMONDALE MOOR   NZ:637108
An oval stone ring 32 m across with low stones seldom more than 0·5 m high, and set radially towards the centre. Excavation in 1968 only produced flints. [J. Radley, *YAJ*, 42 (1969), 240.]

14   CROWN END, Westerdale   NZ:668075
A large irregular walled enclosure measuring some 240 m by 400 m covers the eastern end of Westerdale Moor and has a scatter of circular huts within it. At one point is a circular embanked enclosure 40 m in diameter with walls 0·5 m high and entrances on the east and west. A kilometre to the west (at NZ:658070) a linear earthwork consisting of a bank, ditch and counterscarp cuts across the top of the ridge between the Esk and the Baysdale Beck as though intended to make a promontory fort. Between this earthwork and the settlement described above are nearly 200 small cairns. Excavation has failed to produce any burials. [F. Elgee, *Early Man in North East Yorkshire* (1930), 140.]

15   DANBY RIGG, Danby   NZ:710065
A trapezoidal spur with precipitous slopes on most sides is cut off on the south by the Double Dike, a low linear work of three banks and two ditches. Five hundred metres north is a single stone wall crossing the width of the spur. Between the two structures is a circular bank of earth and stones 18 m in diameter, which enclosed a robbed grave, and some small stone cairns. On the north side of the stone wall is a concentration of about 300 small stone cairns that are usually interpreted as burial mounds although no burials have been found.

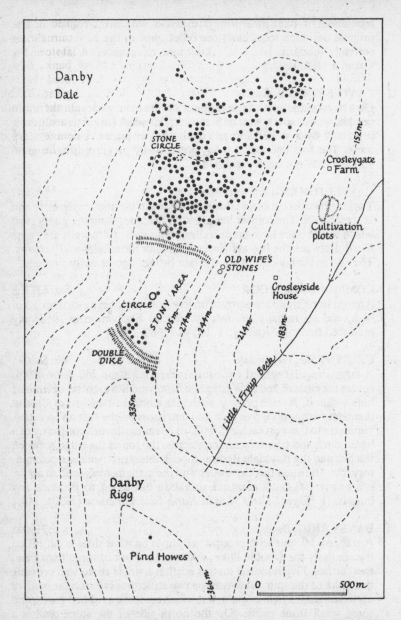

Fig 32. Settlement site on Danby Rigg, Yorkshire, North (after F. Elgee). The black dots represent stone cairns

Alternative interpretations such as clearance mounds and iron age industrial waste need further investigation. Among the cairns stood a stone circle, 12 m in diameter, of which only one broad flat stone 1·5 m high is still standing. Traces of a surrounding earthen bank are still visible, and excavations in the nineteenth century produced two collared urns from the centre. Two ordinary round barrows can also be seen amongst the cairns, close to the southern wall. On the eastern slope of the spur and a little south of Crosleygate Farm are traces of Celtic fields (NZ:718064). It is probable that the monuments extend in time from about 1700 BC to the first century AD. [F. Elgee, *Early Man in North East Yorkshire* (1930), 134.]

16   DEVIL'S ARROWS, Boroughbridge   SE:391666
Three massive and naturally fluted blocks of millstone grit march across a field along an almost straight line on a north-south axis. They have heights of 5·5 m (north), 6·4 m and 6·9 m (south). They seem to have been quarried at Knaresborough 10 km away, and the task of dragging them to Boroughbridge would have been colossal. They should probably be seen as part of the Thornborough/Hutton Moor religious complex that existed in this part of Yorkshire at the end of the neolithic and beginning of the bronze age.

17   DRUID'S ALTAR, Malham Moor   SD:949652
At a height of more than 360 m in the Pennines is a ruined cairn on which stood three (originally four) stones of an oval ring measuring 4 m by 3·5 m. The ring belongs to a type of stone circle common in Scotland known as a 'four-poster'. It is well south of the rest of its type. [A. Raistrick, *YAJ*, 29 (1929), 356.]

18   DUGGLEBY HOWE, Kirby Grindalythe   SE:881669
This is one of the largest round barrows in northern Britain and dates to the late neolithic period. Measuring about 36 m in diameter and 6 m high, it was trenched by J. R. Mortimer in 1890. At the centre was a grave pit 2·7 m deep and about 3 m square, with a shallower grave on the east. In these pits were the crouched remains of ten adults and children. With them were a neolithic bowl of Grimston ware, long bone pins, an antler mace head, and a convex polished flint knife 2 mm thick. A mound of chalk rubble covered the burials. In it were some twenty-two cremations, whilst other cremations in the outer mound bring the total to fifty-three and suggest beaker influence in the area. Only about half the barrow has been dug, so it is possible that other burials remain to be found. [J. R. Mortimer, *Forty Years' Researches* (1905), 23.]

19   ELBOLTON CAVE, Thorpe   SE:008616
On the western slope of Elbolton Hill a deep pit-like entrance leads

into a cave that seems to have been a temporary refuge during the closing years of the neolithic around 2300 BC. Pieces of Mortlake pottery, food vessels and collared urns have been found. Skeletons of a later date were also present. [N. Newbigin, *PPS*, 3 (1937), 216.]

20 FOLKTON TA:059777
This small round barrow was built to cover the remains of a male and female burial with a bell beaker. The skeletons seem to have been reburied in prehistoric times after the skulls had been removed. They were covered with a mound of flints. Outside this, but inside two concentric surrounding ditches, were the burials of four adults and a child. Between the concentric ditches was a further child burial accompanied by a bone pin and three chalk 'drums'. One of these touched the child's head whilst the others were at his hips. The 'drums' measure 10–12 cm in diameter and are now in the British Museum. Their geometric decoration includes stylized face patterns reminiscent of megalithic art, yet their presence in a child's grave suggests that whilst they might be endowed with protective religious powers, they could equally be toys. [W. Greenwell, *Archaeologia*, 52 (1890), Pl. 1, 2.]

21 GRASSINGTON SD:995655 to SE:004654
On the moors north of Grassington are a series of prehistoric field boundaries and hut circles. On High Close and Sweetside the fields can be up to 120 m long and 22 m wide with lynchets a metre high separating them. On Lea Green the fields are even bigger, often 90 m by 150 m, with hut enclosures scattered amongst them. The best village is at the north end of Lea Green, where excavations have produced iron age and Roman occupation material.

22 GREAT AYTON NZ:595115
On the northern edge of the Cleveland Hills are an extensive but scattered group of neolithic and bronze age cairns. At the grid reference above is a cairn with a tent-like stone chamber which was empty when excavated. The mound itself produced collared urns and an incense cup. A bank of stones 75 m long and up to 8 m wide runs north-west from the cairn. There is an oval enclosure on its north side. Two ring cairns lie south-east of the chambered cairn. One has produced three cremations. [R. H. Hayes, *Scarborough Dist. Arch. Soc. Res. Rep.*, 7 (1967).]

23 HANGING GRIMSTON, Thixendale SE:810608 (centre)
Originally eighteen round barrows lay in an arc around a long barrow. Most of them have now been destroyed. At SE:808608 is the long barrow excavated by J. R. Mortimer in 1868. Now ploughed, it is only 1 m high, but was originally 24 m long and 15 m wide, and had side

ditches 8 m wide and 1·8 m deep. At the eastern end a palisade trench held a wooden facade with a ritual pit at its centre. Four bowls of neolithic Grimston ware were found, together with the jaws of twenty pigs, but no signs of human burials.

Of the round barrows, now mostly flattened, one (at SE:806613) covered eleven burials. The primary skeleton of a young man was accompanied by a beaker. All the burials lay within a limestone circle covered by the barrow mound. More beakers were found in the other barrows, together with collared urns, a food vessel, a stone battle-axe, jet buttons and numerous flints. [J. R. Mortimer, *Forty Years' Researches* (1905), 96.]

24 HEDON HOWE, Burythorpe   SE:784665
Excavated by J. R. Mortimer in September 1893, this round barrow contained five contemporary stone cists, one at the centre and the others in cruciform plan around it. The central cist contained the remains of three skeletons and cremation with a food vessel. Two of the other cists contained single skeletons, the rest were empty. Pottery in the mound included neolithic Grimston ware and a beaker, and other finds included joints of meat and flint implements. [J. R. Mortimer, *Forty Years' Researches* (1905), 346.]

25 HELPERTHORPE LONG BARROW   SE:963679
Most of this barrow was removed for marling more than a century ago. It is still about 30 m long and 14 m wide. When opened by Mortimer in 1868 three circular pits at the higher west end were empty, but a smaller pit near the centre of the mound contained a cremation. Much of the floor of the barrow was covered with wood ash. Side ditches were examined and shown to be 1·8 m deep, 4 m wide at the top and 0·9 m at the bottom. [J. R. Mortimer, *Forty Years' Researches* (1905), 333.]

26 HIGH BRIDESTONES, Eskdale cum Ugglebarnby   NZ:850046
These two stone circles, both about 10 m in diameter, are now extensively damaged. Only three stones remain standing in each ring, the tallest 2 m high. Outside the circle to the north are three outlying stones; a single stone stands to the south. Adjoining the circles is the **Flat Howe** barrow with its kerb of retaining stones.

27 HUTTON MOOR, Hutton Conyers   SE:353735
Three ploughed henge monuments exist close together at Hutton Moor and within 2 or 3 km of the river Ure. All have suffered badly from agricultural activities. At Hutton Moor there is a circular bank with internal and external ditches, and entrances at the north and south. The site measures about 170 m in diameter. To the south is a

second henge at **Cana** (SE:361718) of about the same diameter with similarly positioned entrances and ditches. Between the two sites are half a dozen barrows of which the finest is north of Copt Hewick Hall at SE:348724. The **Nunwick henge** was discovered by aerial photography, but is still visible (SE:323748) as a circular bank about 1 m high. It has an internal ditch 13·5 m wide and 1·8 m deep, but no external ditch. It, too, has north- and south-facing entrances. [D. P. Dymond, *YAJ*, 38 (1955), 425; 41 (1961), 98.]

28 INGLEBOROUGH, Ingleton   SD:742746
At 716 m above sea-level this is the highest hillfort in southern Britain, and although it contains hut circles, this desolate, windswept height hardly seems a suitable place for permanent occupation. The fort is pear-shaped and encloses about 6 ha. Its single wall 4 m thick is made of millstone grit constructed with transverse lines of upright slabs passing through it at 2 m intervals dividing it into sections which are filled with rubble. Sadly, parts of the walls have been reduced by use as a quarry for a modern cairn on the summit. The main entrance seems to have been on the south-western side, though other gaps at the north and east may also be original. [A. King, *Early Pennine Settlement* (1970), 74.]

29 IRON HOWE, Snilesworth   SE:527951
On the southern tip of Cow Rigg at a height of about 300 m above sea-level is a group of about 300 cairns, lying between plots, enclosures and occasional huts. Most of the cairns are between 3 and 5 m in diameter and tend to be quite low. Many cairns of this type have been excavated elsewhere in Yorkshire but have failed to produce burials. Perhaps they should be considered as the bases of raised funeral pyres on which the bodies were burnt.

About 2 km of prehistoric walling have been measured at this site. [J. McDonnell, ed., *History of Helmsley, Rievaulx and District* (1963), 39.]

30 JOHN CROSS RIGG, Fylingdales   NZ:905025
It is claimed that there are some twelve hundred very small mounds on Fylingdales Moor, which are usually interpreted as part of a large cemetery. On the western slope of Grey Heugh Slack near its junction with Biller Howe Dale are many shallow oval pits and these may help to explain the mounds as upcast from quarrying activity. The association of a powerful earthwork 0·8 km long and 30 m broad consisting of four banks and three ditches cutting off the majority of the mounds from the main hill spur reminds one of the great iron age industrial site at Michelsberg near Kelheim in Bavaria. A lack of obvious settlements and field systems in the area makes this one of the puzzle sites of Britain. [F. Elgee, *Early Man in North East Yorkshire* (1930), 157.]

31 KEPWICK LONG BARROW   SE:492904
This barrow is about 34 m long, 9 m at its widest point and 1 m high. It is
highest at the eastern end, beneath which a deposit of human bones
was found by Greenwell. The core of the barrow was of stones, and
beneath these lay the disarticulated remains of at least five individuals,
including three young people, together with two flint flakes. [F. Elgee,
Early Man in North East Yorkshire (1930), 47.]

32 LOOSE HOWE, Ugthorpe   NZ:703008
This fascinating barrow, at the considerable height of 430 m above sea-
level, was excavated by F. and H. W. Elgee in 1937. Today it stands
2 m high and 18 m across. Its great interest centres on the fact that it
contained a burial in a tree-trunk coffin, accompanied by a dug-out
canoe, also carved from a tree-trunk. Both were 2·7 m long. As the
barrow was opened gallons of water poured out, indicating that the site
was waterlogged. 'The contents of the coffin proved to be a wet, black,
greasy substance in which the outline of the internment was
untraceable . . . a small fragment of shoe showing two lace holes
indicated the position of the left foot . . . The remains of a bronze
dagger occurred in the vicinity of the left hip.' Hazel husks indicated an
autumn burial. The corpse had been laid on a bed of rotted rushes,
reeds or straw. Beneath the head had been a pillow of grass or straw.
Linen fibre from the coffin suggests that the corpse was clothed in that
material. Both the coffin and its lid seems to have been designed as
canoes – quite remarkable when it is considered that the nearest
navigable water is 5 km away at the foot of an extremely steep hillside.
They may be dated to about 1700 BC. Almost at the centre of the
barrow was a much disturbed cremation in a broken collared urn, with
a pygmy cup, stone battle-axe, bronze dagger blade and crutch-headed
pin. It probably dates from the late bronze age. [H. W. and F. Elgee,
PPS, 15 (1949), 87.]

33 MAIDEN CASTLE, Harkerside Moor   SE:023981
On the slope above the river Swale is a circular banked enclosure 90 m
across with an external ditch. From an entrance on the eastern side is
an avenue of tumbled drystone walling stretching for about 110 m. Just
north of the end of the avenue is a large round barrow that is probably
contemporary, though there is no record of its contents.

NUNWICK HENGE, see Hutton Moor.

34 ROULSTON SCAR, Hood Grange   SE:514816
The largest of the promontory forts of north-east Yorkshire, it encloses 21 ha. A spur on the south-west is cut off by a rampart 3 m high
with a ditch on the north-east side. This is continued as a terrace on the
south-east along the valley side.

35 SCAMRIDGE, Allerston   SE:892861

This is an almost rectangular barrow 50 m long lying east–west. It is
3 m high at the eastern end, which is 16 m wide. At this end of the
barrow and along the centre lay a trench with a floor of yellow clay 12 m
long and 1 m wide. In it lay the scattered remains of about fourteen
persons, those at the eastern end completely burnt in position. At the
western end of the trench a cairn of stones may have acted as a flue or
chimney to the surface of the barrow. The whole mound, which is 48 m
long, was built of limestone boulders and was enclosed within a drystone wall. [W. Greenwell, *British Barrows* (1877), 484.]

36 SELSIDE, Horton   SD:777772

Along the lower eastern slope of Park Fell, south from SD:775780 and
below the trees, is an extensive area of Celtic fields which stretch east
across the B6479 and the railway. At SD:777772 are a series of circular
huts about 6 m in diameter, each in a walled enclosure. There is a pond
nearby, and plenty of springs on the hillside amongst the fields.

37 SHARP HOWES, Folkton   TA:049777

A linear cemetery of five round barrows excavated by Canon Greenwell. From north to south they are as follows:

1 A cremation in a cist with a food vessel, flint knife and bone pin.
   Nearby was a scattered cremation, whilst another pit held an inhumation.
2 No record of contents.
3 The structure of this mound was interesting. At the centre was a
   mound of earth, covered by one of chalk and held in place by a wall
   of chalk with an entrance in its southern side. Under the mound was
   a skeleton and a food vessel, as well as an empty grave.
4 South-west of the last. This small barrow covered four graves. In one
   was the skeleton of a man with a flint knife. The others held a
   cremation, further flint knives and a food vessel.
5 To the south-east was a barrow built for a woman, buried with a food
   vessel. It seems to have been constructed on a platform of chalk,
   with a mound of chalk blocks above held in place with a chalk wall
   similar to no. 3. This was covered in turn with earth and an outer
   casing of chalk rubble.

[W. Greenwell, *Archaeologia*, 52 (1890), 5.]

38 STANWICK, Stanwick St John   NZ:180115

Although this is the largest hillfort in Britain, Stanwick is by no means
the most impressive. Most of the site is low-lying and its great size is
masked by belts of trees and undulating countryside. A small fort
called The Tofts is the nucleus of an extensive system of fortified
enclosures which have been interpreted by Sir Mortimer Wheeler, the

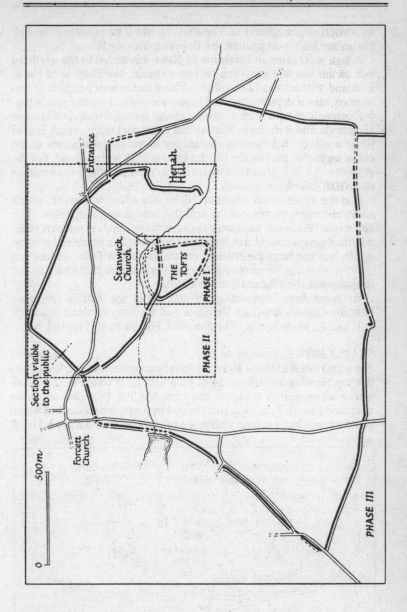

Fig 33. The Stanwick earthworks, Yorkshire, North

excavator, as the capital of Venutius, in which he prepared the Brigantes for his revolt against the Romans after AD 50.

A few years later an extension of 50 ha was added to the northern side of the fort and including part of a stream, the Mary Wild Beck. The new rampart was 12 m wide at its base and at least 3 m high. It was fronted with a drystone wall of limestone slabs. In front was a flat-bottomed ditch with vertical sides, cut into the solid rock. It was some 12 m wide and 4 m deep. Part of this excavated ditch, north-east of Forcett village, has been preserved for viewing. Excavations at the entrance to this part of the fort found the ditch waterlogged. On the bottom was a well-preserved sword in a wooden scabbard and a human skull with sword-cut wounds.

Perhaps about AD 69 a further 240 ha was added to the site, with a great enclosure to the south, but this was never completed. The gateway on the south was commenced with overlapping rampart ends, but the Romans attacked before it was finished. The whole site of some 300 ha was too large for efficient control from The Tofts, and we can only imagine that Venutius was too inexperienced in hillfort command to withstand the efficient forces of Rome.

At some time between AD 69 and AD 74 the British Governor Petillius Cerialis attacked Venutius and his followers and Stanwick fell. [R. E. M. Wheeler, *The Stanwick Fortifications* (1954).]

39 STAPLE HOWE, Scampston   SE:898749

A natural hill stands out from the main escarpment of the Wolds, its flat top forming a platform 54 m long and 12 m wide. With a small spring about 270 m away to the east, the hill provided an easily defended site. At first it was surrounded by a wooden palisade in which stood an oval hut 9 m long with stone or chalk walls and a gabled roof;

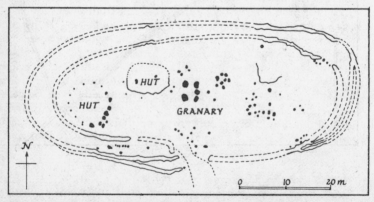

Fig 34. Staple Howe, Yorkshire, North (after T. C. Brewster)

inside were a clay oven and hearth. Later two round huts and a possible granary took its place. These huts had stout timber walls with thatched roofs and south-east-facing porches. As well as hearth and oven the larger hut also contained a loom. A five-post structure that might have been a granary stood on the highest part of the hill. Considerable quantities of burnt grain came from the farm, giving a radiocarbon date of 440 ± 150 BC. The bones of cattle, goats, sheep and pigs indicate that the farmer kept stock as well as hunted wild animals and fished. Two bronze razors suggest a date around 500 BC. The positions of the huts are clearly marked. [T. C. Brewster, *Staple Howe* (1963).]

40 THOMPSON'S RIGG, Allerston   SE:882922
On the south-east slope of the moor are more than a hundred small mounds of the type so common to this part of Yorkshire. They may be burial mounds, but some doubt exists.

41 THORNBOROUGH, East and West Tanfield   SE:585795
There is a concentration of religious sites between the Ure and the Swale in the vicinity of Ripon. Here can be found six henge monuments, a cursus and numerous barrows (see also Hutton Moor).

The Thornborough henges lie in a line of three, of which the central is the most accessible, although the northern, protected by trees, is the best preserved. All three circles have an approximate diameter of 275 m, and have the remains of massive banks with ditches inside and outside. There are entrances at the north-west and south-east of each circle. Excavation of the central circle in 1952 showed the ditches to be about 20 m wide and 3 m deep. Each was separated from the bank by a broad berm 12 m wide. The bank was constructed of large boulders, but had been given a coating of white gypsum crystals, perhaps to resemble similar monuments in the chalk country. Under the central circle were the ditches of a cursus that ran from the north-east to south-west, ending in the disused gravel pit south-west of the circle where it can still be seen in section. It had already gone out of use at the time when the central circle was constructed over it. The southern circle has been disturbed by gravel working but is still intact. Scattered amongst the henges are a number of barrows, including the Centre Hill barrow (SE:287791), still a metre high; it produced a skeleton with a food vessel and flint knife lying in a tree-trunk coffin. Three other barrows, the Three Hills, lie east of the northern circle and south of the road (about SE:286801.) Excavation by W. C. Lukis produced cremation burials. [N. Thomas, *YAJ*, 38 (1955), 425.]

42 THREE HOWES, Cockayne   SE:633983
Along the summit of the hill are four cairns of stones in a curving line. They vary in size from 10 to 24 m in diameter and from 1 to 3 m high.

The southernmost cairn produced two cremations in collared urns when they were dug into in the nineteenth century.

43 VICTORIA CAVE, Langcliffe   SD:838650

A large entrance leads into three chambers which were occupied during the last part of the ice age as a hyenas' den. Amongst their litter were the bones of hippopotamus, woolly rhinoceros and elephant. In higher layers were the bones of bear, fox and red deer, indicating a change in climate. Two antler points, one decorated, which can be dated to the upper palaeolithic, and a barbed red deer antler harpoon from the mesolithic hint at continuity of occupation, and many Roman finds show that the cave was lived in at that time also.

Four hundred and fifty metres north of the Victoria Cave is the Jubilee Cave (SD:838656), a small cavern with two entrances, which has produced neolithic, bronze age, iron age and Roman pottery. [J. W. Jackson, *British Caving* (1953), 180, 235.]

44 WESTERN HOWES, Westerdale   NZ:682023

Of the three barrows, the largest covered two collared urns, one containing a cremation, incense cup, bone pins and stone battle-axe. Both urns were covered by a mound of stone. The smallest barrow held a cremation, but there is no record for the third mound. [*Gentleman's Magazine*, 15 (1863), 548.]

45 WHARRAM PERCY, Wharram   SE:837636

A line of six barrows was opened by J. R. Mortimer in 1866. From north-east to south-west they covered:

1 A cremation burial. This barrow is a little east of the next five.
2 A child's cremation and food vessel.
3 A crouched burial in a decayed boat-shaped wooden coffin; also a cremation with food vessel, flint and bone tools.
4 An inverted collared urn and cremation.
5 A central stake marked the grave of a fourteen-year-old child with jet ear plugs.
6 An inverted collared urn containing a cremation at the centre, with an upright urn above it, also holding a cremation burial.

[J. R. Mortimer, *Forty Years' Researches* (1905), 44.]

46 WILLERBY WOLD, Willerby   TA:029761

One of the crematorium long barrows peculiar to Yorkshire, it measured 40 m long, 11 m wide and 1·2 m high, although it is now under plough. It is flanked by ditches on the north and south sides.

Excavations in the nineteenth century by Greenwell and from 1958 to 1960 revealed a trapezoidal mortuary enclosure, defined by a narrow ditch with a concave setting of wooden posts at the eastern end and a ritual pit at the centre. The wooden posts were burnt down and the bones of several exposed corpses were laid in a crematorium trench along the central spine of the barrow and covered with chalk rubble and timber. The barrow mound was then thrown up and the crematorium trench fired. It acted like a horizontal kiln reaching a temperature of around 1200° C. A radiocarbon date for the timber of the posts was about 3000 BC. [T. G. Manby, *PPS*, 29 (1963), 173.]

47 WILLERBY WOLD HOUSE, Willerby   TA:015763
Most of the round barrows on this part of the Wolds were dug by Canon Greenwell, including this one, almost opposite the House. Originally 13 m in diameter and about 0·5 m high, it was found to contain two skeletons in a grave pit. The bodies had probably been burnt on the spot; a shallow ditch had surrounded the funeral pyre. Later a beaker burial had been dug down through the primary one. Close to the edge of the barrow were four beautifully decorated bronze flat axes of Irish type, probably contemporary with the primary burials. [W. Greenwell, *Archaeologia*, 52 (1890), 2.]

48 WINDYPITS, Scawton
In or near the valley of the river Rye between Duncombe Park and Arden are a series of natural fissures in the limestone which were used for beaker burials. All are difficult to enter and it must be stressed that only experienced potholers should attempt them. **Buckland's Windypit** (SE:588827) was first explored by William Buckland in 1821. It contained six human skulls and beaker sherds. **Antofts Windypit** (SE:582829) seems to have been a burial chamber for eight people, with fragments of four or five beakers radiocarbon dated to 1790 ± 150 bc. **Ashberry Windypit** (SE:571849) also produced beaker material, including a flint knife and bone pin. One chamber contained Romano-British objects, amongst them a bronze trumpet brooch, bangle, chain, armour and bone spoons. [J. McDonnell, ed., *History of Helmsley, Rievaulx and District* (1963), 18.]

49 YEARSLEY LONG CAIRN, Gilling East   SE:603742
A damaged cairn 45 m long, 12 m wide and 2·5 m high was built of sand retained by a stone kerb. On the old land surface was a paved area where the burials were probably laid. A cist burial containing a food vessel and flints was later added to the mound.

50 YOCKENTHWAITE, Buckden   SD:899794
Probably a cairn circle since the stones are set edge to edge. The ring is 7·5 m in diameter and contains twenty limestone blocks. A gap facing south-east may be an entrance, but it is probably modern. There are four more stones outside the circle, but concentric to it, on the north-west. [A. Raistrick, *YAJ*, 29 (1929), 355.]

YORKSHIRE, SOUTH

1 CARLWARK, Sheffield   SK:260815
High on Hathersage Moor above Burbage Brook is a fort that occupies
a rocky outcrop of millstone grit only 0·9 ha in extent. The fort is
rectangular with steep sides everywhere except on the west. Traces of
stone walls crown these steep slopes running from rock outcrop to outcrop. Only on the lower west end of the promontory is there a massive
defence 3 m high, consisting of a well-built stone wall nine or ten
courses high backed by a massive dump of turf. The wall has collapsed
back on to the turf, and is probably close to its original height. At the
end of a hollow gully at the southern end of this rampart is an inturned
gateway 1·5 m wide. There is another simple gap in the eastern side.
Excavation failed to produce a date for construction, and re-use in the
Roman period should not be ruled out. [C. M. Piggott, *Antiquity*, 25
(1951), 210.]

2 ROMAN RIG, Sheffield to Mexborough
This linear earthwork stretches from Sheffield along the northern side
of the river Don as far as the river Dearne, and may have been a
frontier work built by the Brigantes against the Coritani, or even
against the Roman advance. Much of its course is heavily built over,
but good stretches can be found with diligent searching. It begins about
SK:358880 and runs north-east through Grimesthorpe, passing east of
Wincobank hillfort to Hill Top (SK: 397927). At this point it forks into
two, the western line running 1 km east of Scholes Wood hill-slope fort
to Wentworth Park, where a 1 km section runs down to Dog Kennel
Pond, marked by two banks and a central ditch. At SK:423984 it can be
picked up again and runs to SK:443992. It finally ends west of Mexborough Hospital. The eastern fork ran through Greasbrough and is
clearly visible from SK:417961 to Upper Haugh. It turns east here and
ends today at SK:448981.

3 SCHOLES WOOD, Rotherham   SK:395953
Because of its position, there is some doubt whether this is a prehistoric fort. The site is overlooked by high ground on most sides and lies in a
hollow on the north-eastern slope of a sandstone ridge. The enclosure
is oval in shape, 0·4 ha in extent, and with a single rampart, ditch and

counterscarp providing the defence. The bank still stands about 1 m high. There is an entrance on the north-east. [F. L. Preston, *Derbys. Arch. J*, 74 (1954), 11.]

4 WINCOBANK, Sheffield   SK:378910

This is an oval fort of about 1 ha in the middle of industrial Sheffield. It is surrounded by a rampart, ditch and counterscarp on all sides except the north-east, where the ditch and counterscarp have been destroyed. There is an entrance on the north-east, where one end of the bank widens out and the other runs across it for 10 m forming an out-turned entrance.

Wincobank was excavated in 1899 by J. Howarth, who found that the stone rampart was 5·5 m thick, with a drystone revetment at front and rear. Timbers passed through from back to front and at some point these had been badly burnt, fusing the stones of the wall together in a partially vitrified state.

It is worth observing that the Roman fort at Templeborough faces Wincobank from across the river Don, 2·5 km away. [F. L. Preston, *Derbys. Arch. J*, 74 (1954), 1.]

1   ALMONDBURY CASTLE HILL, Huddersfield   SE:153141

The castle built by Henry de Laci about AD 1150 obliterates much of
this interesting hillfort. This early Brigantian stronghold has a complicated history, which has been partially unravelled by excavation. It
began as a small unditched univallate enclosure of 1·1 ha occupying the
south-western end of the hill. The entrance was a simple gap with a
wooden guard chamber on one side. The enclosure fell into decay and
a group of undefended round houses were built over it. Early in the
seventh century BC a univallate fort was built following the lines of the
earlier enclosure with a ditch and counterscarp bank. The rampart
itself was of stone topped by a wooden fence.

About fifty years later the rampart was extended to enclose the
whole hilltop (2·2 ha) and an outer rampart and ditch were constructed; the whole being entered at the north-west end through an
overlapping gateway without guardrooms.

Around 550 BC the ramparts were increased in height and width, the
ditches re-dug and additional banks and ditches added in the south and
east. A rectangular annexe was added at the north-east end, containing a two-roomed building. At the same time a bank was thrown up
enclosing 13 ha around the foot of the hill (destroyed by the medieval
work). There seem to have been lean-to buildings against the inner
wall of the main rampart.

The fort was abandoned after it caught fire, apparently by spon-
taneous combustion inside the ramparts, perhaps about 500 BC. The
ditch separating the Victoria Tower from the rest of the fort is medieval. [W. J. Varley, in D. W. Harding, *Hillforts* (1976), 119.]

2   BAILDON MOOR, Baildon   SE:138403 (centre)

The moor flattens out to the north of Dobrudden Farm. Here there are
at least sixteen boulders marked with cup-and-ring marks and
meandering lines. Many of them are flush with the ground and diligent
searching is required to locate them. Cemented into the wall near the
caravan site is a good example (137400); another, north-east of the
path, seems to be a forgery. There is a bell-pit south-east of the farm
(SE:138399) and on its southern edge is a boulder with a complex
design. Whether the designs are early or late in the bronze age se-

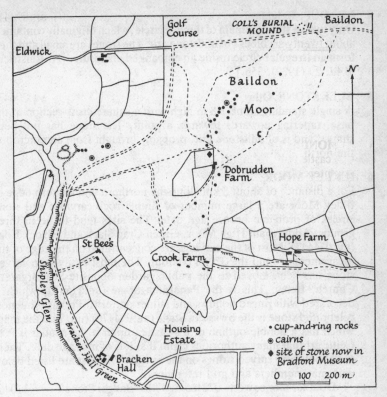

Fig 35. Cup-and-ring in the Baildon area, Yorkshire, West
(after B. M. Marsden)

quence is a matter of controversy. Claims have been made that the
Baildon series are late, but in the absence of related dating material it
is better to keep an open mind.

3 BRADLEY MOOR, Bradleys Both   SE:009476
A circular cairn of stones standing 2·4 m high has a long tail running
west, making a total length of about 70 m. At 18 m from the eastern
end is a stone cist 2 m long and almost 1 m wide with a massive
capstone. On the floor of the cist was a smaller slab which covered
fragments of unburnt adult human bone. Above the slab were traces of
a cremation. To the south of the cist and in the body of the mound were
some upright stones, three of which may have been a false entrance
to the tomb, whilst others suggest a hidden facade.
      There is a robbed round barrow 35 m south of the long cairn.
[A. Butterfield, *YAJ*, 34 (1939), 223.]

4 BRADUP, Keighley   SE:090440
Only twelve stones remain of this 9 m circle, which originally contained
about twenty-six blocks of millstone grit. The stones are small and they
form an irregular circle inside an embanked enclosure. [A. Raistrick,
YAJ, 29 (1929), 356.]

5 BULL STONE, Otley   SE:206435
A single standing stone 1·8 m high with a square cross-section at the
base, tapering upwards towards a point. The stone has not been
shaped and is of millstone grit, probably brought from an outcrop to
the north.

6 ILKLEY MOOR
For a distance of about 8 km along the northern and western edge of
Ilkley Moor are a large number of simple rock carvings and stone
circles of probable bronze age date. The sites tend to lie in three
groups, Addingham High Moor, Green Crag Slack and Rivock Edge
(SE:074447). Most of the carvings are concentrated on the edge of the
escarpment around the 320 m contour. The most easily seen carved
stone has been moved to the public garden opposite St Margaret's
Church, Ilkley. This is the **Panorama Stone** (SE:115472) which is
decorated with ringed hollows and ladder patterns. Perhaps the most
celebrated stone is the **Swastika Stone** (SE:094470) (no. 7 on the map)
which has a double outline of a swastika upon it. So similar is it to
Celtic art that many authorities claim that it is of iron age date. There
are about forty carved stones on the moors. The best are listed below
with map numbers and grid references.

1	Doubler Stones west	072465	13	Badger Stone	110460
2	Doubler Stones east	076466	15	Barmishaw Stone	112464
5	Piper Stone	084471	18	Willy Hall's Wood	115465
7	Swastika Stone	094470	20	Hanging Stones	128467
9	Panorama Rocks	104470	28	Pancake Stone	133462
10	Silver Well Stone	104465	30	Idol Rock	132458

There are at least eight stone circles on the moors, mostly the surrounding kerbs of destroyed burial cairns. Examples worth finding are on the
eastern side of the moor:
Twelve Apostles Circle (SE:126451) The collapsed remains of a large
circle, now reduced to twelve stones, set in a bank of earth 15 m in
diameter.
Grubstones Circle (SE:136447). The kerb of a destroyed cairn, of
which twenty stones, set edge to edge, survive. It is 10 m in diameter
and has been destroyed on the south side.
Horncliffe Circle (SE:134435). An oval ring of forty-six stones set edge
to edge, with traces of a smaller circle in the centre which may surround a burial.

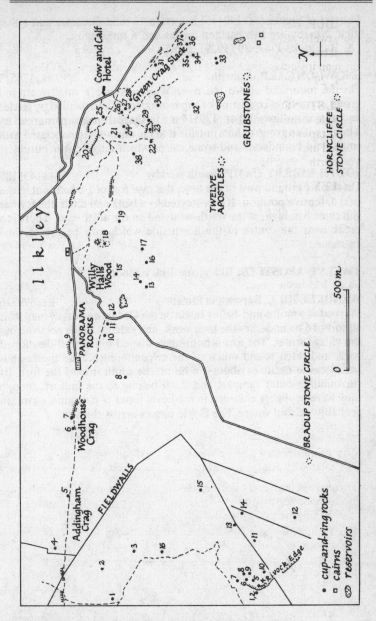

Fig 36. Cup-and-ring rocks on Ilkley Moor, Yorkshire, West
(after B. M. Marsden)

Skirtful of Stones (SE:140446) is a cairn 11 m in diameter and 1·8 m high. Nearby are two earthen circles and a small cairn.
[A. Raistrick, *YAJ*, 29 (1929), 356.]

7   **SNOWDON CARR, Askwith**   SE:178513
On the moorland above the river Washburn are a small scattered group of carvings consisting of cup marks, some surrounded by circles and numerous lines. At SE:179514 is a D-shaped enclosure marked by a bank, with a group of huts outside it to the north-west associated with small field boundaries and some cairns which might cover burials.

8   **SOUTH KIRKBY CAMP, South Kirkby**   SE:435105
On sloping ground west of the town this oval fort of 1·8 ha is not in the best defensive position. It is protected by a bank and ditch, the former still some 3 m high, at the south-west and on the north-east. There is a break near the centre of the north side which may be the original entrance.

TWELVE APOSTLES, Ilkley, see Ilkley Moor.

9   **WENDELL HILL, Barwick in Elmet**   SE:399376
Marked as a motte-and-bailey castle on the Ordnance Survey map, this hillfort of 6 ha underlies the later work, and extends to the north across the village street. The fort is hour-glass shaped with a well-developed bank and ditch round much of the circumference. The motte-and-bailey castle occupies about 1·6 ha on the south side of the fort. Its surrounding outer rampart and ditch belong to the hillfort, though they were probably enlarged in medieval times. An original entrance probably existed where The Boyle passes across the site.

WALES

ANGLESEY (part of Gwynedd)

1 BARCLODIAD-Y-GAWRES, Llangwyfan   SH:328708
(Department of the Environment, key from Beaumaris Castle; take a torch). This barrow was excavated in 1953 and subsequently restored with a modern concrete roof enabling the burial chambers to be visited. A passage 6 m long leads into a central chamber with a single side chamber on the east, and a double side chamber on the west. The tomb had been used as a stone 'quarry' in the eighteenth century and most of the contents removed, though the cremated remains of two people were found in the western chamber. A number of wallstones in the tomb are decorated with lozenges, chevrons, spirals and zig-zag patterns. Three stand in the entrance passage and the others in the east and west chambers. The art style is similar to that found in the Boyne area of Ireland. [T. G. E. Powell and G. E. Daniel, *Barclodiad-y-Gawres* (1956).]

2 BEDD BRANWEN, Llanbabo   SH:361850
According to the *Mabinogion*, the beautiful Queen Branwen, daughter of Llyr, was buried in a square grave on the banks of the Alaw; local tradition associates the site with this ruined cairn first excavated in 1813 and again in 1967–8. The barrow had been surrounded by a kerb 19·5 m in diameter. At its centre was a small standing stone and near this a central cist was found in 1813 containing an inverted cinerary urn and cremation. In 1967 Frances Lynch found further urns in the central area. This had been surrounded by a ring cairn and covered with a mound of turves. There seems to be no doubt that all the urns were buried at the same time. [F. Lynch, *Arch. Cambrensis*, 120 (1971), 11.]

3 BODOWYR, Llanidan   SH:462683
Three upright stones 1·5 m high, with a mushroom-shaped capstone which measures 2·4 m by 1·8 m, stand on the faintest trace of a mound. Of two other stones, one formed part of the chamber walls and that on the east was clearly an entrance sill. [RCHM, *Anglesey* (1937), 103.]

4 BRYN-CELLI-DDU, Llanddaniel-fab   SH:508702
(Department of the Environment). Restoration has left this barrow curiously truncated, but from the front everything appears normal; a

circular mound 26 m in diameter is held in position by a revetment of large stones. Entered on the east through a stone doorway, a roofed passage 7·5 m long leads into a polygonal chamber about 2·5 m across. A single pillar stone stands in the chamber and is presumably of ritual significance since it serves no structural purpose. One of the wallstones of the chamber has an incised spiral on its face. Fragments of cremated and unburnt human bone were found in the chamber and passage. Along the north side of the passage is a low bench. Excavations between 1925 and 1929 showed that the history of the site is complex. Beneath the barrow mound was a circle of fourteen stones and at the centre was a pit covered by a recumbent stone slab. Lying next to this was a stone decorated with an incised meandering pattern. (A replica of this can be seen at the back of the barrow.) The revetment circle of the barrow stands in a buried ditch which is considered to be the remains of a henge monument that pre-dated the burial mound. In front of the entrance (marked by five small stones) were the sockets for five posts; behind them was a pit containing the skeleton of an ox and beside the entrance were two hearths.

Clearly ritual associated with the site was detailed and complicated. Perhaps we should see it not only as a tomb, but also as a temple at which relatives of the dead came to worship, perhaps entering the passage and leaving gifts on the bench at its side. [W. J. Hemp, *Archaeologia*, 80 (1930), 179.]

5 BRYN-GWYN, Llanidan   SH:462669
About 400 m south-west of Castel Bryn-Gwyn are two massive stones that once formed part of a circle of about eight stones. One of the stones is 4 m high and 3 m wide, the other about 3 m square. There are faint traces of a surrounding bank and ditch; the latter, about 110 m in diameter, can still be made out. [RCHM, *Anglesey* (1937), 103.]

6 BRYN-YR-HEN-BOBL, Llanedwen   SH:519690
This is 'the hill of the old people'. It is a kidney-shaped mound 5·5 m high and about 135 m in diameter. On the eastern side is a hollow containing the entrance to the burial chamber, a cell only 2·1 m long, 1 m wide and 1·6 m high. The capstone projects to form a porch over what seems to have been a broken notched entrance stone. Hemp, excavating in 1929, claimed to have found traces of a second chamber on the south-west side. This is disputed. In front of the entrance was a large horned forecourt bound by a number of irregular walls and ceremonially blocked by large stones and dirty soil mixed with neolithic pottery fragments, stone implements, bones and charcoal. Attached to the south horn of the barrow was an unusual stone-revetted terrace almost 100 m long, 12 m wide and a little under a metre high. Although built after the barrow, it seems to have been

broadly contemporary. An inverted cinerary urn covering a cremation was found near its southern end. [W. J. Hemp, *Archaeologia*, 85 (1935), 253.]

7   CAER Y TWR, Holyhead   SH:218830
The extremely rocky summit of Holyhead Mountain has been defended where necessary by a thick drystone wall, enclosing 7 ha. The wall still exists on the north and west sides, standing to a height of 3 m and width of 4 m, running from crag to rock outcrop. Nearby is a breach where the wall may have been deliberately thrown down, perhaps by the Romans. In the north-east corner is an entrance which follows a long and fairly level gully. There are no signs of guard chambers. The site is unexcavated and no huts have been found. [RCHM, *Anglesey* (1937), 24.]

8   CASTEL BRYN-GWYN, Llanidan   SH:464671
An area 54 m in diameter is enclosed by a bank some 3·6 m high and 12 m wide. Inside, the ground level is 3 m higher than outside, where excavation has revealed a surrounding ditch and an entrance causeway on the south-west side. Neolithic pottery and flints confirm that the site was begun early, perhaps as a henge monument, but was refashioned as a defensive work in the first century AD. (G. J. Wainwright, *Arch. Cambrensis*, 111 (1962), 25.]

9   DINAS GYNFOR, Llanbadrig   SH:391951
A craggy headland on the north coast of Anglesey is protected by sea cliffs 60 m high on three sides and a steep slope on the south-west with marsh land at the foot. This southern slope is defended by two walls of limestone blocks running between crags and broken by an incurved entrance in the middle of the south-west side, and a second gate at the top of a rocky gully that climbs up from Porth Cynfor. [RCHM, *Anglesey* (1937), 37.]

10   DIN DRYFOL, Aberffraw   SH:395725
Originally two large stones marked the entrance to this tomb. Only one is still standing, 3 m high and 2·8 m wide. Excavation revealed the hole for the other 2 m to the north. The burial chamber stretches about 9 m to the west and now consists only of one large side wall stone 3·5 m long and 1·5 m high with a capstone resting against it. There are other stones partly buried close by, including one that may represent a cross-slab dividing a segmented gallery. [RCHM, *Anglesey* (1937), 2.]

11   DIN SYLWY, Llanfihangel-Din-Sylwy   SH:586815
This is a roughly oval hillfort overlooking the sea and surrounded by a drystone wall of massive limestone blocks; it encloses about 7 ha. The

ground slopes away steeply on all sides, and the fort wall, which is about 2·4 m thick, is set slightly back to allow a berm all the way round, though no ditch. There are two entrances, one on the south approached by a terraced track with inturned entrance passage 4·5 m wide, and the other on the west at the end of a precipitous narrow ledge. The fort was occupied by the Ordovices during the Roman period. [RCHM, *Anglesey* (1937), 83.]

12   LLANDDYFNAN BARROWS, Llanddyfnan   SH:509788
This important pair of barrows, the larger one visible from the road, were both excavated in 1909. The eastern barrow covered a horseshoe-shaped chamber containing the crouched skeleton of a man of about thirty, buried with a serrated flint flake and covered by a slab of stone. It was probably of early bronze age date, although in the neolithic tradition. The larger barrow to the north-west failed to produce an obvious primary burial, but held seven secondary burials in cremation urns, and a small cist containing burnt bone. All the urns are of late bronze age date. [RCHM, *Anglesey* (1937), 49.]

13   LLANDEGFAN   SH:554739
A tall, thin menhir in a conspicuous position north of the road. It is 3 m high and 1 m wide at the base, where some packing stones are still visible.

14   LLANRHWYDRYS   SH:334906 and SH:334904
Two good standing stones of schist can be found on either side of Pen-yr-orsedd. The northern is nearly 4 m high and 1·5 m wide. The southern is 2·5 m high and 1 m wide. There is a damaged barrow with a rubbing stone at its centre at the corner of the road (SH:341902).

15   LLIGWY, Penrhos-Lligwy   SH:501860
This tomb has one of the largest capstones in Britain, weighing around 25 tonnes, and measuring 5·5 m long, 4·5 m wide and 1 m thick. It is supported on only three of its eight wallstones and the burial chamber seems to have been created by digging a pit beneath it to make a room almost 2 m high. The entrance was probably at the eastern end. Excavations in 1908 found the fragmentary remains of between fifteen and thirty persons of all ages, numerous animal bones, mussel shells and pottery fragments of neolithic and bronze age date. There is no sign of the original barrow mound. [E. N. Baynes, *Arch. Cambrensis*, 9 (1909), 217.]

16   MAEN ADDWYN, Llanfihangel-Tre'r-Beirdd   SH:461834
This standing stone beside the road is of probable bronze age date and gives its name to the village. It is 3·2 m high, 1 m wide and nearly a metre thick.

17 PANT-Y-SAER, Llanfair-Mathanfarn-Eithaf   SH:509824
A complicated site excavated in 1874 and 1930 which revealed a
rectangular stone-built burial chamber, open on the south-west side
and partly covered by a capstone 4 m square. This chamber stands in a
rock-cut pit almost 1 m deep, 4 m long and 3 m broad. The 1874
excavation showed that an oblong cist had been cut into the filling of
the pit, and that it contained at least two crouched burials. More
extensive excavations in 1930 in the covering cairn, which is kidney-
shaped, found the bones of another thirty-six adults, nine children and
nine infants, together with neolithic pottery. Between the drystone
horns at the western end of the barrow were the remains of a forecourt.
[W. L. Scott, *Arch. Cambrensis*, 88 (1933), 185.]

18 PLAS MEILW, Holyhead Rural   SH:227809
(Department of the Environment). Two tall thin standing stones both
about 3 m high, 0·9 m wide and 20 – 30 cm thick, stand 3·3 m apart on a
north-east axis. There is a tradition that a stone cist containing bones,
spearhead and arrowheads was found between the stones. The whole
site was supposed to have stood within a circle of stones. Only excavation might decide if there is any truth in the legend. [RCHM, *Anglesey*
(1937), 23.]

19 PLAS NEWYDD, Llanedwen   SH:519697
On the edge of the lawn in front of Plas Newydd House stands a very
large stone burial chamber devoid of all signs of a covering mound.
The main chamber measures about 3 m by 2·7 m and is crowned by a
massive capstone more than a metre thick and measuring some 3·5 m
by 3 m. It was probably entered from the south-west, where there is a
smaller antechamber, whose capstone is broken and partly lies on the
ground. [RCHM, *Anglesey* (1937), 56.]

20 PRESADDFED, Bededern   SH:348809
Two burial chambers lie 2 m apart in a meadow. The southern one has
a capstone 3·2 m by 2·4 m supported on three upright stones; the
northern one has collapsed and only two uprights remain. There is no
sign of the covering mound, but it is probable that the two chambers
were joined together as a continuous gallery. [RCHM, *Anglesey*
(1937), 18.]

21 TREFIGNATH, Holyhead   SH:259805
Until recently this was thought to be a continuous gallery grave divided
into four chambers, but excavations in 1977–9 have shown that the site
is of more than one period. The earliest structure was a simple box-like
tomb at the west end set in a small round cairn. Then a larger chamber
with tall portal stones was built to the east of it, this tomb having a long

cairn and deeply recessed forecourt. Finally a third chamber was built into this forecourt, with its own dry-built forecourt at the east end. The cairn was edged with drystone walling and the junction of the second and third cairns can be clearly seen, for the walls have been consolidated and restored. The modern excavations produced plain and decorated pottery, but no burials. [F. Lynch, *Archaeology in Wales* (1979).]

22 TRE-GWEHELYDD, Llantrisant   SH:342832
A standing stone originally called Maen-y-Gored. It is 2·5 m high and 1 m wide. It is broken into three pieces and is held together with metal straps.

23 TRWYN DU, Aberffraw   SH:352679
A small cairn stands on a rocky headland above the mouth of the river Ffraw. When it was excavated in 1956 it became clear that the mound had been retained by a kerb of upright stones and covered a D-shaped grave of possible beaker date, but no burial was found. A D-shaped setting of stones surrounded the grave. To the west of the cairn and partly overlain by it was an extensive Maglemosian working site dated by radiocarbon to about 6800 bc. Charred hazelnuts lay among the remnants of a stone industry – mainly blunted points and scrapers with a few microburins. [R. B. White, *Arch. Cambrensis*, 127 (1978), 16.]

24 TY MAWR, Holyhead Rural   SH:212820
Although iron age in character these huts on Holyhead Mountain are all probably of Roman date. Consequently I only mention that two groups exist, with fourteen huts in one and half a dozen in the other. Hearths and slabs marking the positions of beds are visible in some of them, and one produced copper slag, suggesting that it was used by a metal worker. [RCHM, *Anglesey* (1937), 25.]

25 TY MAWR, Holyhead Rural   SH:254810
A good menhir 2·7 m high, 1·2 m wide and 0·4 m thick.

26 TY-NEWYDD, Llanfaelog   SH:344738
Only the chamber area of this passage grave survives. This consists of a capstone, 4 m long by 1·5 m wide, resting on three uprights. When the chamber was excavated in 1935 a layer of black earth 5 cm thick was found all over the floor, containing much charcoal. Mixed into this were 110 pieces of white quartz, a barbed and tanged arrowhead and beaker pottery, but no signs of human burials. [RCHM, *Anglesey* (1937), 65.]

CLWYD

1 BONTNEWYDD CAVE, Cefn   SJ:009712
This small cave above the road was partially excavated in 1872 when a few crude quartzite implements of Aurignacian and Mousterian types were found, together with bones of various types of bears, a rhinoceros, and a human skull with lower jaw. The site is currently under re-excavation.

2 BRENIG, Mynydd Hiraethog   SH:985576
While the Llyn Brenig reservoir was under construction between 1973 and 1976 extensive excavations took place in the Fechan valley. More than fifty archaeological sites were identified and some of them have been restored by the Welsh Water Authority who have laid out two trails for visitors. From the car park a short trail of less than an hour leads first to a mesolithic camping site (marked by a large stone) where radiocarbon dates indicate that a probable summer camp existed about 5700 BC. Close by is a bronze age barrow called Boncyn Arian (Money Hillock), whose central grave, dated to about 1600 BC, was ringed by a drystone wall and stake circles. The whole was covered by a mound of earth, into which later cremations were placed, two in urns.

A short distance south is a ring cairn that was probably designed about 1680 BC for funeral ritual of some kind. A circle of posts enclosed a low ring of stones, in the centre of which ceremonies took place, perhaps involving the exposure of corpses, the performing of burial rites and the depositing of charcoal, possibly representing burnt wooden offerings. No actual burials took place for a century and a half until three cremations in urns were added to the cairn, one with a flint knife and pottery ear plugs.

For more active walkers a two-hour trail, only suitable in fine weather, leads south past other archaeological sites, some of which are relatively recent in date. A kilometre south of the car park is a restored platform cairn, built on top of a bronze age living site. Under a large stone the cremated remains of an adult and child were buried in an urn. A massive ring of stones was built above this with an open central area dominated by a large post. This centre was filled in at a later date to form a low platform. A small mound of stones on the north-east side was added later to cover an urn.

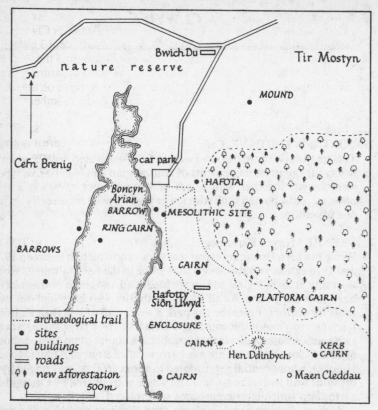

Fig 37. Archaeological trail at Brenig, Clwyd

The trail leads past the ruins of a medieval farm, Hen Ddinbych, east to a bronze age cairn with a stone kerb built over a possible prehistoric hut, whose posts have been restored There is another kerbed cairn west of Hen Ddinbych. A guide pamphlet with map is available at the site.

3 CAER DREWYN, Corwen   SJ:087444
A circular fort of 3·2 ha is protected by a stone-built wall with traces of a rampart walk. There are additional defences above the eastern entrance where the fort is overlooked from higher ground. On the west where the defences are slighter is an inturned entrance. Traces of circular huts can be seen in the annexe by the eastern entrance and just inside the west entrance.

4 CASTEL CAWR, Abergele   SH:937768
There are a number of forts along the west side of the river Clwyd. This
one is small and overgrown with trees. Its walls still stand 3 m high in
places, with a ditch more than 1 m deep. They surround the west and
north-east sides of a triangular site, whilst the south is naturally precipitous and needs no artificial strengthening. The entrance on the south-
east is 9 m wide and is protected by a single guard chamber.

5 CEFN-YR-OGOF, Cefn   SJ:023705
There are four caves high above the Elwy at the point where it is joined
by the Meirchion. One of these is 9 m long and divides into two narrow
passages. It was first dug in 1830 when the bones of a number of extinct
animals, including reindeer, hyenas and cave bears were found. A
human skull, jaw and long bones were also discovered together with
flint flakes. It probably dates from the upper palaeolithic period,
perhaps 12,000 BC.

6 DINAS BRAN, Llangollen   SJ:223430
A fort of 1·7 ha dominated by a medieval castle. The defences of the
iron age fort consist of double lines of banks and ditches nearly 50 m
apart on all sides except the north, where the natural hillslope is
sufficient protection. Two enclosures are thus formed, although most
of the outer one is on a steep slope and of little use. A bronze age
socketed axe was found within the fort in 1918. [E. Davies, *Prehistoric
and Roman Remains of Denbighshire* (1929), 252.]

7 DINORBEN   SH:968757
This important hillfort has been destroyed by quarrying and is no
longer worth visiting. [H. N. Savory, *Excavations at Dinorben, 1965–9*
(1971).]

8 FFYNNON BEUNO, Tremeirchion   SJ:085725
Two small caves lie side by side. The lower one has been used as a
cattle shelter in recent times, but when excavated in 1885 the remains
of hyenas and other ice age animals were found together with tools of
Aurignacian and Solutrian types, sealed below layers of stalagmite.
The upper cave (Cae Gwyn) is long and tunnel-like and has produced
the bones of lion, bear, rhinoceros and deer, as well as Aurignacian
tools.

9 FOEL FENLII, Llanbedr-Dyffryn-Clwyd   SJ:163601
The 'iniquitous and tyrannical king Benlli lived here about AD 450.
After opposing St Germanus he and his city were consumed by fire
from heaven', so the legend goes. Roughly oval, the hillfort is of 10 ha,
with strong ramparts on all sides, double or treble as the nature of the

hillside requires. The only certain entrance is at the west end; it is inturned. The gap on the south is likely to be recent. In the south-western quarter of the site are about two dozen hut platforms – not easily seen because of heather – all unexcavated. There is a spring close to the centre of the fort. The site is probably of more than one period but only excavation can sort it out. [J. Forde-Johnston, *Arch. Cambrensis*, 114 (1965), 152.]

10   GOP CAVE, Trelawnyd   SJ:086801

This rock shelter below the great cairn on Gop Hill has two entrances. One leads into a chamber 14 m long, 4 m wide and about 2·4 m high. Bones of deer, reindeer and the inevitable hyenas were found by Boyd Dawkins in 1886–7. The cave was re-used in neolithic times, when traces of hearth and occupation were left, together with the burials of fourteen individuals. Six more human skeletons were found in the side passages of the adjacent **North West Cave,** and quite recently more neolithic burials were found in a new chamber. Numerous microliths have been found in the caves.

11   GOP-Y-GOLEUNI, Trelawnyd   SJ:086802

At a height of 250 m above sea-level, this is considered to be the largest cairn in Wales. It is some 12 m high and 100 m in diameter. Mining from the top in 1886–7 showed that it is constructed of limestone blocks. No burial was found but some bones of ox and horse were uncovered. The great size of the Gop suggests that it might contain a passage grave like those of Anglesey and the Dublin area. [E. Davies, *Prehistoric and Roman Remains in Flint* (1949), 156.]

12   LLWYN BRYN DINAS, Llanrhaeadr-ym-Mochnant   SJ:172247

This heart-shaped fort of about 3 ha stands at a height of 270 m above the Tanat valley. It is a simple contour fort with a single rampart and ditch, broken by an inturned entrance on the south-east, and another on the west, approached by a sunken road.

13   MOEL ARTHUR, Llandyrnog   SJ:145661

This round-topped hill is 455 m above sea-level and looks out over the Vale of Clwyd. The Offa's Dyke long-distance footpath passes through it. The site consists of a fort of about 2 ha enclosed by two ramparts and ditches with a counterscarp. It has been built by throwing rock outwards from a quarry ditch. The narrow entrance on the north-east is defended by a claw-like internal formation that may cover guard chambers.

14   MOEL HIRADDUG, Dyserth   SJ:063785

This important fort is rapidly being destroyed by quarrying. Its limestone hill stands some 264 m above sea-level and looks north-west across the Clwyd to the sea. The site is a long, narrow ridge where a single wall encloses 8 ha. On the east are two further walls, each of rubble with drystone facings. Both circular and rectangular huts have been found inside. The gate at the north-west had guard chambers. Digging in 1872 accidentally produced fragments of a bronze shield and a broken iron sword blade. These seem to have been amongst the debris of a battle involving the collapse of the middle rampart. As they are datable to the early first century AD we can perhaps see them as evidence of intertribal warfare. [C. H. Houlder, *Flints. Hist. Soc.,* 19 (1961), 1.]

15 MOEL-TY-UCHAF, Llandrillo   SH:056372
High on the moor is a circle of forty-one closely set stones. It measures 12 m in diameter and may have an entrance on the south. At the centre is a large oval stone and what seems to be the remains of a stone cist which has been damaged by an early excavation.

16 MOEL-Y-GAER, Bodfari   SJ:095708
Sited on a small hill above the river Wheeler, this is a semicircular fort with a steep undefended scarp on the east. On the west there is a rampart, ditch and counterscarp, with a second defence lower down the hill slope. The entrance through both ramparts is on the north-east, close to the scarp, and turns both inwards and outwards.

17 MOEL-Y-GAER, Llanbedr   SJ:149618
This 'fort on a rounded hill' is some 4 ha in extent. It is defended by double ramparts on all sides except on the level ground to the north-east where there are three. There are two entrances, one on the west and one on the north-east. Both are inturned, the latter with the gaps in the outer and middle ramparts some 30 m north of the central gap, thus involving a change of direction upon entry. Excavations were carried out in 1849.

18 MOEL Y GAER, Rhosesmor   SJ:211691
This is a simple contour fort of 2·4 ha with a single complete circuit rampart and partial ditch, broken by an entrance on the south-east side where the inturned rampart ends almost certainly enclose guard chambers about 4·5 m by 3 m in size, plus an intermittent outer bank and ditch, apparently unfinished.

The site was extensively excavated in 1972–4 in preparation for the construction of a storage reservoir. The rampart was shown to be of two periods. First, probably in the fourth century BC, a facade of timbers between 0·6 m and 0·9 m apart had been set up, with stone walling between them, backed by stone and soil. This rampart stood

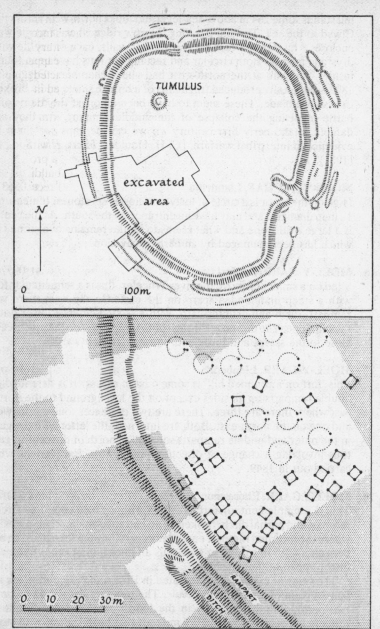

Fig 38. Map and plan of Moel y Gaer, Rhosesmor, Clwyd

1·7 m high, and was probably heightened by a breastwork. In front was a flat berm 3·5 m wide and a ditch 2·7 m deep, which was incomplete and probably served only as a quarry. By the third century BC this rampart had slumped forward over the berm. It was re-capped with clay and stones, and a new wooden breastwork was constructed on top. There was no ditch this time, but the hill slope was scarped in places. Outside the rampart two palisades were found, one having defended an earlier settlement, the other probably constructed as extra defence for the latest rampart.

Inside the early palisaded enclosure circular buildings with roofs supported on rings of posts were constructed, most with a projecting porch. When the rampart was first built the internal buildings included circular houses with walls of rammed stakes and rectangular four-post buildings. The two types occupied different areas of the fort: the four-posters curving in rows with the rampart.

There seems to have been a period of desertion before the final rampart was constructed, probably accompanied by rectangular buildings with wooden sleeper foundations.

Pottery from the site was scarce, but largely of early iron age types. Considerable numbers of pebbles, suggesting sling warfare, were found in connection with the defences. [G. Guilbert, *Antiquity*, 49 (1975), 109.]

19 NAID-Y-MARCH, Holywell   sj:167753
There are two small standing stones south of the road from Panasaph to Brynford. They stand 7·5 m apart, one being 1·2 m high, the other only 0·7 m.

20 PENBEDW PARK, Cilcain   sj:171679
Five of an original eleven stones survive of this 27 m diameter circle. Trees mark the positions of missing stones. Some 215 m to the west is a massive outlying stone 1·5 m high, which seems to be an integral part of the circle. A note of caution must be sounded since there is a slight possibility that the circle is an eighteenth-century folly. There is a barrow in the next field. Food vessel pottery has been found in it.

21 PENYCLODDIAU, Nannerch   sj:129677
This very large fort of 20 ha is on a summit of the Clwydian Range and lies astride the Offa's Dyke footpath. In spite of its size it is of simple construction and is surrounded by a single stone wall and ditch which in places measures 12 m from crest to ditch bottom. The rampart is duplicated across the northern end for additional strength. There are entrances at the south, with a guard chamber on the eastern side of the inturn, and on the north-east, where a hornwork seems to prevent cattle from straying over the edge of the valley to the south.

22   PEN-Y-CORDDYN-MAWR, Llanddulas   SJ:914765
Sited on a massive limestone outcrop east of the river Dulas this hillfort
of 12 ha is naturally protected by strong high cliffs on all sides except
the north. Across the weaker northern part of the plateau are two
stone-revetted ramparts without ditches. Further north still another
rampart defines an annexe of 6 ha. There are three entrances into the
main enclosure, each at the heads of gullies, one with a long inturn and
guard chambers. A steep path on the eastern side links a spring with a
small postern gate. There are circular hut sites inside the fort. It has
been suggested by A. H. A. Hogg that the fort began as the larger
enclosure of 17 ha, but was later reduced to the 12 ha site. Its history
ended with extensive slighting. Beneath its ruins a fragment of Roman
Samian pottery was found. [W. Gardner, *Arch. Cambrensis*, 10
(1910), 79.]

23   RHOS DOMEN, Cornwal   SJ:900640
A group of four unexcavated barrows set in a line on either side of the
road.

24   TY-FFOS, Tyfos   SJ:028387
A large low cairn is surrounded by a fourteen-stone kerb circle. The
circle may originally have been free standing before the cairn was built.

DYFED

1 BEDD-YR-AFANC, Meline   SN:113346
This long barrow is 18 m long, 10·5 m and about 0·6 m high. Along its centre runs a gallery grave 10·5 m long and 2·5 m wide. There are short rows of stones parallel to the gallery on each side. [G. E. Daniel, *Prehistoric Chamber Tombs* (1950), 203.]

2 BOSHERSTON, Bosherston   SR:971948
This little promontory fort of about 2 ha lies on a ridge between two submerged and silted estuaries that are now fishponds. It is cut off by three parallel lines of defence. The outermost consists of two strong banks and ditches, then comes a single strong rampart joined to the former by banks at either end. On the inside is a damaged bank and ditch, which probably marks the earliest occupation on the site. All the defences are cut by a simple entrance gap towards their southern end. A small excavation produced a ring-headed pin of iron age A type. [I. Ll. Foster and G. E. Daniel, eds., *Prehistoric and Early Wales* (1965), 134.]

BUCKSPOOL DOWN CAMP, see Flimston Castle.

3 CARN GOCH, Llandeilo   SN:691243
This is a strong hillfort of 10·5 ha in a rectangular enclosure that straddles a ridge above the river Towy. There are massive drystone walls, 20 m wide, lined with upright slabs across each end of the ridge and lesser ramparts along the sides. At the north-east is the main straight-through entrance and there are two small gates in each of the side ramparts. Other gaps are likely to be relatively recent. A round hut platform is probably contemporary with the fort, but can scarcely have been the only structure in so large a refuge. Two rectangular foundations are later in date.
On the north side of the fort is a long cairn.

4 CERRIG Y GOF, Newport   SN:040390
An irregular round barrow some 10·5 to 12 m in diameter with the remains of five rectangular burial chambers around the edge. The largest of these is 2·4 m long, 1·8 m wide and 1·5 m high. Four capstones still remain, though only one is in its original position. The

mound has been damaged by Fenton (and others), who dug into it in 1811, finding pottery, bones, charcoal and pebbles. [RCHM, *Pembrokeshire* (1925), no. 811.]

5 **CLEGYR BOIA, St David's**   SM:737252
On a rocky outcrop are the ramparts of a small rectangular iron age fort about 100 m long and 25 m wide. In places the natural rock forms the defence. Although excavation failed to date the fort securely, it did reveal two neolithic house foundations, one oval and one rectangular. Two sides of the larger house had been cut into the rocky hillside and two rows of posts supported a timber roof. Numerous cattle bones suggest that the occupants were livestock farmers; they seem to have used polished stone axes and pottery that has distinct Irish associations. [A. Williams, *Arch. Cambrensis*, 102 (1953), 20.]

6 **CRAIG GWRTHEYRN, Llanfihangel**   SN:433402
Trees surround the steep-sided knoll that is crowned by this small fort of 1·3 ha above the river Teifi. The wall is strongly built of stone quarried from an external ditch. There is an entrance on the southwest defended by two curving barbicans of wall and the unexpected presence of chevaux-de-frise.

7 **FLIMSTON CASTLE, Castlemartin**   SR:930946
There are three promontory forts quite close together within the Pembrokeshire Coast National Park. Unfortunately they also lie within the Castlemartin firing range and access on weekdays during summer is sometimes restricted. From the car park (SR:926946) the first fort to the east is Flimston Castle, a limestone peninsula dramatically penetrated by the Devil's Cauldron, a natural collapsed cavern riddled with caves, arches and passages. The peninsula is defended by two banks and ditches, with a third line some 20 m outside. The whole is pierced by a wide central entrance. No huts have been traced with certainty inside.

Half a kilometre east is **Crocksydam Camp** (SR:936943), where a single stone bank cuts off a less pronounced peninsula. A hut can be found inside. East again for 1·5 km, but still within the artillery range, is **Buckspool Down Camp** (SR:954934). Here a single rampart cuts off a narrow bridge of rock. Two outer banks are also present. Inside are two possible circular huts.

8 **FOEL TRIGARN, Whitechurch**   SN:158336
This fort takes its name from the three great bronze age cairns which crown a summit of the Prescelly mountains. Just over an hectare is ringed with a stone and earth wall on the west, and a natural scarp on the east. There is a semicircular enclosure outside this to the west, and

another to the north. There are no ditches. A number of entrances are of simple gap types. In each enclosure are circular hut foundations. Excavations in 1899 produced beads and pottery dating from the earliest iron age up to Roman times. [S. Baring-Gould, *Arch. Cambrensis* (1900), 189.]

9 GORS FAWR STONE CIRCLE, Mynachlog-ddu   SN: 134294
This circle 22 m in diameter lies low on the common. Sixteen of its stones survive and these are graded in size towards the south-south-west. Two tall stones lie 134 m north-north-east of the circle. Alexander Thom considers that these stones are aligned on midsummer sunrise over Foel-Drych hilltop to the east.

10 LLANDDEWI GAER, Llanddewi Velfry   SN: 144160
On the edge of an escarpment above the Afon Marlais, a semicircle of three rows of banks and ditches cut off a tiny area out of all proportion to their size. The original entrance would have been inside the scarp to the north. There is a second fort, **Caerau Gaer,** 0·2 km further west, surrounded by a single rampart and ditch with an extra line of defence on the north-east facing Llanddewi Gaer. There are two gaps, of which the north-eastern seems the more likely to be prehistoric.

11 LONG HOUSE, Mathry   SM: 846334
A well-formed polygonal burial chamber in which three out of seven wallstones support a capstone 4·5 m by 2·7 m. The gaps between the wallstones have been filled with smaller stones in recent times to enable the tomb to serve as a sheep shelter. There is no sign of a covering mound. Locally the site is known as Carreg Samson. [G. E. Daniel, *Prehistoric Chamber Tombs* (1950), 201.]

12 MEINI GWYR, Llandissilio East   SN: 142267
A circular bank 36 m in diameter and a metre high is broken by a narrow entrance on the west. On the inner slope of the bank are two stones, all that remain of the original seventeen. Excavation in 1938 failed to find any internal features save for a middle bronze age hearth with a few pieces of pottery.

13 PEN DINAS, Aberystwyth   SN: 584804
This hour-glass-shaped fort is situated on a ridge between the rivers Rheidol and Ystwyth. Two peaks are enclosed and it is clear that originally they were separate enclosures. At first the northern summit was surrounded by ramparts with a timber revetment and ditch. Fairly soon afterwards the southern crest was more substantially fortified with a stone-faced rubble bank and ditch some 3 m deep. There were entrances at the north and south with gates supported by four posts. A

period of decay or deliberate destruction may have followed before the
southern fort was remodelled. Eventually both forts were joined
together with a new revetted wall across the saddle between the peaks
and around the northern fort. An entrance to the enlarged enclosure
with a four-post gateway was constructed midway along the east side.
This final stage dates from the first century BC. A number of round
buildings have been traced, though the interior has been damaged by
ploughing. [C. D. Forde and others, *Arch. Cambrensis,* 112 (1963),
125.]

14   PENTRE IFAN, Nevern   SN: 099370
One of the best-known tombs in south Wales, the exposed chamber
stands 3 m high, its capstone supported on three uprights. Two of these
on the south form portal stones for a lower doorstone. There is a
semicircular forecourt, originally of two stones on either side of the
portals. The destroyed mound was once about 40 m long by 17 m
broad. [G. E. Daniel, *Prehistoric Chamber Tombs* (1950), 199.]

15   PONT-DDU, Llangynog   SN: 314139
Within 1·5 km are a number of standing stones close to the river Afon
Cywyn. Nothing can be said of them except that they average 2 m tall.
They occur at SN: 308148, 312141 and 314139. Such stones occur all
over the south-west, and whilst many may be prehistoric, we should be
under no illusion that they are all ancient in origin. Some have been set
up in modern times for the cattle to rub themselves on.

16   ST DAVID'S HEAD, St David's   SM: 723279
A rocky headland of 2·5 ha is defended by a drystone wall about 100 m
long running north to south and originally 3 m wide and 4 m high. East
of this are two banks of rubble with possible ditches between them.
There is an entrance gap 2·3 m wide. Not far inside the entrance are
seven circular hut foundations averaging 7 m in diameter. S. Baring-
Gould found indeterminate pottery, spindle whorls and beads
amongst them in 1898. East of the fort ancient boundary walls form
large enclosures that may have been associated with stock rearing.
There are hut circles amongst them. [S. Baring-Gould, *Arch. Cambrensis,* 16 (1899), 105.]

17   YSBYTY CYNFYN CHURCH STONE CIRCLE   SN: 752791
We can probably see a survival of a tradition of sacred rites here.
Ysbyty churchyard is surrounded by a circular bank. The church is
built into the western side of it, and the rest has been damaged by a
wall. Five stones of a circle survive. Only the block on the north, 3·3 m
high, is clearly in its original position. Two others are in use as

gateposts to the churchyard, and have been moved from their original positions, and the remaining two have been built into the churchyard wall, though they may be in their original places. [W. F. Grimes, in I. Ll. Foster and L. Alcock, eds., *Culture and Environment* (1963), 127.]

GLAMORGAN

ARTHUR'S STONE, Llanrhidian, see Maen Ceti.

1 THE BULWARK, Cheriton   ss:443927

Situated on the eastern tip of Llanmadoc Hill with steep slopes to the
north and the ground falling to the east, this is the most westerly
example of the multiple enclosure hill-slope forts so far recognized.
There is an oval inner enclosure some 120 m by 90 m defended by a
bank and ditch and with a broad entrance on the east. There is a second
enclosure outside this, providing a wide penning area everywhere
except on the north. This is entered on the south-west, opposite what
may have been the earliest line of defence, running north to south.
There are further defences of a cross-ridge nature both to the east and
to the west. [A. Fox, *Arch. J*, 109 (1952), 1.]

2 CAERAU, Ely, Cardiff   st:134751

This is a triangular multivallate fort of 5 ha. Its defences are covered
with bushes and its interior is used as a children's playground. On the
north and south-west are triple ramparts and ditches, generally reduced to scarps and terraces. On the east is one massive bank and
ditch, broken by two entrances, each leading from different areas of
ground. The southern entrance is inturned on the east, whilst the
eastern entrance is inturned on both sides and is occupied by the
modern road to the church. A third entrance at the western apex of the
fortification is probably medieval and related to the ring-work now in
the north-eastern corner. Banks suggesting the foundations of buildings inside the fort probably date from the middle ages. [R. J. C.
Atkinson, *Prehistoric Society Swansea Guide* (1965), 20.]

3 CASTLE DITCHES, Llantwit Major   ss:960674

The Afon Col-huw cuts off a triangular promontory fort which is
defended by three ramparts and ditches and steep slopes on the north
and south. Unfortunately the earthworks are very overgrown and not
easy to see.

4 CAT HOLE CAVE, Ilston   ss:538900

Fifteen metres above the floor of a wooded valley is a rock shelter 18 m deep occupied by upper palaeolithic people of the group known as Creswellians, who made blade tools and hunted animals of late glacial type around 10,000 BC. First excavated in about 1864, the site was subjected to further examination in 1958 and 1968 when at least two stone age occupations were recognized, the later being mesolithic. The cave was used again in bronze age times for burial purposes, and medieval occupation has also been recorded. [RCHM, *Glamorgan*, I, 1 (1976), 19.]

5 CRUGYRAFAN, Glyncorrwg   ss:920954
This barrow is of interest since the central mound is surrounded by a ditch 28 m in diameter and a berm, causing it to resemble a bell-barrow. A clayey mound is crowned by a modern stone cairn that replaces an earlier one. When excavated in 1902 traces of a cremation were found in a cist, together with a bone copy of an early bronze age ogival grooved dagger. [RCHM, *Glamorgan*, I, 1 (1976), 95.]

6 DUNRAVEN, St Bride's Major   ss:887728
The Trwyn-y-Witch headland rises steeply above Dunraven Bay. In the iron age it was defended as a promontory fort with double ramparts, probably approached through an entrance now destroyed by erosion. There are traces of a south-facing rampart near the crest of the spur. On its northern slope are about ten hollows and ledges on which iron age houses may have stood. The spur also contains a number of good rectangular medieval pillow mounds (artificial rabbit warrens).

7 GOAT'S CAVE, Paviland   ss:437858
Most easily reached from the sands at low tide but cut off at high tide, this cave is famous for the discovery in January 1823 by Dean William Buckland of the 'Red Lady of Paviland'. This skeleton, deliberately covered with red ochre, was subsequently identified as a young man of about twenty-five buried in an extended position beside a mammoth skull. It was accompanied by mammoth ivory points and hundreds of late Aurignacian stone implements. Unfortunately the early date of the excavation made it impossible to be sure that the man and tools were of the same date. Recently a radiocarbon date for the skeleton of 16,510 bc and a date of 26,650 bc for animal bone for the cave floor would make it appear that the tools belong to an occupation about 10,000 years earlier than the burial. The cave was later used in the mesolithic, neolithic and Roman periods. [T. Molleson and R. Burleigh, *Antiquity*, 52 (1978), 143.]

8 HARDING'S DOWN, Llangennith   ss:434907
A group of three rather weak enclosures, of which one is unfinished. Harding's Down West is oval in shape, about 0·6 ha in size, and

defended by a bank, ditch and counterscarp. There is an entrance on the north-east and an annexe of almost the same size as the main enclosure. There are traces of huts in the West enclosure including one which measured 10 m in diameter after excavation. The rampart is revetted in stone with a V-shaped ditch, and a gate was hung between four large posts.

Harding's Down East seems to have been intended as an enclosure of 0·9 ha, but after it had been marked out only parts of its circumference, mainly on the east, were actually dug. To the north of the East Site is a small circular enclosure protected by a strong bank, ditch and counterscarp. The entrance is approached by a slight hollow way. [RCHM, *Glamorgan*, I, 2 (1976), nos. 687, 688 and 686.]

9 HIGH PENNARD, Pennard   ss:567864
Situated high on the cliffs which protected it to the west and south is a promontory fort defended by two lines of rampart and ditch, broken by rocky outcrops. Presumably the inner enclosure was for houses and the outer, some 46 m by 18 m, for stock. Excavation has revealed a timber gateway with guard hut, and shown that occupation continued into Roman times [RCHM, *Glamorgan*, I, 2 (1976), no. 702.]

10 THE KNAVE, Rhossili   ss:432864
A semicircular cliff-castle defended by the sea on the south and west and by two ramparts and ditches. The ramparts are made of limestone blocks and are broken by entrances on the western side, the inner one of which utilizes the natural rock outcrops and turns inwards on its eastern edge. Pottery from excavations in 1938 was of Glastonbury type. [RCHM, *Glamorgan*, I, 2 (1976), no. 699.]

11 MAEN CETI, Llanrhidian   ss:491905
Described as one of 'the three wonderful works of Britain' and often known as Arthur's Stone, this is the remains of a circular ring cairn some 23 m in diameter, with a burial chamber at the centre. The capstone is massive, having once been estimated at 30 tonnes, but the western quarter has now broken off. Even so a block 4 m long by 2 m wide and 2·2 m thick still survives, supported on some four of the ten chamber wallstones. The burial chamber is rectangular and divided into two sections. It is possible that this vault has always been free standing and was never covered by a mound. It is unexcavated. [RCHM, *Glamorgan*, I, 1 (1976), 31.]

12 MAES Y FELIN, St Lythans   st:101723
Great slabs of gnarled mudstone from a rectangular chamber 2 m long, 1·5 m wide and 1·8 m internal height. It lies at the eastern end of an east-west mound some 27 m long, 11 m wide and 1 m high. Although

unexcavated, material cleared from the chamber in 1875 included human remains and pottery of a coarse type. [RCHM, *Glamorgan*, I, 1 (1976), 39.]

13 **NASH POINT, Marcross**   ss:915684
A track by a wood-filled valley leads to a promontory fort protected by four ramparts separated from each other by flat-bottomed ditches. The entrance is reached from a terraced trackway, but the interior has been almost entirely eroded away.

14 **PARC-LE-BREOS CWM, Pen-maen** (Fig 39, p. 338)   ss:537898
This site was first recognized as a long barrow when the northern end was quarried for road metal in 1869. Then followed an excavation by Sir John Lubbock, which revealed the plan of the forecourt and burial chambers and some two dozen skeletons 'much broken and in no regular arrangement'. The site was taken into guardianship by the Department of the Environment in 1960 and excavated by Professor R. J. C. Atkinson. The tomb contains a central passage with two side chambers on either side built of thin limestone slabs with drystone walling between them. At the entrance to the passage and to three of the side chambers are low sill stones. The capstones have long since disappeared. The cairn and the horned forecourt are bounded by two parallel walls of drystone. Apart from the burials found in 1869, the only other finds in the tomb have been pieces of undecorated neolithic pottery. [R. J. C. Atkinson, in *Archaeology in Wales,* I (1961), 5.]

15 **THURBA FORT, Rhossili**   ss:422870
A rocky promontory on the western extremity of Gower provides the site for a small but strong cliff castle. It seems to have been built in two phases. At first an oval area was defended on the east and north by a broad stone wall. Within were three stone hut sites. An entrance at the south-west leads to a narrow strip of land in which two other possible houses stood. Later two lines of bank and ditch 30 m apart were built across the neck of the promontory. There is a modern field wall on the eastern bank. Other earthworks have been damaged by the ruined limeworks. [C. Fox, *Board of Celtic Studies Bulletin*, 8 (1937), 364.]

16 **TINKINSWOOD, St Nicholas** (Fig 40, p. 339)   st:092733
This well-known chambered barrow was excavated and restored by John Ward in 1914. The mound is almost rectangular, measuring 40 m long and 17 m wide, and is held in position by a drystone revetment wall. Halfway along the northern side is a stone-lined cist about 2·9 m square lined with thin upright slabs. It is probably secondary to the main barrow and contained no human burials. Between horns at the eastern end of the barrow is a trapezoidal chamber 5 m long and 3·5 m

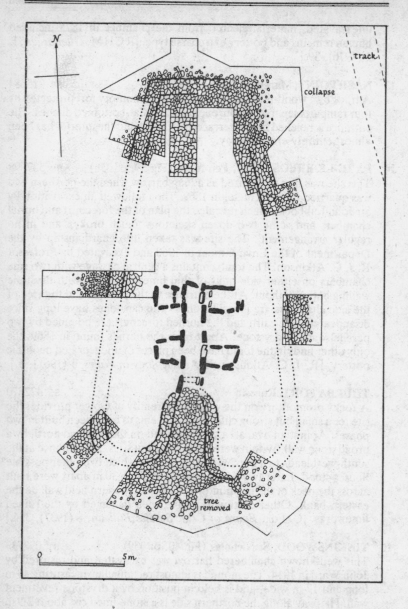

Fig 39. Parc-le-Breos Cwm, Glamorgan (after R. J. C. Atkinson)

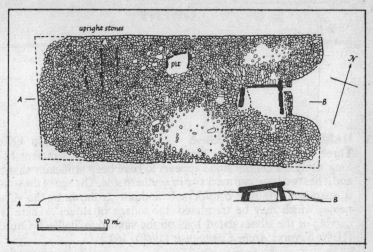

upright stones

pit

A

B

N

A

B

0   10 m

Fig 40. Plan and section of the chambered long cairn, Tinkinswood, Glamorgan (after J. Ward)

wide. It is entered from the forecourt at its north-east corner, by a slab-lined passage 0·8 m wide. The capstone is believed to be the largest in Britain, weighing some 40 tonnes. The southern wallstone of the chamber was destroyed by early stone robbers. Burials included at least fifty persons, twenty-one female, sixteen male and at least eight children. Pottery was of undecorated neolithic type together with fragments of a bell beaker, suggesting a late use of the tomb. [RCHM, *Glamorgan*, I, 1 (1976), 36.]

GWENT

1 HAROLD'S STONES, Trellech   so:499052
Three tall, pointed stones beside the road form an alignment 12 m
long. Only the central stone appears to have been artificially shaped,
and it has two large cup marks on its southern side. The age of the stones
is unknown, although considerable antiquity is shown by the village
name, which may be translated 'the village of stones'. There is a
carving of the stones dated 1689 on the sundial in Trellech Church.
[H. N. Savory, *Arch. Cambrensis* (1940), 169.]

2 HESTON BRAKE, Portskewett   st:506887
Hiding behind a clump of bushes is a much disturbed cairn, at least
21 m long and lying east-west, with an unroofed chamber set in the
eastern end. Two tall portal stones lead into a passage 4 m long and a
chamber of 3 m length. Both passage and chamber are 1·5 m wide and
would form a continuous gallery if it were not that the burial chamber
is offset northwards after half a metre. This suggests that the passage
may have been added to an existing chamber. Skeletons were found
when the tomb was excavated in August 1888. [G. E. Daniel, *Prehistoric Chamber Tombs* (1950), 212.]

3 LLANMELIN, Caerwent   st:460925
This is an oval enclosure of 1·2 ha surrounded by a double rampart,
ditch and counterscarp, and an elongated annexe on the south-eastern
side. A. H. A. Hogg suggests that the site first consisted of a single
elongated oval defence almost all of which was destroyed when the
present double defence was laid out. The new inner rampart was a
massive drystone wall 5 m thick with a berm separating it from a ditch.
The outer defence was a dumped bank and ditch. The entrance was
asymmetrical. The west side was composed of the ends of the ramparts
and ditches, the east by a long inturn. The gate hung on two posts at the
inner side of the fort. The annexe, consisting of a series of rectangular
enclosures ranged along the east side of the approach, was added later.
It most resembles medieval fishponds, but was presumably accom-
modation for livestock. The material found is of the iron age B culture.
Suggestions that this was the capital of the Silures before they were

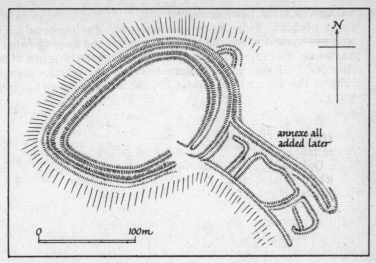

Fig 41. Llanmelin, Gwent (after V. E. Nash-Williams)

moved down to Caerwent should be treated with extreme caution. [A. H. A. Hogg, *Hill-forts of Britain* (1975), 237.]

4 SUDBROOK CAMP, Portskewett ST:505873

Immediately above the Severn Tunnel at a constriction of the Severn estuary, this promontory fort is triangular in shape, the sea cliff forming the southern side whilst the north-west and north-east are protected by three banks and ditches. The inner rampart is of glacis type backed by a revetment of stone, as at Maiden Castle. The site was occupied by the Roman army from about AD 60 until their final defeat of the Silures soon afterwards.

5 TWYN-Y-GAER, Cwnyoy SO:294219

Standing at the end of the Fwthog ridge at 426 m above sea-level, Twyn-y-gaer encloses some 1·8 ha. Its history is fairly complex. It consists of an oval enclosure divided into three sections by two cross-banks and ditches. These sections may be termed eastern, central and western. At first it seems that the central and western sections together formed a single fort with a palisaded annexe on the east. Later the eastern annexe was defended with a bank and ditch and became part of the main fort. Eventually, both the middle and eastern sections were abandoned and only the roughly circular western section survived. There were inturned entrances to the eastern and western areas with complicated histories. [L. A. Probert, in G. C. Boon and J. M. Lewis, eds., *Welsh Antiquity* (1976), 105.]

6   Y GARN LLWYD, Newchurch West   ST:447968
Lurking behind a hedge are the ruined remains of a chambered tomb, with two upright stones flanking the entrance and forming either a narrow square entrance or the dividing wall between two parts of the chamber. Both suggestions indicate links with the Severn–Cotswold culture. The site has been damaged by the road and remains unexcavated.

GWYNEDD

1 BACHWEN, Clynnog   SH:407495
Surrounded by ugly iron railings is a megalithic burial chamber in which four upright stones about 1 m high support a large triangular capstone. This is particularly interesting since the upper surface of the capstone is indented with about 110 cup marks, each about 5 cm in diameter and 2 cm deep. There are two shallow grooves each of which links three of the cup marks. Eight more cups can be seen on the eastern ridge of the capstone. The monument may belong to the portal dolmen family, which are often associated with cup marks. [RCHM, *Caernarvonshire,* II (1960), 55.]

2 BARCOLDIAD-Y-GAWRES, Caerhun   SH:716716
This cairn, whose name means 'the giantess's apronful', stands at 396 m in a natural hollow. The cairn is an oval mass of boulders with a cist on the northern side about 2·5 m long and 1·2 m wide. It is now about 1·2 m high. [RCHM, *Caernarvonshire,* I (1956), 36.]

3 BRYN CADER FADER, Llandecwyn   SH:648353
A long walk from Eisingrug (SH:615345) east to Moel-y-glo and then along a boggy and difficult track north-eastwards leads to a highly dramatic cairn circle of small stones, out of which protrude fifteen long pointed stones like teeth or a crown of thorns. Inside is a low cairn with a central burial cist. Outside is a ring of boulders.

4 CAER EUNI, Llandderfel   SJ:000413
Long, narrow and oval in shape, Caer Euni lies on a high ridge, and is surrounded by a stone rampart with a wide ditch and pronounced counterscarp. Fused stonework at the western side may be an example of vitrification. The bank of an earlier fort can be seen about halfway along the length of the fort earthwork, together with traces of some two dozen hut circles. There are entrances at the north-east and south. The former has both single and twin hornworks. There is a good kerb circle and a ring cairn at 993410.

5 CAPEL GARMON, Llanrwst   SH:818542
(Department of the Environment). Lying east-west in a hollow, Capel

Garmon is a wedge-shaped long barrow some 28 m long and 13 m wide at the broad east end. Excavation showed that it was surrounded by a revetment wall which was intentionally buried beneath the barrow mound. At the eastern end well-developed horns stood on either side of a false entrance composed of two slabs of slate. The true entrance is on the south side, where a passage almost 5 m long leads into a rectangular antechamber, from which roughly circular chambers open on the east and west. These chambers are about 3 m wide and that on the west has a large capstone still in position. When excavated the entrance passage was still blocked as it had been after the last burials had been made in the tomb. Finds included neolithic pottery and beaker fragments, flints and disturbed human bones. [W. J. Hemp, *Arch. Cambrensis*, 82 (1927), 1.]

6 CARNEDDAU HENGWM, Llanaber   SH:614205
Here are two long cairns, the northern one 33 m long and about 18 m wide, with at least two burial chambers. At the west is a large capstone. The southern barrow is larger, 57 m long and 21 m wide. It has two chambers, one a portal dolmen, at the eastern end, and one in the centre approached by a passage from the north. Both cairns have been badly robbed, but there is evidence to suggest that the southern is a multi-period construction. [E. G. Bowen and C. A. Gresham, *History of Merioneth*, 1 (1967), 9.]

7 CARN FADRUN, Llaniestyn   SH:280352
Good boots and determination are needed to visit this fort dominating the Lleyn peninsula. The climb is remarkably steep, though the effort will be rewarded for the enthusiast. The summit is defended by a tumbled stone wall enclosing a triangular area of 5 ha, later extended to 10·5 ha by adding a rectangular area on the north. On the west stood a small Norman castle of the twelfth century. Ancient trackways lead up to gates on the north and south. The revetment of the northern gate may be relatively modern, though in places the fort wall still stands 2 m high. There are a number of round and rectangular huts inside the fort, some built up against the defensive walls. It is impossible to say whether these belong to the first fort or the period of its extension, or even the Norman castle. There is a well in the western half of the northern extension. Beside the first period wall, near the centre of the fort, is a robbed bronze age stone cist that was probably the first feature on the site. Without excavation the fort cannot be dated, but the northern extension probably belongs to the late Roman period. There are numerous huts on the hill slopes outside the fort, especially on the northern side. [RCHM, *Caernarvonshire*, III (1964), 69.]

8 CASTELL ODO, Aberdaron   SH:187284
This not very impressive fort is important because of the excavations of

1958–9. Approximately circular in plan, double banks enclose less than 1 ha. The banks stand 1·5 m high in places, but have been damaged. Inside were nine or ten round timber houses, which were later burnt. Their inhabitants used pottery of iron age A type. The fort was abandoned for a short period, after which a stone bank was heaped up on the line of the present outer bank. There were probably circular stone huts inside, but these were destroyed when the fort was rebuilt. This rebuild consisted of revetting the existing bank and building another one 20 m inside it. More round huts were built, but no pottery seems to have been used. There was a gate on the north-east 1·7 m wide. Next, the ramparts, which could only have been about 1·5 m high, were slighted, though the fort continued to be occupied and more houses were built over the ruins. This final slighting may have taken place about AD 78. [L. Alcock, *Arch. Cambrensis*, 109 (1960), 78.]

9 **CIST CERRIG, Treflys**   SH:543384
Only three stones, looking like a great armchair, survive of this fine portal dolmen, whose burial chamber lay to the west. The two uprights of the portal and the door slab survive. No trace of the covering cairn remains. Twenty-three metres to the south-east is an outcrop of rock with a sloping face on which fifteen cup marks can be traced. Study shows that these have been pecked rather than ground out of the rock surface. [F. Lynch, in T. G. E. Powell, ed., *Megalithic Enquiries* (1969), 129.]

10 **COETAN ARTHUR, Llanystumdwy**   SH:499413
Sometimes called Ystum Cegid Isaf, this passage grave is half buried in a field wall. Five upright stones, the largest 2 m high, support a thin capstone. The chamber has been restored, more or less in its original position. The entrance was on the north side, and a drawing of 1769 shows that there was a passage nearly 5 m long, with two capstones that led up to it. Although the capstones have gone, traces of the passage wallstones can still be seen on both sides of the field wall. There is little doubt that this was once a passage grave with a circular covering mound perhaps 18–20 m in diameter. [RCHM, *Caernarvonshire*, II (1960), 238.]

11 **CONWAY MOUNTAIN, MYNYDD-Y-DREF, Conway**   SH:760778
A roughly rectangular stone-walled fort of 3 ha, strongly protected on the north by the precipitous nature of the ground, is enclosed on the other sides by a single stone rampart, and encloses about sixty circular huts. In the southern side is a simple entrance passage 2·4 m wide. Excavation has shown that this was probably crossed by a wooden bridge. In the south-west corner of the fort is a separate stone enclosure, entered from outside, containing traces of six huts, some of which

have been excavated. The southern wall of this enclosure had been modified and traces of an earlier version can be seen outside. [W. E. Griffiths and A. H. A. Hogg, *Arch. Cambrensis*, 105 (1956), 49.]

12   CORS-Y-CARNEDDAU, Llanfairfechan   SH:717747
A group of four cairns, now divided by a wall. The most important cairn is 18 m in diameter and 2·4 m high with a deep hollow at its centre. The smallest one, little more than a setting of boulders, is a ring cairn. [RCHM, *Caernarvonshire*, I (1956), 125.]

13   CORS-Y-GEDOL, Llanddweye-is-y-craig   SH:603228
This is a very irregular cairn about 25 m long with the remains of a burial chamber at the eastern end. The chamber seems to have been rectangular in plan with a very large capstone lying diagonally between an upright back stone and the ground to the west. Another upright stone, perhaps forming the north wall of the chamber, stands slightly to the east of this and suggests that the capstone has slipped westwards. Only excavation might decide the matter.

An area about 630 m by 450 m to the east of the burial chamber is occupied by hut circles surrounded by a rough enclosure wall. Finds suggest that they belong to the Roman period. [W. E. Griffiths, *J Merioneth Hist. and Record Soc.*, 2 (1956), 293.]

14   CREIGIAU GWINEU, Rhiw   SH:228274
This hillfort is egg-shaped in plan and measures some 120 m by 55 m. A stone rampart partly surrounds the rocky mass and at least one hut circle may be seen in the eastern half. The view from here is superb. [RCHM, *Caernarvonshire*, III (1964), 100.]

15   DINAS DINLIE, Llanwrog   SH:437563
This rounded hill beside the sea was once enclosed by a double rampart, now eroded away on the west side. The inner bank, which encloses 1·5 ha, rises between 1·8 m on the south and east to 6 m on the north. The outer bank is lower and weaker and is separated from it by an intervening ditch. There is a simple straight-through entrance at the south-east corner. On the inside can be seen hut hollows and a mutilated mound, which may have been a round barrow. It has been suggested that the fort formed an iron age beachhead with a sheltered harbour, now silted up, in the marshland to the north. [RCHM, *Caernarvonshire*, II (1960), 190.]

16   DINAS DINORWIG, Llanddeiniolen   SH:549653
Although half covered by trees, this is an impressive fort of 1·2 ha, sited on a ridge above a tributary of the Seiont. The site consists of an inner wall 3·4 m thick, surrounded by two massive banks of earth and

rubble, now between 6 m and 9 m high. A track leads obliquely through the rampart on the north-west to a gateway in the stone wall. There is a second blocked gate in the wall on the north-east. It has been suggested that this wall is earlier than the ramparts which enclose it and probably of early iron age date, while the ramparts together with a triangular annexe on the north might date to immediately before the Roman conquest. The name of the fort has been interpreted by some as 'the fortress of the Ordovices' which recalls the tribe that occupied the area in Roman and earlier times. There are three stone 'guns' on the site, of nineteenth-century date. [W. Gardner, *Arch. Cambrensis*, 99 (1947), 231.]

17 DINAS EMRYS, Beddgelert   SH:606492
Although begun in the early iron age, this attractive little hillfort is largely post-Roman in date. Artificial defences run between craggy outcrops to enclose about 1 ha, with a single entrance on the south-west. On that side is a small outer enclosure. Nowhere are the defences even a metre high. The dominant feature of the site is the base of a twelfth-century tower. South-west from it is a pool, an artificial cistern constructed to supply the settlement with water and dated by excavation to the fifth or sixth century AD. Dinas Emrys figures in a number of legends, particularly that of Nennius, who recorded magical events associated with Vortigern and Ambrosius (Emrys in Welsh). Excavations show that the fort was occupied at the time mentioned in the legend. [RCHM, *Caernarvonshire,* II (1960), 25.]

18 DINLLAEN, Edern   SH:275416
A long narrow peninsula of 5·6 ha is cut off by two cross-dykes 60 m apart that form a promontory fort. Sadly all the earthworks are badly disfigured by quarrying and a golf course. The main advantage of the fort would have been its control over a good harbour. [RCHM, *Caernarvonshire,* III (1964), 34.]

19 DRUID'S CIRCLE, Dwygyfylchi   SH:722746
The Druid's Circle (Meini Hirion) is the jewel amongst a number of ruined cairns and circles on a low saddle 700 m east of the Craig Lwyd axe factory. On a bank of boulders 26 m in diameter were thirty stones; ten still remain standing, some as much as 1·8 m high. At the south-west is a gap in the bank with two large door stones. At the centre of the circle was a cist containing an inverted food-vessel and the cremated remains of a ten-year-old child, perhaps a sacrifice. North-west of the cist was a pit with a second food-vessel and child cremation. A third pot with whetstones and a cremation nearby were also found in the centre when the circle was excavated in 1958.

A ring cairn lies 145 m south-west of the Druid's Circle. The central area was empty but a cremation and urn came from the edge of the circle. Further east from the Druid's Circle are more cairns and a tiny boulder circle of five stones, only 3 m in diameter. (See Cors-y-Carneddau.) [RCHM, *Caernarvonshire*, III (1964), 111.]

20 DYFFRYN ARDUDWY, Llanenddwyn   SH:589229
(Department of the Environment). Situated on the hillside above the sea, this chambered cairn is of two periods of construction. First a small rectangular stone chamber 2·7 m long and 2 m high was constructed with two portal stones on either side of a high closing slab and roofed with a single capstone. This had been covered by a cairn of water-rolled stones; it was at least 3 m in diameter and is clearly marked on the ground today. Although the chamber was empty when excavated in 1961, a pit in front of the entrance contained pieces of undecorated neolithic pottery.

A second, larger, stone burial chamber was constructed to the east of the first. It was 3·6 m long, 2·4 m wide and 1·5 m high, with two wallstones on either side, an end stone and a low sill stone that only slightly blocked the opening. The cairn of the eastern chamber was rectangular in plan and extended westwards to incorporate the whole of the earlier tomb. Finds in the eastern chamber included neolithic and bronze age pottery, which was also found in the forecourt to the east. The forecourt had been carefully blocked in prehistory, and

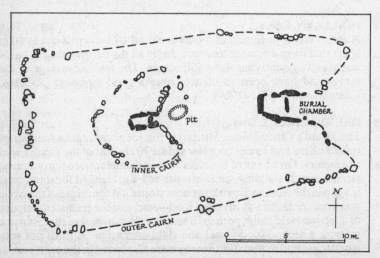

Fig 42. Dyffryn Ardudwy, Gwynedd

much of this remained intact in 1961. [T. G. E. Powell, *Archaeologia*, 104 (1973), 1.]

21   FOUR CROSSES, Abererch   SH:399385
A small closed rectangular burial chamber with no sign of an original mound. The chamber measures 1·3 m by 0·8 m and is 1·5 m high on its northern side. The eastern stone probably formed the entrance since it is only 1 m high and does not support the capstone. The pentagonal capstone is a large slab 2·6 m by 2 m and 0·6 m thick. Nothing was found in the chamber when the stones were straightened in 1936.

North-east of the burial chamber are two standing stones: one (SH:400389) is 1·7 m high, the other (SH:400388) is of similar height but not so massive. [RCHM, *Caernarvonshire*, III (1964), 16.]

22   GAERWEN, Llanwnda   SH:501583
Between the farm at Hafoty Wern-las and Bod-Angharad are a number of small hutted settlements and field banks dating from the iron age and Roman periods. About 150 m north-east of Hafoty Wern-las is a quadrangular walled enclosure containing a circular hut 7 m in diameter and two rectangular foundations, one of which was a blacksmith's workshop. On the other side of the road are the remains of four circular huts. Other groups can be seen at SH:501585, SH:504579 and SH:505580. [RCHM, *Caernarvonshire*, II (1960), 226.]

23   GARN BODUAN, Boduan   SH:311394
Although surrounded by trees, this large hillfort of 10 ha is not itself wooded. It crowns a rocky eminence and contains a number of springs that would have been useful for the occupants of the 168 round houses that stood inside it. It was originally surrounded by a wall 3 m thick enclosing 10 ha. This was later made slightly larger by taking in part of the western slope of the hill with a more massive wall 4 m thick, which still stands 2 m high. There were two entrances; that on the south-east was apparently the more important, but is badly ruined. That at the north-east is well preserved and is about 3 m wide. The houses were built of upright slabs or laid stones, sometimes both together. Excavation of four of them failed to produce dating material. Crowning the summit on the eastern side is a small fort 70 m long and 30 m wide, built in a neater style with steeply battered faces. Access to the top of the rampart is by a flight of steps formed of long stones jutting from the inner face. There were two entrances, one badly damaged on the south, and another blocked in antiquity on the west. There was a house immediately inside this entrance. Excavation produced slight evidence of a late Roman date, as well as dark age pottery. This is compatible with the legendary association of the fort with Buan who lived about AD 600 or 650. [RCHM, *Caernarvonshire*, III (1964), 22.]

24 GWERN EINION, Llanfair   SH:587286
A rectangular burial chamber forming a portal dolmen, with five
wallstones supporting a sloping capstone 2·7 m long. The whole has
been built into a drystone wall and is used as a cattle shelter. There is
no sign of a mound. [G. E. Daniel, *Prehistoric Chamber Tombs*
(1950), 196.]

25 HENDRE WAELOD, Llansantffraid-glan-Conway   SH:793748
Here is a very fine portal dolmen above the banks of the river Conway.
two portal stones 1·7 m high stand at the south-eastern end of a low
chamber. The entrance is closed by a thin stone slab that rises up to the
capstone; this is a massive block 3 m long and 1·5 m thick, and rests on
the ground at the northern side. The remains of the long cairn that
covered the tomb survive in the hedgerow. [F. Lynch, in T. G. E.
Powell, ed., *Megalithic Enquiries* (1969), 140.]

26 LLANBEDR   SH:585269
Inside the church is a stone slab with a megalithic spiral design 0·3 m
across. Two stones stand 90 m north-west of the church and west of the
A469, and may have survived from a stone circle. One is 3 m high, the
other 2 m. They are known as Meini Hirion.

27 LLETY'R FILIAST, Llandudno   SH:772829
An oval barrow mound about 25 m long has been partly quarried away
at the southern end, exposing a ruined burial chamber. The chamber
may originally have been rectangular. Today the four wallstones are
open on the eastern side. A broken capstone is partly in position on the
west. [G. E. Daniel, *Prehistoric Chamber Tombs* (1950), 191.]

28 MAEN-Y-BARDD, Caerhun   SH:740718
The Bard's Stone stands at over 300 m above sea-level. Four stones
form a rectangular chamber with blocked entrance facing west and a
single square capstone. There are traces of a long cairn on either side of
a modern wall. Nearby are the remains of a burial cist and adjoining
mound (SH:741718). To the west along the lane are two fine standing
stones: Ffon-y-Cawr, The Giant's Stick at SH:738717, and another at
SH:736716. [RCHM, *Caernarvonshire*, I (1956), 37.]

29 MOEL GOEDOG and TRACKWAY, Morfa Harlech   SH:614325
Here is a small circular fort about 230 m in diameter, enclosed by
double banks except on the north, where there is a third bank. There
must have been a timber palisade to make the defence really effective.
The gap on the south-west was most probably the original entrance. At
SH:616322 are two groups of huts and traces of field boundaries. They
may be contemporary with the fort. To the south-west (at SH:610324)
are two ring cairns, one of which was recently excavated and restored.

Running north and south to the west of the fort is an ancient trackway that may date back to bronze age times when metal prospecting was taking place. Its course is marked by a series of standing stones, such as Carreg (SH:599309) and the tallest example, which is at SH:602313. At least five more stones can be found between this last site and the fort. There is a strongly built hut circle at SH:605324 with signs of cultivation terraces close by.

30 MYNYDD CEFN AMWLCH, Penllech SH:230345
A wedge-shaped capstone is supported by three upright stones to make a roughly rectangular chamber, which may have been closed by a fourth stone now lying beside the monument. To the north-west a further flat stone might have been the capstone of another chamber. It is possible that a mound 8·5 m in diameter once covered the tomb. Legend says that the tomb was once removed, but the cattle bellowed continually until it was re-erected! [RCHM, *Caernarvonshire*, III (1964), 8.]

MYNYDD-Y-DREF, Conway, see Conway Mountain.

31 PEN-Y-DINAS, Llanaber SH:607209
On a small spur looking west over Egryn Abbey is an unusual oval fort of 0·2 ha. The walls have stone facings filled with earth and rubble and are 4·5 m wide. There is a second rampart on the north and west with traces of a third. The entrance on the north-west is sunken and a bridge must have existed there. It is inturned and guard chambers probably existed. It is approached by a road from the north, which seems to be original, though the rectangular hut foundations beside it are likely to be medieval. Below the fort on the south side, but above the stream, is an enclosed hut site. [O. G. S. Crawford, *Arch. Cambrensis*, 75 (1920), 99.]

32 PEN-Y-GAER, Llanbedr-y-Cennin (Fig 43, p. 352) SH:750693
The interest of this site lies mainly in the existence of chevaux-de-frise for defence. These were groups of pointed stones set on end close together to make approach difficult. The fort is of at least two periods, and has two walls of stone around it, except on the south and a short distance on the north where an additional line exists. The walls, of massive construction, are 4·5 m thick. There is an original entrance on the west; that on the south is recent. The chevaux-de-frise lie in two broad areas to the west and south. The southern group can be found between the outer and middle rampart, suggesting that the outer rampart was constructed later. [RCHM, *Caernarvonshire*, I (1956), 100.]

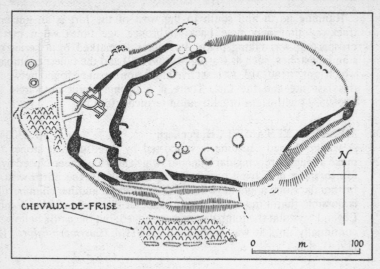

Fig 43. Pen-y-Gaer, Gwynedd

33 RHOSLAN, Llanystumdwy   SH:483409

A single large capstone 3·5 m long and 2·7 m wide is supported on four wallstones. The chamber is open to the south. There is no trace of a covering mound.

34 TAN-Y-MURIAU, Rhiw-with-Llanfaelrhys   SH:238288

One of the most interesting tombs on the Lleyn peninsula, with a portal dolmen at the north-western end. Above the typical H-shaped closed 'doorway' is a massive capstone, 4 m by 3 m and 1·5 thick at the northern end. The chamber has lost its sidestones, and the cairn itself has been removed to make field walls. To the south-east, 7·5 m down the slope, is a side chamber, entered from the west, and from this point the cairn is well preserved for a further 27 m southwards. There are early reports of a third chamber but this is unconfirmed. It has been suggested that the portal dolmen formed part of an early cairn about 8 m long, and that the rest of the mound is a later addition. This might be confirmed by excavation. [T. G. E. Powell, ed., *Megalithic Enquiries* (1969), 132.]

35 TRE'R CEIRI, Llanaelhaearn (Fig 44, opposite)   SH:373446

The most dramatic and impressive of all the British hillforts. The 'town of the giants' is on the most easterly of the three peaks of Yr Eifl. It is an irregular oval enclosure 450 m above sea-level, 290 m long and 100 m wide. The walls of the fort survive largely intact. They are

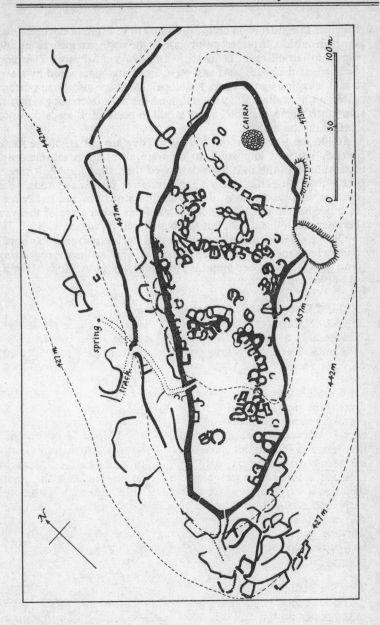

Fig 44. Tre'r Ceiri, Gwynedd

353

irregular in construction and vary from 2 m to 3·5 m in thickness and 4 m high outside. In places, particularly at the north, a rampart walk and ramps up to it still exist. There are five gateways into the fort. The main ones are at the south-west and west. Both are approached by steep tracks climbing up the rocky hill slope. There are also three postern gates, each less than 1 m wide. Of these the most interesting is that at the north where the lintel stone is still in position. It leads down to springs on the hillside.

Inside the fort are about 150 huts. They are not all of the same period, but it is impossible to separate all of them satisfactorily. Excavations in the past have destroyed their stratigraphy. It seems likely that the earliest huts were circular in plan. Later huts were circular with subdivisions, then D-shaped structures and finally rectangular buildings. Occupation material has dated some of them to between AD 150 and 400, but some may well be earlier.

On the sides of the hill are numerous enclosures, probably small paddocks connected with sheep and cattle, since no querns suggesting corn grinding have been found at Tre'r Ceiri. [A. H. A. Hogg, *Arch. J,* 117 (1960), 10.]

YSTUM CEGID ISAF, see Coetan Arthur.

POWYS

1 BEACON RING, Trelystan   SJ:265058
This oval fort of 2 ha stands on the highest part of the Long Mountain
at 408 m above sea-level. It is very strongly defended by a single bank
and ditch. The rampart may have been of box construction. Quarry
scoops were visible prior to the afforestation of the site. There is an
original entrance on the south side 15 m wide, and that on the north
may also be original. [C. J. Spurgeon, in F. Lynch and C. Burgess,
eds., *Prehistoric Man in Wales and the West* (1972), 336.]

2 THE BREIDDIN, Bausley   SJ:292144
This is a jagged volcanic peak above the river Severn, rising to 365 m
above sea-level. There are precipitous slopes on the elongated north-
west side, whilst the south-east is protected by two tumbled walls of
stone, which for a short distance north of the entrance become three
walls, only the third having a ditch. The entrance cuts diagonally across
the ramparts from the east, creating a stone-lined passage. Outside the
entrance amongst the trees are traces of Celtic fields and a small
isolated enclosure, perhaps for cattle (at SJ:298140).

The site has been excavated twice and a clear sequence of construction is now apparent, beginning in the mid eighth century BC and
continuing throughout much of the iron age. At first the inner rampart
was formed by a double row of posts filled with a bank of rocks and
stones, which was destroyed by fire. Rectangular huts may have existed. In the iron age a more substantial rampart was constructed,
faced with stone at back and front, and associated with round huts of
mid-fourth-century date, each about 6 m in diameter. Two hundred
years later they had been replaced by rectangular buildings roughly
2·5 m by 3 m. Whether these were barns or granaries we cannot tell.
The entrance was slighted, probably by the Romans, after which the
fort was deserted for many years. It was reoccupied perhaps in the later
second century, possibly for as long as three hundred years. [C. R.
Musson, in D. W. Harding, *Hillforts* (1976), 293,]

3 BURFA CAMP, Burva   SO:290613
This large fort of 8 ha is thickly forested. An east-facing spur above the
Hindwell Brook is crowned by multiple stone-revetted ramparts and

ditches, especially on the north-west by the entrance, where there is a strong second line of defence forming a barbican. The inner rampart is inturned. There is another simpler entrance on the north-east. While the fort remains forested it is impossible to try to interpret its history, which is likely to be long and complicated.

CAER EINON, Llanelwedd, see Gaer Fawr, Llanelwedd.

4 CASTELL DINAS, Talgarth   so:178302
This spur stands at the northern end of the pass from Crickhowell to Talgarth. It is well defended, with massive double ramparts on the southern side where the slopes are less steep. There is an oblique entrance on the north. The fort is divided into two by a cross-bank, which seems to make provision for animals. The Normans constructed a motte within the hillfort.

5 CASTLE RING, Evenjobb   so:266636
Just west of Offa's Dyke, facing south-west 335 m above sea-level, is a circular site with double ramparts enclosing 8 ha. There is an entrance at the north-west with extended ramparts, which protect the track entering the fort.

6 CEFN CARNEDD, Llandinam   so:016900
This splendid fort crowns a narrow, oval hill 277 m above sea-level, and encloses about 6 ha. All the strong defences lie on the north-west side of the hill. The natural steepness of the south-east makes them almost unnecessary. There are three ramparts on the north side: the inner and outer banks are rather slight affairs, but between them is a more massive bank. There are faint lines of a single rampart on the south-east. The entrance at the north-east end is inturned, with traces of an annexe outside it to the east. The gate at the south-west was formed where the outer and middle ramparts merge and swing inwards. It seems likely that the fort began as a smaller enclosure of 1·6 ha occupying the south-western half of the ridge, and traces of a dividing bank can just be made out on aerial photographs. Later the higher end was cut off by a straight cross-dyke clearly visible today, possibly isolating an area of Romano-British occupation. [C. J. Spurgeon, in F. Lynch and C. Burgess, eds., *Prehistoric Man in Wales and the West* (1972), 339.]

7 CEFN Y CASTELL, Middletown   sj:306134
An exposed contour fort on the summit of Middleton Hill. Oval in shape and enclosing 0·8 ha, it is surrounded by a bank of earth and stones. There are entrances at the north-east and south-west ends, with long inturns. Traces of quarry scoops exist inside the fort, but

there is little sign of an external ditch. A low bank south of the south-west entrance forms a small annexe. It has its own central entrance. [C. J. Spurgeon, in F. Lynch and C. Burgess, eds., *Prehistoric Man in Wales and the West* (1972), 332.]

8   CERRIG DUON, Glyntawe   SN:852206
A great block of sandstone almost 2 m high called 'Maen Mawr' (large stone) dominates this egg-shaped ring of twenty-two stones, standing above the river Tawe. There are two small stones behind Maen Mawr to the north which mark the axis of the circle. Aubrey Burl believes these to be directional indicators, though Thom considers that they marked the rising of the star Arcturus in 1950 BC. North-east of the circle is an irregular avenue 46 m long of very low stones, 5 m wide close to the ring; it does not reach the ring, however, but would pass on its south-eastern side if projected. [W. F. Grimes, *PPS*, 2 (1936), 108.]

9   CRAIG RHIWARTH, Llanrhaiadr   SJ:057270
A hillfort of 16 ha defended by a precipitous cliff on the south and a ruined stone wall across the north. The latter has two entrances, one in the middle and another at the west end. Inside are an uncounted number of circular huts built in hollows, sometimes with smaller huts apparently inside larger and presumably earlier ones.

10   CRUG HYWELL, Llanbedr   SO:225206
This well-preserved pear-shaped fort crowns the Table Mountain at 451 m, well below the summit of Pen Cerrig-calch to the north-west. It is surrounded by a single strong stone-built rampart and ditch with a counterscarp bank that curves round the ditch ends up to the inturned entrance on the curving west side.

11   CWRT-Y-GOLLEN, Crickhowell   SO:236167
On the northern bank of the Usk close to the Regimental Museum is a standing stone 1·8 m high. Nothing is known about it, but it is quite impressive.

12   DAN-YR-OGOF, Abercraf   SN:838161
This is a show cave with spectacular stalactites and natural arches, but above it is the Bone Cave in which bronze age and Roman remains have been found. A bronze razor, sword blade and gold bead were left by the bronze age inhabitants.
    Today the cave has been filled with dioramas of prehistoric life including rather garish models of cave bears, sabre-toothed tigers and a bronze age family group. [E. J. Mason, *Ogof-yr-Esgyrn, Bone Cave* (1979).]

13   FFRIDD FALDWYN, Montgomery   so:216970

A complicated fort of at least four periods. After a neolithic occupation the oval hilltop was defended by a double palisade dated to the
third century BC. This was rebuilt in timber lacing with a second outer
line of defence, and a bridged gateway, all of which were vitrified when
fire swept round the fort. During the early first century BC the whole
fort was rebuilt on a larger scale to enclose 4 ha with a stone-revetted
bank and ditch, although parts of the original fort including the gate
were strengthened at this time. With the Roman advance of *c*. AD 50
hasty repairs were carried out before the site was finally abandoned.
Only the southern part of the fort has been excavated, and this remains
incomplete. [A. H. A. Hogg, in I. Ll. Foster and G. E. Daniel, eds.,
Prehistoric and Early Wales (1965), 140.]

14   FOUR STONES, Walton and Womaston   so:245608

Four glacial boulders with flattened faces on the inner sides have been
arranged to form a square setting 5·2 m across. It is neither a true circle
nor a megalithic tomb, but is one of the enigmatic group of monuments
christened by Burl a 'four-poster' and found mostly in Scotland and
northern England. There is another setting of four standing stones
2 km north-east at so:262609

15   GAER FAWR, Guilsfield Without   sj:223130

The earthworks on this ridge are obscured by woodland. The fort is
roughly rectangular in shape with three ramparts on the western side
and two on the east. There are entrances at the south and north-east.
The ends of the inner rampart are inturned, and probably contain
guard chambers. At the south the rampart ends form a long entrance
passage. A tiny bronze boar of Roman date was found in the hillfort.

16   GAER FAWR, Llanelwedd   so:058531

There are two circular forts on south-facing spurs of Carneddau: Gaer
Fawr to the west and Caer Einon a kilometre to the east. Each is about
1 ha in area, with steep slopes and crags to extend the defences. Gaer
Fawr has multiple defences of stone and an oblique barbican-type
entrance. Caer Einon has a slightly inturned entrance.

17   GIANTS GRAVE, Glascwm   so:141544

This is one of a number of large barrows in the area. Situated in a
saddle between two hills, it is about 30 m in diameter. Its contents are
not known. Three kilometres to the west are two more barrows on
either side of the river Edw at Hundred House.

18   GWERNVALE, Crickhowell   so:211192

On the north side of the A40 are the remains of a long cairn in the

Cotswold–Severn tradition, overlying a small neolithic settlement. The cairn was horned, with a forecourt and false portal at the eastern end. Along the south side were two lateral chambers, with traces of a third at the damaged western end. Another single chamber lay on the north side. Traces of burial survived only in the chamber on the south-east. Six post-holes in the forecourt suggest that some sort of mortuary structure stood there during the life of the tomb. [W. Britnell, *Antiquity*, 53 (1979), 132.]

19 LLANGYNIDR, Llanfihangel Cwmdu so:156204
Close to the track along the valley bottom of the Usk, this is the largest standing stone in the area. As with all the other stones its date of erection is unknown, but assumed to be prehistoric.

20 LLANMYNECH HILL, Llanmynech sj:265220
This, the largest hillfort in Wales, encloses 57 ha, but is badly preserved. It is steep sided and needs little actual defence. On the north and east sides double banks and ditches existed, but they have been frequently disturbed by quarrying and houses. On the west side there is a single rampart which was later utilized as part of Offa's Dyke. It is also the national boundary. There were two inturned entrances at the north, one in the centre of the ramparts and one (damaged) on the north-east. Perhaps gaps on the south and west were also simple entrances. The interior is now a golf course and has been much disturbed by quarrying since Roman times, so that it is now difficult to distinguish particular features. No hut sites have been recognized. A. H. A. Hogg has pointed out that this is the only fort in the area large enough to have been Caratacus's headquarters. [C. Fox and W. J. Hemp, *Arch. Cambrensis* (1926), 395.]

21 MAEN SERTH, Llansanffraidd sn:944698
Close to the old coach house above a cliff is a standing stone just over 2 m high. It has a cross incised on it which may support the tradition that it marks the site of the murder of Einion Clud in the twelfth century AD. As such stones were a common feature of the bronze age, it may be that it was erected in prehistoric times and the cross added in the twelfth century.

A kilometre to the west is the cairn **Clap-yr-arian** (sn:936699) from which a perfect battle-axe of Prescelly bluestone came.

22 PEN-Y-CRUG, Fennifach so:029303
Sited on a rounded moorland hilltop north-west of Brecon with three (and in places four) banks and ditches and a counterscarp bank. There is an entrance on the south-east side. There may have been an earlier enclosure on the site as there is a slight bank which forms an annexe

south of the fort and seems to join up with another minor bank on the inside of the enclosure. Parts of the rampart have been damaged by quarrying.

23 PIPTON CAIRN, Pipton
so: 160373

At the end of a spur above the Wye is a trapezoidal cairn about 30 m long with a drystone revetment. It is horned at the northern end where two upright stones side by side form a false entrance. There are two burial chambers, both on the western side. One has a long curved passage and antechamber before the burial chambers proper, which lie roughly north and south down the spine of the barrow. This resembles Arthur's Stone, Dorstone, in Herefordshire. The second chamber further south is a simple rectangular structure with no passage. Clearly more than one tradition of building is represented in this tomb. [H. N. Savory, *Arch. Cambrensis*, 105 (1956), 7.]

24 RHOS-MAEN, Glascm
so: 143579

This circular earthwork 24 m in diameter is reputed to have once had thirty-six stones standing upon it. Only a few remain today, in an area that has been ploughed and greatly disturbed. None of the stones are buried in the ground and there is evidence that most have been moved in recent times. [W. F. Grimes, in I. Ll. Foster and L. Alcock, eds., *Culture and Environment* (1963), 131.]

25 RHOS-Y-BEDDAU, Llangynog
sj: 058303

A difficult site to find as it is overgrown with rushes. It consists of a stone circle on the west, 12 m in diameter, of which about nine stones remain, none higher than 75 cm. To the east of the circle is a double avenue of stones, 48 m long and about 3 m apart. Heights vary between at little as 10 cm and 45 cm. About 42 m away from the eastern end of the avenue and to the north-east is a ruined cairn recognizable by the surviving fragments of its kerb stone. This site is important because of the comparative rarity of stone rows in Wales, but it is of interest only to the enthusiast. [W. F. Grimes, in I. Ll. Foster and L. Alcock, eds., *Culture and Environment* (1963), 120.]

26 TRECASTLE MOUNTAIN, Trecastle
sn: 833311

Two circles of stones stand 45 m apart. The larger is 22 m in diameter and is made up of a ring of eighteen small stones surrounding a low central mound. Hollows for other stones can still be detected. The second circle, also with small stones, is only 8 m in diameter. Four stones stood in a line to the west, but only two remain. [W. F. Grimes, in I. Ll. Foster and L. Alcock, eds., *Culture and Environment* (1963), 135.]

27 TŶ ILLTUD, Llanhamlach   so:098263

Set off-centre in an oval cairn is a rectangular burial chamber with three wallstones and a low capstone sloping forwards. There seems to be part of a rectangular forecourt or antechamber to the north. Most of the wallstones are decorated with faint incised patterns, mostly crosses, some in lozenges, some with circles at the ends of their arms, and amongst them a few people have spotted writing, notably the date 1312. The decorations are almost certainly medieval, and I would go along with Longueville Jones, who in 1867 considered them 'only the work of shepherd boys (for sheep commonly congregate on the mound)'. [G. E. Daniel, *Prehistoric Chamber Tombs* (1950), 214.]

28 TY ISAF, Talgarth   so:182291

This is a trapezoidal mound 30 m long and about 16 m wide at the northern end. It is enclosed by double drystone revetment walls which form horns and curve inwards to a false doorway at the north. About halfway along the barrow were a pair of side chambers opening from

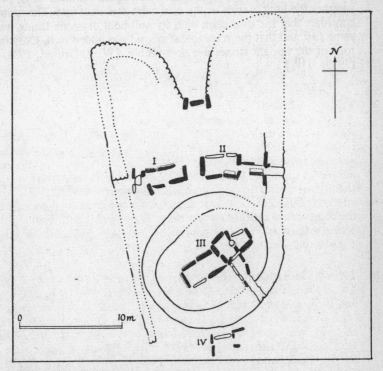

Fig 45. Ty Isaf, Powys (after Grimes)

the east and west. The western chamber (I on the plan) contained the crushed bones of seventeen individuals, neolithic pottery, leaf-shaped arrowheads and a polished axe. Only one skeleton could be recognized in the eastern chamber (II), but pieces of at least six neolithic bowls were present. In the passage leading to the chamber were the remains of two articulated skeletons. At the southern end of the barrow was another rectangular chamber (IV). which had contained part of a bronze age cremation urn and burnt boxes. Between the two side chambers and the end chamber was a curious feature: an oval cairn surrounded by double drystone walls had been incorporated into the long barrow. It had an entrance passage 4·5 m long leading into a transepted burial chamber (III) aligned diagonally across the long barrow from south-west to north-east. This burial chamber was in three parts, a central section 2 m long, with a small chamber leading out of it to the east of similar size, and a bigger chamber to the west 3 m long. The broken bones of a number of individuals were found on the floors together with neolithic pottery. In the entrance passage were parts of two articulated adults. Archaeologists continue to debate whether the long barrow or the oval cairn was built first. The writer considers that the oval cairn with its well-built drystone facing wall came first and that the trapezoidal mound was added to it. Only the tops of the upright stones are now visible. [W. F. Grimes, *PPS*, 5 (1939), 119.]

List of References

Alcock, L., 'By South Cadbury is that Camelot', London, Thames & Hudson, 1972.

Allcroft, A., Earthwork of England, London, Macmillan, 1908.

Ashbee, P., Ancient Scilly, Newton Abbot, David and Charles, 1974.

Ashe, G., ed., Quest for Arthur's Britain, London, Pall Mall, 1968; Paladin, 1971 (paperback).

Atkinson, R. J. C., Prehistoric Society Swansea Guide, 1965;
Stonehenge, Harmondsworth, Penguin Books, revised edn, 1979.

Atkinson, R. J. C., and others, Excavations at Dorchester, Oxon, vol. 1, Oxford, Ashmolean Museum, 1951.

Bateman, T., Vestiges of the Antiquities of Derbyshire, 1848.

Beckensall, S., Prehistoric Carved Rocks of Northumberland, Newcastle-upon-Tyne, Frank Graham, 1974.

Boon, G. C., and Lewis, J. M., eds., Welsh Antiquity, Cardiff, National Museum of Wales, 1976.

Bowen, E. G., and Gresham, C. A., History of Merioneth, vol. 1, Dolgelly, Merioneth Historical Record Society, 1967.

Brewster, T. C. M., The Excavations of Staple Howe, Malton, Yorkshire, East Riding Archaeological Committee, 1963.

British Association for the Advancement of Science, Birmingham and its Regional Setting, BAAS, 1950.

Brooks, R. T., and Fulcher, E. A., Archaeological Guide to Epping Forest, Loughton, Conservators of Epping Forest, 1979.

Burgess, C., and Miket, R., Settlement and Economy in the Third and Second Millenia BC, Oxford, British Archaeological Reports, 1976.

Burl, A., Prehistoric Avebury, New Haven and London, Yale University Press, 1979;
Rings of Stone, London, Frances Lincoln (distributed by Weidenfeld & Nicolson), 1979;
Stone Circles of the British Isles, New Haven and London, Yale University Press, 1976.

Clarke, R. R., East Anglia, London, Thames & Hudson, 1960.

Clifford, E. N., Bagendon, a Belgic Oppidum: Excavations of 1954–56, Cambridge, Heffer, 1961.

Coles, J. M., and Simpson, D., eds., Studies in Ancient Europe, Leicester, Leicester University Press, 1968.

Crawford, O. G. S., Air Survey and Archaeology, London, HMSO (Ordnance Survey Professional Papers, no. 7), 1924;
Long Barrows of the Cotswolds, Gloucester, 1925.

List of References

Crawford, O. G. S., and Keiller, A., *Wessex from the Air,* Oxford, Clarendon Press, 1928.

Cunliffe, B. W., *Excavations at Fishbourne 1961–1969,* London, Society of Antiquaries, 1971;
Hengistbury Head, London, Elek, 1978.

Cunliffe, B. W., and Rowley, T., eds., *Oppida, the Beginnings of Urban Civilization in Barbarian Europe,* Oxford, British Archaeological Reports, 1976.

Cunnington, M. E., *Woodhenge,* Devizes, G. Simpson, 1929.

Curwen, E. C., *The Archaeology of Sussex,* 2nd ed., London, Methuen, 1954.

Daniel, G. E., *The Prehistoric Chamber Tombs of England and Wales,* Cambridge, CUP, 1950.

Davies, E., *Prehistoric and Roman Remains in Flint,* 1949;
Prehistoric and Roman Remains of Denbighshire, Cardiff, 1929.

Dixon, P., and Borne, P., *Crickley Hill and Gloucestershire Prehistory,* Gloucester, Gloucester County Council, for the Crickley Hill Trust, 1977.

Dobson, D. P., *Archaeology of Somerset,* London, Methuen, 1931.

Dyer, J., *Hillforts of England and Wales,* Princes Risborough, Shire, 1981;
Southern England: An Archaeological Guide, London, Faber, 1973.

Dymond, C. W., *Worlebury, an Ancient Stronghold in Somerset,* 1902.

Elgee, F., *Early Man in North East Yorkshire,* Gloucester, 1930.

Forde-Johnston, J., *Hillforts of the Iron Age in England and Wales,* Liverpool, Liverpool University Press, 1976.

Foster, I. Ll., and Alcock, L., eds., *Culture and Environment,* London, Routledge & Kegan Paul, 1963.

Foster, I. Ll., and Daniel, G. E., eds., *Prehistoric and Early Wales,* London, Routledge & Kegan Paul, 1965.

Fowler, P. J., and others, *Cadbury Congresbury, Somerset, 1968,* Bristol, University of Bristol Department of Extra-mural Studies, 1970.

Fox, A., *South-West England,* London, Thames & Hudson, 1964.

Fox, C., *Archaeology of the Cambridge Region,* Cambridge, CUP, 1923.

Greenwell, W., *British Barrows,* Oxford, 1877.

Grinsell, L. V., *The Ancient Burial Mounds of England,* 2nd ed., London, Methuen, 1953;
Archaeology of Exmoor, Newton Abbot, David & Charles, 1970;
Archaeology of Wessex, London, Methuen, 1958;
The Cheddar Caves Museum, 1969;
Dorset Barrows, Dorchester, Dorset Natural History and Archaeological Society, 1959;
Prehistoric Sites in the Quantock Country, Taunton, Somerset, Somerset Archaeological and Natural History Society, 1976;
The Rollright Stones and their Folklore, St Peter's Port, Guernsey, Toucan Press, 1977;
Somerset Barrows, 2 vols., Somerset Archaeological and Natural History Society, 1969–1971;
Stonehenge Barrow Groups, Salisbury, Salisbury and South Wiltshire Museum, 1979;
White Horse Hill and the Surrounding Country, London, St Catherine Press, 1939.

Harding, D. W., *The Iron Age in the Upper Thames Basin*, Oxford, Clarendon Press, 1972.

Harding, D. W., ed., *Hillforts:Later Prehistoric Earthworks in Britain and Ireland*, London, Academic Press, 1976.

Hoare, R. C., *Ancient History of South [and North] Wiltshire*, 2 vols., London, 1812–19.

Hogg, A. H. A., *Hill-forts of Britain*, London, Hart-Davis, MacGibbon, 1975.

Houlder, C., *Wales: An Archaeological Guide*, London, Faber, 1975.

Jackson, J. W., *British Caving*, 1953.

Jenkinson, R. D. S., *Creswell Crags Visitors' Centre Research Reports No. 1*, 1978.

Jesson, M., and Hill, D., *The Iron Age and its Hillforts*, Southampton University, 1971.

Jessup, R., *South-East England*, London, Thames & Hudson, 1970.

Jewell, P. A., ed., *The Experimental Earthwork on Overton Down, Wilts.*, London, British Association for the Advancement of Science, 1963.

King, A., *Early Pennine Settlement*, Clapham via Lancaster, Dalesman Publishing, 1970.

Lawson, A., *Prehistoric Earthworks in Norfolk*, London, Prehistoric Society, 1978.

Longworth, I., *Yorkshire*, London, Cory, Adams & Mackay (Regional Archaeology Series), 1965.

Lukis, F. C., *A Brief Account of the Barrows near Bircham Magna, Norfolk*, 1843.

Lynch, F., *Archaeology in Wales*, 1979.

Lynch, F., and Burgess, C., eds., *Prehistoric Man in Wales and the West*, Bath, Adams & Dart, 1972.

McDonnell, J., ed., *History of Helmsley, Rievaulx and District*, York, Stonegate Press, for the Yorkshire Archaeological Society, 1963.

Marsden, B. M., *Burial Mounds of Derbyshire*, 1977.

May, J., *Prehistoric Lincolnshire*, Lincoln, History of Lincolnshire Committee, 1976.

Mercer, R., *Hambledon Hill, a Neolithic Landscape*, Edinburgh, Edinburgh University Press, 1980.

Miles, W. A., *The Deverel Barrow*, 1826.

Mortimer, J. R., *Forty Years' Researches in British and Saxon Burial Mounds of East Yorkshire*, London, 1905.

O'Neil, B. H. St J., *Isles of Scilly*, London, HMSO (Ministry of Works Official Guide), 1949.

Pearce, S., *Devon in Prehistory*, [Exeter, Royal Albert Memorial Museum, 1979].

Phillips, C. W., *Map of the Trent Basin Showing the Distribution of Long Barrows*, Ordnance Survey, 1933.

Piggott, S., *West Kennet Long Barrow: Excavations 1955–56*, London, HMSO, 1962.

Pitt-Rivers, A. L., *Excavations in Cranborne Chase*, 4 vols., privately printed, 1887–98.

Powell, T. G. E. and Daniel, G. E., *Barclodiad y Gawres*, Liverpool, Liverpool University Press, 1956.

Powell, T. G. E., ed., *Megalithic Enquiries in the West of Britain,* Liverpool, Liverpool University Press, 1969.

Pull, J. H., *Flint Miners of Blackpatch,* London, Williams & Norgate, 1932.

Richmond, I., *Hod Hill,* vol. 2, *Excavations Carried out between 1951 and 1958,* London, British Museum, 1968.

Rivet, A. L. F., ed., *The Iron Age in Northern Britain,* Edinburgh, Trustees of the Edinburgh University Press, 1966.

RCHM, *Long Barrows in Hampshire and the Isle of Wight,* London, HMSO, 1979;
Stonehenge and its Environs, London, HMSO, 1979.

Savory, H. N., *Excavations at Dinorben 1965–9,* Cardiff, National Museum of Wales, 1971.

Smith, I. F., *Windmill Hill and Avebury: Excavations by Alexander Keiller 1925–39,* London, OUP, 1965.

Spratt, D. A., ed., *The Archaeology of Cleveland,* Middlesbrough, Middlesbrough Borough Council Recreation and Amenities Department, 1979.

Stanford, S. C., *Archaeology of the Welsh Marches,* London, Collins, 1980;
Croft Ambrey: Excavations carried out for the Woolhope Naturalists' Field Club, The author, 1974;
The Malvern Hillforts, Archaeological Committee of the Malvern Hills Conservators, 1973.

Stead, I. M., *The Arras Culture,* 1979.

Sutcliffe, R., Ed., *Chronicle: Essays from Ten Years of Television,* London, BBC, 1978.

Thom, A., *Megalithic Sites in Britain,* London, OUP, 1967.

Thomas, N., *Guide to Prehistoric England,* 2nd ed., London, Batsford, 1976.

Varley, W. J., *Cheshire before the Romans,* Chester, Cheshire Community Council, 1964.

Wadmore, B., *Earthworks of Bedfordshire,* Bedford, 1920.

Wainwright, G. J., and Longworth, I. H., *Durrington Walls: Excavations 1966–1968,* London, Society of Antiquaries, 1971.

Wainwright, R., *A Guide to the Prehistoric Remains in Britain,* vol. 1, *South and East,* London, Constable, 1978.

Wheeler, R. E. M., *Maiden Castle, Dorset,* London, OUP, 1943;
Report on the Excavations . . . in Lydney Park, Gloucestershire, London, Society of Antiquaries, 1932;
The Stanwick Fortifications, London, Society of Antiquaries, 1954.

Wheeler, R. E. M. and T. E., *Verulamium: A Belgic and Two Roman Cities,* London, OUP, 1936.

Williams-Freeman, J. P., *Introduction to Field Archaeology as Illustrated by Hampshire,* London, Macmillan, 1915.

Worth, R. H., *Dartmoor,* new ed., Newton Abbot, David & Charles, 1967.

Wymer, J., *Lower Palaeolithic Archaeology in Britain,* London, John Baker, 1968.

ABBREVIATIONS

Ant. J	*Antiquaries' Journal*
Arch. Ael.	*Archaeologia Aeliana*
Arch. Cambrensis	*Archaeologia Cambrensis* (Cambrian Arch. Society)
Arch. Cantiana	*Archaeologia Cantiana* (Kent Arch. Society)
Arch. J	*Archaeological Journal*
BAR	*British Archaeological Reports*
Beds. AJ	*Bedfordshire Archaeological Journal*
Berks. AJ	*Berkshire Archaeological Journal*
Derbys. Arch. J	*Derbyshire Archaeological Journal*
D of E pamphlet	Department of the Environment guide pamphlet
East Anglian Arch.	*East Anglian Archaeology*
Flints. Hist. Soc.	*Flintshire Historical Society*
J Anthrop. Inst.	*Journal of the Anthropological Institute*
J Brit. Archaeol. Assn	*Journal of the British Archaeological Association*
J Merioneth Hist and Record Soc.	*Journal of Merioneth Historical and Record Society*
J R Inst. Cornwall	*Journal of Royal Institution of Cornwall*
P Cambs. Ant. Soc.	*Proceedings of the Cambridge Antiquarian Society*
PDAES	*Proceedings of the Devon Archaeological Exploration Society*
PDAS	*Proceedings of the Devon Archaeological Society*
P Hants. FC	*Proceedings of the Hampshire Field Club*
PIWNHS	*Proceedings of the Isle of Wight Natural History Society*
PPS	*Proceedings of the Prehistoric Society*
PPSEA	*Proceedings of the Prehistoric Society of East Anglia*
Proc. Dorset NHAS	*Proceedings of the Dorset Archaeological and Natural History Society*
PSAL	*Proceedings of the Society of Antiquaries of London*
PSAN	*Proceedings of the Society of Antiquaries of Newcastle-upon-Tyne*
P Somerset AS	*Proceedings of the Somerset Archaeological Society*
P Suffolk Arch. Inst.	*Proceedings of the Suffolk Archaeological Institute*
PUBSS	*Proceedings of the University of Bristol Spelaeological Society*
RCHM	Royal Commission on Historical Monuments (various counties)
Records of Bucks	*Records of Buckinghamshire*
Report Royal Inst. Cornwall	*Report Royal Institution of Cornwall*

Scarborough Dist. Arch. Soc. Res. Rep.	Scarborough and District Archaeological Society Research Report
Surrey AC	Surrey Archaeological Collections
Sussex AC	Sussex Archaeological Collections
T Berwick FC	Transactions of the Berwick Field Club
TBGAS	Transactions of the Bristol and Gloucester Archaeological Society
TCWAAS	Transactions of the Cumberland and Westmorland Antiquarian and Archaeological Society
TLCAS	Transactions of the Lancashire and Cheshire Antiquarian Society
TLMAS	Transactions of the London and Middlesex Archaeological Society
Trans. Birmingham AS	Transactions of Birmingham Archaeological Society
Trans. Devon Assn	Transactions of the Devonshire Association
Trans. Newbury and District Field Club	Transactions of the Newbury and District Field Club
T Shrop. AS	Transactions of Shropshire Archaeological Society
T Woolhope Club	Transactions of the Woolhope Club (Herefordshire)
Univ. London Inst. Arch. Bulletin	University of London Institute of Archaeology Bulletin
VCH	Victoria County History (various counties)
WAM	Wiltshire Archaeological and Natural History Magazine
YAJ	Yorkshire Archaeological Journal

GLOSSARY

Adulterine castle A castle built without licence, usually during the reign of Stephen (1135–54).

Aldbourne cup A small pottery cup of the early bronze age, decorated with lines and dots, and found in barrows (2300–1700 BC)

Ard A primitive plough that has no mouldboard or other means of turning the soil and consists simply of a share of stone or hard wood.

Atrebates A Belgic tribe centred on Hampshire, Berkshire and west Sussex, with capitals near Chichester, Winchester and Silchester.

Awl A small metal tool used for pricking or boring.

Barbican An inturned entrance passage to a hillfort, with gates at either end, which can be guarded from a rampart walk above.

Barrow A long or round burial mound constructed of earth or stones.

Bâton-de-commandement Palaeolithic object of carved deer antler with a perforation in the side; of unknown use – possibly ceremonial or used for straightening arrows.

BC and bc BC is used for 'corrected' radiocarbon dates, whilst bc is retained for uncorrected dates. (Radiocarbon dates before 1200 BC have to be calibrated and set several centuries earlier.)

Beaker A finely made drinking vessel with S-shaped profile, decorated with cord impressions or a notched tool. The type originated in the Rhinelands and developed in Britain about 2500 BC with bulbous bodies and long necks. Beakers are sometimes classified according to shape; for example, long-necked beaker, short-necked beaker and bell beaker, the latter looking like an inverted bell.

Belgae An iron age people who came to Britain from the area of modern Belgium around 120 BC and dominated south-eastern England prior to the Roman conquest.

Bell-barrow See Introduction, page 36, Fig 3.

Berm Flat space separating the bank from the ditch in a barrow or hillfort.

Bronze age Period when metallurgy was introduced into Britain, divided into early period, 2300–1700 BC; middle period, 1700–1300 BC; and late period, 1300–800 BC.

Burh Fortified place of Saxon date; often a reused hillfort.

Capstone Large stone forming the roof of a burial chamber.

Catuvellauni A native tribe of the late iron age based on the Chilterns. They led the main resistance to Caesar in 54 BC. After overcoming the Trinovantes of Essex they became the major power in south-east England with a capital at Colchester.

Causewayed camps See Introduction, page 36

Celtic fields See Introduction, page 41

Chambered tombs See Introduction, page 35

Chevaux-de-frise Sharp stones set on end in front of the walls of a hillfort to act as an added defence. (See Pen-y-Gaer, page 351.)

Cist A grave lined with slabs of stone in the shape of a box.

Cliff castle See Introduction, page 34

Collared urn A pottery jar with high collar used at first for food storage, but later used almost exclusively for cremation burials (1700–1300 BC).

Corbelling Layers of stones overhanging each other to form the roof of a stone chamber.

Cordonned ware Iron age pottery with horizontal ribs or cordons decorating it.

Counterscarp bank A bank on the outside of a defensive ditch, often produced as a result of ditch clearance.

Courtyard house See Introduction, page 33.

Cove Three stones arranged in U-shaped setting, usually at the centre of a stone circle or henge monument of neolithic and bronze age date.

Cup-and-ring marks See Introduction, page 40.

Currency bars Sword-shaped bars of iron in graded lengths believed to have been used as a form of currency prior to the introduction of coins about 100 BC.

Cursus See Introduction, page 38

Deverel-Rimbury culture A culture found in southern England at the end of the middle bronze age, characterized by stockaded enclosures, new metal-working styles and pottery.

Disc-barrow See Introduction, page 36, Fig 3.

Dobunni A non-Belgic tribe of the late iron age living between the Severn and the Cotswolds, with a probable capital at Bagendon, Gloucestershire.

Duck-stamped ware Iron age pottery from the west Midlands decorated with S-(ducks) or V-patterns between two parallel lines.

Dumnonii A non-Belgic iron age tribe living in Devon and Cornwall.

Durotriges A non-Belgic tribe centred on Dorset and Somerset.

Entrance grave See Introduction, page 35.

Faience beads Blue glazed beads of glass-like composition, usually considered to be of early bronze age date.

False portal An imitation doorway in the end of a long barrow. The true entrances are usually at the sides.

Fécamp defence A Belgic method of hillfort defence consisting of a dumped bank and wide, flat-bottomed ditch; introduced into south-east England during the first century BC.

Fogou A stone-lined underground passage associated with iron age habitations, usually in Cornwall, and probably used for storage rather than defence.

Food vessel Pottery vessel of early bronze age date, with thick bevelled rim and lavish decoration, most common in Yorkshire and Ireland. Usually found with burials and assumed to have been containers of food for the dead.

Forecourt Paved area in front of the entrance to a chambered long barrow or passage grave, where funerary ritual was probably performed.

Gallery grave A neolithic chambered tomb in which the entrance passage runs into the burial chamber without clear separation. It may have side chambers (transepts), as in the Severn-Cotswold group, or a short chamber under a round mound (entrance grave). The simplest gallery graves occur under round barrows in the Peak District.

Grape cup See Incense cup.

Glacis A rampart of loose rubble.

Grimston-Lyles Hill ware Early neolithic pottery found in the north of England and Ireland dating from around 3600 BC.

Halberd An early bronze age dagger-like blade fixed at right angles to a wooden handle. Perforated models made of gold and amber were worn on necklaces as halberd pendants.

Hallstatt The first culture of the iron age in Europe, around the eighth century BC, named after a town in Austria.

Hand axe Unsatisfactory name given to multi-purpose oval or pear-shaped tool of flint or stone, used during the lower palaeolithic period from about 350,000 BC.

Henge monument See Introduction, page 38.

Hillfort See Introduction, page 33.

Hollingbury rampart A type of hillfort defence named after the site in Sussex (qv); it consists of two parallel rows of fences, filled with chalk, and linked together by horizontal timbers.

Hollow way A sunken trackway that has cut deeply into the hillside due to constant use.

Iceni Non-Belgic late iron age tribe who occupied Norfolk and Suffolk.

Incense cup A small pottery cup often found with early bronze age cremation burials.

Iron age The period from about 700 BC to the Roman Conquest, when iron was the main metal used for making tools and weapons, although some bronze and flint continued in use. Sometimes divided into three phases, the early, Hallstatt (q.v.) or A; the middle, La Tène (q.v.) or B; and the final C phase from about 120 BC related to the arrival of the Belgae in south-east England. These phases may also be divided regionally; for example, south-western B or north-eastern A.

La Tène The second iron-using culture of Europe (fifth to first centuries BC) named after a site in Switzerland.

Long barrow See Introduction, page 35.

Lynchet See Introduction, page 41.

Megalithic Made of large stones.

Megalithic yard According to Professor A. Thom a measurement equivalent to 2·72 feet used in the construction of stone circles.

Menhir A single standing stone.

Mesolithic The period following the final ice age until the introduction of agriculture and pottery-making in Britain from 10,000 to 4000 BC.

Microliths Minute flint implements used during the mesolithic period.

Miz-maze A maze cut into the turf. The name is local to Sussex and Hampshire.

Mortlake ware A form of neolithic pottery with thick rims and heavy decoration; it is named after a vessel found in the river Thames at Mortlake.

Mortuary enclosure An enclosure or chamber in which corpses were collected together until sufficient had accumulated to allow the construction of a long barrow. This barrow was sometimes built over the enclosure.

Motte-and-bailey castle Typical Norman castle earthwork, consisting of a tall conical castle mound (motte) surrounded by a ditch and an outer yard (bailey) enclosed by a bank and ditch.

Multivallate A hillfort having more than one line of rampart and ditch.

Neolithic The new stone age in which man first practised agriculture, made pottery and constructed ceremonial monuments such as causewayed camps and long barrows (4000–2300 BC).

Oppidum See Introduction, page 34.

Orthostat Upright stones, often surrounding a burial mound.

Palaeolithic The earliest period of man's existence in Britain, ending around 10,000 BC at the close of the final ice age.

Passage grave Stone passage leading into a roughly circular burial chamber, covered by a circular mound of earth.

Peristalith Stone retaining wall or kerb around a burial mound.

Pillow-mound A rectangular mound of earth believed to have been constructed as an artificial rabbit warren at any time between the twelfth and early nineteenth century.

Pond-barrow See Introduction, page 36, Fig 3.

Portal dolmen Burial chamber entered through a high porch of two upright stones, often blocked by a door slab. Found in western Britain.

Porthole A circular hole cut into two upright blocks of stone to form an entrance to a burial chamber. (See Avening, Gloucestershire, page 138.)

Pound See Introduction, page 32.

Promontory fort See Introduction, page 34.

Pygmy cup An incense cup, found in early bronze age burials; its precise use is unknown.

Quoit Cornish name for stone burial chamber.

Revetment Wall of stone, timber of turf used to hold a rampart or mound in position.

Ring cairn A low circular cairn with an open space at its centre where burials were made.

Ring mark An engraved or pecked circle on a stone. See also Cup-and-ring marks.

Romano-British The native British population showing clear signs of influence by the Romans during their occupation.

Samian ware Glossy, red-coated pottery imported into Roman Britain from southern Gaul.

Sarsen A form of micaceous sandstone often used for the construction of stone circles and chambered tombs.

Saucer-barrow See Introduction, page 36, Fig 3.

Scarping A slope that has been artificially steepened.

Stater Iron age coin.

Terret A metal ring that formed part of a chariot or cart, and through which a horse's reins passed.

Timber lacing Horizontal cross-timbers used to tie front and back fences of a hillfort rampart together.

Trilithon Three stones, two upright and one across the top, as at Stonehenge (page 283).

Trinovantes A late iron age tribe centred on Essex and frequently at war with the Catuvellauni.

Univallate A single line of defence, one bank and ditch.

Vitrification This occurs where the stone walls of a fort have been subjected to intense heat by burning the timber lacing, thus causing them to fuse together.

Windmill Hill folk One of the best known groups of neolithic people in southern England, named after the causewayed camp near Avebury.

Index of Sites

Three Stone Burn, Northumberland cm 205
Threlkeld Knott, Cumbria ss 94
Thundersbarrow Hill, Sussex W hf 253
Thursley Common, Surrey rb 238
Tidcombe, Wilts. lb 284
Tilshead Old Ditch, Wilts. lb 284
Tilshead White Barrow, Wilts. lb 284
Tinglestone Barrow, Glos. lb 149
Titterstone Clee, Shropshire hf 221
Toots Barrow, Glos. lb 149
Towthorpe Plantation, Humberside rb 179
Towtop Kirk, Cumbria ss 94
Treen Dinas, Cornwall hf 78
Tregeare Rounds, Cornwall hf 78
Tregiffian Cornwall rb 78
Trencrom, Cornwall hf 78
Trendle Ring, Somerset hf 229
Trethevy Quoit, Cornwall cb 79
Trevelgue Head, Cornwall hf 79
Trippet Stones, Cornwall cm 79
Trowlesworthy Warren, Devon ss 116
Trundle, The, Sussex W hf 253
Twelve Apostles, Yorks. W cm 310

Uffington Castle, Oxon. hf 213
Uffington White Horse, Oxon. tf 214
Uley Bury, Glos. hf 149
Upper White Horse Stone, Kent cb 185
Upton Great Barrow, Wilts. rb 285
Upwey Ridgeway, Dorset rb 132
Urswick Stone Walls, Cumbria ss 94

Valley of Stones, Dorset fs 132
Veryan Barrow, Cornwall rb 79
Victoria Cave, Yorks. N ca 304

Waitby, Cumbria ss 95
Walbury, Berks. hf 57
Wallbury Camp, Essex hf 136
Wambarrows, Somerset rb 230
Wandlebury, Cambs. hf 62
Wapley Camp, Hereford & Worcester hf 172
Wappenbury, Warwicks. hf 257
Warbstow Bury, Cornwall hf 79
Warham Camp, Norfolk hf 196
Warton Crag, Lancs. hf 187
Waulud's Bank, Beds. cm 52

Wayland's Smithy, Oxon. cb 214
Weasenham Plantation, Norfolk rb 196
Weetwood Moor, Northumberland cr 205
Wendell Hill, Yorks. W hf 312
West End Common, Surrey rb 239
Western Howe, Yorks. N rb 304
West Hill, Northumberland ss 206
West Kennet, Wilts. cb 285
West Rudham, Norfolk lb 196
West Tump, Glos. cb 150
West Wycombe, Bucks. hf 60
Wharram Percy, Yorks. N rb 304
Whispering Knights, Oxon. cb 216
Whitehawk, Sussex enc 245
Whiteleaf, Bucks. rb 61
Whitelow, G Manchester rc 153
Whitesheet Castle, Wilts. hf 285
White Sheet Hill, Wilts. enc 286
White Sheet Hill Long Barrow, Wilts. lb 286
Whiteshoot Plantation, Hants. rb 164
Whitfield's Tump, Glos. lb 150
Whitmoor Common, Surrey rb 239
Wick Barrow, Somerset rb 230
Willerby Wold, Yorks. N lb 304
Willerby Wold House, Yorks. N rb 305
Willy Howe, Humberside rb 180
Wilsford, Wilts. rb 286
Wilson Scar, Cumbria cm 95
Winchester, Hants. tc 164
Wincobank, Yorks. S hf 307
Windover Hill, Sussex E fm rb 245
Windmill Hill, Wilts. enc 286
Windmill Tump, Glos. cb 150
Windrush Camp, Glos. hf 151
Windypits, Yorks. N ca 305
Winklebury Hill, Wilts. hf 288
Winterbourne Stoke, Wilts. lb rb 288
Wisley Common, Surrey rb 239
Withypool Stone Circle, Somerset cm 230
Wolstonbury, Sussex W hf 254
Woodbury Hill, Hereford & Worcester hf 172
Woodhenge, Wilts. cm 289
Woolbury Ring, Hants. hf 164
Wooler Fort, Northumberland hf 206
Wor Barrow, Dorset lb 132